Teaching
Life Writing Texts

Modern Language Association of America
Options for Teaching
Joseph Gibaldi, Series Editor

For a complete listing of titles,
see the last pages of this book.

Teaching Life Writing Texts

Edited by
**Miriam Fuchs and
Craig Howes**

The Modern Language Association of America
New York   2008

© 2007 by The Modern Language Association of America
All rights reserved. Printed in the United States of America

For information about obtaining permission to reprint material from MLA book
publications, send your request by mail (see address below), e-mail
(permissions@mla.org), or fax (646-458-0030).

LIBRARY OF CONGRESS CATALOGING-IN-PUBLICATION DATA

Teaching life writing texts / edited by Miriam Fuchs and Craig Howes.
    p. cm. — (Options for teaching ; 21)
  Includes bibliographical references and index.
  ISBN: 978-0-87352-819-1 (alk. paper)
  ISBN: 978-0-87352-820-7 (pbk. : alk. paper)
  1. English language—Rhetoric—Study and teaching.   2. Autobiography—
Authorship.   3. Biography—Authorship.   I. Fuchs, Miriam, 1949–
II. Howes, Craig, 1955–   III. Modern Language Association of America.
PE1404.T3944 2007
808'.0420711—dc22   2007022805
ISSN 1079-2562

Cover illustration of the paperback edition: *Self Portrait*, by Ellen Carey. 1986.
Polaroid 20×24 Color Positive Print. Courtesy of the artist and Jayne H. Baum,
New York, New York

Published by The Modern Language Association of America
26 Broadway, New York, NY 10004-1789   www.mla.org

Contents

Interdisciplinary Approaches

Gendered and Sexual Orientation Approaches

Illness and Disability Approaches

Acknowledgments

We would like to thank the anonymous readers and the MLA Publications Committee, whose suggestions at various stages of the process have helped to improve this volume. We wish also to cite Joseph Gibaldi, director of book acquisitions and development, for his early and sustained encouragement of our project.

The initial idea came from a roundtable panel on life writing pedagogy at the second International Auto/Biography Association Conference at the University of British Columbia in Vancouver (2000). Chaired by David Parker, the panel included Margaretta Jolly, Alfred Hornung, and Thomas R. Smith. We would also like to thank Sidonie Smith and Julia Watson for their ongoing commitment to the pedagogy of life writing in their many important publications.

Susanna Egan and G. Thomas Couser have been very helpful and supportive, and, as he has for many others, Paul John Eakin has served as our mentor, critic, and friend throughout.

The English Department of the University of Hawai'i at Mānoa, chaired by Cristina Bacchilega, has made this volume possible through its support for the activities of the Center for Biographical Research. In the College of Languages, Linguistics, and Literature, Dean Joseph H. O'Mealy has given us ongoing assistance. Finally, we gratefully recognize the Board of the Biographical Research Center, the nonprofit organization that supports the activities of the center. Special mention goes to the board member George Simson, director emeritus of the center and the founder of *Biography: An Interdisciplinary Quarterly.*

Miriam Fuchs wants to thank Alan S. Holzman for twenty-five years. Craig Howes would like to thank Sara Collins and Seth Howes for sharing the ride. And we both thank Stan Schab, managing editor for the Center for Biographical Research, for making every page of this book better. We're delighted to have the opportunity to acknowledge his support and to express publicly our appreciation. We dedicate this volume to him.

Miriam Fuchs and Craig Howes

Introduction

The past thirty years have nurtured a rapid growth in the number and variety of courses and programs that study life writing from literary, philosophical, psychological, and cultural perspectives. In literary studies alone, biography, hagiography, autobiography, memoir, testimonio, diary, oral history, genealogy, group biography, and a host of other related genres have become the texts selected for a whole range of general and specialized courses. The Modern Language Association responded to this emergence by revising the way it categorized literary studies. Once the purview of the Executive Committee on Nonfiction Prose Studies, such texts are now represented by the Division on Autobiography, Biography, and Life Writing, which since 1991 has sponsored sessions at every annual convention.

This expansion goes beyond disciplinary labels. Even a cursory look at academic gatherings around the world reveals sessions and entire conferences explicitly concerned with life writing texts and issues. This should not be surprising, for much of the significant recent critical and theoretical work on gender, race, sexual orientation, class, disability, the status of indigenous peoples, and postcolonial politics and aesthetics focuses its attention on biographical and autobiographical texts, which foreground issues of identity, subjectivity, memory, agency, history, and representation.

1

This concern with representation also accounts for the many interdisciplinary and comparative studies that draw together life writing and the visual and plastic arts, photography, and film; life writing and trauma studies and narrative psychology; or life writing and anthropology—and specifically ethnography and autoethnography. University presses have been adding life writing criticism and theory from many disciplines to their scholarly lists. The 2007 *Directory of the Association of American University Presses* lists more than eighty presses in the United States and Canada that publish in the fields of biography or autobiography, and some of them have separate series featuring life writing studies. Autobiographies and biographies also continue to appear on regional and trade publishers' lists appealing to a more general readership. And, as always, national and international trade-publishing houses market innumerable as-told-to books, ghostwritten autobiographies, and life accounts for celebrities whose reputations make their books potential best sellers.

Interest in life writing is also international in scope. Scholars who study, teach, and write about biography and autobiography do so in virtually all the languages represented by MLA and in all the communities from which those languages emerge. To take one fairly representative example, the more than five hundred subscribers to the International Autobiography and Biography Association electronic discussion list (IABA-L) represent six continents and forty countries. Given the widespread interest in life writing not only as a field in itself but also as a source of texts for study in many other fields, we believe that this collection will prove useful to an already large and ever-growing number of instructors in a variety of institutions and communities.

Biography, Autobiography, Oral History

Although certain texts and approaches have aged remarkably well, over the past generation the study of life writing has greatly expanded the nature and range of its subject matter. These changes have often questioned the assumptions at work in traditional approaches to defining and teaching biography as a genre. Such a mainstream course, offered in an English department, would start with the gospels or Plutarch, then move on to saints' lives. After some John Aubrey or Isaak Walton, the class would read selections of Samuel Johnson's *Lives of the Poets* and James Boswell's *Life of Johnson*. Thomas Carlyle's comments on heroes would represent nineteenth-century biography, and Lytton Strachey's cool, savage dissection in *Eminent Victorians* of this great-man biographical tradition would bring the course to a close. Sometimes the instructor might forge ahead into psychoanalysis or literary modernism. Sigmund Freud's work on Leonardo and case studies of living patients or Virginia Woolf's fictional biography *Orlando* might have been discussed.

A number of generic assumptions were implicit in such a survey. Biographies were about prominent people: historically significant persons, the nobility, celebrities, and, to a great degree, writers—largely because they wrote or were the subjects of large numbers of documents, the source of choice for most biographers. Classroom activities might have included defining the heroic or exemplary life, recognizing the telling or humanizing detail, and exploring the life-and-times approach to biography in an attempt to gain a sense of an era through the narrative of one or more of its prominent figures. Selection, veracity, point of view, and so forth were also studied. Only when the course turned the corner into the twentieth century would depth psychology and the new biography shift the focus to a conception of biography as a genre of interrogation or revelation. If the biographer's task had become to identify the secret, the key, or the motive behind later behavior, then what is not observable, rational, predictable, or acceptable might also have become the biographer's quarry.

This impulse to study a life because the person is already recognized as an outstanding or defining historical agent is, however, permeated by well-worn Western cultural assumptions. The venerable notions that history is the collected biographies of admirable or notorious individuals and that the way to understand shared social experience is by studying a "representative" prominent life are philosophically and historically problematic. In fact, lives other than the admirable and notorious have always been recorded, and in forms other than the familiar monograph—in genealogies, oral narratives, postcontact written accounts, postcolonial texts, resistance literature, and increasingly today in videos and on Web sites. As the texts featured in many of the courses in this volume suggest, these tensions between canonical and emergent texts, between the Great Man and the formerly unrepresented person, are making the study of biography a far more nuanced and wide-ranging activity.

The fortunes of autobiography in the classroom over the last thirty years can also be seen as the consequences of this distancing from eminent lives. There is no real need to provide a history for this progress: Sidonie

Smith and Julia Watson's introduction to *Women, Autobiography, Theory: A Reader*, the essays collected in that volume, and their more recent book *Reading Autobiography: A Guide for Interpreting Life Narratives* are excellent accounts of the ongoing interplay between the study of autobiographical texts and contemporary feminist, poststructuralist, postcolonial, and narrative theory. A few especially important influences on the teaching of autobiography should, however, be mentioned—first, the highly successful efforts of Philippe Lejeune, Paul John Eakin, Smith and Watson, and others to establish a poetics for autobiography and, second, the influence of James Olney, not only through his critical work, but also through his landmark National Endowment for the Humanities summer seminars on life writing for university faculty members.

Challenges to the literary canon and the growing impact of cultural studies in literature departments have also powerfully stimulated critical and theoretical work on autobiography. One of Edward Said's starting points for *Orientalism*, Karl Marx's oft-quoted observation that "they cannot represent themselves, [therefore] they must be represented," has often been the state of affairs that life writing has sought to change. With the emergence of identity politics in the second half of the twentieth century, women, indigenous peoples, the economically disenfranchised, persons with disabilities, ethnic and racial minorities, and gay, lesbian, and transgendered peoples began individually and collectively to find ways to write their lives. Their publications have brought to light complexities in how scholars and the general public have come to understand collaboration, ghostwriting, transcribed and translated editions, as well as changes produced by editing conventions. "Autobiography by people who do not write," which Lejeune covers in a chapter in *On Autobiography*, "throws light on autobiography written by those who do" and reveals among other things "the secrets of fabrication and the functioning of the 'natural' product" (187), which no longer looks natural to discerning readers.

Communication technologies of the twenty-first century are also enabling new modes of social and political interaction. Technologies establish and realign constituencies formed by migrations, religious struggles, nationalisms, and evolving relations of identity and community. As critics and scholars study these developments, students in our life writing classes will confront literary, cultural, political, philosophical, ethical, and genetic issues relative to identity and identity practices, and our pedagogies and instructional materials will make increasing use of electronic data in and across classrooms. These modalities will challenge how we teach the interactions of ethics, politics, and identity.

Any ethnographic or autoethnographic approach to life writing must determine how the text came into existence and explore the relationship between the person who has led the life and the person or persons recording and preparing it for publication. Close study of oral history shakes any remaining easy assumptions that life writing is primarily a means for preserving an individual life. In testimonio, for instance, the person who bears witness is often doing so on behalf of a community under siege, and many narratives produced by indigenous peoples insist on this distinction from the start. The subject tells the story of a people; what is personal or idiosyncratic is of secondary value. As the proliferating theoretical work on ethnography and autoethnography demonstrates, the whole discipline or practice of gathering and publishing such narratives always takes place on highly contested ground, because of political assumptions often implicit in the methodology and because of different understandings of such concepts as narrative, translation, and the representativeness of the informant. The implications of telling, collecting, editing, and distributing life stories are fundamental concerns in many of the classrooms our contributors describe.

Teaching Life Writing Texts

This volume shows some of the ways that life writing is being taught at over forty postsecondary institutions. The three familiar generic divisions—biography, autobiography, and oral history—continue to be relevant, but as life writing theory and criticism have evolved over the past few decades, even those courses that concentrate on one genre tend to confront and then explore the limitations of any single designation. Some instructors begin with the assumption that life writing genres invariably intersect, and they develop their teaching approaches on this foundation. This pedagogy is in keeping with ongoing critical and theoretical practice. Title—though not subtitle—to the contrary, the journal we edit, *Biography: An Interdisciplinary Quarterly*, regularly publishes essays on biography and autobiography, reviews books in both fields, includes biographies and autobiographies in its "Reviewed Elsewhere" feature, and lists critical and theoretical work on all life writing genres in its annual annotated bibliography of life writing. As for *A/B: Auto/Biography Studies*, the American publication largely devoted to literary and cultural studies, and *Auto/Biography*, the British publication that was concerned primarily with subjects in social science, the slash in both titles insists on the distinctiveness and the inseparability of the genres. (The title of the Australian journal *Life Writing* is self-explanatory.) Volumes and guides published in the past few years also explore parallels and reciprocal relations among all life writing genres. To mention only the most prominent, the two-volume *Encyclopedia of Life Writing*, edited by Margaretta Jolly, stands as a landmark contribution not only to the recognition of autobiography's and biography's shared status as narratives, regardless of field, region, time, or subject, but also to the consideration of biography, autobiography, and other genres as bound together in highly significant critical and theoretical ways.

Certain critical and theoretical texts of the last sixty years have been especially influential in providing frameworks for selecting texts to be discussed and taught together. Georg Misch's prescriptive *History of Autobiography in Antiquity*, translated into English in 1950, proclaimed standards for autobiographical writing. Georges Gusdorf's 1956 essay "Conditions and Limits of Autobiography," which was translated and published in English by Olney in 1980, delineated the genre as a distinct product of Western culture, particularly in its mix of Christian and classical traditions and its emphasis on individual self-awareness.

By the 1970s, though, Olney was already reconsidering these canonical impulses in his own book, *Metaphors of Self: The Meaning of Autobiography*, and then in his influential edited collection, *Autobiography: Essays Theoretical and Critical*, which contained discussions of African American writing, women's autobiographies, autobiographies of film stars, and the fictional aspects of life writing. In the late 1980s and early 1990s, Eakin's *Fictions of Autobiography: Studies in the Art of Self-Invention* and *Touching the World: Reference in Autobiography* and Smith's *A Poetics of Women's Autobiography: Marginality and the Fictions of Self-Representation* and *Subjectivity, Identity, and the Body: Women's Autobiographical Practices in the Twentieth Century* were of central importance in altering the way we look at life writing narratives and in expanding life writing canons. Smith and Watson's coedited *De/Colonizing the Subject: The Politics of Gender in Women's Autobiography*, *Getting a Life: Everyday Uses of Autobiography*, and *Interfaces: Women/Autobiography/Image/Performance* set off extensive dialogues exploring the rhetoric of gendered self-presentations; *Interfaces* also contains a useful appendix of Web resources and a model syllabus for courses in women's visual and performance autobiography.

And yet, though life writing is now widely taught, attention to pedagogical issues has been largely confined to the field of education theory. Considerable research examines the use of personal narratives in children's and adult education programs and at postsecondary institutions as well. Peter Abbs's *Autobiography in Education*, James Britton's *Language and Learning*, and various works by Jerome Bruner, Robert J. Graham, Sue Middleton, and others describe student-centered approaches to using autobiography as a teaching tool. In *Framing Identities: Autobiography and the Politics of Pedagogy*, Wendy S. Hesford examines the intersections of pedagogy and cultural politics by drawing on Mary Louise Pratt's idea of a contact zone to study representational dialogues occurring on college campuses inside of and outside the classroom. More in line with our own collection, which offers suggestions on specific teaching materials as well as on general concepts and developments, is *Teaching and Testimony: Rigoberta Menchú and the North American Classroom*, edited by Allen Carey-Webb and Stephen Benz. Contributors to the volume not only use classroom narratives and analyses of methods and curricula but also rethink strategies for both beginning and experienced teachers.

Estelle C. Jelinek, known for her early study *The Tradition of Women's Autobiography: From Antiquity to the Present* and for her anthology *Women's Autobiography: Essays in Criticism*, sets forth her pedagogical approach in "Teaching Women's Autobiographies." Jelinek, though, considers pedagogical issues and curriculum design for courses that emphasize the students' own life writings. Alluding to the difficulties of this kind of approach, Martin A. Danahay cites an invitation to solipsism as one of the dangers of writing autobiography in and for the classroom. In "Teaching Autobiography as Cultural Critique," he describes the importance of using life writing texts to challenge students' uncritical ideas concerning the genre as well as history and culture. Along these lines, several essays in *Women's Personal Narratives: Essays in Criticism and Pedagogy*, edited by Lenore Hoffman and Margo Culley, make an even earlier case for using diaries, journals, oral testimonies, and autobiographies in both freshman and upper-level courses. H. Porter Abbott's essay "Autobiography, Autography, Fiction: Groundwork for a Taxonomy of Textual Categories" assesses other difficulties in the life writing classroom—in his case, whether to distinguish or adhere to traditional genre distinctions at all. The students who enjoyed reading assigned books by Benjamin Franklin and Jean-Jacques Rousseau, for instance, were mainly interested in the authors' histories, and they read these autobiographies as biographies that just happened to be written by their central subject. Students interested in literary techniques and writing as a deliberate act were often highly critical of the very same books. As Abbott does in his 1988 essay, many contributors to this volume describe how they draw on students' existing expectations of genre and uncritical interpretations to increase awareness of autobiography as strategy and performance.

Nancy K. Miller, Margaretta Jolly, and Shoshana Felman have also written on life writing pedagogy in ways that prefigure our volume. The chapter "Teaching Autobiography" in Miller's *Getting Personal: Feminist Occasions and Other Autobiographical Acts* compares teaching an evening class made up primarily of adult women in a New York City public university with a similar class she customarily taught at Barnard College and Columbia University. The result is part self-examination and part analysis of the impact of gender, race, and class on determining specific reading and writing assignments. In "Teaching Carolyn Steedman's *Landscape of a Good Woman*" Jolly likewise describes how she has adapted methodologies to different class situations, specifically an adult education class for women centering on Carolyn Kay Steedman's *Landscape for a Good Woman*. Felman's "Education and Crisis; or, The Vicissitudes of Teaching," the first chapter of Felman and Dori Laub's *Testimony: Crises of Witnessing in Literature, Psychoanalysis, and History*, is a cautionary lesson for instructors who choose materials that students will experience as especially painful or controversial. Felman found herself unprepared for her Yale students' emotional responses to the testimonies of Holocaust survivors, and she records how she improvised strategies for alleviating the crisis in the classroom situation. *Teaching the Representation of the Holocaust*, Marianne Hirsch and Irene Kacandes's volume in the MLA Options for Teaching series, is the most comprehensive resource for approaches to teaching this central life writing subject. The contributors present historical and theoretical views, discuss individual texts and films, and give special attention to the emotional responses that such materials elicit.

In addition to the volumes previously mentioned, Smith and Watson's collection *Women, Autobiography, Theory: A Reader* includes a final section, "Politics and Pedagogy," featuring essays by bell hooks, Smith, Shirley Geok-lin Lim, Barbara Harlow, Nancy K. Miller, and Nancy Mairs, all foregrounding the effect of marginalization on identity formation and autobiographical writing. Hooks examines race, Lim discusses Asian women, Harlow refers to resistance movements, Miller to class, and Mairs to physical disability, reminding us that all these factors necessarily shape students' attitudes and reactions to the texts that we ask them to read. And in *Reading Autobiography* Smith and Watson establish pedagogy as their primary concern:

> At the graduate level, this text offers a comprehensive introduction for students engaging primary texts or doing intensive theoretical work in life writing. At the undergraduate level this text is a handbook to accompany survey, period, or multicultural courses on autobiography, memoir, personal narrative, or literary history more broadly. (xi–xii)

Our own contributors often cite this guide, which comprehensively goes over definitions, history, constitutive elements, genres, and general suggestions for class assignments.

Our volume builds on and complements these earlier efforts. The essays here identify and describe courses for every level of postsecondary instruction. Methods and theoretical perspectives from a broad range of educational institutions and geographic locations reflect the history and politics of where these instructors teach, as well as their beliefs and professional interests. Student demographics and our contributors' own biographies clearly shape the contours of their courses. Gender and racial concerns also affect class dynamics.

Many of these essays grapple with texts that represent disability, illness, abuse, and depression; ethnic, sexual, and racial discrimination; crises and catastrophes; witnessing and testimonials; human rights violations; and genocide. Some of the contributors draw heavily on literary and cultural theory to describe their efforts; others share their assignments and weekly syllabi. Some do both. We hope that these essays will help instructors in their own course preparations. All of us try to meet students' expectations while challenging our classes to reassess them. We all wish to sharpen the ways our students read and interpret genre, judge authors and their central subjects, and apply what they read to their own lives. And we all want our students to encounter and appreciate life writing originating from outside their own social, economic, ethnic, religious, and national borders.

In its organization, this volume adheres less to the traditional categories than to the groupings suggested to us by current scholarship, as represented by the more than forty essays we have selected. In this way, *Teaching Life*

Writing Texts seeks to foreground the many overlapping relations between genres and disciplines that are virtually unavoidable in life writing narratives and courses. The classes described here are taught in social science, humanities, cultural studies, and language departments and at every level of postsecondary education. Through various life writing texts, contributors to this volume introduce freshmen and sophomores in English and other humanities disciplines to the challenges of critical writing and reading, to narration and narrative problems, to questions in ethics, and to methods of research. Juniors and seniors take life writing courses in liberal studies, modern languages, communications, gender studies, women's studies, media studies, art history, and comparative literature. The MA and PhD courses described in this volume are designed for students not just in English concentrations but in art, art history, and cultural studies. As the institutional affiliations and geographic distribution of our contributors suggest, a wide variety of educational institutions offer life writing: private colleges, liberal arts colleges, small institutions, large state universities, and adult programs located in the United States, Canada, Australia, Great Britain, Germany, Eritrea, and South Africa, to mention only the regions specifically represented in this volume.

We think that readers will discover many approaches that are new to them and that will stimulate further innovation. The teaching creativity represented here arises from the fact that biography, autobiography, and oral history texts are taught not only as regular program offerings but as units within more generally defined classes and as special-topics classes. Probably as a result of such innovation, we received fewer descriptions than expected of traditional courses in confessional and conversion life writing, canonical biography, American autobiography, and life writing set within national traditions and histories but many descriptions with rationales and texts unfamiliar to us.

In this collection, we have attempted to provide a general survey of life writing courses offered throughout postsecondary institutions and often in disciplines other than English. Courses in English departments frequently examine the nature of the poststructural and postcolonial *I* voice, plot, narrative, memory, reference, resemblance, performativity, gender, ethnicity, race, and ethics. In other disciplines, life writing can also provide the texts for language study, research procedures, editing, transcribing oral history, translation studies, anthropology, ethnography, social history, and even encounters with English in interdisciplinary curricula. Our selection of contributors seeks to reflect the range, depth, and diversity of instruction in the field today—qualities that will undoubtedly become more pronounced in the years ahead.

Current trends in life writing theory and criticism suggest that, increasingly, instructors will be designing courses that respond to developments in media and genre studies. Film and video have become major sources of life narrative texts, as special issues of *Biography: An Interdisciplinary Quarterly* on the biopic (2000) and on narrative cinema as autobiographical act (2006) suggest. While a number of the essays in this volume draw on Internet resources for their texts and for class management, we are also certain that the proliferation of personal Web pages, blogs, and life writing exchange centers like *MySpace* is leading to courses that will devote themselves entirely to *Lives Online*—the title of a 2003 *Biography* special issue. The commodification of life writing texts is also attracting critical attention. Scrapbooking, trade-publication guides for conducting family history, do-it-yourself genealogy databases, memoir clubs and writing circles, contracted ghostwritten autobiographies for corporate leaders or even the corporations themselves, commercially prepared video biographies for weddings, anniversaries, and funerals—all these trends speak to the importance of life writing in contemporary culture. Finally, while courses devoted to the actual practice of life writing lie outside the focus of this volume, distinctions between literary and cultural studies, creative writing, and composition and rhetoric are blurring and often disappearing, as scholars, writers, and students explore new ways to create and engage with texts. Critical and theoretical work in life writing is exploring many of these new genres and forms of publication; though not represented prominently in this volume, classes devoted entirely to these areas will, in the future, be integral parts of curriculum design and pedagogy.

The Essays in This Volume

While the implied gap between part 1, "Generic Approaches," and part 2, "Cultural Approaches," might initially seem definitive, the subdivisions within each part gesture to affinities between the parts. Part 1 groups essays under the headings "Literary Studies" and "Interdisciplinary Approaches." Part 2 is divided into "Times and Places," "Ethnographic and Autoethnographic Approaches," "Gendered and Sexual Orientation Approaches," and "Illness and Disability Approaches." Emphasis is the distinguishing factor.

While cultural concerns are prominent in the book's first half, the courses tend to provide structures for exploring ideas of genre and genre theory pertinent to all forms of life writing narratives. And while generic distinctions are often crucial in part 2, "Cultural Approaches" courses often note the formation of new genres in direct response to social conditions and historical developments.

Generic Approaches

The essays in part 1 describe courses in which life writing genres—their working definitions, histories, problems, and critical and theoretical literature—provide the starting point for the instructors' pedagogic and textual choices. Roger J. Porter leads off the section entitled "Literary Studies" with an account of using life writing in a lower-division course to introduce students to narrative forms and issues. Thomas R. Smith's "Slipping Away, Sliding Around" shows how reading canonical autobiographies with contemporary multicultural autobiographies displays the unstable nature of genre and genre terminology. Through readings in biographical fiction, David Houston Jones helps students recognize that biography itself is generically less stable than they might expect, mass-market biographies and celebrity culture to the contrary. The personal appeal of journals and other forms of self-recording informs Suzanne L. Bunkers's course in diaries and diarists. Students in this lower-division class examine diaries, novels in the form of diaries, film adaptations of diaries, and on-line diary Web sites to appreciate diaries as historical documents as well as a distinctive literary form and channel of individual expression. Gary Totten's upper-division course in travel writing, which covers historical and contemporary readings, asks students to see travel writers as self-narrators who reshape themselves as they change geographic locations. The next two essays examine life writing genres within literary periods. Alison Booth's lecture class on Victorian lives uses library and computer research to illustrate the importance of life writing genres for late-nineteenth-century British writers. David Caplan's course in modernist American literature contains a unit on life writing to demonstrate that the modernist dictum on impersonality did not prevent writers of that period from covertly using autobiographical and biographical forms.

Voice, identity construction, and narrative constructions of truth from various perspectives shape other life writing classes in literary studies.

Martin A. Danahay's course, Autobiography: The Subject of Drugs, attends to ways that topics considered risky for autobiographers to write about shape various narratives. James W. Pipkin's course in American sports autobiographies shows students how voice and identity formation are profoundly influenced by the social and political atmosphere of a specific culture and period. The British scholars John Mepham and Sarah Sceats focus their MA course at Kingston University on writing personae and truth values in relation to postmodernism, postcolonialism, gender theory, and late-twentieth-century trauma theory. Gabriele Helms's course emphasizes nontraditional forms of representation; students look at Canadian life writing authors who have altered the genre by shifting its boundaries in response to contemporary events and culture. Organizing his graduate course around a number of well-known writers, Timothy Dow Adams has students read an autobiography and biography of each person; soon, students are reassessing their former assumptions about genres as they begin to ask whether these writing forms can ever be discrete. Concluding this section, Craig Howes's essay describes a course for MA and PhD students that introduces biographical, autobiographical, and oral-history texts as stimuli for larger projects in literary and cultural studies. The creating and interpreting of filmed, televised, and online life representations also become topics for investigation.

The courses under discussion in "Interdisciplinary Approaches" carry students into more than one subject area by creating bridges between different departments and fields of study. The first few essays demonstrate how life writing can serve in lower-division courses as a conduit to other subjects and debates. Students in Cynthia Huff's freshman course read unpublished autobiographical manuscripts to practice their reading and writing skills and to think critically about what goes into the making of an English curriculum. Kristine Peleg's composition course has a life writing unit based on a central text that introduces issues of oral transmission, transcription, translation, editing, and collaboration. By assigning her graduate students memoirs, letters, and literacy narratives that lend themselves to primary and secondary research, Katrina M. Powell also employs life writing to direct efforts in interdisciplinary scholarship.

Other essayists explicitly link different subject areas, or they describe ideas that could shape units in larger courses or become themes for full courses. Kenneth Womack's students read life writing theory to shed light on the autobiographical dimensions of the Beatles' recordings and to develop methods for applying literary criticism to nonliterary productions.

Taking Pierre Loti as his example, Thomas J. D. Armbrecht suggests that examining nonliterary artistic productions by life writing authors can help us understand their literary narratives, while Julie F. Codell connects artists' literary narratives to their art. The art history and literature majors who take Codell's class read autobiographies by Victorian artists as analytic tools for assessing the artwork—an approach not customarily taken by contemporary art historians. Also pairing autobiography and art, Frances Freeman Paden presents Felix Gonzalez-Torres's installations as texts for demonstrating that the visual arts can be metaphorical narratives about the lives (and in Torres's case, the death) of their creators. Miriam Fuchs ends this section with a graduate seminar that introduces the mediums of life writing and life imaging to explore tensions between traditional and experimental modes of representation; the course then traces how autobiographical and biographical representations have come to resemble each other.

Cultural Approaches

Part 2 of the collection contains essays that emphasize life writing pedagogy in relation to cultural and historical developments. The contributors whose essays appear in "Times and Places" suggest that the traditional habits of linking life narratives to national traditions have been changing. By exploring orally transmitted material or works by marginalized persons that require the discussion of power and politics from various cultural angles, the essays grouped under "Ethnographic and Autoethnographic Approaches" deal explicitly with issues of ethics and justice in and outside the classroom. The "Gendered and Sexual Orientation Approaches" section highlights embodiment, sexuality, and gender, whereas the teachers contributing to "Illness and Disability Approaches" show how they examine life writing within the body of current theorizing and debates in illness and trauma studies.

In the first essay in "Times and Places," Michael W. Young proposes combining Canadian and United States authors for an undergraduate course in early American and Canadian life writing. Kathleen Boardman sees her American autobiography class as countering "classic" texts by emphasizing Native American, minority, and ethnic writing and in the process by raising questions of collaboration, ghostwriting, and oral transmission. The two essays that follow concentrate on events over the past decade that have influenced life writing curricula in Australia. Examining referentiality, subjectivity, and memory, Richard Freadman's course on growing up in Australia projects all of these themes against a background of national, racial, and colonialist issues. Gillian Whitlock and Kate Douglas also stress location, but, by taking a postcolonial view of Australia, Canada, and South Africa, their course also investigates the broader dimensions of settler literature and indigenous life writings. Judith Lütge Coullie, who teaches at the postgraduate level in South Africa, describes her efforts to encourage students to see and appreciate, through autobiographical, theoretical, and critical readings, the relations between oral-performance texts and written life narratives in the context of apartheid and South Africa's contemporary history. The next essay shifts to the modern Middle East and North Africa, as Julia Clancy-Smith explains the colloquium she has taught since the late 1980s. In particular, she shows how discussions of identity have evolved with theories in historiographical, autobiographical, and political narratives; language practice, ethnolinguistics, and translation studies; cultural studies and postcolonialism; and even with the availability of archival photographs and films. The remarkable course that ends this section describes online interaction between students at the University of Washington and the University of Asmara in Eritrea. Sandra Chait and Ghirmai Negash found that after autobiographical exchanges, their students (graduate and undergraduate) better understood the dynamics of cultural and technological positionality and could effectively apply those ideas to the assigned life narratives.

Daniel Heath Justice opens the section entitled "Ethnographic and Autoethnographic Approaches" by outlining an undergraduate course on indigenous life narratives from North America that pays special attention to ethical teaching practices. Working with slave narratives in courses for undergraduate and graduate students, Joycelyn K. Moody describes the challenges she faces when teaching these texts in an environment of post-structuralism and in response to students' own fixed ideas about history and historical truths. Sarah Brophy explains how incorporating slave narratives—in this case *The Interesting Narrative of the Life of Olaudah Equiano*—into other classes shows students ways in which oppressed people have often used life writing for both expressive and critical purposes. Concentrating on intercultural studies and oral narratives, Iulia-Karin Patrut's course starts with the Eastern European tale of the walled-up wife. Students read theory in ethnography and folklore, then apply what they have learned to explore the cultural and female representations invoked by this narrative. And by concentrating on identity formation and diversity, Joanne Karpinski leads students in her lower-division seminar, Discerning Diversity in American Lives, to engage with ideas of justice and community by reading individuals' life narratives, family stories, and testimonies.

The courses taught by Jeraldine R. Kraver and Gail Y. Okawa are firmly grounded in ethnography. Kraver teaches ethnographies alongside current theory and helps students recognize the strategies that marginalized people use in recording and disseminating their stories. Recounting her experiences with a class in ethnic autobiography at a midwestern university, Okawa explains why, over time, she has come to approach the subject differently: by adopting an ethnographic perspective, she finds that she teaches more successfully. In this section's final essay, "Teaching Testimony: A New, Ex-Centric Design Emerges," Arturo Arias discusses the ethical and political considerations that cause him to teach testimonios in classrooms where he also teaches fiction, memoirs, poetry, essays, and historical novels. To ensure that students gain a complex understanding of how testimonios reveal colonialist abuses, Arias's pedagogy is based on comparative genre study.

"Gendered and Sexual Orientation Approaches" contains four essays about diverse classes, institutions, and locations: an undergraduate course in a small northeastern American college; a seminar at a midwestern American university; an adult education course at the University of Exeter; and a master's-level class at the University of York in England. Susannah B. Mintz opens the section with her women's autobiography course at Skidmore College. By focusing on the theme of embodiment, she covers important texts; by stressing the impact women's literature has had on the field of life writing, she accounts in part for what gets taught. Margaretta Jolly describes teaching British students from three constituencies: the Workers' Educational Association, a continuing-education class, and a graduate program. Taking as her example a single feminist text, Jo Spence's *Putting Myself in the Picture*, Jolly outlines various pedagogies for successfully working with very different students. At Saint Louis University, Georgia Johnston's course, Taking Queer Positions: Teaching Queer Lives, formally and historically traces the evolution of gay and lesbian representations from the seventeenth century to the present, noting motifs emerging for self-expression and self-censorship. Trev Lynn Broughton describes her graduate class for British students interested in learning about gender and women's literature through a multidisciplinary approach. The goal is to explore how life narratives by or about women are related to the politicizing of intimacy through media exposure and controversy.

"Illness and Disability Approaches" brings the contributors' section of *Teaching Life Writing Texts* to a close. As G. Thomas Couser points out, narratives about such circumstances add a further element of diversity that is often missing from multicultural agendas. Couser assigns nonmajors as well as English majors readings that extend class discussion to current ethical and public policy debates. In a women's and gender studies program, Hilary Clark offers her course, Women's Depression Memoirs: Healing, Testimony, and Critique, to study the psychology, politics, history, and changing attitudes related to this particular genre. Finally, Leigh Gilmore describes an undergraduate course where the focus is on trauma narratives that, because they have led to controversy and scandals, now provide the means for examining current methods of recording, evaluating, and teaching trauma.

Two additional features supplement the course descriptions included in this volume. At the end of each of the two main divisions that categorize the volume, we have supplied bibliographic resources that complement, but do not repeat, the works cited in the individual essays. And our final section, "Life Writing Resources for Teachers," points to periodicals, online resources, and centers, programs, and organizations that provide additional and ongoing support for the teaching and practice of life writing.

The purpose of this collection is twofold: to suggest the range and creativity of life writing in various departments and programs throughout the world and to share the experiences of our contributors as sources of encouragement for new and veteran instructors of life writing. We recognize that even with over forty contributors, readers will discover gaps in our coverage. We anticipate, though, that the gaps themselves may prove as suggestive and valuable as the materials we do provide. Some contributors are new to the academy whereas others have been theorizing and teaching life writing for many years. Their diverse points of view are indicative of the excitement of life writing research and teaching. As autobiography, biography, oral narrative, and various combinations of life writing genres are increasingly recognized, valued, and taught, the field will continue to expand and flourish as a space for examining literature, culture, history, politics, and pedagogy.

Works Cited

Abbott, H. Porter. "Autobiography, Autography, Fiction: Groundwork for a Taxonomy of Textual Categories." *New Literary History* 19 (1988): 597–615.

Abbs, Peter. *Autobiography in Education*. London: Heinemann, 1974.

Boswell, James. *Life of Johnson*. 1791.

Britton, James. *Language and Learning*. London: Lane, 1970.

Carey-Webb, Allen, and Stephen Benz, eds. *Teaching and Testimony: Rigoberta Menchú and the North American Classroom*. Albany: State U of New York P, 1996.

Carlyle, Thomas. *On Heroes, Hero-Worship, and the Heroic in History*. 1841. Berkeley: U of California P, 1993.

Danahay, Martin A. "Teaching Autobiography as Cultural Critique." *CEA Critic* 54.2 (1992): 8–20.

Eakin, Paul John. *Fictions in Autobiography: Studies in the Art of Self-Invention*. Princeton: Princeton UP, 1985.

———. *Touching the World: Reference in Autobiography*. Princeton: Princeton UP, 1992.

Equiano, Olaudah. *Olaudah Equiano: The Interesting Narrative and Other Writings*. Ed. Vincent Carretta. New York: Penguin, 2003.

Felman, Shoshana. "Education and Crisis; or, The Vicissitudes of Teaching." *Testimony: Crises of Witnessing in Literature, Psychoanalysis, and History*. Ed. Felman and Dori Laub. New York: Routledge, 1992. 1–56.

Freud, Sigmund. *Leonardo da Vinci: A Study in Psychosexuality*. Trans. A. A. Brill. New York: Vintage, 1947.

———. *Three Case Histories*. Trans. James Strachey. New York: Collier, 1963.

Gusdorf, Georges. "Conditions and Limits of Autobiography." Olney, *Autobiography* 28–48.

Hesford, Wendy S. *Framing Identities: Autobiography and the Politics of Pedagogy*. Minneapolis: U of Minnesota P, 1999.

Hirsch, Marianne, and Irene Kacandes, eds. *Teaching the Representation of the Holocaust*. New York: MLA, 2004.

Hoffman, Lenore, and Margo Culley, eds. *Women's Personal Narratives: Essays in Criticism and Pedagogy*. New York: MLA, 1985.

Jelinek, Estelle C. "Teaching Women's Autobiography." *College English* 38 (1976): 32–45.

———. *The Tradition of Women's Autobiography: From Antiquity to the Present*. New York: Twayne, 1986.

———, ed. *Women's Autobiography: Essays in Criticism*. Bloomington: Indiana UP, 1980.

Johnson, Samuel. *Lives of the Poets*. 1779–81.

Jolly, Margaretta, ed. *Encyclopedia of Life Writing: Autobiographical and Biographical Forms*. 2 vols. London: Dearborn, 2001.

———. "Teaching Carolyn Steedman's *Landscape for a Good Woman*: A Comparative Perspective on Pedagogy and Life Writing in British University and Adult Education Contexts." *A/B: Auto/Biography Studies* 10 (2002): 35–40.

Lejeune, Philippe. *On Autobiography*. Ed. and fwd. Paul John Eakin. Trans. Katherine Leary. Minneapolis: U of Minnesota P, 1989.

Miller, Nancy K. "Teaching Autobiography." *Getting Personal: Feminist Occasions and Other Autobiographical Acts*. New York: Routledge, 1991. 121–42.

Misch, Georg. *A History of Autobiography in Antiquity*. Trans. E. W. Dickes. 2 vols. 1907. London: Routledge, 1950.

Olney, James, ed. *Autobiography: Essays Theoretical and Critical*. Princeton: Princeton UP, 1980.

———. *Metaphors of Self: The Meaning of Autobiography*. Princeton: Princeton UP, 1972.

Pratt, Mary Louise. *Imperial Eyes: Travel Writing and Transculturation*. London: Routledge, 1992.

Said, Edward W. *Orientalism*. New York: Vintage, 1979.

Smith, Sidonie. *A Poetics of Women's Autobiography: Marginality and the Fictions of Self-Representation*. Bloomington: Indiana UP, 1987.

———. *Subjectivity, Identity, and the Body: Women's Autobiographical Practices in the Twentieth Century*. Bloomington: Indiana UP, 1993.

Smith, Sidonie, and Julia Watson, eds. *De/Colonizing the Subject: The Politics of Gender in Women's Autobiography*. Minneapolis: U of Minnesota P, 1992.

———, eds. *Getting a Life: Everyday Uses of Autobiography*. Minneapolis: U of Minnesota P, 1996.

———, eds. *Interfaces: Women/Autobiography/Image/Performance*. Ann Arbor: U of Michigan P, 2002.

———. *Reading Autobiography: A Guide for Interpreting Life Narratives*. Minneapolis: U of Minnesota P, 2001.

———, eds. *Women, Autobiography, Theory: A Reader*. Madison: U of Wisconsin P, 1998.

Spence, Jo. *Putting Myself in the Picture: A Political, Personal and Photographic Autobiography*. London: Camden, 1986.

Steedman, Carolyn Kay. *Landscape for a Good Woman*. New Brunswick: Rutgers UP, 1986.

Strachey, Lytton. *Eminent Victorians*. London: Chatto, 1918.

Woolf, Virginia. *Orlando: A Biography*. London: Hogarth, 1928.

Part I

Generic Approaches

Literary Studies

Roger J. Porter

Introduction to World Narrative

For many years I have taught autobiography in a variety of configurations (I once called such a course From Saint Augustine to Saint Genet). The present course reflects my interest in using autobiographical writing explicitly to raise questions of narrative for introductory literature students. I chose the genre of life writing to examine such issues as self-representation, rhetorical strategies, authorial voice, plotting, and autobiographical intention, especially because questions of the construction of the subject, the referential nature of autobiographical language, and the truth status of storytelling all come to the fore.

For the most part, the students in this course were sophomores, many of whom were taking it as one of the two mandatory genre courses preparatory to enrolling in the English major, while others were taking it to satisfy a distribution requirement. At Reed College nonmajors often perform as brilliantly as majors. Given the intellectual drive and the commitment to rigor that characterizes Reed students, I designed this introductory course, taken by many science and social science majors as well as by those intending to study literature, to meet Reed's expectations of challenging and significant quantities of reading, demanding assignments, and students' desire for theoretical as well as critical approaches to texts. Students are encouraged to engage in intellectual debate, and the "conference" (or seminar) approach to classroom work insures that students participate in vigorous give-and-take.

This semester course of approximately thirteen weeks is one of several beginning-level courses the English department offers each year as introductions to narrative. Others typically focus on prose fiction. My intention was to use life writing or autobiography as the vehicle for understanding how stories are shaped to particular authorial ends. Since even the most sophisticated students tend to believe that autobiographical writing is an "accurate" or "true" picture of one's life, that the writing depicts exactly what happened, autobiography shows students how a life story is constructed to create specific self-images or to serve certain functions in the life at the time of the writing. Much of the course introduces students to the notion of narrativity as a performance and suggests how distinctions between the living author, the narrator, and the depicted "I" constitute and reveal what is at stake when one condenses a life into a text. For that reason the course begins with Vladimir Nabokov's *Speak, Memory*. This work rapidly persuades students that textual lives become aesthetic constructs, and the initial critical readings by Barrett Mandel, G. Thomas Couser, Sidonie Smith ("Performativity"), and Paul John Eakin (*Fictions*) assigned along with *Speak, Memory* enhance the Nabokovian position. Even a less aestheticized narrative makes the point: our second text, Philip Roth's *Patrimony*, along with readings by Timothy Dow Adams and Nancy K. Miller, also addresseses the inevitability of the writer imposing a deliberately self-serving view, in this case of Roth's relation to his father.

The emphasis of the course was partly on strategies writers employ to depict the self, including the rhetoric of self-representation, problems of truth and fictionalizing (Mandel's essay in week 1 stresses the complex connection between fact and artifact), the relation of performativity to identity, and the uses of memory on the one hand and selectively gathered evidence (photos, letters, archival materials, documents, and records) on the other to narrate personal experience.

But other issues were central to the course, namely, gender and the self in relation to the family or stories of an other (Eakin's notion of "relational selves" figures here). I divided the reading list into male and female autobiographers, with the idea of testing whether, by the end of the semester, distinctions in approaches to life writing according to gender were evident, problematic, or nonexistent. Such issues did not always play themselves out in neat packages. The male writers are no less concerned than the women writers with delineating relationships, nor do they especially characterize themselves in terms of an imperial self. Roth, Paul Auster, Georges Perec, and Art Spiegelman (with readings by Sturrock and by Young) all search to understand themselves through a depicted relationship to difficult or missing fathers. Perec, Spiegelman, and Binjamin Wilkomirski all write about the Holocaust and approach that experience as survivor, victim, or observer of another's plight. Eakin's work in *How Our Lives Become Stories* was, in this sense, a useful antidote to the position held by a number of the critics we read from Sidonie Smith and Julia Watson's significant collection *Women, Autobiography, Theory*, who tend to emphasize the greater degree to which women autobiographers stress relationality rather than individuality and a goal-oriented perspective.

Binjamin Wilkomirski's *Fragments: Memories of a Wartime Childhood* provided the most interesting class in the first half of the semester. I did not tell students ahead of time that Wilkomirski's claim that he had been in a concentration camp during the war had been effectively challenged— indeed had proved to be a falsification. I gave students Phillip Gourevitch's article from the *New Yorker* citing the evidence for the revisionist position, urging them to read it only after they had finished the memoir. That produced a fierce class, in which students debated the "truth" issue of life writing and tried to account for why Wilkomirski might have fabricated his claim. Many students reported feeling betrayed by the author, a response that provoked a discussion of the relation of writer to reader and the issues inherent in Philippe Lejeune's "autobiographical pact." Could one still find the account powerful, or was it now "reduced" to the status of fiction? *Fragments* proved, as much as any text in the course, to be a heuristic device through which to raise the perennial theoretical questions of authenticity and reference.

Maus provided an opportunity to examine autobiography in a visual medium, but because Spiegelman is a highly literate artist, we analyzed the way history and biography emerge through the conjunction of images and language. Several of the autobiographies in the first half of the semester challenged conventional notions of sequential life writing. Perec, for example, writes two parallel accounts, one a fragmentary plotting of his childhood, the other an allegorical narrative of the Holocaust perceived through the Olympic ideal in Tierra del Fuego. Auster depicts an absent father through missing or edited photographs. Michel Leiris understands his self through images of two seventeenth-century paintings by Lucas Cranach the Elder representing wounding and self-wounding. Such experimental narratives were useful to undercut notions that life writing is necessarily formulaic in its plotting. To this end the theoretical readings by Judith Butler, Eakin ("Narrative"), and Smith ("Universal Subject") raised questions regarding chronology, the amalgamation of external history and internal psychological process, and the importance of the body in self-representation. We kept returning to autobiographical theory not only in the secondary readings but also as it was embedded in the primary texts; Leiris, in his afterword to *Manhood*, theorizes autobiography as much as Nabokov does, and Leiris's famous afterword to *Manhood*, "The Autobiographer as Torero," which develops out of his guilt at not having suffered in the war, links him with Perec and Spiegelman in their self-conscious insistence on theorizing the genre even as they enact it.

That the male life writers could not be characterized in ways early feminist theorists of the genre proposed challenged, if not undermined, simplistic gender distinctions. Nevertheless, the positions staked out by theorists in the second half of the course—including essays by Shari Benstock, Rita Felski, Susan Stanford Friedman, Helen M. Buss, and Anne E. Goldman excerpted from *Women, Autobiography, Theory* (Smith and Watson)—were valuable for leading the class to examine what, if anything, is distinctive about women's life writing (see also Smith, "Autobiography" and "Woman's Story"). One of the issues that interested some of my students concerned the relevance of ethnographic or anthropological modes of criticism for the discursive analysis of life writing, especially when the autobiography contained significant amounts of biographical material.

Corresponding to the excitement sparked by Wilkomirski earlier, our class on Kathryn Harrison's *The Kiss* was the high point of the second half of the semester. The work inevitably raised questions about the ethics of revelation and of privacy when others are implicated. Such questions have come to the forefront of autobiographical discussion, led by Eakin's recent work ("Breaking Rules"). Because Harrison writes about a time in her life when she was close to the age of my students, her resistance to blaming her father and her willingness to take responsibility for her incestuous relation with him proved especially contentious in class, but such discussions were framed by the ethical issues regarding the act of writing as much as by the sexual facts themselves. Since Virginia Woolf writes about her own sexual molesting by her stepbrother, it was interesting to compare analogous narrative accounts from the early and the late twentieth century. Another payoff of the course was seeing how a theoretical text such as Felski's "On Confession" could illuminate both Woolf's and Harrison's writing. One of my pedagogical assumptions was that a critical text, even though directed at a specific work, could beneficially apply throughout the syllabus.

Another interplay of texts involved writers in a cross-cultural context. Both Eva Hoffman and Maxine Hong Kingston may be said to write autobiography in a condition of exile. Hoffman immigrated from Eastern Europe at an early age, first to Canada and later to the United States, whereas Kingston was born and grew up in California, but each writer concerns herself with the power of the family culture—Polish and Chinese respectively—from a position increasingly removed from the roots of that culture. Though both their texts (read with selections by Wong and Smith [*Poetics*]) are written in English, the way language (whether native or ancestral) functions to define consciousness is paramount in each work. Hoffman's autobiography is entitled *Lost in Translation*, but Kingston's work is likewise about translation—of her mother's sensibility to the child's experiences and expectations and of the child's Americanness to a state of filial respect and to the integration of older ways through a reconstruction of the stories and myths that define the familial culture.

In some ways the central text in the second half of the course was Mary Gordon's *The Shadow Man: A Daughter's Search for Her Father*. Gordon discovers that her father, who died when she was a young girl, was not Catholic, as she believed, but Jewish; yet he was profoundly and vocally anti-Semitic, and he edited a pornographic magazine. Unraveling his deceptions and secret life, Gordon wrestles with her sense of betrayal, and the text narrates her readjusting (to) his revised image and the discovery of herself as separate from the father. Gordon's work raised a crucial problem of narrativity for the course. Her work represents the most comprehensive depiction I know in autobiography of the process of unearthing the past through research. "Digging up the past" and "digging up the dirt" are no empty metaphors; late in the text Gordon describes her discovery of her father's grave site and her decision to have his bones removed to be reinterred in a cemetery of her own choice. *The Shadow Man* narrates how one discovers a past when memory falsifies or when the past lies beyond one's own life. Gordon implicitly conveys her belief that had the father written his own life, it would have been nothing but fabrication. Only a view from outside could reach even a simulacrum of truth about him, which is why,

I believe, she makes the *process* of detection central to her project. Her text is the autobiography of her investigation as much as it is the life of her father. Everything she discovers stems from what she calls "the insufficiency of memory" (164). Gordon's memory is as untrustworthy as her father himself, and, because she regards it as an unreliable resource, she turns to empirical research to capture the past. The more she searches in the documents of his life, the more she feels like "a detective in the department of magical realism" (xxii). If the man she remembers is nothing like the man who emerges from the archives, then both their identities are subject to emendation—his as the godlike hero, hers as the dutiful acolyte.

She tracks him down at the National Archives in Washington, DC, and then in Cleveland, where she visits local libraries, and scans city directories, high school yearbooks, synagogue records, and local histories of his hometown. Each discovery turns up, as it were, a new father. In the process she becomes the shadow woman, impersonating him in her mind, imagining his point of view about the world, and assuming his anxieties and desires. Gordon's motive—her need to know the father and to know why she needs to know him—drives her inquiry and leads her from record to record, depository to depository, despite a nagging conviction that she ought to leave him in peace to keep concealed what he worked so hard to hide and to let his bones lie.

I dwell at length on Gordon because her work raises important problems of memory distortion and the necessary compensation in narrative for that lack of accuracy. Her focus on telling the story of the story, and even on her dogged research, only emphasizes what life writing generally performs, namely, a shaping motive for constructing a story that involves one's self even as it incorporates significant others who may or may not turn out, in the telling, to be all we remember them as having been.

Appendix

Sample Essay Assignments from Introduction to World Narrative: Autobiography

First essay, five pages. Examine in detail the last several pages of *Speak, Memory* and relate them to the "stab of wonder" passage on page 298. Suggest in what ways these final meditations by Nabokov and the metaphors that issue from them characterize the kind of autobiographer or memoirist you take him to be.

Second essay, seven pages. Write an essay analyzing the form that Perec has chosen for his work. What connection do you find between this form, or the language of the work, and Perec's subject matter? Or, write an essay that considers how Leiris's

"Afterword: The Autobiographer as Torero" illuminates his text. In what way(s) does this theoretical meditation clarify Leiris's autobiographical intention and performance? You might make use of the critical essays you are reading this week.

Third essay, eight pages. This paper is on a text we will not read in class. You may choose from among Gertrude Stein, *The Autobiography of Alice B. Toklas*; Richard Wright, *Black Boy*; or Carolyn Steedman, *Landscape for a Good Woman: A Story of Two Lives*. The topic is up to you, but you should write about the text partly in relation to a theoretical issue that has come up in class discussion or in the critical reading.

Works Cited

Adams, Timothy Dow. "Design and Lie in Modern American Autobiography." *Telling Lies in Modern American Autobiography*. Chapel Hill: U of North Carolina P, 1990. 2–16.

Auster, Paul. *The Invention of Solitude*. 1982. New York: Penguin, 1988.

Benstock, Shari. "Authorizing the Autobiographical." Smith and Watson, *Women* 145–55.

Bruss, Helen. "A Feminist Revision of New Historicism to Give Fuller Readings of Women's Private Writing." Smith and Watson, *Women* 222–31.

Butler, Judith. "Introduction to *Bodies that Matter*." Smith and Watson, *Women* 367–79.

Couser, G. Thomas. "Introduction: Authority, Autobiography, America." *Altered Egos: Authority in American Autobiography*. New York: Oxford UP, 1989. 13–27.

Eakin, Paul John. "The Autobiographical Imperative: 'I Have to Write.'" Eakin, *Fictions* 275–78.

———. "Breaking Rules: The Consequences of Self-Narration." *Biography: An Interdisciplinary Quarterly* 24.1 (2001): 113–27.

———. *Fictions in Autobiography: Studies in the Art of Self-Invention*. Princeton: Princeton UP, 1985.

———. *How Our Lives Become Stories: Making Selves*. Ithaca: Cornell UP, 1999.

———. "In Talking about the Past We Lie with Every Breath We Draw." Eakin, *Fictions* 3–9.

———. "Narrative and Chronology as Structures of Reference and the New Model Autobiographer." *Studies in Autobiography*. Ed. James Olney. New York: Oxford UP, 1988. 32–41.

———. "Relational Selves, Relational Lives: Autobiography and the Myth of Autonomy." Eakin, *How* 43–98.

———. "Self-Invention in Autobiography: The Moment of Language." Eakin, *Fictions* 181–227.

———. "'The Unseemly Profession': Privacy, Inviolate Personality, and the Ethics of Life Writing." Eakin, *How* 142–86.

Felski, Rita. "On Confession." Smith and Watson, *Women* 83–95.

Friedman, Susan Stanford. "Woman's Autobiographical Selves." Smith and Watson, *Women* 72–82.

Goldman, Anne. "Autobiography, Ethnography, and History: A Model for Reading." Smith and Watson, *Women* 288–98.

Gordon, Mary. *The Shadow Man: A Daughter's Search for Her Father*. New York: Random, 1996.

Gourevitch, Phillip. "The Memory Thief." *New Yorker* 14 June 1999: 48–68.

Harrison, Kathryn. *The Kiss*. New York: Random, 1997.

Hoffman, Eva. *Lost in Translation: A Life in a New Language*. New York: Penguin, 1989.

Kingston, Maxine Hong. *The Woman Warrior: Memoirs of a Girlhood among Ghosts*. New York: Knopf, 1976.

Leiris, Michel. *Manhood: A Journey from Childhood into the Fierce Order of Vitality*. Trans. Richard Howard. New York: Grossman, 1963.

Lejeune, Philippe. "The Autobiographical Pact." *On Autobiography*. Ed. and fwd. Paul John Eakin. Trans. Katherine Leary. Minneapolis: U of Minnesota P, 1989. 3–30.

Maechler, Stefan. *The Wilkomirski Affair: A Study in Biographical Truth: Including the Text of* Fragments: Memories of a Wartime Childhood. Trans. John E. Wood. New York: Schocken, 2001.

Mandel, Barrett. "Full of Life Now." *Autobiography: Essays Theoretical and Critical*. Ed. James Olney. Princeton: Princeton UP, 1980. 49–72.

Miller, Nancy K. "Childless Children: Bodies and Betrayal." *Bequest and Betrayal: Memoirs of a Parent's Death*. New York: Oxford UP, 1996. 23–56.

Nabokov, Vladimir. *Speak, Memory*. New York: Vintage, 1989.

Perec, Georges. *W; or, The Memory of Childhood*. Trans. David Bellos. Boston: Godine, 2003.

Roth, Philip. *Patrimony: A True Story*. New York: Simon, 1991.

Smith, Sidonie. "Autobiography, Criticism, and the Problematics of Gender." Smith, *Poetics* 3–19.

——. "Performativity, Autobiographical Practice, Resistance." Smith and Watson, *Women* 108–15.

——. *A Poetics of Women's Autobiography: Marginality and the Fictions of Self-Representation*. Bloomington: Indiana UP, 1987.

——. "The Universal Subject, Female Embodiment, and the Consolidation of Autobiography." *Subjectivity, Identity, and the Body: Women's Autobiographical Practices in the Twentieth Century*. Bloomington: Indiana UP, 1993. 1–23.

——. "Woman's Story and the Engenderings of Self-Representation." Smith, *Poetics* 44–62.

Smith, Sidonie, and Julia Watson. "Introduction: Situating Subjectivity in Women's Autobiographical Practices." Smith and Watson, *Women* 3–52.

——, eds. *Women, Autobiography, Theory: A Reader*. Madison: U of Wisconsin P, 1998.

Spiegelman, Art. *And Here My Troubles Began*. New York: Pantheon, 1991. Vol. 2 of *Maus: A Survivor's Tale*.

——. *My Father Bleeds History*. New York: Pantheon, 1986. Vol. 1 of *Maus: A Survivor's Tale*.

Sturrock, John. "The New Model Autobiographer." *New Literary History* 9 (1977): 51–63.

Wilkomirski, Binjamin. *Fragments: Memories of a Wartime Childhood*. Trans. Carol Brown Janeway. New York: Schocken, 1996.

Wong, Sau-ling Cynthia. "Immigrant Autobiography: Some Questions of Definition and Approach." Smith and Watson, *Women* 299–315.

Woolf, Virginia. *Moments of Being*. Ed. and introd. Jeanne Schulkind. New York: Harcourt, 1976.

Young, James. "The Holocaust as Vicarious Past: Art Spiegelman's *Maus* and the After-Images of History." *Critical Inquiry* 24 (1996): 666–99.

Thomas R. Smith

Slipping Away, Sliding Around: Teaching Autobiography as— and Not as—History and Genre

To accommodate the teaching of literary works that are not easily categorized by period or as canonical works of poetry, drama, or fiction, undergraduate course offerings in English at many universities include upper- and sometimes lower-level courses loosely constituted in terms of genre. My own university, Penn State, calls such courses Studies in Genre and Exploring Literary Forms. These two courses and others with similarly vague rubrics such as Texts, Authors, Contexts; Literature and Society; and Literature and Culture allow instructors flexibility in choosing infrequently taught texts and in designing courses to treat topics not usually encountered in courses devoted to periods, major authors, and canonical genres.

Unlike many state university systems, Penn State campuses offer most of their courses and majors from the same catalog. Apart from an upper-level course titled Biographical Writing that may or may not treat autobiography as a species of biography, no course treats autobiography on its own as an object of study.

Wanting to teach an upper-level course devoted solely to autobiography, I therefore chose to teach the Studies in Genre course. The catalog description reads: "English-language texts exemplifying particular genres, with attention to critical theories, historical development, rhetorical strategies, and social, cultural, and aesthetic values" (*2002–04* 518). The title and description carry with them several assumptions that are not necessarily helpful in the case of autobiography. Most obviously, since the course has to be constructed around the topic of genre, the question of what autobiography is must be addressed. Second, the course rubric assumes that the literary texts chosen may be fruitfully understood as conforming to or varying from a generic ideal. One task might be to isolate and describe this ideal, for even if such an ideal does not actually exist, one may be extrapolated from the various texts. And third, the course rubric assumes that, like biological species, genres show development over time—the terms "social, cultural, and aesthetic values" suggesting the mechanisms of change.

Anyone who tries to define autobiography as a genre realizes quickly how difficult it is to do so. "In talking about autobiography," James Olney writes,

> one always feels that there is a great and present danger that the subject will slip away altogether, that it will vanish into thinnest air, leaving behind the perception that there is no such creature as autobiography and that there never has been—that there is no way to bring autobiography to heel as a literary genre with its own proper form, terminology, and observances. (4)

By animating it, Olney captures the elusiveness of the "genre" of autobiography. Can a single genre include works so disparate as Harriet Jacobs's *Incidents in the Life of a Slave Girl*, William Wordsworth's *The Prelude*, Michel de Montaigne's *Essais*, and Maxine Hong Kingston's *The Woman Warrior*? Philippe Lejeune's famous definition of autobiography as "[r]etrospective prose narrative written by a real person concerning his own existence, where the focus is his individual life, in particular the story of his personality" (4) immediately rules out *The Prelude* and Montaigne. Kingston's work, subtitled *Memoirs of a Girlhood among Ghosts*, at least initially appears to fall into Lejeune's category of "[g]enres closely related to autobiography," one of which is memoir (4). Despite its including the stories of her mother and of other relatives, doesn't it focus on an individual life? And however elliptically, doesn't it tell the story of Kingston's personality? Is Jacobs's text the only autobiography as defined by Lejeune?

Nonetheless, autobiography is well suited for Studies in Genre precisely because it resists the comparative and evaluative judgments of literary works entailed by the idea of genre. This slipperiness of autobiography throws the idea of genre itself into relief. Teaching a broad range of auto-biographies written across centuries by people in disparate cultures encourages the interrogation of genre as a theoretical construct, for, even if autobiographies are chosen to illustrate the genre, the result will hardly be more specific than "writings with a varying degree of focus on the author's life." Students may in fact appreciate the power of self–life writing as a mode of discourse because it flouts categories of understanding that the teacher and other commentators bring to bear on it. (I use "mode" here in Gérard Genette's sense, as a kind of writing that transcends genre [71].)

With these considerations buzzing in my head, I constructed an upper-level course that tried to do justice to the history of autobiography as well as to its protean, genre-busting qualities. My chief tactic is to dramatize the inevitable conflict between the concept of genre as a source of literary meaning and value and the multifariousness of autobiographi-cal writing and its resistance to generic rules. My pedagogical objectives are to teach students how the idea of genres influences literary percep-tions, for good or ill, and to have students explore classic and contempo-rary autobiographies with and without genre as a heuristic principle. I therefore offer a history of autobiography conceived of as a genre and a survey of such a history's limitations, which are exposed when works are clearly autobiographical in intent but not easily placed into a history of the genre, except as outliers or instances of Lejeune's "closely related" genres.

Accordingly, the first eight weeks move chronologically through sev-eral classic autobiographical texts: Augustine's *Confessions* (in translation), *The Book of Margery Kempe* (in translation), Rousseau's *Confessions* (in translation), *The Autobiography of Benjamin Franklin*, John Stuart Mill's *Autobiography*, Harriet Martineau's *Autobiography*, and Jacobs's *Incidents in the Life of a Slave Girl*. The last eight weeks treat contemporary, mostly American, autobiographical works: Maya Angelou's *I Know Why the Caged Bird Sings*, Richard Rodriguez's *Hunger of Memory*, James McBride's *The Color of Water*, Rigoberta Menchú's *I, Rigoberta Menchú* (in translation), Reinaldo Arenas's *Before Night Falls* (in translation), Sara Suleri's *Meatless Days*, and Kingston's *The Woman Warrior*.

The students are a mix of junior and senior English majors and upper-level students who need a 400-level course outside their major. My Penn State campus, Abington, is a small college of about 3,200 day and evening students located in a wealthy neighborhood of a nineteenth-century streetcar suburb about thirteen miles north of the center of Philadelphia. Despite its surroundings and history as a former upper-class girls' boarding school, most Abington students are working- and middle-class. They often work up to twenty-five hours per week at part-time jobs, and many are young adults who have served in the military or started a family. Some are nontraditional students returning to college, having left during their first or second year for a host of reasons. Because many students have limited time, I assign selected chapters of Augustine, Rousseau, Mill, Martineau, and Menchú. The other texts are read in full.

Since I want students to discover for themselves the limitations of genre as a concept, I do not announce this either at the outset or during the course. The chronological organization, however, raises the issue naturally, as students encounter *The Book of Margery Kempe* immediately after Augustine's *Confessions*. How could such different books both be autobiographies? Students easily see that Augustine and Kempe share a religious and personal focus, but the differences in the personal concerns, and in the texts' narrative styles and means of organization, make it hard to determine just what autobiography is. At this point, I talk about the dangers of making generalizations based on a limited number of cases. So we suspend our discussions of definition as we move on through Rousseau, Franklin, Mill, Martineau, and Jacobs. Students soon sense that the model of the growth of the writer's identity is powerful, but since they still have Kempe before them, they cannot wholly accept the premise that autobiography requires a narrative of developing identity.

Later encounters with Angelou, Rodriguez, McBride, Menchú, Arenas, Suleri, and Kingston make it even more clear that a developmental model is but one way to organize an autobiographical work. Nonetheless, students see the power of that model persisting, as one of the many understandings of what autobiography can be. The variety and force of these autobiographies help students understand that the "problem" is not the texts' violations of the rules of genre but the inadequacy of the idea of genre itself when applied to autobiographical writing. In fact, students are generally happy to accept each autobiography on its own as a representation of the experience and sensibility of the writer, instead of worrying about the autobiographies' similarities with "classics" of the genre. Individualist sympathies lead students not only to uphold the freedom of autobiographers to interpret experience as they choose but also to defend their own right to appreciate autobiographies without trying to make them conform to strict generic expectations.

Students prepare three essays, midterm and final exams, and an oral presentation on one autobiographer. The first essay covers works by Augustine, Kempe, Rousseau, Franklin, Mill, Martineau, and Jacobs. Suggested topics include the supposed necessity of a major life change in autobiography, the role of religion in at least two texts, the role of gender in shaping autobiographies, the role of plot in autobiography, and the influence of one or more texts on another. The second assignment treats Jacobs again, but adds Angelou, Rodriguez, McBride, and Menchú. Suggested topics include mixed identity, the burden of oppression, the contrast between life in the twentieth century and earlier centuries as depicted in the autobiographies to be discussed, and the difference between autobiography and memoir. The final essay covers Menchú again, along with Arenas, Suleri, and Kingston. Topics include truth versus fiction in autobiography, the role of shock value in reading autobiography, politics and autobiography, the idea of the relational self in autobiography, and the organization of Kingston's book compared with the chronological arrangement of many autobiographies.

The midterm includes short-answer questions about textual details and a paragraph asking students to explain how reading one document, critical essay, or book chapter has changed their understanding of an autobiography. The first part of the final exam asks for paragraph-length responses to questions designed to determine if students have completed the readings. The second part asks them to define autobiography in a short essay, using at least three texts read in the course, or to write a portion of their own autobiography in such a way as to illustrate three criteria of autobiography that they must choose. The short essay and the autobiographical passage ask students not to define autobiography as a genre in an all-inclusive way but to select characteristics of the books they have read to construct their own working definition of autobiography.

I meet individually with students to work out suitable topics for oral presentation. In class sessions, we collectively build a chart of the rhetorical situations of each autobiographer, limiting our analysis to purpose, topic, and audience. This exercise helps students organize their understanding of the autobiographies by relating one to another, dramatizes the variety among the autobiographies, and encourages comparing autobiographies without using a generic ideal as a yardstick.

Works Cited

Angelou, Maya. *I Know Why the Caged Bird Sings*. 1969. New York: Bantam, 1971.
Arenas, Reinaldo. *Before Night Falls*. Trans. Dolores M. Koch. 1993. New York: Penguin, 1994.
Augustine. *The Confessions*. Trans. Maria Boulding. 1997. New York: Vintage, 1998.
Franklin, Benjamin. *The Autobiography and Other Writings*. Ed. and introd. Kenneth Silverman. New York: Penguin, 1986.
Genette, Gérard. *The Architext: An Introduction*. Trans. Jane E. Lewin. Berkeley: U of California P, 1992.
Jacobs, Harriet A. *Incidents in the Life of a Slave Girl Written by Herself*. Ed. and introd. Jean Fagan Yellin. Cambridge: Harvard UP, 1987.
Kempe, Margery. *The Book of Margery Kempe: A New Translation, Contexts, and Criticisms*. Ed. and trans. Lynn Staley. Norton Critical Edition. New York: Norton, 2001.
Kingston, Maxine Hong. *The Woman Warrior: Memoirs of a Girlhood among Ghosts*. 1975. New York: Vintage, 1989.
Lejeune, Philippe. "The Autobiographical Pact." *On Autobiography*. Ed. and fwd. Paul John Eakin. Trans. Katherine Leary. Minneapolis: U of Minnesota P, 1989. 3–30.
Martineau, Harriet. *Autobiography*. Ed. Maria Weston Chapman. 1877. 2 vols. Boston: Houghton, 1879.
McBride, James. *The Color of Water: A Black Man's Tribute to His White Mother*. 1996. New York: Riverhead, 1997.
Menchú, Rigoberta. *I, Rigoberta Menchú: An Indian Woman in Guatemala*. Ed. and introd. Elisabeth Burgos-Debray. Trans. Ann Wright. New York: Verso, 1984.
Mill, John Stuart. *Autobiography*. 1873. New York: Collier, 1909. 6 Apr. 2001. *Bartleby.com Great Books Online*. 16 Sept. 2001 <http://www.bartleby.com/25/1>.
Montaigne, Michel de. *Essays*. Trans. and introd. J. M. Cohen. London: Penguin, 1993.
Olney, James. "Autobiography and the Cultural Moment: A Thematic, Historical, and Bibliographical Introduction." *Autobiography: Essays Theoretical and Critical*. Ed. Olney. Princeton: Princeton UP, 1980. 3–27.
Rodriguez, Richard. *Hunger of Memory: The Education of Richard Rodriguez*. 1982. New York: Bantam, 1983.
Rousseau, Jean-Jacques. *The Confessions of Jean-Jacques Rousseau*. 1782. Trans. W. Conygham Mallory. 2005. *eBooks@Adelaide*. Univ. of Adelaide Lib. 5 Sept. 2001 <http://etext.library.adelaide.edu.au/r/rousseau/jean_jacques/r864c>.
Suleri, Sara. *Meatless Days*. 1989. Chicago: U of Chicago P, 1991.
2002–04 Undergraduate Degree Programs Bulletin. University Park: Pennsylvania State U, 2002.
Wordsworth, William. The Prelude, *1799, 1805, 1850: Authoritative Texts, Context and Reception, Recent Critical Essays*. Ed. Jonathan Wordsworth, M. H. Abrams, and Stephen Gill. New York: Norton, 1979.

David Houston Jones

Life Writing and Biographical Fiction: Contemporary Teaching and Learning Strategies

Philippe Lejeune's work on the theorization of autobiography has undoubtedly played a crucial role in redefining the genre as an area worthy of serious academic attention. His notion of the "pacte autobiographique" ("autobiographical pact"), in particular, has generated much stimulating debate and continues to provide a model definition (although a disputed one) of autobiography (*Le pacte*).[1] While contemporary debates also consider new forms of writing like autofiction, and Lejeune has moved on to consider Internet and audio life histories, Lejeune's 1976 book is important both for its pioneering impetus and for its desire to create rigorous generic definitions.[2] The present essay considers a phase of anxiety arising in student learning when classification of potentially (auto)biographical texts is first explicitly approached. The phenomenon is understood here both as a teaching and learning problem with serious practical consequences and in terms of what it may tell us about questions of genre classification.

In what follows, I refer to an optional second- or final-year course in which students of modern languages and joint-degree programs chose a number of texts involving life writing issues. While some, like André Gide's *Si le grain ne meurt* and Jean Genet's *Journal du voleur*, are voiced in the first person and appear to function as autobiographical narratives, others, like Pierre Michon's *Vies minuscules* and Pascal Quignard's *Albucius*, are narrated principally in the third person and raise important questions about the status of third-person biographical narrative. I want now to set out some of the learning experiences that arose, evaluating the relevance of existing genre theorizations for contemporary writing that problematizes the biographical.

Genet's *Journal du voleur* represents a fascinating test case for readerly assumptions concerning biographical attribution. Although students responded critically to many aspects of the text, most did not volunteer reactions as to the text's autobiographical status and only appeared to consider the question of whether it is an autobiography in the course of the seminar or tutorial itself. Responses to the question were for the most part strongly affirmative, and, most interestingly, in many cases this judgment was considered to represent a self-evident truth. The assessment of whether the text is an autobiography was presented in varying ways, from a tentative expression of opinion to, more commonly, a form of almost condescending bemusement. One such reaction presented autobiographical attribution as not only indisputable but also wholly obvious in any reading of the text: "It *is* a first-person narrative signed by the author, Jean Genet, after all."

The *self-evident* classification of biographical narrative has extremely interesting implications for our understanding of life writing texts and resonates with Lejeune's theorizations. The relation of identity between author, protagonist, and first-person narrator is a crucial part of Lejeune's early definition of autobiography in *Le pacte autobiographique*. That relationship, we learn, must be confirmed by proper name; that is, by the use of the author's own name in the text: "l'identité du *nom* (auteur-narrateur-personnage)" ("identity of name [author-narrator-character]"; 26).[3] In subsequent seminar discussion, a number of readers cited the information on the book's cover as evidence for Lejeune's definition: the name "Jean Genet" immediately follows the title *Journal du voleur*, suggesting a "journal intime" associated with Genet's lived experience through the idea of theft. Although such an assumption mimics the early reception of the text (the thief announced in the title being associated by Sartre with Genet himself), it is questioned by the very debatable relation between Genet's life narrative and the account given in the *Journal* and, more important, by the liberties taken in the text with reference.

Lejeune's autobiographical pact is founded on the possibility of reference to the existence of the author in the real: "la biographie et l'autobiographie sont des textes *référentiels*. . . . Tous les textes référentiels comportent
donc ce que j'appellerai un '*pacte référentiel*'" ("biographies and autobiographies are *referential* texts. . . . All referential texts involve what I will
call a 'referential pact'" [*Le Pacte* 36]). In the *Journal du voleur*, meanwhile,
the narrator shifts between identities and cannot be solidly identified with
the author and protagonist by name, contravening the conditions of the
autobiographical pact and, therefore, of the referential pact. Most prob-
lematically, the text displays a reflexivity that undermines the narrator's reliability: "Ce que j'écris fut-il vrai? Faux? Seul ce livre d'amour sera réel.
Les faits qui lui servirent de prétexte? Je dois en être le dépositaire. Ce n'est
pas eux que je restitue" ("Was what I wrote true? False? Only this book of
love will be real. What of the facts that served as its pretext? I must be their
repository. It is not they that I am restoring"; Genet 113; Frechtman 100).
Such a demotion of reference cannot be accommodated within Lejeune's
early theories.

Rather than a viable autobiography, then, the *Journal* produces a critique of the assumptions of autobiography. As readers, we expect coherent
chronology, expressive language, and a reliable narrator, and yet all three
are systematically downgraded as the text unfolds.[4] The expectation of
each is expressly cultivated in a narrative that thrives on baffling chronological references, frantic scene changes, and self-undermining narratorial
asides. The most fascinating, if disconcerting, aspect of seminar discussion
concerns the blind spot that "unreliable" narrative moments became in student readings. It was apparent that the failure to recognize narratorial un-
reliability was atypical and that many of the students had little difficulty in
recognizing such problems in overtly fictional texts. Genet's work plays on
the readerly expectation of reference in life writing: the anxiety with which
readers apprehend the instability of viewpoint in the *Journal du voleur*
counterbalances the inordinate confidence with which they instinctively
classify the text as self-evidently autobiographical, alerting us to the extraordinary suspension of critical scrutiny that (auto)biographical writing
may produce.[5]

The *Journal*, meanwhile, may shed further light on the genre classification of third-person, biographically orientated texts. Pierre Michon's *Vies
minuscules* is instructive in what it may tell us about recent writing in
French that operates at the edge of biography as a genre category and

whose manipulation of narrative voice problematizes genre classification through self-conscious textual strategies. Michon's "vies" are fascinating as teaching texts because of their emphatic foregrounding of a narrator whose narrative is subsequently undercut and problematized by a third-person protagonist. In the "Vie d'André Dufourneau," for example, our primary expectation is again one of reference: we expect the narrator to function as the conduit for a more or less coherent life narrative that refers principally to Dufourneau. As the narrative develops, however, the assumption is progressively frustrated. We realize that many of the scenes, like Dufourneau's arrival at the house of the foster family, are artifacts of the narrator's imagination: "Je me plais à croire qu'il arriva un soir d'octobre ou de décembre, trempé de pluie ou les oreilles rougies dans le gel vif; pour la première fois ses pieds frappèrent ce chemin que plus jamais ils ne frapperont" ("I like to think that he arrived one evening in October or December, soaked by the rain or with ears reddened by the sharp frost; for the first time his feet trod this path that they will tread no more"; 15).

The same avowed fictionalization applies to the scene in which Dufourneau is taught to read and write by the narrator's grandmother: "*J'imagine* un soir d'hiver" ("*I imagine* one winter evening"; 15; my emphasis). And years after Dufourneau's departure, the narrator's interpretation of the silence that follows Dufourneau's last letter is still more capricious: "Un définitif silence y succéda, que je ne peux et ne veux interpréter que par la mort" ("A final silence followed, which I can only and wish only to interpret as (his) death"; 28). While "je . . . peux" might represent a narrator piecing together the facts of a life in the only possible way, "je . . . veux" once more emphasizes the excessively thin factual basis of the narrative and the narrator's disconcerting readiness to admit that his story is largely a fiction.

In contrast to the sensation of certainty pervading the readings of Genet that I discussed earlier, Michon's narrative strategies usher in a more explicit form of doubt, and anxiety, regarding genre categorization. The highly misleading signpost of "journal" in Genet's title seems to authorize a particular mode of reading, whereas Michon's text provides insufficient information about the readerly position to be adopted. The label "vie" does not, at least for this particular student readership, carry the clear practical instruction inferred from that of "journal." The "well, obviously" response that we considered earlier is replaced, in the encounter with Michon, by the perplexed question, How are we supposed to read the text?

The question as to whether the text is to be read as biography, autobiography, or fiction again fails to be posed, and the absence of the question no longer signals its perceived redundancy but rather a lack of readerly orientation concerning genre categories.

Dufourneau's death clarifies the exploitation of the assumptions of biography taking place behind the unstable façade of the "vie." The narrator's grandmother, in the text's conclusion, believes that Dufourneau, years after emigrating to Africa, has been killed by his own workers: "Elise pensait en secret que Dufourneau avait succombé de la main d'ouvriers noirs" ("Elise secretly thought that Dufourneau had died at the hands of black workers"; 29). Instead of consolidating the sense of reference that Lejeune advocates, the claim to verisimilitude is presented purely as the narrator's desire to believe this particular version of events, whose fictionality is acknowledged: "l'hypothèse la plus romanesque—et, j'aimerais le croire, la plus probable—m'a été soufflée par ma grand-mère" ("The most Romanesque—and I would like to believe, the most likely—hypothesis was whispered to me by my grandmother"; 29). The alleged probability of such an imaginative reconstruction can only exacerbate its fictional basis: probability, like hypothesis, can have no place in an account whose raison d'être is simply the desire to tell stories.

The intractable problem that we encounter here is the fictional status of Dufourneau's story in a narrative that purports to be biographical in basis. Each individual text in Michon's book functions under the sign of the "vie," setting up the possibility of reading the work biographically. The resulting play between first-person narrator and inscrutable protagonist leads to a dramatic loss of confidence in both: Dufourneau remains a shadowy character whose narrative is dreamed up at the whim of the narrator. The narrator's wild equivocations over the truth status of his narrative—"et j'ose croire un instant, sachant qu'il n'en fut rien" ("and I dare to believe for a moment, knowing that such was not the case"; 19)—culminate in the admission that Dufourneau is a decoy, leading back only to the figure of the narrator: "Mais parlant de lui, c'est de moi que je parle" ("But speaking of him, it is of myself that I speak"; 19).

Michon, like Genet, implicitly invokes a genre that his text conspicuously fails to live up to. While students' readings of Genet sometimes display a marked insensitivity to narrative phenomena that they would recognize in other contexts, one of the problems raised in Michon's work stems from the status of the genre of biography in critical accounts. Biography remains undertheorized and lower in profile than autobiography, in part perhaps because of the success of Lejeune's work on autobiography.[6] Even entitling every short text in the book "Vie" may be insufficient to alert students to the subliminal presence of biography, in which case much of Michon's tricky manipulation of viewpoint will be lost. The problem is that of the "intention" that Lejeune sees as underpinning the autobiographical pact: we respond, as readers, to an implicit narrative intention that appears to guarantee the affiliation of text to generic category, whether fiction, biography, or autobiography. Once this judgment is made, the questioning of genre categories becomes disproportionately difficult. Although student readers of Michon may miss the problematization of life writing in *Vies minuscules*, readers of Genet tend to blank out the problems and inconsistencies of narrative viewpoint in favor of simplistic genre classification. Dilemmas like these can cause a dramatic stalling in student learning, but the experiences to which I have referred also make possible, in the long term, a greater awareness of the complexity of the role of the narrator in establishing the text's conventions.

Michon's work, meanwhile, may alert readers to a contemporary current of experimentation around the question of the biographical. The problems that student readers experience with texts like *Vies minuscules* in fact reproduce tensions between the genre of biography, biographical fiction, and theory. While Michon is concerned to work with "minor lives" in *Vies minuscules*, in *Vie de Joseph Roulin* he trades on the celebrity that is still largely unproblematically associated with the subjects of biography, apparently offering a revisionist biography of Vincent Van Gogh by reference to Van Gogh's postman. In such ways, Michon's work interrogates the monolithic presence of the biographical subject through the idea of the *petites gens*, replacing the cultural visibility of the biographical subject with the provocative obscurity that plays in the margins of biographical discourse.

Notes

1. All translations are mine unless otherwise stated.

2. For more recent work on autobiographical writing, see Laouyen. For Lejeune's work on audio life histories, see *Je est un autre*, and on Internet life writing, see *"Cher écran."*

3. For Lejeune's subsequent modifications of this definition, see *Je est un autre* 8–10 and *Moi aussi* 9–10 and "Le Pacte autobiographique (bis)."

4. For a detailed study of the role of reference in readerly expectations concerning autobiography, see Eakin 30.

5. Although Lejeune questions the categorization of Genet's text as autobiographical, his critique focuses not on reference but on chronology. Lejeune's claim that the journal focuses on a single childhood event is reminiscent of Sartre's account rather than Genet's text (*L'autobiographie* 19). On Genet and autobiography, see also Sheringham.

6. In Shelston's account of biography, for example, we are frequently "embarrassed by a form which is 'non-literary'"; see also Madelénat 9.

Works Cited

Eakin, Paul John. *Touching the World: Reference in Autobiography*. Princeton: Princeton UP, 1992.

Frechtman, Bernard, trans. *The Thief's Journal*. By Jean Genet. New York: Grove, 1964.

Genet, Jean. *Journal du voleur*. 1949. Paris: Gallimard, 1982.

Gide, André. *Si le grain ne meurt*. Paris: Gallimard, 1928.

Laouyen, Mounir, ed. *Nouvelles autobiographies*. Spec. issue of *L'esprit créateur* 42.4 (2002): 1–96.

Lejeune, Philippe. *L'autobiographie en France*. Paris: Colin, 1971.

——. *"Cher écran": Journal personnel, ordinateur, Internet*. Paris: Seuil, 2000.

——. *Je est un autre: l'autobiographie, de la littérature aux médias*. Paris: Seuil, 1980.

——. *Moi aussi*. Paris: Seuil, 1986.

——. *Le Pacte autobiographique*. Paris: Seuil, 1976.

——. "Le Pacte autobiographique (bis)." *Moi aussi* 21–36.

Madelénat, Daniel. *La biographie*. Paris: PUF, 1984.

Michon, Pierre. *Vie de Joseph Roulin*. Paris: Verdier, 1988.

——. *Vies minuscules*. Paris: Gallimard, 1984.

Quignard, Pascal. *Albucius*. Paris: P. O. L., 1990.

Sartre, Jean-Paul. *Saint Genet: Comédien et martyr*. Paris: Gallimard, 1952.

Shelston, Alan. *Biography*. London: Methuen, 1977.

Sheringham, Michael. *French Autobiography: Devices and Desires, from Rousseau to Perec*. Oxford: Clarendon, 1993.

Suzanne L. Bunkers

Diaries and Diarists

A few years ago, I developed and began teaching English 213, Diaries and Diarists, a four-credit undergraduate general education literature course designed to be writing-intensive and to appeal to a wide range of students.[1] Few courses in my department focused on forms of life writing. Thus, when my university redesigned its general education program, it was a propitious time to create an entire course that centered on life writing and also made use of my work on diary writing. Like my research for *"All Will Yet Be Well": The Diary of Sarah Gillespie Huftalen, 1873–1952*; *Diaries of Girls and Women: A Midwestern American Sampler*; and *Inscribing the Daily: Critical Essays on Women's Diaries*, the course Diaries and Diarists explores ways that diaries both document the experiences of individuals and families and function as life writing forms where self-representation is at the core of the writer's work.

Diaries can provide valuable insights into individuals' self-images, the dynamics of families and communities, and the nature and kinds of cultural contributions that individuals have made. The diary's appeal can be traced to its expansiveness and flexibility. The diary can incorporate a variety of writing styles. It can range from being formal and stylized to conversational and idiomatic. It can also envelop a variety of themes; for example, the need for self-affirmation, the conflict between duty and desire, the quest for knowledge, the wish to make one's mark on the world, or the coming to terms with change and loss. Because it is expansive and flexible, the diary can be studied simultaneously as a historical document, a therapeutic tool, and a form of literature. Moreover, the form and content of a diary are inevitably shaped not only by its writer's personality but also by her or his experience of race, ethnicity, class, age, sexual orientation, and geographic setting (Bunkers, Introduction).

Contrary to stereotypes, diaries have not necessarily been the intensely secretive texts that come to mind when most present-day readers imagine diaries with little locks and keys. Although many manuscript diaries are private in the sense that they are not published, these texts are sometimes meant to be shared with family members and close friends. Occasionally, a diary even functions as a collaborative text, with more than one person writing in it or with one family member (often a female) writing what is intended as a family record, an artifact of material culture that will be treasured by many generations. For these reasons, the diary occupies a unique place in literature and history as a text that can be both personal and communal.[2]

Starting from this theoretical framework, the course focused on each diary's format, context, purpose, and possible audience(s) to examine not only what diaries say but also what they do not say. The course also addressed the following questions: Why are we drawn to read about another person's daily experiences? What makes diaries appealing to writers, young and old? What can diaries tell us about why individuals write in diaries, and why they (and others) preserve those diaries and make them available for others to appreciate? What is the author's relation to the diary once it is edited and published? How are the designs and forms of diaries related to their content? How can the diary function as both an individual and community text?

Student registration the first time I taught Diaries and Diarists set the pattern for enrollments in subsequent semesters: eight first-year students, seven second-year students, four third-year students, and ten fourth-year students—with many different majors.

Kimberly Nielsen, an MFA graduate student in creative writing, participated as my teaching intern, and the course we planned was based on team-taught individual class sessions. Then Kim and I developed this course description:

Keeping a diary is a personal activity that has a public appeal. In this course, which will be a four-credit writing-intensive course, students will study various kinds of diaries and will keep diaries themselves. Novels such as Graham Greene's *The End of the Affair* and Helen Fielding's *Bridget Jones' Diary*, each of which features the diary format, will be analyzed in conjunction with viewing and analyzing their film adaptations. The Holocaust will be explored in the context of the various editions of *The Diary of a Young Girl*, supplemented by the documentary film *Anne Frank Remembered*, and other Holocaust testimonies. Course participants will study excerpts from *"All Will Yet Be Well,"* the diary kept by an Iowa farm woman and teacher, Sarah Gillespie Huftalen, for more than seventy-five years, as well as excerpts from other diaries by "ordinary" people. Tristine Rainer's *The New Diary*, *The Freedom Writers' Diary*, and Esmé Raji Codell's *Educating Esmé: Diary of a Teacher's First Year* will round out the course readings and provide contextual background for the intensive writing to be done.

As outlined below, each course text served a specific purpose. Tristine Rainer's *The New Diary* functioned as a how-to text that offered many practical ideas for specific kinds of diary entries. For example, students could list and discuss the significance of stepping-stones (i.e., turning points) in their lives. Alexandra Johnson's *Leaving a Trace: On Keeping a Journal* offered students additional diary-writing possibilities, including such topics as key influences, hidden lessons, secret gifts, and unfinished business.

Our Diaries and Diarists syllabus outlined specific reading assignments followed by related diary-writing assignments. I was able to provide each student with a complimentary copy of my *"All Will Yet Be Well."* This text struck many students as the most difficult reading because its style and content spanned 1873–1952. After reading the diary, students wrote responses to this assignment: "Create a brief portrait in words of one individual in Sarah's diary other than Sarah herself. See what you can discover about that individual's life (and Sarah's life) through what Sarah says about this individual." Students had the option of writing from another individual's point of view, creating a dialogue between another individual and Sarah, or creating an unsent letter written by either Sarah or another individual discussed in Sarah's diary.

Several weeks later, when we discussed *The Freedom Writers' Diary*, by the Freedom Writers, and Codell's *Educating Esmé: Diary of a Teacher's First Year*, students gained insights into the ways in which contemporary students' and teachers' diaries paralleled and differed from Sarah Gillespie Huftalen's diary. As class members analyzed diaries written for different readers during different historical eras, students assessed how each diarist's consciousness of purpose and audience influenced when, what, and how she or he wrote. Just as important, students saw that patterns emerging in a diary might be linked to its format (e.g., a five-year diary measuring four-by-six inches that permits the diarist to make one four-line entry each day), sometimes as the result of the ways in which a diarist subverts a rigid format (e.g., writing outside the allotted number of lines, crossing out formatted dates) or invents an individual format (e.g., sewing together eight-by-eleven-inch loose-leaf pages into a packet of diary pages or using unlined pages of varying sizes and gathering them into a folder). Students discovered that one task of the careful reader is to observe how the diarist creates and maintains the text. By doing so, the reader can "map" a diary and learn how a diarist works.

Finally, students began to interpret how a diarist might use encoding in a text. *Encoding*, as I use the term, means the transmission of the writer's message in an oblique rather than direct manner. Encoding can take a variety of syntactic and semantic forms. For example, a diarist might speak indirectly by deleting the pronoun *I* from the text or by contradicting one statement with another. A diarist might deviate from standard American English sentence structure or orthography—particularly in the case of pre-twentieth-century diaries—or use a sophisticated code of visual symbols. A diarist might employ silences in choosing not to write explicitly (or at all) about such taboo subjects as sexuality, pregnancy, labor, and childbirth.

My students' analysis of encoding grew more sophisticated when we compared editions and English translations of Anne Frank's *The Diary of a Young Girl*. During class discussions, each student selected one diary entry that she or he deemed important, paraphrased the entry, and explained how it illustrated a central theme in the diary. By recognizing how editors and translators shaped the publication history of Anne Frank's diary and contributed to ongoing discussions about ownership and copyright, students came to appreciate the distinction between the artifacts—that is, the volumes and loose-leaf pages that compose Anne Frank's diary—and the diverse (and sometimes contentious) ways in which these artifacts have been transformed into print.

Graham Greene's *The End of the Affair* and Helen Fielding's *Bridget Jones' Diary* allowed students to analyze how authors could incorporate various diary formats into works of fiction. Moreover, the opportunity to view film adaptations of these two novels gave students a framework for comparing diary formats in fiction and in film.

Because I wanted to provide students with an opportunity to examine the burgeoning world of the online diary, which intrigued me but which I had not yet had time to explore fully, I encouraged students to investigate *The Emily Project* (marblehead.net/Emily), *Diarist.net* (diarist.net/registry), *The World Diary Project* (worlddiaryproject.com), and other Web sites that provide links to thousands of online diaries. Students who opted to keep diaries online during the semester learned that keeping such a diary means that each entry might be accessible to a large readership. Reconceptualizing the diary as well as the act of diary keeping becomes inevitable because timeworn assumptions that a diary is kept only for the diarist and that it is an intensely secretive and private enterprise are unworkable when exploring the phenomenon of the online diary.[3]

As a writing-intensive general education course, Diaries and Diarists required that each student complete a minimum of twenty-five pages of polished writing. One component of this writing consisted of entries in what Kim Nielsen and I called a "professional diary"; namely, one in which each student drafted responses to subjects discussed during class sessions— responses that the students revised and expanded into personal-reflection essays.

Finally, each student developed a course project (see appendix) that involved selecting a published or unpublished diary (or a form of life writing that used the diary format as its basis) to be analyzed in depth. A number of students who had kept diaries in childhood or adolescence chose their own diaries, thereby adding a self-reflexive component to their course projects. Each student prepared a written report as well as an oral presentation in which he or she described the diary's format, defined possible encoding techniques used by the diarist, and evaluated the purposes that the diary might have served for its writer and its reader. At the end of the semester, each student submitted a portfolio that contained written assignments, along with his or her self-assessment and course evaluation.

Appendix

Final Project

Select a diary (or a form of autobiography that uses the journal-diary format) as the basis for your analysis. The diarist should intrigue you enough to spend sufficient time with him or her in order to discover the value of the diarist's text, to gain the extended confidence to read and analyze it, and to compare and contrast it to other diaries you've read, in or out of class, or to journals you've kept. Analyze the diary by using techniques you've learned in class and in Tristine Rainer's *The New Diary*. In your analysis you should

> Define the diarist's purpose and format and audience.
> Analyze the diction and syntax, the changes and circumstance, the audience, and the risks the writer takes.
> Describe the diary modes used by the diarist: subjective or objective, cathartic, descriptive, intuitive, reflective.
> Compare and contrast the devices used by the diarist with those you've already seen or used: lists, portraits, maps, guided imagery, altered points of view, epistles, dialogue.
> Evaluate ways in which the writing is affected by historical, personal, or institutional circumstances.
> Draw conclusions on how the diary functions for its writer and for you as its reader.

Notes

I would like to thank Kimberly Nielsen for her fine work as the teaching intern in Diaries and Diarists. Above all, I would like to thank the students who participated in the course.

1. Founded in 1868, Minnesota State University, Mankato, is a comprehensive public university located 85 miles southwest of Minneapolis–St. Paul. Two-thirds of the university's 14,000 students come from Minnesota. The student body represents 48 states of the United States and includes 600 international students from 70 countries.

2. Among the secondary sources I've recommended to students on the generic, formal, and historical dimensions of diaries are Bunkers (*Diary of Caroline Seabury*, "Whose Diary"); Buss; Culley; Fothergill; Gannett; Hogan; Huff; Lejeune ("*Cher écran*," "How Do Diaries"); Podnieks; Sinor; Temple and Bunkers; and Wink; and the articles by Bloom, by Lejeune, and by Temple in Bunkers and Huff.

3. For more on online diaries, see Lejeune, "*Cher écran*."

Works Cited

Anne Frank Remembered. Dir. John Blair. Culver City: Columbia TriStar, 1996.

Bloom, Lynn Z. "'I Write for Myself and Others': Private Diaries as Public Documents." Bunkers and Huff 23–27.

Bunkers, Suzanne L., ed. *"All Will Yet Be Well": The Diary of Sarah Gillespie Huftalen, 1873–1952*. Iowa City: U of Iowa P, 1993.

——. *The Diary of Caroline Seabury, 1854–1863*. Madison: U of Wisconsin P, 1991.

———. Introduction. *Diaries of Girls and Women: A Midwestern American Sampler.* Ed. Bunkers. Madison: U of Wisconsin P, 2001. 3–40.

———. "Whose Diary Is It, Anyway? Issues of Agency, Authority, Ownership." *A/B: Auto/Biography Studies* 17.1 (2002): 11–27.

Bunkers, Suzanne L., and Cynthia Huff, eds. *Inscribing the Daily: Critical Essays on Women's Diaries.* Amherst: U of Massachusetts P, 1996.

Buss, Helen M. "Pioneer Women's Diaries and Journals: Letters Home / Letters to the Future." *Mapping Our Selves: Canadian Women's Autobiography in English.* Montreal: McGill-Queen's UP, 1993. 37–60.

Codell, Esmé Raji. *Educating Esmé: Diary of a Teacher's First Year.* Chapel Hill: Algonquin, 2001.

Culley, Margo C., ed. *A Day at a Time: The Diary Literature of American Women from 1764 to the Present.* New York: Feminist, 1985.

Fielding, Helen. *Bridget Jones' Diary.* New York: Viking, 1998.

Fothergill, Robert. *Private Chronicles: A Study of English Diaries.* London: Oxford UP, 1974.

Frank, Anne. The Diary of Anne Frank*: The Critical Edition.* Ed. David Barnouw and Gerrold Van Der Stroom. Trans. Arnold J. Pomerans and B. M. Mooyaart. New York: Doubleday, 1989.

———. The Diary of Anne Frank*: The Definitive Edition.* Ed. Otto H. Frank and Mirjam Pressler. Trans. Susan Massotty. New York: Doubleday, 1995.

———. *The Diary of a Young Girl.* Ed. Otto Frank. New York: Pocket, 1972.

———. *Scientific Edition of* The Diary of Anne Frank*: Fifth Amended Print.* Ed. David Barnouw and Gerrold Van Der Stroom. Amsterdam: Netherlands Inst. for War Documentation, 2003.

Freedom Writers. *The Freedom Writers' Diary: How a Teacher and 150 Teens Used Writing to Change Themselves and the World around Them.* New York: Main Street, 1999.

Gannett, Cinthia. *Gender and the Journal: Diaries and Academic Discourse.* Albany: State U of New York P, 1992.

Greene, Graham. *The End of the Affair.* 1951. New York: Penguin, 1991.

Hogan, Rebecca. "Engendered Autobiographies: The Diary as a Feminine Form." *Autobiography and Questions of Gender.* Spec. issue of *Prose Studies* 14.2 (1991): 95–107.

Huff, Cynthia. "'That Profoundly Female, and Feminist Genre': The Diary as Feminist Praxis." *Women's Studies Quarterly* 17.3–4 (1989): 6–14.

Huftalen, Sarah Gillespie. *"All Will Yet Be Well": The Diary of Sarah Gillespie Huftalen.* Ed. Suzanne L. Bunkers. Iowa City: U of Iowa P, 1993.

Johnson, Alexandra. *Leaving a Trace: On Keeping a Journal.* Boston: Back Bay, 2002.

Lejeune, Philippe. *"Cher écran": Journal personnel, ordinateur, Internet.* Paris: Seuil, 2000.

———. "How Do Diaries End?" *Biography: An Interdisciplinary Quarterly* 24.1 (2001): 99–111.

———. "The 'Journal de Jeune Fille' in Nineteenth-Century France." Trans. Martine Breillac. Bunkers and Huff 107–22.

Podnieks, Elizabeth. *Daily Modernism: The Literary Diaries of Virginia Woolf, Antonia White, Elizabeth Smart, and Anaïs Nin.* Montreal: McGill-Queen's UP, 2000.

Rainer, Tristine. *The New Diary: How to Use a Journal for Self-Guidance and Expanded Creativity.* Los Angeles: Tarcher, 1999.

Sinor, Jennifer. *The Extraordinary Work of Ordinary Writing: Annie Ray's Diary.* Iowa City: U of Iowa P, 2002.

Temple, Judy Nolte. "Fragments as Diary: Theoretical Implications of the Dreams and Visions of 'Baby Doe' Tabor." Bunkers and Huff 72–85.

Temple, Judy Nolte, and Suzanne L. Bunkers. "Mothers, Daughters, and Diaries: Literacy, Relationship, and Cultural Context." *Nineteenth-Century Women Learn to Write.* Ed. Catherine Hobbs. Charlottesville: UP of Virginia, 1995. 197–216.

Wink, Amy L. *She Left Nothing in Particular: Nineteenth Century Women's Diaries.* Knoxville: U of Tennessee P, 2001.

Gary Totten

Teaching Travel Writing as Life Writing

Frances Bartkowski argues that travelers choose their "place," "routes," and "questions" and that in their travel texts "the writing of their displacement lead[s] them to a re-shaped sense of self " (101). Travel literature allows writers not only to narrate their encounters with the unfamiliar but also to theorize the personal implications of their journeys. Travel's effects on writers' lives and selves are also evident through reference to literary and cultural texts that have allowed the writers, as Bartkowski says, to "name" and "preconceive" a place (21). Travel writers' decisions regarding place, route, and purpose, the preconceptions and literary-cultural repertoire that affect the travel experience, and the reshaped sense of home and self that results from the journey make travel writing a significant act of life writing. In an upper-level, semester-long undergraduate course on the American road narrative, I ask students to consider these aspects of travel in relation to issues of race, class, and gender. This approach reveals how travel writing not only provides insight into the life and perspective of the writer but also encourages the reader's reshaping of self through reflection about his or her experiences in relation to those of the travel writer.

Although most of the students are English majors, the course also attracts students from other departments. Some of the students have an interest in and experience with travel through study-abroad programs. And yet, while students may have had valuable international travel experiences, they are less likely to have traveled much within the United States or to have encountered the nation's racial or socioeconomic differences. By approaching American road narratives as instances of life writing, I am able to expose students to the wide range of life circumstances and experiences in the United States and to encourage them to consider their own experiences, travel-related or otherwise, in the broader context of American culture.

I first discuss the historical links between travel and life writing and how the two modes share concerns about self-creation and empowerment. Mary Louise Pratt's *Imperial Eyes: Travel Writing and Transculturation* provides a theoretical framework for this discussion. As Pratt notes, travel writing's "heterogeneity and its interactions with other kinds of expression" suggest that there is room in such narratives for various concerns (11), including the construction and reshaping of the self. Pratt notes how the woman traveler of the late eighteenth and early nineteenth centuries took up autobiography, "the form that had become canonical and authoritative in the bourgeois era," and constructed herself "as the protagonist of her travels and her life" (171). To illustrate this idea, I have students read Sarah Kemble Knight's journal of her journey by horseback from Boston to New York in 1704 and consider how she claims the role of protagonist in her life by casting herself as such in her travel narrative.

Olaudah Equiano's *Interesting Narrative of the Life of Olaudah Equiano: Written by Himself* provides another example of the overlapping concerns of travel text and autobiography. The text illustrates Pratt's argument that the first slave autobiographies are "self-descriptions" conforming "to a degree . . . with western literary institutions and western conceptions of culture and of self" and opposing "official ideologies of colonialism and slavery (which, among other things, excluded Africans from western conceptions of culture and of self)" (102). Pratt suggests that Equiano's narrative "*engage*[s] western discourse of identity, community, selfhood, and otherness," using a "transcultural" dynamic (102)—a term she uses to describe how "subordinated or marginal groups select and invent from materials transmitted to them by a dominant or metropolitan culture" (6).

As students encounter Equiano's transcultural negotiation of identity, they gain experience with these shared agendas of travel and life writing and are prepared to consider the connections between subjectivity and movement, a major concern for the "diasporic," "nomadic," and "migratory subjects" of many contemporary texts (Smith and Watson 29). As Caren Kaplan argues, while "displacement" may not be "universally available," "desirable," or "evenly experienced" for all "subjects," "[t]he prevalence of metaphors of travel and displacement" in contemporary literary and cultural criticism reveals an ongoing fascination with the "experience of distance and estrangement" (1).

Once I have established the overlapping concerns and strategies of travel and life writing, I discuss the reshaping of self that often occurs in travel writing and that makes such texts significant acts of life writing. I ask students to identify the writer's preconceptions before and during the travel experience and then to compare these preconceptions with the insights the writer gains during and after the journey. This comparison allows students to track the writer's reshaping of self and the aspects of travel that have affected this change.

The course texts are chosen to illustrate varying preconceptions, expectations, and insights that affect the textual self-construction. For example, Mary Morris journeys from New York to San Miguel, Mexico, to escape the weariness and isolation of her American life and to find "a place where the land and the people and the time" are "connected" and life "make[s] sense . . . again" (4). Morris experiences a sense of power as a woman traveling alone, becoming what Julia Watson calls "a moving point of perception," who "attempts to elude the strictures of definition as 'woman' that would immobilize her" (159). Or as Sidonie Smith notes, travelers (particularly women travelers) use mobility "to alter the terms of identity" (25). But Morris also experiences the fear that she might "spend [her] entire life alone, without a true traveling companion" (211). As Morris makes her complicated journey through fear, loneliness, empowerment, and unfamiliar cultural and physical landscapes, students become aware of the physical and emotional aspects of travel that contribute to a reshaping of the self. Although Morris may not achieve the coherence she seeks, realizing near the end of her time in Mexico that she "wander[s] the world" in a constant "flux" (175), she does achieve an expansion of self. Her reshaped sense of self, accomplished through her travel experiences, allows her to imagine that, like the eagle that first fascinated her as a young girl growing up in the Midwest, she is "rid of [her] body . . . the first woman to be granted this privilege, to be sacrificed to the sun . . . and free to fly" (244).

Students experience a much different self in Simone de Beauvoir's *America Day by Day*. As Beauvoir departs France, she believes that she will have to remake her self to comprehend American culture and feels as if she is "leaving . . . [her previous] life behind" (3). During the flight from Paris to New York, she experiences the sensation that she has "escaped" herself. "I am nowhere: I am *elsewhere*," she insists (3). As Beauvoir works to "reincarnate" the "phantom" of her self in America (7), she depends on scenes and images from American films, the texts on which she has relied, in Bartkowski's words, to "name" and "preconceive" the United States (21). These preconceptions act as a screen that colors her experiences with people, institutions, and material culture, and, as I have noted elsewhere, "perpetually distance" her from America and thwart the remaking of self that she desires (145). Beauvoir returns to France without experiencing the essence of American culture and consequently without experiencing the self-transformation she had expected—a result that shows students how the reshaping of travelers' selves is determined by preconceptions and expectations.

Unlike Morris or Beauvoir, in *South of Freedom*, a narrative of his journey from Minneapolis to and through the 1950s South, Carl Rowan recounts the reshaping of self that occurs for travelers of color within what Pratt would term the "contact zones" of culture: "the space of colonial encounters . . . in which peoples geographically and historically separated come into contact with each other and establish ongoing relations, usually involving conditions of coercion, radical inequality, and intractable conflict" (Pratt 6). Rowan returns to the South of his childhood with both trepidation and optimism, wondering what "old wounds" the experience will reopen (8), but hoping that a "New South" may have arisen in his absence (14). Before he travels far below the Mason-Dixon Line, however, he finds that the Old South is alive and well (15), not only through the persistence of institutionalized racism, but also because of the doubt racism produces, which Rowan experiences in his uncertainty about where he can safely buy gas, use the restroom, or eat a meal (16). He also experiences a heightened awareness of his dress and skin color, emphasizing, as Kris Lackey observes, how the subjectivity of black travelers is "dominated by awareness and fear of the white observer who wields both psychological and material power" (119). Rowan's travel narrative details his attempts to overcome doubt and self-consciousness so that he can accomplish his purpose, which is to document for his white military buddy Noah Brannon (and all the Noah Brannons of the world) what the South is like for African Americans.

At several points in his narrative, Rowan is forced to reflect on the markers of identity on which he has relied to both define his self and ensure his mobility, particularly in situations where he is forced to insinuate a false identity, implying that he is a "government man," or to amplify his true identity—by showing his naval reserve card—in order to demonstrate his value as a human being, buy a newspaper, or gain passage on a train (208, 249). Near the middle of his journey, he begins to feel the "weariness" of negotiating jim crow and realizes that he cannot "live a black life and write about it as a black man, and then wipe away the effects with a smug shake of the head" (139). The weight of travel's cultural work descends on him at the conclusion of his travels, manifested through a "mental tiredness" and "a fatigue of the soul that came from probing into the mores of the South for more than a month" (245). He concludes that the contact zones he navigates exist not only below the Mason-Dixon Line but also in the minds and attitudes of his fellow Minnesotans, placing the entire country "south of freedom" (263). To borrow Pratt's words, he wonders, given the "asymmetrical relations of power" in the United States, whether "interlocking understandings and practices" (Pratt 7) favorable to all races are possible, even in the North. "In our common hour of tribulation," he concludes, "as we stumble to a common destiny, I only hope the Noah Brannons really care" (270). Rowan moves somewhat beyond the doubt he expresses at the beginning, but his travel experiences and conclusion suggest that, despite progress, United States dominant culture still threatens black subjectivity.

While the class discussion and assignments tend to focus on the experience of the travel writers, I also ask students to compare their own post-travel views of home, nation, and self to those of the writers. In small groups or in writing assignments, I ask them to consider questions such as the following: How do race, class, and gender affect these views (both the students' and the writers')? How do issues of power and mobility intersect with race, class, and gender, and how does this affect life experience and life writing? What do your answers to the previous questions reveal about the intersections between life and travel experiences and the act of life and travel writing? Although I have illustrated my approach with specific texts, the questions I pose can be applied to other works to reveal the ways in which travel, life writing, and experience intersect when we consider how travel reshapes the self.

Works Cited

Bartkowski, Frances. *Travelers, Immigrants, Inmates: Essays in Estrangement*. Minneapolis: U of Minnesota P, 1995.

Beauvoir, Simone de. *America Day by Day*. 1952. Trans. Carol Cosman. Berkeley: U of California P, 1999.

Equiano, Olaudah. *The Interesting Narrative of the Life of Olaudah Equiano: Written by Himself*. 1791. Ed. Robert J. Allison. Boston: Bedford, 1995.

Kaplan, Caren. *Questions of Travel: Postmodern Discourses of Displacement*. Durham: Duke UP, 1996.

Knight, Sarah Kemble. *The Private Journal of a Journey from Boston to New York in the Year 1704. Kept by Madam Knight*. 1825. Albany: Little, 1865.

Lackey, Kris. *RoadFrames: The American Highway Narrative*. Lincoln: U of Nebraska P, 1997.

Morris, Mary. *Nothing to Declare: Memoirs of a Woman Traveling Alone*. New York: Picador, 1988.

Pratt, Mary Louise. *Imperial Eyes: Travel Writing and Transculturation*. London: Routledge, 1992.

Rowan, Carl. *South of Freedom*. 1952. Baton Rouge: Louisiana State UP, 1997.

Smith, Sidonie. *Moving Lives: Twentieth-Century Women's Travel Writing*. Minneapolis: U of Minnesota P, 2001.

Smith, Sidonie, and Julia Watson. "Introduction: Situating Subjectivity in Women's Autobiographical Practices." *Women, Autobiography, Theory: A Reader*. Ed. Smith and Watson. Madison: U of Wisconsin P, 1998. 3–52.

Totten, Gary. "Simone de Beauvoir's *America Day by Day*: Reel to Real." *Issues in Travel Writing: Empire, Spectacle, and Displacement*. Ed. Kristi Siegel. New York: Lang, 2002. 135–49.

Watson, Julia. "Unspeakable Differences: The Politics of Gender in Lesbian and Heterosexual Women's Autobiographies." *De/Colonizing the Subject: The Politics of Gender in Women's Autobiography*. Ed. Sidonie Smith and Watson. Minneapolis: U of Minnesota P, 1992. 139–68.

Alison Booth

Teaching "The Lives of the Victorians": A Historical Approach to Changing Conventions of Life Narrative

For over two decades I have taught in a large English department at a selective public university in the United States, offering courses on the Victorian novel, women writers, and other subjects to undergraduates who tend to be motivated and well prepared. Intermittently I have included nonfiction prose and poetry on my reading lists, sensing that the students have become overly accustomed to reading novels (as their tendency to refer to all literary works as "novels" would suggest). Given my research interests in feminist and narrative theories, I inevitably followed the turn to studies of autobiography in the 1980s, and by the mid-1990s I was working on a book-length study of collective biographies of women. It seemed an ideal time to design a course that would heighten students' awareness of the many forms of life narrative in historical perspective. As in all of my courses, I would try to interfuse matters of form and of history and to approach each work in the contexts of changing literary and social conventions. Instead of focusing on contemporary or twentieth-century autobiography in the manner of most undergraduate courses dealing with life writing, I would introduce a long history of biography as well as autobiography in a course dedicated to several genres of writing in nineteenth-century Britain.

The Victorian period, like our own, produced an outpouring of life writing. Then as now, the public was eager, but the critics had many reservations about the worthiness of the auto/biographical subjects, the quality of the texts or talents of the writers, and the character of the audience. My readings in the history of biography and biography studies showed me that the field had had a definitive phase at the beginning of the twentieth century with the British modernists and their rejection of the standard Victorian tribute to an eminent man. Academic criticism of biography, which predated the development of studies of autobiography, gave prominence to the modernists' claims that biography is a literary art rather than a branch of history or moral pedagogy and that it should present a psychologically accurate portrait rather than a eulogy or a chronicle of deeds. Could I encourage students to recognize their current assumptions about life writing and to place these in historical perspective? Are the many "lives" of celebrities or cultural and political figures that are disseminated today aligned in some ways with Victorian models of life narrative? Would it be possible to engage students in reading and writing a kind of collective biographical history of the Victorian period? Could they gain a critical and theoretical perspective on life writing that would make them better interpreters of any similar texts that they encounter? My experiences of the course have answered these questions largely in the affirmative.

In designing the course, I chose readings for generic variety and appeal, as well as for interrelated themes concerning identity, self-development, and social reform or progress. Our department was offering no undergraduate course specifically on Victorian cultural history, a flourishing field, and I hoped through remedying this omission to expand students' conception of an age that continues to shape Anglo-American culture in the twenty-first century. At the same time I hoped to spark students' enthusiasm for research and the tools available in a good library—from the Internet to special collections. The course, meeting twice weekly for a semester with an enrollment of twenty-five to seventy-five (with a graduate assistant for enrollments above forty-five), does assume that students have access to computers and digital resources and that the instructor can readily set up a course Web site and e-mail discussion list. It does not rely on extended lecturing or on technology such as *PowerPoint* in the classroom, though it could use either or both. The collaborative writing and the creation of an online archive of student work could benefit from setting up "e-folio" software that allows participants continuing access to ongoing projects (next time I teach the course I will set this up, so that the growing collection of Victorian biographies over several semesters will have a more accessible format and public face). But the "middle-tech" model of the course has suited my teaching style and the limited time I have each semester for course planning and teaching.

I comment below on the texts for the course before providing an interpretative gloss on the syllabus and its intentions and effects; sample assignments follow. First, I relied on *The Longman Anthology of British Literature*'s separate volume on the Victorian period because it provides historical background, various short examples of life writing, and biographical material on a range of writers (Henderson and Sharpe). (Other presses such as Norton also have anthologies that would serve the purpose.) Second, I compiled a selection of out-of-print, out-of-copyright materials; students downloaded these short lives or essays on biography from the class Web page (a course packet of photocopies is a good alternative). Third, bearing in mind a reasonable reading load for undergraduates, I arranged thematic phases of the readings as well as a cluster of longer works in fiction, biography, and poetry that present a female bildungsroman: *Jane Eyre: An Autobiography* (Brontë), *The Life of Charlotte Brontë* (Gaskell), and the autobiographical epic *Aurora Leigh* (Browning). *Father and Son* (Gosse) offers a complementary auto/biography focused on masculine development. The Longman anthology also provides excerpts of longer life writing. Although it is unfortunate to excerpt such wonderful works, doing so keeps down the students' expenses in acquiring texts and in the time allowed gives students a comprehensive impression of the diversity and interdependence of Victorian public figures. Whenever possible I set up comparisons between one or more versions of the same life or a similar narrative pattern.

In addition to an unusual perspective on biographical history, this course presents a distinctive model for teaching life writing through innovative assignments. My goals are to overcome any tendency to passive learning and any reluctance students might have to get their hands dirty in research and writing, biographical or otherwise. I also seek to build a sense that we are learning together and that they write to communicate to peers as well as to the instructor. The first step in forming the teamwork of the course is the e-mail list of all registered students. Given that many of their courses rely on e-mail and everyone's mailbox is crowded, I make each student responsible for a short weekly commentary five times during the semester. Posted to the entire class, these commentaries can lead to productive debates and always help me prepare my classes with their responses in mind. In class, I ask students to elaborate on these commentaries, as one of several strategies to make a midsize course resemble a discussion seminar.

Beyond the commentaries, the students have four written assignments. The first research assignment is to read or view three or more biographies on the *Biography* Web site (biography.com) and to view one hour's programming of the Biography Channel on television. Their answers to specific questions about the lives they review help them connect Victorian life writing to the welter of self-development narratives in developed countries today. Students discover that some of the same topoi or plot elements recur in many of the biographical representations and that celebrity biography tends to present a public front and to serve the aim of praise or eulogy that Edmund Gosse ("Custom") and others deplored in previous centuries of life writing. The second research assignment, again requiring a report on a few hours of independent investigation of one or several texts, sends them to the archives rather than to contemporary media. This research, along with readings and discussions, increases their interest in and knowledge of what the Victorians were "really like," beyond a few notions about their being proper and repressed. To help them research a work published during the Victorian period, we hold a class session in our special-collections library and in a computer lab, and the librarians offer their assistance in finding sources. A more extensive project is a collaboration of two or three students on a three-page biography of a Victorian person (the subjects are chosen from a list, and students must consult at least four sources of different kinds). These biographies are uploaded to a folder on our Web page, so that we ultimately produce our own collective biography of Victorians. I ask students to read all the contributions, but they must post a review of three of them on our class e-mail list; the reviews are constructive comments on the substance of the biographies as well as the manner in which they are written. Students learn a great deal about the conventions and potential of life writing from comparing the techniques of several works in the same genre or on the same subject, especially when they have tried to write in that mode themselves. They learn not to take nonfiction as transposition of objective fact. They each write in addition a longer essay focused on one of the works on the syllabus or on another work by one of the Victorians we have encountered. The specific topic and argument are their own choice. A final exam, along with the various assignments and commentaries, is designed to ensure that students have read and thought about the texts in the course.

The argument that emerges as the students progress from week to week is shaped in simultaneous reference to our own context, to the Victorian period, and to a degree to the characterizations of the Victorians and of life writing that we have inherited from the modernists. Early in the semester, in addition to unsettling some of the students' preconceptions about the Victorian period, I ask students to write in class their own "lives" in three or four sentences addressed to me as the audience. We then discuss such common ingredients of an auto/biography as names, birth or place, education, journeys or deeds, relationships, and glimpses of character or appearance that individualize the subject. The tension between a person's uniqueness and the common narratives and social types—a theme throughout the course—becomes clear in discussing John Stuart Mill's rhetoric: like Saint Augustine or the early biographers deplored by Gosse in "The Custom of Biography," Mill insists that he is average—a typical subject—and that his education and conversion are representative (1097, 1099–101). Nevertheless, Mill is a Victorian in his belief in self-development and social progress, which (as he insists in *On Liberty*) require that society allow scope for individual "originality" (1078–83). Thomas Carlyle's hero worship of the captains of industry provides a contrast to the liberal individualism of Mill as well as an anticipation of Samuel Smiles's modeling of the self-made man (*Self-Help* is a collective biography featuring industrialists and inventors). As Margaret Oliphant points out in "The Ethics of Biography," Carlyle practiced an ancient mode of biography, that of eulogy or the "enthusiast's" hero worship, and she finds it ironic that Carlyle himself was then subjected (by James Anthony Froude) to a new mode of biography, the "cynic's" (80–84), that is, the critical debunking mode of the modernists. Students recognize that since the Victorians, lives are widely expected to be realistic, revealing psychological depths and ordinary flaws in the subject. Yet they find in their own research project that celebrity biographies may be idealized or stereotyped, following schematic narrative patterns and inviting admiration and praise—for the living as much as for the dead.

Several sets of readings are devoted concurrently to a characterization of the Victorian social spectrum, from the very poor to the middle and upper classes; to filling out the students' pictures of public and private, domestic and foreign spaces in the nineteenth-century British perspective;

and to gathering writings of lives in various modes. The modes include Henry Mayhew's ethnography, the impersonal confession and ironic biography of Florence Nightingale, the communal narration of Elizabeth Gaskell's spinster "amazons" in the loosely autobiographical *Cranford*, and the voyages and personal narratives of explorers and of Charles Darwin. The varied voices as well as the issues of self-development and collective change that these texts raise provide a context for *Jane Eyre*, which the students read with pleasure and seldom for the first time in my course. The novel's romance plot is defamiliarized by their greater awareness of the upheavals of science, religion, social roles, and politics in contemporary Britain. In a context that emphasizes spiritual autobiography as the template for *Jane Eyre*, students are more likely to realize that Elizabeth Gaskell's *Life of Charlotte Brontë* relies on techniques and conventions of hagiography and novels. We attend to Gaskell's then-innovative documentation of regional environment, as well as her "collaboration" with Brontë's personal writings. Noting that literary biography has predominated in the canon of life writing, we turn to Elizabeth Barrett Browning's experiment in the Künstlerroman, her verse novel with plot elements that converge with *Jane Eyre*. As always, the authors of the readings become subjects for our biographical study—hence the glimpse of Robert Browning's dramatic monologues of artists and the biographical sketches of Brontë and Gaskell.

Since our first reading of Mill's *Autobiography*, the issue of conversion and the substitution of culture for a childhood faith (be it utilitarianism or orthodox religion) has run through many discussions, and it guides the turn to men's lives in the later weeks of the course. Arguably the two greatest debts we owe to the nineteenth-century traditions studied in this course are the rise of (canonical) life narratives of (middle-class) women and the rise of (popular) belief in art and literature or aestheticism. Thus two great autobiographers committed to the reform of taste present a fine contrast: John Ruskin and Oscar Wilde. Gosse, an ally of the Bloomsbury debunkers of Victorians and their biographies, writes a compelling memoir of a father who was both a devout religious dissenter and a devout scientist and traces a loss of family faith and conversion analogous to Mill's. The formal, stylistic, and tonal difference between Mill and Gosse shows the long way that life writing had come in half a century. And finally, as a reminder of the many generic modes of first-person and third-person portraiture and as a complement to earlier works of poetry, we consider

Alfred Tennyson's portraits of the artist ("Mariana," "The Lady of Shalott," "Ulysses") and his elegy, *In Memoriam*, which, like other works in the course, tells a story of collective moral evolution, recovery, and intersubjectivity.

As Mill says, a flaw in his own life must be a flaw in life itself; that is, the *representation* of his experience is *representative*. And yet, as Lytton Strachey writes in the preface to *Eminent Victorians*, "Human beings are too important to be treated as mere symptoms of the past" (10). Having met many Victorians and having written and read a variety of representations of them, some of them by and about the same subjects, students recognize the artfulness or selectivity of any life writing. They become more conscious of the influence of shared stories, as well as cultural context, on the construction of their own life stories. The course models a way to approach cultural history through the evolving conceptualizations of a tradition in interrelated genres. And I believe students gain a respect for the historical distance and unknowability of an era in the past. Whether my goals are realized completely, I have been pleased by the warm response to the course. Each time I teach it, I am curious to watch new Victorian personae emerge in high relief on our collaborative monument to a period that remains a lively part of our history.

Appendix

First Research Assignment (2 Pages)

Read or view three or more biographies on biography.com and watch one hour of biography (commercial breaks count) on the Biography Channel or other channel; this may include more than one program and may be about one person or several.

What *kinds* of information do these four or more "lives" include (major events, trivial details, how the subject felt, what the public's opinion was)? How much of the entire life span do the biographies cover? Is there a narrator or interviewer, or is the biography presented as documentary information? How is the audience supposed to feel about the subject?

In writing your paper, consider the following questions:

Is each of the biographies a story of progress, change, conversion or recovery, trauma, survival, or noble failure? If not one of these common types, is there another structure or motive for telling about this person?

How far—geographically, socially, and so forth—did each person move from where he or she started? Does classified identity, such as race or gender or nationality, make a difference in each life? Are there any subjects who are not American?

Why do you think the presenters of these biographies regarded each of these subjects as noteworthy or narratable? Are the reasons different for different subjects? Does the representation of each person seem fair, slanted, sketchy or superficial, probing, justifiably critical?

Collaborative Writing Assignment (3 Pages)

You and your coauthor must research, write, and revise a short biography of a Victorian figure; the challenge is to make your biography *concise and interesting*. Each coauthor must consult one complete biography (birth to death) of the subject; it may be short (such as those from the *Dictionary of National Biography*) or long. Another reference *must* be a primary source, such as a collection of letters, a diary, an obituary, an autobiography, or a memoir by someone who knew the subject. You and your cobiographer should agree on the most important characteristics and events in the subject's life and decide on an interpretative angle. How will you compromise between "granite and rainbow" (as Woolf puts it)?

Second Research Assignment (2 Pages)

This report will be based on a text published in a book or periodical during the Victorian period (1837–1901) that you have examined in its original format by consulting the following resources (in order of decreasing preference): in special collections; on microfilm; or as an electronic text, if the text has been digitized with original characteristics (appearance of the pages). Look closely at such aspects as cover- and title-page design; the introduction or preface, if any; the advertisements or other matter on the end pages; illustrations; placement in the periodical or volume; and so on. Though the text you decide on may not necessarily be a biography or autobiography, memoir, or review, it should emphasize life narrative in some respect (progress, development, quest, social constraints, and so on). You should write a brief, detailed, and lively formal as well as physical description and briefly comment on the significance of the text itself.

Works Cited

Brontë, Charlotte. *Jane Eyre*. 1847. Ed. Richard J. Dunn. Norton Critical Edition. New York: Norton, 2000.

Browning, Elizabeth Barrett. *Aurora Leigh*. 1856. Ed. Margaret Reynolds. Norton Critical Edition. New York: Norton, 1995.

Darwin, Charles. "From *The Voyage of the Beagle*." Henderson and Sharpe 1245–54.

Gaskell, Elizabeth. *The Life of Charlotte Brontë*. 1857. Ed. Elisabeth Jay. Harmondsworth: Penguin, 1998.

———. "Our Society at Cranford." Henderson and Sharpe 1413–28.

Gosse, Edmund. "The Custom of Biography." *Anglo-Saxon Review* 8 (1901): 195–208.

———. *Father and Son*. 1907. Ed. Peter Abbs. Harmondsworth: Penguin, 1989.

Henderson, Heather, and William Chapman Sharpe, eds. *The Victorian Age*. New York: Longman, 2003. Vol. 2B of *The Longman Anthology of British Literature*. David Damrosch, gen. ed. 2nd ed. 2 vols.

Mayhew, Henry. "From *London Labour and the London Poor*." Henderson and Sharpe 1068–73.

Mill, John Stuart. "From *Autobiography*." Henderson and Sharpe 1095–1104.

——. "From *On Liberty*." Henderson and Sharpe 1075–86.

Nightingale, Florence. "Cassandra." Henderson and Sharpe 1498–514.

Oliphant, Margaret. "The Ethics of Biography." *Victorian Biography*. Ed. Ira Bruce Nadel. New York: Garland, 1986. n. pag.

Ruskin, John. "From *Praeterita*." Henderson and Sharpe 1488–98.

Smiles, Samuel. *Self-Help*. 1859. Ed. Peter W. Sinnema. Oxford World's Classics. Oxford: Oxford UP, 2002.

Strachey, Lytton. *Eminent Victorians*. 1918. Twentieth Century Classics. Harmondsworth: Penguin, 1987.

Tennyson, Alfred, Lord. "From *In Memoriam*." Henderson and Sharpe 1165–94.

——. "Mariana," "The Lady of Shalott," "Ulysses." Henderson and Sharpe 1139–46, 1150–51.

Wilde, Oscar. "From *De Profundis*." Henderson and Sharpe 1926–33.

Woolf, Virginia. "The New Biography." *Granite and Rainbow*. London: Hogarth, 1958. 149–56.

David Caplan

Modernist American Literature and Life Writing

Anyone who teaches modernist life writing must confront the fact that several of its major authors detested the very notion of life writing. "[T]he emotion of art is impersonal," T. S. Eliot famously observed, "[a]nd the poet cannot reach this impersonality without surrendering himself wholly to the work to be done" (*Selected Prose* 44). Eager to discourage biographical readings of "Hugh Selwyn Mauberley," Ezra Pound wrote, "Of course, I'm no more Mauberley than Eliot is Prufrock." Instead, the poem should be classified as "a study in form" (180). Such canonical statements helped establish the familiar vocabulary of modernism—*impersonality, personae, form, tradition*—with a list of fallacies to avoid.

I respond by teaching the texts as a series of questions about how literature is written, read, and studied. Instead of repeating a tired series of oppositions (New Critical versus poststructuralist, aesthetics versus politics, etc.), I ask students to consider a number of dialectical, creative interactions: genre and experimentation, theory and practice, and the lived life and artistic performance—in William Butler Yeats's phrase, "the bundle of accident and incoherence that sits down to breakfast" and "an idea, something intended, complete" (509). Like modern literature itself, modernist life writing is worth studying because of its power to unsettle what we think we know. Brilliantly complicating self-evident "facts," it defamiliarizes language and our notions of how language and culture work.

To understand my specific strategies, you should know something about the students I teach. About half come from Ohio; seventy-five percent receive need-based aid, and ninety-five percent aid of some kind. My best students tend to be Ohio-born merit scholars, often from smaller towns, who are just starting to define themselves, rather shyly, as intellectuals. The American literature seminar alternates annually between modern (the twentieth-century up to World War II) and contemporary (postwar). Ohio Wesleyan University is a classic liberal arts college; it has no graduate programs. The English department's twelve full-time faculty members typically offer about twenty-five classes each semester, a number that includes many sections of the freshman writing seminar. Discussion-based classes teach students to read literature closely. Because the department offers only a few classes in theory and no literature surveys, my students are less confident when asked to consider the development of forms across historical periods or the philosophies of literature and culture. My imperfect strategy is to assign primary texts that raise such developmental issues, then guide discussion to them.

The Autobiography of Alice B. Toklas, for example, introduces the major players and movements of international modernism, including many of the authors we will read, such as Eliot, Pound, and Ernest Hemingway. A crucial moment in modernity inspires an important class discussion: midway through *The Autobiography*, Gertrude Stein describes the wild scene that erupted at the opening night of *Le sacre du printemps*, when the crowd's hisses and applause drowned out the music. "[O]ur attention," Stein wrote,

> was constantly distracted by the man in the box next to us flourishing his cane, and finally in a violent altercation with an enthusiast in the box next to him, his cane came down and smashed the opera hat the other had just put on in defiance. It was incredibly fierce. (137)

As preparation, I assign the relevant portions of Thomas Forrest Kelly's *First Nights: Five Musical Premieres*, which includes several contemporary reviews of the performance (258–339). Stein, Kelly notes, attended the second performance, not the opening night; the incongruity between the historical record and Stein's representations outrages some students and amuses others (293–94).

At this point, we begin to talk about genre, although many are unfamiliar with the word. After introducing the term, I ask the students what defines two well-known examples: a sitcom such as *Seinfeld* and a drama such as *Law and Order*. A sitcom such as *Seinfeld* is funny, they say; each episode lasts for a half hour, during which a few main characters pursue comically intertwined plots. A drama such as *Law and Order* is serious. The show's gravity outweighs the occasional wry quip. In a typical episode, two detectives investigate a crime, someone is charged, and a trial ensues. Whereas *Seinfeld* begins with the main character, a stand-up comedian, delivering a joke, *Law and Order* usually starts with the discovery of a corpse. With a little prodding, the students define generic conventions so obvious that they remain nearly invisible. In both sitcoms and dramas, commercials appear at regular intervals and have little, if anything, to do with the show. If a criminal is caught in the first few minutes of *Law and Order*, we know he is either innocent or that a major complication will follow; otherwise, the program will not last for an hour. (For this reason, many viewers find the rare multishow episode deeply unsatisfying.)

The conversation turns less predictable when I ask for definitions of *autobiography*, *biography*, and *novel*. We consider the task from several perspectives, including rhetorical, philosophical, and phenomenological. Which devices do the forms typically use? What kinds of truth claims characterize the forms? What does it mean when we say a book "reads like a novel"? What expectations do the forms inspire? What should a novel, an autobiography, or a biography *never* do?

After generating a list of characteristics, I ask the obvious question: is *The Autobiography of Alice B. Toklas* a novel, autobiography, or biography? As Stein generates nearly every kind of reaction except indifference, the responses passionately vary. Students offended by Stein (and there are always several) charge that by writing her companion's autobiography, she composed a biography manqué, an endeavor they find offensively presumptuous. Others more sympathetic to Stein basically agree but suggest that the structure expresses Stein's intimacy with Toklas. Stein, after all, mentions how "terribly touched" she was when H. P. Roché noted that "she would have a biography" (Stein 45). Those arguing for novel cite the book's final paragraph, in which Stein asserts, "I am going to write it for you. I'm going to write it as simply as Defoe did the autobiography of Robinson Crusoe" (252). Regardless of the results, my purpose remains to have students formulate notions of what novels, autobiographies, or biographies do and to test their theories against the texts they confront.

We also debate whether Stein violates, revises, extends, or reproduces generic conventions. Praising *The Autobiography of Alice B. Toklas*, the novelist Jeanette Winterson rhetorically asks of Stein, "what has she done but take a genre and smash it?" (53). For Winterson, genres gain energy when a writer is "able to take a well-known, well-worn form, formula almost, and vitalise it by disrespecting it" (55). Scholars of genre caution that many genres are mixed and combinatory and that writing a novel-autobiography-biography (or a "fictional essay in 29 tangos," as Stein's great admirer Anne Carson composes) does not "smash" a genre but demonstrates its flexibility.[1] Life writing, then, does not prescribe rules that a new work must follow but proposes a Wittgensteinian set of "family resemblances" that a new generation might reconfigure.

My methods for teaching Langston Hughes and Eliot similarly encourage students to consider the implications of assigning (consciously or unconsciously) genre or genres to a text. Hughes's "Theme for English B" slyly interrogates a familiar kind of life writing: the freshman "theme" essay. Asked to present unmediated experience, *"And let that page come out of you—/ Then, it will be true,"* the unnamed speaker responds with a mixture of tact and impudence: "I wonder if it's that simple?" (409). Many students assume that the poem expresses Hughes's experience, but its "facts" differ from those of Hughes's life.[2] By tracing the route the speaker takes home to the "Y, / the *Harlem* Branch Y" (409; my emphasis), the poem details the cultural geography that distinguishes student from instructor by race. Especially when read as part of "Montage of a Dream Deferred" and not in isolation as many anthologies present it, "Theme for English B" shows how life writing techniques arise in specific institutional settings and power relations.

Paired with "Montage of a Dream Deferred," *The Waste Land* offers an extended meditation on the issues we have discussed. Following a class devoted to explicating the poem's structure, we reread the poem and read a few supplementary texts: Valerie Eliot's introduction to the facsimile edition, which provides an excellent outline of Eliot's life at the time he wrote and edited the poem; Eliot's widely anthologized "Tradition and the Individual Talent"; and a brief excerpt from *The Use of Poetry and the Use of Criticism*, which considers how "some forms of ill health" may "produce an efflux of writing" (137). Each student also writes a three-page response to the following question:

> Eliot's comments on *The Waste Land* and on creativity in general seem self-contradictory. Some promote a theory of art's impersonality; others espouse a belief that art arises from and seeks to relieve personal suffering. Take a passage of no more than eight lines not yet discussed in class and argue which theory (or theories) best describes it. If none fit, propose your own.

The class that follows is usually one of the most productive, moving several students to write final papers on the ideas it generates. While "Theme for English B" deconstructs the notion of authorial sincerity, *The Waste Land* hides sexual and religious autobiography in plain view. If Stein "redefined autobiography as the ultimate Trojan horse" (Winterson 49), Eliot and Pound seem more anguished than playful about the genres they mix. "By the banks of Leman I sat down and wept," the poet confesses, before again invoking Saint Augustine (*Waste Land* 140). I encourage the students to take such lines seriously, to see the complications that arise when a commitment to "impersonality" meets a desperate need to "shore" "fragments" "against my ruins" (*Waste Land* 146)

Notes

1. See Cohen, especially 17–20.

2. Hughes was born in Joplin, Missouri, not Winston-Salem. He attended school in Lawrence, Kansas; Lincoln, Illinois; and Cleveland, Ohio—not in Winston-Salem—and was enrolled at Columbia University and graduated from Lincoln University. He did not take classes at City College of the City University of New York (see Rampersad and Roessel's chronology of Hughes's life in *The Collected Poems* 8–20).

Works Cited

Carson, Anne. *The Beauty of the Husband: A Fictional Essay in 29 Tangos.* New York: Knopf, 2001.

Cohen, Ralph. "Do Postmodern Genres Exist?" *Postmodern Genres.* Ed. Marjorie Perloff. Norman: U of Oklahoma P, 1989. 11–27.

Eliot, T. S. *Selected Prose of T. S. Eliot.* Ed. Frank Kermode. New York: Harcourt, 1975.

——. *The Use of Poetry and the Use of Criticism: Studies in the Relation of Criticism to Poetry in England.* Cambridge: Harvard UP, 1933.

——. The Waste Land: *A Facsimile and Transcript of the Original Drafts.* Ed. and introd. Valerie Eliot. New York: Harcourt, 1971.

Hughes, Langston. *The Collected Poems of Langston Hughes*. Ed. Arnold Rampersad and David Roessel. New York: Vintage, 1994.

Kelly, Thomas Forrest. *First Nights: Musical Premieres*. New Haven: Yale UP, 2000.

Pound, Ezra. *The Letters of Ezra Pound, 1907–1941*. Ed. D. D. Paige. New York: Harcourt, 1950.

Stein, Gertrude. *The Autobiography of Alice B. Toklas*. 1933. New York: Vintage, 1990.

Winterson, Jeanette. *Art Objects: Essays on Ecstasy and Effrontery*. New York: Vintage, 1997.

Yeats, William Butler. *Essays and Introductions*. New York: Macmillan, 1986.

Martin A. Danahay

The Subject of Drugs

Autobiography: The Subject of Drugs is a junior-level class that is open to English majors and nonmajors. I therefore have a mixture of students, some of whom are familiar with literary theory and analysis and about a third of whom are not. My students are traditional college age for the most part, though a fair number are returning students or people who have stretched their higher education over a decade or two. Many of the students work as well as attend university and thus often take classes well beyond the conventional four years. As a result, my students tend to be experienced and fairly sophisticated politically but do not necessarily know much about academic discourse. I therefore introduce theory by supplying references as we discuss and analyze texts, and I send students off to the library or direct them to our university's excellent, subscription-only online sources for further reading beyond the primary texts. The students are required to write four papers that can either be critical analyses of one of the assigned texts or research papers into the historical background of a particular drug.

Drugs have become an increasing part of autobiography, since the genre itself explores extreme states of experience and consciousness— witness Leigh Gilmore on "trauma" and the "limits" of autobiography or

Laurie Stone's collection of memoirs. Autobiographies like Jerry Stahl's *Permanent Midnight: A Memoir*, which was turned into a movie starring Ben Stiller (1998), plumb the depths of degradation brought about by heroin addiction, whereas Ann Marlowe's *How to Stop Time: Heroin from A to Z* presents the view that heroin could be a "recreational" drug rather than a devastatingly addictive substance. These diametrically opposed texts are both based on personal experience. Clearly, then, although autobiography is a powerful and effective way to convey an individual's experience, a wider context is needed to evaluate conflicting claims.

I use the term *subject* in the title of my course to signal the affiliation of my approach to autobiography with theoretical accounts of identity that question the stable, autonomous self (e.g., Smith and Watson; Gilmore; or Lenson). Like many working in the field of autobiography studies, I follow Paul de Man's argument that autobiography is a "figure of understanding" that can be found in texts whether they advertise themselves as autobiographies or not (67–81). After the Romantic period, the subject of autobiography can be detected in any text with a title page, so that *David Copperfield* could be read as Dickens's autobiography, as William Spengemann did. Autobiography as a "figure of understanding" from the Romantic period onward can be found in texts that do not at first glance appear to fit within the strict boundaries of the genre.

The trajectory of James Frey's *A Million Little Pieces* is instructive in this regard. I assigned the book shortly after it was published and was thrilled in the spring of 2005 when the author agreed to talk to my class by speakerphone. Frey spoke to my class for over an hour, and several students brought in friends and partners who had struggled with addiction. It was an inspirational event for all concerned. Frey's book was then catapulted into best-seller status by being chosen as an Oprah's Book Club selection, sending sales into the millions. In January 2006, however, allegations emerged that his memoir was heavily fictionalized when crucial details of arrests and other incidents could not be verified. It emerged subsequently that Frey had at first labeled his text fiction but that his publisher had decided to publish it under the rubric of memoir. This is just one example of many such revelations about first-person narratives that were initially marketed as autobiography but were later revealed to be largely or completely fictional.

The uncertainty over the boundaries of autobiography and fiction is compounded in drug memoirs. From Thomas De Quincey onward, the author of a drug narrative is suspect because memory is faulty to begin with; recollection inevitably involves some element of re-creation and revision. If the author has been taking drugs, then recollection must be filtered through the psychoactive effect of the drug ingested and its long-term effects on memory.

The hybrid nature of autobiography as a "figure of understanding" is evident in the earliest text in the class by Humphrey Davy. I do not give the students the first sections of his book, which concern his researches into phlogiston, but rather the first-person narratives appended to the end of the text in which the "subject of autobiography" is allowed to speak in the first person. Increasingly science defined itself as objective to distinguish itself from such subjective texts as autobiography, but, even as late as Sigmund Freud's text on cocaine, the first person can still be found in a scientific text. Freud experimented with cocaine on himself and wrote about his own reaction to the drug in terms that show the changing attitudes to both drugs and subjectivity between Davy's text and the late nineteenth century—a period that saw the first legislation against drugs and the definition of some drugs as addictive and illegal. For complex professional and cultural reasons, after Freud scientists no longer wrote about drugs in the first person.

In the twentieth century I no longer deal with scientific texts, which attempt to erase the "subject of drugs" in favor of material and physical description. I focus instead on certain key figures and place them in historical context. Thus students read not only Aldous Huxley's *The Doors of Perception* but also his *Brave New World* to chart his remarkable change in attitude toward drugs. Anticipating in many ways Peter Kramer's *Listening to Prozac*, in *The Doors of Perception* Huxley views mescaline as enhancing his personality, especially his visual imagination. This view leads students to consider Huxley's connection with the psychedelic movement of the 1960s, including cultural references to him made by, for example, the Doors. My class reflects a cultural studies approach to his text that views it as embedded in history, not as an isolated aesthetic object. Hunter Thompson's *Fear and Loathing in Las Vegas*, with its angry and elegiac view of the 1960s, helps bridge the period between the psychedelic movement and the Just Say No and War on Drugs policies that came later in the 1980s and 1990s.

This approach distinguishes my class from one that assumes not only that autobiography is a discrete genre but also that its boundaries can be clearly demarcated from fiction. At first glance my reading list may appear to contain many texts that are not autobiography. This is true if one approaches autobiography from the perspective of the unified and autonomous self, but for theorists in the field the heuristic of the subject allows for consideration of the cultural and historical formation of forms of consciousness. From the Romantic period on, discussions of drugs and discussions of the subject have addressed the nature of consciousness and whether or not there is an essential and natural identity that is erased or enhanced by the action of drugs. For this reason subjectivity and drugs are closely allied areas of inquiry.

Finally, the title The Subject of Drugs indicates the way in which drugs are personified, essentialized, and made to "speak" for themselves. Drugs are not people, but slogans such as The War on Drugs act as if they were. This use of personification is most obvious in Kramer's *Listening to Prozac*, where it is ambiguous whether the human subject or the drug itself is being listened to as it speaks—Kramer, after all, is listening to "Prozac," not people. He provides the reader with case studies that draw on first-person narratives, but in his own schema it is impossible to differentiate the "real" person from Prozac. In fact, Kramer argues that people speaking under the influence of Prozac are more themselves than when depressed.

Though not autobiography in the conventional sense, this text is a classic example of the difficulties with the "subject of drugs" in determining whether there is a real self that can be separated from the drug. Because such issues cannot be addressed under the rubric of autobiography alone, which imports the expectation that there is a stable, autonomous self that can write the text in the first place, I approach these texts from the theoretical position that the subject is constructed in and through language.

Though I don't assign it as reading, the primary historical source to which I refer is *Emperors of Dreams: Drugs in the Nineteenth Century* by Mike Jay; and, taking my cue from Jay, I begin with poems by William Wordsworth that examine the effects of nature on his consciousness in terms that suggest that nature alters his physical and mental state as something "felt along the blood," as he phrases it in "Tintern Abbey."

From the Romantic period, both De Quincey's *Confessions of an English Opium Eater* and Samuel Taylor Coleridge's "Kubla Khan" provide a link to the history of the British Empire and its involvement in the drug trade. De Quincey was taking a drug that not only was widely used in the nineteenth century but also was an important commodity, alongside spices, tea, coffee, and sugar. In *Confessions*, De Quincey describes a nightmare that has become an important site for analyzing British colonial anxieties (see, e.g., Barrell). A combination of De Quincey's guilt and colonial anxiety leads to this description and other extraordinary statements that gloss over entirely the role of the British themselves in promoting the growth of poppies and the export of the drug.

In Victorian society opium was both widely available and viewed as a social menace. Charles Dickens's *The Mystery of Edwin Drood* contains a famous depiction of an opium den that represents its habitués as sordid wrecks who have been led to their destruction by the evil Chinese influence. Like Arthur Conan Doyle's Sherlock Holmes story "The Man with a Twisted Lip" (1891), Dickens's unfinished tale portrays opium as connected with violence and crime and shows the increasing criminalization of drug use.

Robert Louis Stevenson's *The Strange Case of Dr. Jekyll and Mr. Hyde* acts as a convenient bridge between the nineteenth- and twentieth-century approaches to drugs. Dr. Jekyll is in some sense a chemist, in that he spends his time trying to synthesize a chemical that will separate good from evil. While they did not have the same aim, chemists at large drug companies increasingly came to play an important role in the distillation of old drugs or the creation of new ones. Chemists were behind the two drugs that came to dominate law-enforcement efforts in the twentieth century: cocaine and heroin.

By the dawn of the twentieth century the narratives concerning drugs fall into predictable patterns. They are either, like Huxley's and Thompson's work, attempts to promote various drugs as expanding the horizons of consciousness and as legitimate tools in the exploration of subjectivity, or, like Stahl's *Permanent Midnight*, they are stark tales of the destructive effects of drugs and deeply steeped in shame and self-recrimination. Michael Dransfield's poetry, for example, self-consciously updates Coleridge and examines the experiences of addiction, withdrawal, and despair.

This pattern was broken by the publication of *Listening to Prozac*. Kramer's text marks a profound shift in the perception of drugs, suggesting that, far from distorting consciousness, they could in fact make the "subject of drugs" into a more authentic self. Like the creation of the cyborg as a fusion of human and machine, Kramer's text ushers in the ideal of the psychopharmacological subject who can regulate his or her moods thanks to the new generation of selective serotonin reuptake inhibitors that have revolutionized the treatment of depression.

In *Prozac Nation*, Elizabeth Wurtzel, in contrast, in her own uniquely annoying way, raises a variety of objections to Kramer's definition of a consciousness free from depression as "normal." Wurtzel reminds us that texts such as hers would effectively be medicated away under Prozac and that the need for the drug may mask deeper social problems. She also expresses an anxiety found only marginally in Kramer that her therapist has become a drug pusher akin to purveyors of illegal psychoactive substances.

In the early twenty-first century, "drugs," like "autobiography," names a profoundly contradictory category. Substances with substantially similar effects are denoted legal or illegal depending on how they are perceived, thanks to historical and cultural factors. Narratives about drug use purport to tell the "truth," but strikingly different narratives, from Marlowe to Frey, portray the same substance as everything from harmless to something that produces misery and addiction. The "subject of drugs," like the field of autobiography, is contested terrain in which competing narratives claim to know the "truth."

Works Cited

Barrell, John. *The Infection of Thomas De Quincey: A Psychopathology of Imperialism.* New Haven: Yale UP, 1991.

Davy, Humphrey. *Researches, Chemical and Philosophical, Chiefly concerning Nitrous Oxide, or Dephlogisticated Air, and Its Respiration.* London: Johnson, 1800.

de Man, Paul. "Autobiography as De-facement." *MLN* 94 (1979): 919–30.

De Quincey, Thomas. Confessions of an English Opium Eater *and Other Writings.* 1822. Harmondsworth: Penguin, 2003.

Dickens, Charles. 1870. *The Mystery of Edwin Drood.* Harmondsworth: Penguin, 1970.

Doyle, Sir Arthur Conan. "The Man with a Twisted Lip." 1891. *Sherlock Holmes: The Complete Novels and Stories.* New York: Bantam, 1986. 306–27.

Dransfield, Michael. *Drug Poems.* Melbourne: Sun, 1972.

Freud, Sigmund. "On Coca." 1884. *The Cocaine Papers.* Ed. and introd. Robert Byck. New York: Stonehill, 1975. 47–74.

Frey, James. *A Million Little Pieces.* New York: Doubleday, 2003.

Gilmore, Leigh. *The Limits of Autobiography: Trauma and Testimony.* Ithaca: Cornell UP, 2001.

Huxley, Aldous. *Doors of Perception and Heaven and Hell.* 1959. New York: Perennial, 1990.

Jay, Mike. *Emperors of Dreams: Drugs in the Nineteenth Century.* Sawtry, Eng.: Dedalus, 2002.

Kramer, Peter D. *Listening to Prozac.* Harmondsworth: Penguin, 1997.

Lenson, David. *On Drugs.* Minneapolis: U of Minnesota P, 1999.

Marlowe, Ann. *How to Stop Time: Heroin from A to Z.* 1999. New York: Anchor, 2000.

Smith, Sidonie, and Julia Watson, eds. *Getting a Life: Everyday Uses of Autobiography*. Minneapolis: U of Minnesota P, 1996.

Spengemann, William C. *The Forms of Autobiography*. New Haven: Yale UP, 1982.

Stahl, Jerry. *Permanent Midnight: A Memoir*. 1995. New York: Warner, 1998.

Stevenson, Robert Louis. *The Strange Case of Dr. Jekyll and Mr. Hyde*. 1886. New York: Dover, 1991.

Stone, Laurie. *Close to the Bone: Memoirs of Hurt, Rage, and Desire*. New York: Grove, 1997.

Thompson, Hunter S. *Fear and Loathing in Las Vegas: A Savage Journey to the Heart of the American Dream*. 1971. New York: Vintage, 1998.

Wordsworth, William. "Lines Written a Few Miles above Tintern Abbey." *The Major Works*. Ed. Stephen Gill. New York: Oxford UP, 2000. 131–35.

Wurtzel, Elizabeth. *Prozac Nation: Young and Depressed in America: A Memoir*. New York: Riverhead, 1995.

James W. Pipkin

Sports Autobiographies
and American Culture

The undergraduate literature course Sports Autobiographies and American Culture is the only course in my university's English department that focuses on autobiography, the only course that takes sports as its subject, and one of only two or three courses on popular literature. For these reasons, it is an introductory course in important ways. While many of the students have read a few autobiographies in some of their American literature survey courses or on their own, they have usually not thought about issues raised by the genre itself. They have even less experience with the academic study of sports, and, surprisingly, many do not even consider themselves sports fans but are taking the course because it is an intriguing exception to the traditional offerings in our curriculum.

The first pedagogical question is how to organize such a course. Although the selection of the texts is a basic issue for any course, particularly a course in contemporary literature in which there is less consensus about which works are significant, choosing the list of sports autobiographies adds additional problems because of the uneven quality of the books. Many sports autobiographies are, in the parlance of the trade, "written with a roller." Often they are marketed to take advantage of a championship season and primarily chronicle public achievements with little contribution from the athletes themselves about their private lives. A glance at the chapter headings usually suffices to identify these books because the authors typically devote little attention to their childhood, a fairly reliable sign that the account will be informed by little reflection and only limited insight into the athlete's life outside of sports.

Although my process of selection required reading over a hundred sports autobiographies to find the ones that would provide the best mirror of American culture, other principles also guided my decisions. First, I wanted the readings to have some historical scope. A main theme of the course is that identity is in part a social and cultural construction, and so the works on the reading list are written by athletes whose lives represent touchstones of particular periods in American history. The course begins with Ty Cobb's *My Life in Baseball* and his portrait of pre–World War I America, moves to the boxer Jake La Motta's mean streets of New York City during the Great Depression of the 1930s, Jackie Robinson's jim crow America of the 1940s, Pat Jordan's account of his failure to make it to the major leagues in the Eisenhower 1950s, and several autobiographies focusing on various aspects of the counterculture movements in the 1960s and 1970s, and concludes with the autobiography of a more recent athlete, Dennis Rodman.

James Olney has argued that for many minorities, autobiography has served as the "gateway to the house of literature," and I also wanted the course to reflect the rich chorus of voices that constitute these American "Songs of Myself." What I discovered in my readings was that some of the best sports autobiographies were written by African American basketball players. The combination of being black, extraordinarily gifted physically, and unusually tall often gives these athletes a unique point of view on American culture as well as their own lives. Certainly, Kareem Abdul-Jabbar, the former Lew Alcindor, "writes it slant" in his autobiography *Giant Steps*, and it, along with the autobiographies of Jackie Robinson and Dennis Rodman, allows the students to trace aspects of the civil rights movement and the continuing issue of race relations in America. The autobiographies of the tennis player Billie Jean King and the runner Lynda Huey add the subject of gender to the representation of minority athletes. Another virtue of this diversity is that the readings encourage a discussion of both the sense we have of a uniquely American identity and the distinctive patterns of identity found in works by African Americans, women, and immigrants. To encourage debate about this question, I introduce the students to the anthropologist Laura Bohannon's provocative thesis in her essay "Shakespeare in the Bush," where her attempts to use the plot of *Hamlet* as her contribution to a West African tribe's storytelling ritual turn upside down her assumptions about the universality of great literature. The tribe understands the story perfectly, but, to her surprise, not at all in the way she does. Their interpretation is shaped by their culture, and Bohannon learns that sometimes the only way to the universal is through the concrete and the particular.

Sometimes the off-the-field accomplishments of the athletes promised that their autobiographies would have literary merit. My research had uncovered that many scholars rank Jordan's *A False Spring* as the best sports autobiography. Jordan takes the title of his meditation on failure from Hemingway, and it is not surprising that this successful freelance writer would write a thoughtful life story. Another obvious choice was Bill Bradley's *Life on the Run*, a diary of the last part of one of his seasons as a player for the New York Knicks basketball team. The surprise was that few of my students knew that the former Rhodes scholar, United States senator, and presidential candidate had once been a professional athlete. And the former Notre Dame football player Michael Oriard, the author of *The End of Autumn*, completed his PhD in English at Stanford after he retired from professional football and is now a professor of American literature at Oregon State University.

A third principle of selection also provided a recurring theme of the course. In teaching works like Wordsworth's *Prelude*, Tennyson's *In Memoriam*, and Joyce's *A Portrait of the Artist as a Young Man* in some of my other courses, I introduce my students to the concept that at times of a crisis in culture, when the writer discovers that the actualities of experience no longer correspond to the ruling myths of the culture, the response of the artist is often to turn within and seek in his or her own experience some pattern or design that does adequately explain the world. It seemed no coincidence that some of the most interesting sports autobiographies I researched were written in the 1960s and 1970s. Autobiographies such as the football player Dave Meggysey's *Out of Their League*, an exposé of the cultural connections he found between the dehumanizing violence of professional football and the militarism responsible for the Vietnam War; King's life story, in which what she calls her "split personality" (199) is created by the sexual revolution and questions of sexual orientation; and Oriard's resistance to such cultural upheavals in the *The End of Autumn*, as he attempts to continue "dreaming of heroes" (the title of his later scholarly study of American sports fiction) have real value because of the intense introspection this watershed moment in American history inspired in such otherwise very different athletes. These works underscore for the students that in addition to the subjectivity at the core of each individual, the historical moment shapes identity. Students also recognize that the ruptures, discontinuities, and psychic scars the athletes find in their personal lives map the terrain of the culture as a whole.

The autobiographies chosen to represent this era contribute to another recurring theme in the course: experience as a crucible that can lead to self-definition and self-creation. When the students learn that Oriard became a professor of English and that Meggysey wrote his exposé at the Institute for the Study of Sport and Society, a radical think tank founded by Jack Scott, widely suspected at the time of being part of the underground movement that housed Patty Hearst after she was kidnapped by the Symbionese Liberation Army, they begin to understand the limitations of the stereotype of the dumb jock and to appreciate some of the important ways in which sports mirror the concerns of the larger culture. These examples prepare students for a later discussion about what Malcolm Gladwell calls "physical genius."

In all my literature courses, I continually remind my students that selection is meaning, but the principle is truer of this course than of any other course I teach. As my explanations for the reading list imply, each work develops in a new way some of the issues raised by the previous book and at the same time introduces new subjects so that the various levels of the course build by accretion.

Before exploring specific issues, however, the students need to think about more basic subjects. During the first week of the course, using a combination of lecture and discussion, I introduce them to questions about the form and function of the genre, as well as to some broad scholarly approaches to sports. Drawing on such seminal studies as Georges Gusdorf's "Conditions and Limits of Autobiography" and Roy Pascal's *Design and Truth in Autobiography*, we discuss the key structures of the form—how the work begins, the author's motives for writing the autobiography, his or her principles of selection, point of view, and self-image. In particular, we talk about the implications of defining an autobiography as "a second reading of experience" (Gusdorf 38), which leads us to consider such issues as the "truth" of an autobiography, its subjectivity, and the implications of what the author chooses to omit. I also introduce students to the rhetorical forms of autobiography—confession, apologia, exemplum, exposé, ideological argument, and so on—and encourage them to think about other forms of life writing such as the diary or journal, letters, autobiographical novels, certain documentary films, as well as subcategories of autobiographies such as family histories and trauma autobiographies. Although half the books on the reading list were written by the athlete himself or herself, we also discuss the implications of the fact that many sports autobiographies are coauthored by a professional writer. In the following weeks, when this subject recurs, we pay attention to pertinent information provided in prefaces and forewords, and I share with the students interviews I have had about the subject with professional coauthors, including one or two represented on our reading list.

We consider the current use of *memoir* as a synonym for *autobiography*, as opposed to the word's former more distinct meaning, and whether students can think of any ways in which the two forms remain different. We begin to identify what students consider to be defining traits and issues in American culture that they might expect life stories to reflect—for example, the Horatio Alger rags-to-riches story, the values underlying Benjamin Franklin's model for success in his autobiography, the Emersonian virtue of self-reliance, and Whitman's democratic creed in "Song of Myself." I encourage them to look at the titles of the essays in the collections edited by Albert Stone and Olney and to read the introductory chapter in Herbert Leibowitz's *Fabricating Lives* for ideas about the relation between American identity and values and autobiography as a form.

I give the students an introductory lecture about some influential scholarly books that interpret and conceptualize sports. I first present a brief overview of Allen Guttmann's *From Ritual to Record: The Nature of Modern Sports* and *A Whole New Ball Game: An Interpretation of American Sports*, so students will have a sense of how some of the best scholars ground their theories in a historical context. To provide an overview of scholarly conceptualizations of sports, I contrast Paul Hoch's Marxist interpretation in *Rip-Off the Big Game* with Michael Novak's celebration of sports and its parallels with religion in *The Joy of Sports* and with Bartlett Giamatti's literary analysis of sports' power to re-create the values associated with an Edenic pastoral world in *Take Time for Paradise: Americans and Their Games*. Whatever the differences in these writers' subjects or points of view, however, they all share Giamatti's thesis that we reveal and define ourselves more in our leisure than we do in our work, a key premise of the course.

These early classes on autobiography as a form, the relation between the individual life story and the larger American culture, and general interpretations of sports give the students a context for reading the autobiographies and identify recurring issues that we will analyze as the semester progresses. But their purpose is to provide a context, not to create a template. Each autobiography was selected to raise additional themes, issues, and questions unique to its author or its era.

For example, Ty Cobb subtitles his autobiography *The True Record*, and his defiant, unrepentant account of his life provides a vivid example of the autobiography as apologia. We watch the movie *Cobb*, which focuses on the relationship between Cobb and his biographer Al Stump, so that the students can compare the point of view Cobb takes in his book with the movie's portrait of Cobb, which is based on Stump's biography. Cobb's *My Life in Baseball* offers a vivid example of the significance of what a writer chooses to omit. We discuss the implications of the differences between Cobb's bare-bones announcement in the autobiography that his father was killed and the account in Charles Alexander's biography that reveals that Cobb's mother killed her husband, claiming that she thought he was a burglar when he unexpectedly returned early from a business trip in order to catch his wife, Alexander speculates, with her lover.

Because a major focus of the course is a close textual reading, we concentrate on the language Cobb uses to create a class-based image of himself. Like so many protagonists in American literature, he presents himself as the outsider, not just because he had a fiery temperament but because, he claims, he came from a family of position and property, lived by a chivalric code, and off the field frequented the world of opera, museums, and Detroit's exclusive businessmen's clubs. Central to the identity he constructs are his quotations of Shakespeare and Victor Hugo to establish his distance from what he calls the "animal level" of his teammates and the "bugs" (fans) attracted to the sport (25, 71). Cobb's use of metaphors introduces the students to traditional conceptualizations of sports that range along a spectrum from war to art. We relate Cobb's boasts about the art of stealing and using psychological ploys to the American literary tradition of the trickster and interpret Cobb's stories of besting Babe Ruth in the context of opposing American concepts of the hero found in stories about the trickster and folktales about Paul Bunyan and other titans of strength. The general approach to Cobb's autobiography, as well as those that follow, is that it is a case study for beginning to understand the uses of autobiography as a form, the implications of the way an athlete conceptualizes sports, and the portrait that emerges of the relation between the individual life and the larger culture that shapes it.

Three other autobiographies that focus on race, gender, and recent contemporary developments in sports autobiographies are typical of the following weeks of the course.

The former basketball star Abdul-Jabbar's autobiography, *Giant Steps*, is the first work about the 1960s and 1970s and the best case study about race that we read. We approach it in several different ways. We first use the bildungsroman, the novel of education or initiation, to trace his movement from what he calls "the sanctuary" (9) of his bedroom—he compares it to the Cloisters in his native New York City—to an ever-widening social arena. Because of his interest in jazz and his comparison of the improvisational nature of the distinctively black playground style of basketball to jazz, we contrast the universal pattern of the bildungsroman with the more specific forms of African American culture such as the ex-slave narrative and the blues. Abdul-Jabbar himself introduces the literary context when he asserts that he discovered the design of his own life when he read *The Autobiography of Malcolm X*. In addition to thinking about how his life mirrors in miniature the larger civil rights movement, we consider Elizabeth Schultz's thesis that the blues provides a distinctive cultural form for representing black life. Because some of the early autobiographies we have read focus on the athlete's childhood, we also consider the significance of the emphasis Abdul-Jabbar places on his adolescent years. Drawing on Patricia Meyer Spacks's article "Stages of Self," we discuss the meaning inherent in a culture's privileging of a certain stage in the life cycle. Overall, the emphasis of this case study is on race and cultural identity, but this approach is balanced by a continuing discussion of more general questions relevant to the culture as a whole.

Later in the course we pair the autobiographies of two women athletes from the 1960s and 1970s, Huey and King. Although Huey is unknown to most sports fans while King became a cultural icon, the theme of their life stories is the same: gender conflict. Sports was traditionally viewed as a male "preserve," and both women struggle with what they call their split personalities as they try to create identities as women and as athletes. Both women write about the social construction of beauty and the disparity between the bodies of female athletes and bodies considered conventionally beautiful. A more specific topic is that not only did most women athletes of this era have to deal with questions of sexual orientation, but they also had to face the stigma that society often viewed them as freaks. In addition to opening up the course to a discussion of the issue of gender, these two autobiographies raise the issue of the athlete's body as a site of identity. This general subject develops into a consideration of physical genius, the body as a performative instrument, and the way a culture reads the body.

The course concludes with Dennis Rodman's *Bad as I Wanna Be*. The first approach to this autobiography is to use Daniel Boorstin's distinction between the hero and the celebrity to analyze Rodman's construction of self. We discuss the tension between the traditional and the more contemporary models Rodman uses to present his life. The students recognize his adoption of the rags-to-riches story and his claims to the American celebration of individualism and self-reliance, but they are more interested in his quotation of lyrics from the rock band Pearl Jam, his identification with "grunge" youth, and the more contemporary visual presentation of the book's print on some pages. This book usually provides an energetic debate among students who admire Rodman's self-image because of its appeal to a more contemporary sensibility, students who are more interested in the way Rodman markets himself for his consumer society, and those who are offended by his vulgarity and attempt at sensationalism. The concept of the celebrity allows us to talk about "pose" as opposed to self-image.

The requirements in the course reflect the purpose of its design. Since sports autobiographies are not considered traditional works of literature and the object of the course is not to cover a body of knowledge, there are no examinations. Instead, the students write three short papers and a longer final research paper. The purpose of the short papers is for the students to begin identifying their own interests in the course—changing concepts of the hero, various factors in the construction of identity, the use of literary patterns in the autobiographies, gender conflicts in sports, the body as a site of identity, and so on. Ideally, the short papers become experimental testings of ideas for the final paper, but often the students don't find what most interests them until well into the course, and so the short papers don't serve a larger purpose for them.

Because this is a course in autobiography, the students are required to include some scholarship on this topic in their final paper, and because the most valuable academic scholarship on sports is either historical or inter-disciplinary, students are required to include some historical scholarship and are encouraged, depending on their particular topics, to do some research in religion, sociology, or psychology. Although most students write about the topics we cover in class discussion, some students have pursued subjects that were only briefly considered in class, such as autobiographies by gay athletes, the influence of Islam in Hakeem Olajuwon's autobiography, and the culture of boxing.

Although the design I have chosen for the course allows me to pursue my interests in the counterculture movements of the 1960s and 1970s and in the body as a site of identity, I think that one advantage of teaching sports autobiographies is the wide range of topics—works by famous athletes and unknown athletes; accounts that reveal the distinctive differences between team sports, individual sports, and extreme sports such as marathon swimming; sports as ritual and performance art versus the business, politics, and media-driven image of sports—and the many different possible approaches and disciplinary emphases. But perhaps the main attraction of sports autobiographies is that the athletes' stories about the nature of competition—it is life presented in extremis—and the narrative inscribed in most sports events allow us to see some of the central aspects of culture writ large.

Works Cited

Abdul-Jabbar, Kareem, and Peter Knobler. *Giant Steps.* New York: Bantam, 1983.

Alexander, Charles. *Ty Cobb.* New York: Oxford UP, 1984.

Bohannon, Laura. "Shakespeare in the Bush." *Natural History* 75 (1966): 28–33.

Boorstin, Daniel. *The Image.* New York: Atheneum, 1975.

Bradley, Bill. *Life on the Run.* 1976. New York: Vintage, 1995.

Cobb. Dir. Ron Shelton. Perf. Tommy Lee Jones, Robert Wuhl, Lolita Davidovich, and Ned Bellamy. Warner Bros., 1994.

Cobb, Ty, and Al Stump. *My Life in Baseball: The True Record.* 1961. Lincoln: U of Nebraska P, 1993.

Giamatti, A. Bartlett. *Take Time for Paradise: Americans and Their Games.* New York: Summit, 1989.

Gladwell, Malcolm. "The Physical Genius." *New Yorker* 2 Aug. 1999: 56–65.

Gusdorf, Georges. "Conditions and Limits of Autobiography." Olney 28–48.

Guttmann, Allen. *From Ritual to Record: The Nature of Modern Sports.* New York: Columbia UP, 1978.

———. *A Whole New Ball Game: An Interpretation of American Sports.* Chapel Hill: U of North Carolina P, 1988.

Hoch, Paul. *Rip-Off the Big Game.* Garden City: Doubleday-Anchor, 1972.

Huey, Lynda. *A Running Start*. New York: Quadrangle, 1976.

Jordan, Pat. *A False Spring*. Saint Paul: Hungry Mind, 1998.

King, Billie Jean, and Frank Deford. *Billie Jean*. New York: Viking, 1982.

La Motta, Jake, Joseph Carter, and Peter Savage. *Raging Bull: The True Story of a Champ*. New York: Bantam, 1980.

Leibowitz, Herbert. *Fabricating Lives*. New York: Knopf, 1989.

Meggysey, Dave. *Out of Their League*. Berkeley: Ramparts, 1970.

Novak, Michael. *The Joy of Sports*. New York: Basic, 1976.

Olajuwon, Hakeem. *Living the Dream: My Life and Basketball*. Boston: Little, 1996.

Olney, James, ed. *Autobiography: Essays Theoretical and Critical*. Princeton: Princeton UP, 1980.

Oriard, Michael. *Dreaming of Heroes: American Sports Fiction, 1868–1980*. Chicago: Nelson-Hall, 1982.

———. *The End of Autumn*. Garden City: Doubleday, 1982.

Pascal, Roy. *Design and Truth in Autobiography*. Cambridge: Harvard UP, 1960.

Robinson, Jackie, and Alfred Duckett. *I Never Had It Made*. 1972. Hopewell: Ecco, 1995.

Rodman, Dennis, and Tim Keown. *Bad as I Wanna Be*. New York: Delacorte, 1996.

Schultz, Elizabeth. "To Be Black and Blue: The Blues Genre in Black American Autobiography." Stone 109–32.

Spacks, Patricia Meyer. "Stages of Life: Notes on Autobiography and the Life Cycle." Stone 44–60.

Stone, Albert E., ed. *The American Autobiography*. Englewood Cliffs: Prentice, 1981.

John Mepham and Sarah Sceats

Writing the Self

Writing the Self is a one-semester module in an MA program at Kingston University called Issues in Twentieth-Century Literature. The module engages students in the study of life writing and in debates about the nature of the self through close study of life writing texts and through the students' exploration of the problems of selfhood in their own writing. Teaching is seminar-based and involves extensive discussion of texts and concepts. There are no lectures. The module is assessed by both written presentations and students' own life writing, on which they also write a commentary.

Enrollment usually consists of fifteen to twenty students, who come from different backgrounds and have varying ambitions. Most have degrees in English literature; a substantial minority are over thirty. The majority are British, and the rest come from the United States, Canada, European countries, Africa, and the Middle East. Quite a few are British Asian and Afro-Caribbean. Students from diasporic backgrounds are often interested in investigating their own families' histories of migration and adaptation through life writing.

We familiarize the students with different kinds of twentieth-century life writing, which might include autobiography, memoir, diaries, family history, and fictional autobiography. Students examine textual constructions of self and of life narratives and how these writings involve a variety of genre conventions, narrative strategies, and rhetorical devices. They also consider why life writing seems to demand inventive departure from conventional narrative strategies.

The theoretical basis of the course lies in life writing's implicit deployment of a variety of models of self and assumptions about the shapes, or shapelessness, of lives. We select texts that invite students to reflect on these models and assumptions and to be conscious of them in their own writing. A quotation from Leigh Gilmore sums up our agenda: "Every autobiography is the fragment of a theory. It is also an assembly of theories of the self and self-representation; of personal identity and one's relation to a family, a region, a nation" (12).

These models and assumptions are approached through theoretical debates, though theory is not in itself our main concern. We begin by discussing extracts from Patricia Waugh's *Revolutions of the Word* and find introductions to Sigmund Freud, Anthony Giddens, Erving Goffman, and the idea of the multiplicity of selves suggested in Virginia Woolf's "Street Haunting" to be most helpful. Students are encouraged to read Linda Anderson's introductory text *Autobiography*, with its generally poststructuralist treatment of the self. Our purpose is not to press the claims of any one theoretical approach but to open as many doors as possible so that students can deepen their understanding of whichever theories seem most rewarding or appropriate. Within this framework three themes recur: truth telling, ethical problems, and fictionality.

Our module specifically concerns twentieth-century writers. We assume that new forms of writing and new ways of thinking about the self emerged in the early twentieth century. To give students points of comparison, we have them read slightly earlier texts, such as Woolf's "A Sketch of the Past," Rudyard Kipling's *Something of Myself*, or Edmund Gosse's *Father and Son*. The meta-autobiographical comments of Woolf are highlighted, as she identifies the difficulty of knowing the decisive influences that keep the self in place, like a fish in a stream. She sees an analogy between sketching the past (especially in the freely associative manner that she adopts in "Sketch") and psychoanalytic therapy. She gives space to the present writing I and questions motives for wanting to re-create her past self (the written I) in textual form. Above all, she speculates about memory and "moments of Being" ("Sketch" 70). "A Sketch of the Past" also opens a debate about gender and autobiography. Woolf claimed that there had never been a woman's autobiography, and several feminist writers, such as Anderson, argue that Woolf's writing "flies in the face of conventional modes of representation, producing a multiplicity which cannot be captured within one and the same, the singular 'I' of masculine discourse" (98).

This foundation informs the discussion of a number of texts grouped under the heading life writing and trauma. Explored in recent years by Suzette Henke and Leigh Gilmore, trauma is understood here as the result of events so distressing and disorienting that they shatter the felt coherence of self and life narrative. Life writing is discussed as an attempt to recover from trauma by rebuilding a sense of self-definition and directed life.

We feature two books by British novelists, Tim Lott's *The Scent of Dried Roses* and Martin Amis's *Experience*. Both are nonlinear, nonchronological multiple narratives that combine autobiographical presentation of self with family memoir. At the center of each is the death of a parent. Lott's book is a response to his mother's shockingly unexpected suicide. His mother had been so familiar, yet in death comes to seem a complete stranger. The book is in part a detective story: who is the guilty party who drove his mother to self-destruction? (The author thinks himself a prime candidate.) The book is also an extended reflection on clinical depression, from which both Lott and his mother suffered, and an essay in social history, attempting to reconstruct the culture of his parents' generation of respectable lower-middle-class Londoners. Lott and his mother are presented as typical examples of the postmodern self, fragmented and unfinished. Author and reader endlessly encounter new shocks and discoveries that force revisions of the narratives and undermine confidence in the explanatory frameworks.

Giddens's theories are especially useful here. He sees the posttraditional self as a reflexive project of self-narrativization. Since we constantly revise our own projected life narrative, episodes of life crisis, which disrupt the projection of the narrative into the future, prove particularly difficult.

Amis wrote his memoir *Experience* partly in response to the death of his father, the English comic novelist Kingsley Amis. The book's narrative and rhetorical strategies are complex, experimental, subtle, and sophisticated. Despite its rather chilling tone of emotional detachment and rigorous control, this book is concerned with trauma, as the author responds to a series of difficult life events. An important theme is Amis's attempt "to put the record straight" (7) by challenging inaccurate, unscrupulous, or malicious versions of stories in the press.

But why should the reader trust one telling of a story rather than another? In his account of the "autobiographical pact," Philippe Lejeune addresses truth telling in autobiography as both an epistemological and an ethical issue. The central issue is that of trust. The writer must earn and build the reader's trust. But how can readers be sure that trust is well founded rather than cunningly elicited? Can the modern writer, conscious of the constructions, strategies, and narrative postures involved in textualizing a life, be anything other than calculating, seductive, and manipulative?

We group another selection of works together as diaries, texts written without long-range retrospective contemplation. The diary, especially the daily journal, can seem to offer a more spontaneous, less calculated picture of segments of a life. Bringing the writing I and the written I into close proximity, the diary creates the illusion of an unmediated portrayal of life as it is lived. Students quickly learn, however, that even daily journals narrativize experience and that, as a written text, the diary is open to patterns of meaning making and to attempts (perhaps unconscious) to manipulate the reader.

Derek Jarman, the British filmmaker, painter, and stage designer, was a serial autobiographer. After being diagnosed HIV-positive, he chose to present his life in diary form, first in *Modern Nature* and then in *Smiling in Slow Motion*, published after Jarman's death in 1994. Rarely has an autobiographical text come so close to being the writer's own epitaph. Jarman deliberately chose the diary form as appropriate for the self-making (or self-unmaking) and self-presentation of a dying man, for whom the personal future is likely to be short and unpredictable.

The diary is also central to Lorna Sage's *Bad Blood*, though here the diary is that of her transgressive grandfather, a small-town Anglican priest and sinner, who records his sexual affairs, first with a district nurse and then shockingly with a seventeen-year-old contemporary and friend of his granddaughter. *Bad Blood* is both a memoir about Sage's grandfather and family and an autobiographical account of her childhood and adolescence. The stories converge in the idea of bad blood, inherited from her grandfather and taking the form of unconventionality and sexual transgression. Refusing to adopt her mother's child-wife femininity, Sage aimed to become a literary scholar and academic, as she conspicuously did. Sage's use of her grandfather's diaries raises ethical questions. Is it right to publish a private confessional document? Sage interweaves her reading of this private document with social and cultural history of the suffocating provincial backwater where she grew up in the 1950s. Her life is written as a story of escape and successful self-creation against the cultural odds—a narrative of iconic significance for many women of her generation.

The question of the body in life writing is posed differently in Hilary Mantel's *Giving Up the Ghost*, which tells how a misdiagnosed illness affected her life. In postmodern theory the body is not a biologically determined thing but is culturally constructed (see Bordo). Mantel's body, however, became a trap, constructed by medical incompetence, the cultural arrogance of doctors, and pharmacological accident, as her body and the humiliation of labeling constantly undermined her attempts at self-making. One doctor called her "Little Miss Neverwell" (82). Suffering from endometriosis and later from gross overweight resulting from medication and unable to have children as a result of surgery, Mantel felt trapped in an alien body in which she could not recognize herself. Life writing became a way to seize control over her own script, thereby recovering her sense of agency.

For many writers, self-definition and control begin with (re)locating the self in relation to a revisited familial past. Margaret Forster reveals that research for *Hidden Lives: A Family Memoir* began at the moment after her mother's funeral when she set out on the trail of the concealed illegitimate birth of her grandmother's first daughter. But *Hidden Lives* does much more than simply uncover a family secret or chronicle Forster's investigation into her mother's, grandmother's, and aunts' lives. Like Lott and Sage, she also provides a wealth of social history, writing with painful candor about her relationship with her mother and contrasting her own hunger to extend her horizons with her mother's convention-bound, unquestioning, and ultimately discontented life.

For Linda Grant's Jewish immigrant family, secrecy and self-reinvention were necessary for survival and advancement. Grant's mother also tended to make things up for her own purposes, a tendency later overlaid by genuine inability to remember when she developed dementia (MID). As Grant (re)writes her own life in relation to the excavated familial past, she records the harrowing, grotesque progress of her mother's condition and how she and her sister struggled to deal with it. The attrition of Rose Grant's faculties progressively destroys her self, the work-in-progress. Without memory, this work, and therefore the self, cannot continue, for memory, Grant says, is "everything, it's life itself " (17). Terry Castle's "Courage, Mon Amie" provides another narrative in which exploring family history connects with attempts to solve enigmas in the writer's own self, as Castle links her obsession with World War I to puzzles about her gender identity.

James McBride's *The Colour of Water* introduces questions about migration and hybridity in relation to self-making. Raised by a tough, single-minded Jewish mother and an African American stepfather, McBride delineates both his mother's story and his own. The two narratives come together in McBride's questioning of his identity, focusing on his ethnic mix and childhood confusions about race in the face of his mother's silence on the subject. McBride's self-discovery draws on both the Jewish strand of his history and cultural identity and his black American experiences.

In Sara Suleri's *Meatless Days*, straightforward storytelling gives way to complex running metaphors and shifting narrative positions used to explore the deaths of the writer's mother and sister and political upheavals in her native Pakistan. Students find this the most difficult text to grapple with. An alternative that dwells on the problems of the postcolonial self in the context of a study of Indian writing in English is Amitava Kumar's *Bombay, London, New York*.

We generally include a fictional text that centers on life writing. Anne Michaels's *Fugitive Pieces* prompts discussion of what we call the archaeology of the self. Her imagery—the symbolic resonances of geography, geology, and archaeology; the Holocaust events underpinning the novel; and the biographical theme—all focus attention on the difficulties of writing a life (re)constructed from incomplete or inaccessible historical data. This text inverts the commonplace that auto/biography uses the narrative strategies of fiction. Here in particular, and elsewhere in the course, Nicola King's *Memory, Narrative and Identity* provides a useful reflection on problems of writing and memory.

We have also used W. G. Sebald's *The Rings of Saturn*, which hovers between autobiographical memoir, historical essay, and fiction. Ostensibly an account of a walking tour through the county of Suffolk, with ruminations on a number of loosely associated historical topics, the book can also be read as the account of a self recovering from a bout of incapacitating depression. As the narrator stumbles repeatedly on historical episodes of human cruelty or futility and of death and destruction, he seems unable to escape melancholy reflections. The narration, however, never quite acquaints the reader with the self harboring these thoughts or with the life that contains this journey, making this strange, unclassifiable book the most liminal of life writing texts.

Discussions about the use of photographs in life writing texts occur throughout the course. Some writers provide photographs as evidence for social or family history; more often, they seem to bear more subtle relation to the meanings of the written life. Often photographs seem designed to trigger the reality effect—to authenticate the writing or guarantee that the written discourse is not fiction but refers to real people. Photographs in Carol Shields's *The Stone Diaries*, for instance, offer the only indication that what on the cover is termed a novel may in fact be biographical. Sebald's images also play with these effects, as their amateurish qualities seem to guarantee the nonfictional reality of the narrator whose status is otherwise indeterminate. Jarman uses photographs to stage the self, employing costume and props to take on temporary identity, as though enacting Goffman's theories. In other works, photographs remind the reader of the huge gulf between people's appearances and their inner worlds of confusion and chaos—an insight that, along with others acquired over the semester, returns students to the point of life writing: that it attempts, from confusion, to construct coherent selves and intelligible life narratives.

Works Cited

Amis, Martin. *Experience*. London: Vintage, 2001.

Anderson, Linda. *Autobiography*. London: Routledge, 2001.

Bordo, Susan. *Unbearable Weight: Feminism, Western Culture, and the Body*. Berkeley: U of California P, 1995.

Castle, Terry. "Courage, Mon Amie." *London Review of Books* 24.7 (2002): 3–11.

Forster, Margaret. *Hidden Lives: A Family Memoir*. London: Penguin, 1996.

Freud, Sigmund. "Sigmund Freud from *Civilization and Its Discontents*." Waugh 143–46.

Giddens, Anthony. "Anthony Giddens from *Modernity and Self-Identity*." Waugh 157–60.

———. *Modernity and Self-Identity: Self and Society in the Late Modern Age*. Cambridge: Polity, 1991.

Gilmore, Leigh. *The Limits of Autobiography: Trauma and Testimony*. Ithaca: Cornell UP, 2001.

Goffman, Erving. "Erving Goffman from *The Presentation of Self: Everyday Life*." Waugh 153–56.

Gosse, Edmund. *Father and Son*. 1907. London: Penguin, 1949.

Grant, Linda. *Remind Me Who I Am, Again*. London: Granta, 1998.

Henke, Suzette A. *Shattered Subjects: Trauma and Testimony in Women's Life-Writing*. New York: St. Martin's, 2000.

Jarman, Derek. *Modern Nature: The Journals of Derek Jarman*. London: Vintage, 1991.

——. *Smiling in Slow Motion*. London: Vintage, 2001.

King, Nicola. *Memory, Narrative and Identity: Remembering the Self*. Edinburgh: Edinburgh UP, 2000.

Kipling, Rudyard. *Something of Myself*. 1936. London: Penguin, 1977.

Kumar, Amitava. *Bombay, London, New York*. New York: Routledge, 2002.

Lejeune, Philippe. *On Autobiography*. Ed. and fwd. Paul John Eakin. Trans. Katherine Leary. Minneapolis: U of Minneapolis P, 1989.

Lott, Tim. *The Scent of Dried Roses*. London: Penguin, 1997.

Mantel, Hilary. *Giving Up the Ghost: A Memoir*. London: Fourth Estate, 2003.

McBride, James. *The Colour of Water: A Black Man's Tribute to His White Mother*. 1996. London: Bloomsbury, 1998.

Michaels, Anne. *Fugitive Pieces*. London: Bloomsbury, 1997.

Sage, Lorna. *Bad Blood*. London: Fourth Estate, 2000.

Sebald, W. G. *The Rings of Saturn*. London: Vintage, 2002.

Shields, Carol. *The Stone Diaries*. London: Fourth Estate, 1993.

Suleri, Sara. *Meatless Days*. London: Flamingo, 1989.

Waugh, Patricia, ed. *Revolutions of the Word: Intellectual Contexts for the Study of Modern Literature*. London: Arnold, 1997.

Woolf, Virginia. "A Sketch of the Past." *Moments of Being*. Ed. Jeanne Schulkind. 2nd ed. San Diego: Harcourt, 1985. 61–159.

——. "Virginia Woolf, 'Street Haunting.'" Waugh 149–52.

Gabriele Helms

The Generic Instability of Contemporary Life Writing in Canada

Some of the most exciting innovations in contemporary Canadian auto/biography have come from writers who have self-consciously responded to existing life writing genres. These writers transgress generic boundaries and combine multiple generic conventions; their texts incorporate elements of autobiography, biography, fiction, poetry, drama, critical theory, essay, photography, maps, historical documents, and much more. To signal their generic reconceptualizations, writers such as Fred Wah, Daphne Marlatt, Linda Griffiths and Maria Campbell, and Aritha van Herk have proposed alternative terms to describe their texts: biotext, fictionalysis, theatrical transformation, and crypto-friction respectively. Studying these cross-generic Canadian texts develops an understanding of how important genres continue to be for readers and writers alike. More specifically, close analysis of these texts illustrates how they respond to and influence contemporary Canadian culture.

At the University of British Columbia, I offer a three-credit course for senior undergraduate students built around six autobiographical texts. Forty-five students meet two or three times a week (for a total of three hours) for thirteen weeks. By pairing primary readings with secondary theoretical material drawn from new genre theory, auto/biography studies, and Canadian studies, the course can easily be adapted to work as a more advanced major or honors seminar with a greater theoretical focus.

Theoretical Issues

The theoretical underpinnings of the course come from recent developments in genre theory and auto/biography studies. Unlike earlier studies that understood genres as fixed entities to be described and categorized, new genre theory has since the 1980s focused its attention on the sociability of discourse. New genre theorists understand genre as "a socially standard strategy, embodied in a typical form of discourse, that has evolved for responding to a recurring type of rhetorical situation" (Coe and Freedman 137). While genres may still be identified in terms of textual regularities, critics now focus on how genres can be understood as strategies for achieving particular goals in specific situations. Often referring to Carolyn Miller's groundbreaking essay "Genre as Social Action," they see genres as "situated and strategic" (Coe and Freedman 143).

According to Mikhail Bakhtin and P. N. Medvedev, "every genre has its methods and means of seeing and conceptualizing reality" (133); in other words, genres are neither neutral nor ahistorical. On the contrary, genres are ideologically charged, as they embody values, attitudes, and worldviews. If genres are forms of ideology, "then the struggle against or the deviations from genre are ideological struggles" (Beebee 19). One of these struggles has to do with writers' searches for ways to represent their experiences. In this course, I begin from the premise that the texts under discussion present experience not as providing authoritative evidence but as requiring explanation. Given that experience is not transparent and unmediated but constituted discursively, writers pay special attention to the language and forms chosen to represent experience. I suggest that writers' simultaneous desire to rely on and challenge experience is closely linked with their concurrent resistance to and complicity with genre conventions. The inclusion of multiple generic conventions stages the performative nature of experience, and the texts thus take on performative qualities themselves: they rupture generic boundaries, intervene in the gaps, and reaccentuate and combine traditional genres in new ways. To think about experience and genre in this interconnected way requires a historicized approach that sees all categories of analysis as contextual, contested, and contingent.

While genre knowledge is usually tacit, students in this course make explicit the genre expectations that inform their reading experiences. John Swales argues that the nomenclature for genres can be an important source of insight. Given that "names tend to persevere against a background of substantial change in activity," it is particularly important to recognize the significance of genre naming. Swales suggests that the people who "give genre names to classes of communicative events that they recognize as providing recurring rhetorical action" tend to be those who "have the greatest genre-specific expertise" (55). As Bakhtin points out, "to use a genre freely and creatively is not the same as to create a genre from the beginning; genres must be fully mastered in order to be manipulated freely" (80). The writers discussed in this course expertly and self-consciously place themselves within a history of life writing genres as they create texts that do not fit into existing forms. Instead of expanding our understanding of the term *autobiography* from within, they create a new genre label that signals their engagement with generic traditions.

Course Outline and Readings

Since I cannot assume that my students have any knowledge of life writing in Canada, I ask them to read an introductory overview in the first week, Susanna Egan and Gabriele Helms's "Life Writing." I also provide a brief overview of how the field of auto/biography study has developed over the last three decades, introducing some key terms and concepts (such as autobiographical pact, relationality, and identity) and referring students to Sidonie Smith and Julia Watson's *Reading Autobiography* for follow-up. We revisit these ideas as we discuss each text, building a "toolbox" of critical terminology, as terms and concepts (such as collaboration, embodiment, agency, and ethics) become relevant to class discussion.

Our first auto/biographical reading in week 2 is Michael Ondaatje's *Running in the Family*. Variously described as biography, family saga, oral history, travel journal, memoir, collection of anecdotes, nonfiction novel, and fictionalized portrait, the book reconstructs Ondaatje's family history, especially his parents' early lives in Ceylon (now Sri Lanka). Students pay close attention to the organization of the text, its narrative strategies, voice, and use of photographs to determine what kind of text we are reading. After two epigraphs, a map, and a table of contents, the book opens with an italicized section, which reads like the opening to a novel with a third-person narrator. If we equate the narrator's stance with that of the author, then what we are promised here is a biography. But the first chapter immediately deconstructs such biographical intent, for now we encounter a first-person narrator whom we also presume to be identical with the author of the text.

In the acknowledgments at the end of the text, Ondaatje undermines such generic conventions: "While all these names may give an air of authenticity, I must confess that the book is not a history but a portrait or 'gesture'" (176). He challenges the conventions of traditional life writing genres, but he does not simply reject representation or intentionality. The desire for direct, unmediated access is nevertheless frustrated in *Running in the Family*. Neither individual sources nor their combinations provide the complete history of the Ondaatje family. However, this realization does not so much make family auto/biography impossible as it revises the underlying expectations and draws our attention to the mediated nature of memory. Ondaatje challenges the validity of generic boundaries by evoking them and then transgressing them to examine the purposes they serve and the effects they have on both writers and readers.

Wah's *Diamond Grill*, on the other hand, explicitly refuses familiar genre labels. Published in 1996, it is Wah's first (full-length) prose work, consisting of 132 prose segments that range from five lines to more than five pages. To explore his mixed-race identity, Wah tests and challenges the various ways and codes available to him to write (about) his life, introducing the term "biotext," which he borrows from George Bowering. As Wah has explained in an interview with Ashok Mathur, the term *biotext* works as a "hedge" so that the writing in *Diamond Grill* won't be "hijacked by ready-made generic expectations" (97). As Joanne Saul argues, "'biotext' foregrounds the writer's efforts to articulate him or her self through the writing process. The text itself comes to life" (260). Not only is life constructed and composed when it is written (with memory playing a crucial role in the process), but experience itself is not transparent or authoritative. Experience, Wah writes, becomes the very thing that has to be explained through "poses or postures" ("Interview" 98). And because Wah's understanding of experience cannot be accommodated by existing genres, he needs a new form to represent his way of seeing and conceptualizing reality.

Marlatt shares Ondaatje's and Wah's discomfort with the familiar genres of auto/biography. For one, she is concerned about how the writer comes to represent her own connection with so many others—what Paul John Eakin has discussed as our relational lives. How can a form accommodate such multiplicity and interrelatedness? But furthermore, she insists on the importance of the imaginary in one's life story, proposing in 1990 "fictionalysis" as a new term to suggest "a self-analysis that plays fictively with the primary images of one's life, a fiction that uncovers analytically that territory where fact and fiction coincide" (124). In her introduction to *Readings from the Labyrinth*, a collection of her essays from 1982 to 1996, Marlatt describes her initial discomfort with the idea of an essay collection and her decision to approach it autobiographically by including journal entries, letter excerpts, notes, photographs, and so on. That way, she felt, she could return the "essaying" to the essays: to make them once again into "attempts to read my life and the lives of women close to me in light of theoretical reading about psycho-social conditioning as women, as lesbians, *writing*" (ii). Beverley Curran analyzes the alternative ways of writing in Nicole Brossard's and Marlatt's texts and argues that they signal alternative ways of reading the self (138), which will have an impact on their own and others' auto/biographical writing. In fact, Marlatt's editorial work on Roy Kiyooka's *Mothertalk: Life Stories of Mary Kiyoshi Kiyooka* is an excellent example of serial collaboration that shows Marlatt's rethinking of auto/biographical genres put into practice.

Marlatt leads readers into *Mothertalk* by way of an introduction in which she asserts the personal and historical significance of Mary's stories and then outlines the complex stages of putting this book together, foregrounding and explaining her editorial role and her investment in the project. She describes the complex procedures whereby Mary Kiyoshi Kiyooka's life stories traveled from oral Japanese conversations to the written English that includes her son's memories. When Roy Kiyooka died in 1994 before completing his book, his daughters asked Marlatt to see it into print. *Mothertalk* was published in 1997, and in the introduction, Marlatt attests to her personal accountability but also calls attention to the much more general realization that life stories are always already mediated.

Mothertalk is collaborative life writing that defies familiar definitions of collaboration. Marlatt herself describes only her interaction with Kiyooka's drafts as collaborative, but most of the collaboration in *Mothertalk* is best described as successive or serial, as each listener becomes the speaker of another story shaped by yet another listener (Egan and Helms, "Many Tongues" 50). Each version thus always belongs to at least two people whose sameness and difference inform their struggle for control over the story. The concept of serial collaboration not only emphasizes the crucial relations among multiple speakers, listeners, and contexts but also fore-grounds the succession of multiple versions, their mediated quality, and the processual nature of the life stories collected in *Mothertalk*.

Another example of a hybrid text that explores auto/biographical writing as process and collaboration is Griffiths and Campbell's *The Book of Jessica: A Theatrical Transformation*, which endlessly repeats, as Joanne Tompkins points out, the rehearsal procedure that characterized the ini-tial production of the play *Jessica* at 25th Street House in Saskatoon, as well as the transformations of the text and the relationship between the two women (149). The hybrid form of the text results from its three sec-tions: "Spiritual Things" is Griffiths's retrospective narrative of events leading to the play and the book; "The Red Cloth" presents the carefully edited transcript of conversations between Griffiths and Campbell in 1988; and *Jessica* is the script of the actual play. If we follow Bakhtin in regarding the addressee as a defining characteristic of genre (95), "genre boundaries" in the final book version "become permeable or mobile" (Egan 108). In *The Book of Jessica*, students encounter an auto/biograph-ical text whose generic expectations continue to shift as they read; it re-fuses final answers as it places the students in the middle of multiple cross-cultural misreadings and appropriations. The "theatrical transfor-mation" of the subtitle characterizes not only the processes represented within the text but also the reading process in which the students are asked to engage.

As a way to review the readings of the course and to reflect on the questions about genre conventions, blurring, and instability, students con-sider van Herk's "Blurring Genres: Fictioneer as Ficto-Critic," in which van Herk creates two characters, Aritha van Herk and Hannike Buch—an alter ego who challenges van Herk's understanding that a "book must genre itself, must delineate its boundaries" (14). The two characters' rela-tionship and dialogue playfully, but seriously, enact and explicitly com-ment on the struggle between "the comfort of category" (20) and the "infidelities (genre crime) with other forms" (14). The result is an essay that van Herk describes as "crypto-friction" (14) or "ficto-crypticism" (14) or "ficto-criticism" (39)—writing that is "cryptic and full of friction" (39) and that does not fulfil the genre expectations of either fiction or criticism, let alone auto/biography.

What Do Students Learn from This Course?

I encourage students to study life writing texts not only for the experiences these texts inscribe but also for the specific devices and strategies they employ to represent those experiences. "New means of representation force us to see new aspects of visible reality," Bakhtin and Medvedev point out, "but these new aspects cannot clarify or significantly enter our horizon if the new means necessary to consolidate them are lacking" (134). Generic conventions embody ideologies, and this course enables students to formulate questions and develop reading strategies that help them explore what it means, ideologically speaking, to adopt or challenge genre conventions. Since the texts we study are primarily concerned with blurring genres and unfixing boundaries, the idea of genre may initially appear like an anachronistic concept. Ultimately, however, it becomes clear that writers and texts rely on our understanding of genre even (or especially) if they reject available forms.

Works Cited

Bakhtin, Mikhail M. *"Speech Genres" and Other Late Essays*. Trans. Vern W. McGee. Ed. Caryl Emerson and Michael Holquist. Austin: U of Texas P, 1986.

Bakhtin, Mikhail M., and P. N. Medvedev. *The Formal Method in Literary Scholarship: A Critical Introduction to Sociological Poetics*. Trans. Albert J. Wehrle. Cambridge: Harvard UP, 1978.

Beebee, Thomas O. *The Ideology of Genre: A Comparative Study of Generic Instability*. University Park: Penn State UP, 1994.

Brossard, Nicole. *Journal intime ou voilà donc un manuscript*. Montreal: Les Herbes rouges, 1998.

Bowering, George. *Errata*. Red Deer, AB: Red Deer Coll. P, 1988.

Coe, Richard, and Aviva Freedman. "Genre Theory: Australian and North American Approaches." *Theorizing Composition: A Critical Sourcebook of Theory and Scholarship in Contemporary Composition Studies*. Ed. Mary Lynch Kennedy. Westport: Greenwood, 1998. 136–47.

Curran, Beverley. "Critical Journals: Theory and the Diary in Nicole Brossard and Daphne Marlatt." *A/B: Auto/Biography Studies* 15.1 (2000): 123–40.

Eakin, Paul John. *How Our Lives Become Stories: Making Selves*. Ithaca: Cornell UP, 1999.

Egan, Susanna. *Mirror Talk: Genres of Crisis in Contemporary Autobiography*. Chapel Hill: U of North Carolina P, 1999.

Egan, Susanna, and Gabriele Helms. "Life Writing." *The Cambridge Companion to Canadian Literature*. Ed. Eva-Marie Kröller. Cambridge: Cambridge UP, 2004. 216–40.

——. "The Many Tongues of *Mothertalk: Life Stories of Mary Kiyoshi Kiyooka*." *Canadian Literature* 163 (1999): 47–77.

Griffiths, Linda, and Maria Campbell. *The Book of Jessica: A Theatrical Transformation*. Toronto: Coach House, 1989.

Kiyooka, Roy. *Mothertalk: Life Stories of Mary Kiyoshi Kiyooka*. Ed. Daphne Marlatt. Edmonton: NeWest, 1997.

Marlatt, Daphne. *Readings from the Labyrinth*. Edmonton: NeWest, 1998.

Miller, Carolyn. "Genre as Social Action." *Quarterly Journal of Speech* 70.2 (1984): 151–67.

Ondaatje, Michael. *Running in the Family*. Toronto: McClelland, 1982.

Saul, Joanne. "Displacement and Self-Representation: Theorizing Contemporary Canadian Biotexts." *Biography: An Interdisciplinary Quarterly* 24.1 (2001): 259–72.

Smith, Sidonie, and Julia Watson. *Reading Autobiography: A Guide for Interpreting Life Narratives*. Minneapolis: U of Minnesota P, 2001.

Swales, John M. *Genre Analysis: English in Academic and Research Settings*. Cambridge: Cambridge UP, 1990.

Tompkins, Joanne. "'The Story of Rehearsal Never Ends': Rehearsal, Performance, Identity in Settler Culture Drama." *Canadian Literature* 144 (1995): 142–61.

van Herk, Aritha. "Blurring Genres: Fictioneer as Ficto-Critic." *In Visible Ink: Crypto-Frictions*. Edmonton: NeWest, 1991. 13–42.

Wah, Fred. *Diamond Grill*. Edmonton: NeWest, 1996.

———. "Interview with Ashok Mathur." *Faking It: Poetics and Hybridity. Critical Writings 1984–1999*. Edmonton: NeWest, 2000. 97–104.

Timothy Dow Adams

A + B ≠ B + A:
Teaching Autobiographies
and Biographies in Pairs

> *In biography, it is resemblance that must ground identity; in autobiography, it is identity that grounds resemblance. Identity is the real starting point of autobiography; resemblance, the impossible horizon of biography.*

—Philippe Lejeune

Although I admire the many ways that writers have always combined autobiography and biography—along with such other forms of life writing as memoir, diary, journal, and autobiographical novel—I believe students and instructors on all levels can benefit from courses that try to make distinctions between the genres, so long as those distinctions are not too rigid and do not diminish the value of texts that cannot be made to fit easily into any particular genre. Of course, there are autobiographical elements in any biography and biographical aspects of all autobiographies; however, the popularity of hybrids like James McBride's *The Color of Water* or Michael Ondaatje's *Coming through Slaughter*, which could as easily be classified as biography or autobiography, have led some of my students to assume that there are really no differences in those genres and that all autobiographies and biographies might be read without any regard for their classifications.

With these concerns in mind, I designed and taught a graduate course that paired autobiographies and biographies of the same person. Among the questions I hoped this class could consider, in addition to what we might discover by reading about the same lives in pairs, were readers' expectations for biography as opposed to autobiography, the truth value of each genre, the distinctive characteristics of each genre, and the purpose of classifying texts into genres. While the basic idea of the course was to come to some understanding of the different demands each genre asks of its readers, in the end the class discovered that genre did not have as strong an effect as they had imagined.

This semester-long graduate topics course (as opposed to a seminar) attracted a class ranging from first-year MA and MFA students in English to PhD students from the history department. While some of the students came into the class with a preference for biography or autobiography, most of the class had never even considered the possibility of reading either as a primary text. During the first few class meetings, a number of the students referred to whichever text we were discussing as a novel.

Because I had hoped to show the ways that autobiography is a part of biography and vice versa, the course began with a text that combines autobiography and biography: Steven Millhauser's *Edwin Mullhouse*, a novel about a biographer whose writing is autobiographical. *Edwin Mullhouse* is a parody of the obsessions of some biographers for the minutiae of their subjects and a fictional case study of the biographer's need to control his or her subject. In this instance the fictional biographer goes so far as to literally "take" his subject's life. The class seemed to appreciate the way this novel introduced some of the basic concepts we would be considering, especially the complicated ways in which biographers are connected to their subjects.

As an additional example of the way the two life writing forms interact, I next assigned Art Spiegelman's *Maus: A Survivor's Tale*. The first volume, *My Father Bleeds History*, begins with an autobiographical preface in which Art Spiegelman illustrates the difficulty of living with his father, Vladek Spiegelman, a Holocaust survivor, followed by a series of episodes in which Art acts as his father's recorder, editor, and interpreter. To different degrees, both father and son are survivors. Other sections, including "The Prisoner of Hell Planet," are even more directly autobiographical. The second volume, *And Here My Troubles Began*, focuses on the son's difficulty in dealing with the success of the first volume and with the father's inability to adjust to life after his time in the concentration camps. The universal reaction of my class was positive toward the son but less so toward the father.

Because I wanted the class to consider the way each genre dealt with issues of accuracy, authenticity, documentation, and reception, I deliberately chose texts that have called such topics into question. We began our reading in pairs with Carol Brightman's *Writing Dangerously: Mary McCarthy and Her World*, a biography that includes discussion of the controversy between McCarthy and Lillian Hellman over issues of truthfulness and authenticity, including the McCarthy-Hellman lawsuit and the accuracy of McCarthy's memory as displayed in her *Memories of a Catholic Girlhood*. The class was excited by the idea of treating a literary biography as a text to be studied for its own sake, and in our discussions the general opinion was that the Mary McCarthy of the biography was an admirable character whose life exemplified her courage and iconoclastic stance.

When we turned to McCarthy's *Memories of a Catholic Girlhood*, on the other hand, some of the class found the autobiographical McCarthy to be untrustworthy, manipulative, and less than honorable. Attempts to pin down exactly what passages or scenes in the autobiography gave this negative impression often proved difficult because the students' main concern was that the figure that they had come to admire in the biography was different from the character in the autobiography. I assumed that the biographical McCarthy was seen as more admirable than the autobiographical because of McCarthy's device of including separate italicized interchapters that questioned the accuracy of the original chapters, because of her emphasis on her predilection for misrepresentation, or because of her tone. (I had intended to move next to a pairing of one of Hellman's autobiographies with William Wright's *Lillian Hellman*. Unfortunately, at the time of the course, those texts were not available in paperback editions.)

For the next pairing—Zora Neale Hurston's *Dust Tracks on a Road* and Robert Hemenway's *Zora Neale Hurston*—we began first with the autobiography. Although Hurston's text is often taken to be an exemplar of an untrustworthy autobiography, the class's reaction was very positive. In general students found the persona in the autobiography to be strong and charming; what some people think of as her disingenuousness struck them as a survival mechanism. Turning to the biography, however, which I had anticipated would set the record straight and provide factual information that might undercut the almost universally positive reaction, I was surprised to discover that here the autobiography was seen as the default, the biography serving not to give additional information that might act as a corrective but to provide details that reinforced the view that critics of *Dust Tracks on a Road* were unnecessarily captious.

Initially I'd imagined that most readers would see the autobiography half of each pairing as more trustworthy for personal matters and the biography more useful for historical details. However, as we moved next to a consideration of Michael Reynolds's *Hemingway: The Paris Years* and Ernest Hemingway's *A Moveable Feast*, personal and historical details were equally present in both texts. Reynolds's biography frequently warns of the dangers of accepting anything Hemingway wrote as straightforward nonfiction. Referring to *The Sun Also Rises*, Reynolds asserts that "most of his readers and more than one biographer assumed that all of his fiction was thinly veiled biography, which it never was" (12). The biographer's insistence that neither autobiography nor novel can be read for accurate details of Hemingway's life is further confused by the fact that *Hemingway: The Paris Years* includes numerous instances in which fiction is used to support speculation, frequent ambiguity about the degree to which Nick Adams is a fictional or autobiographical character (followed by attacks on other Hemingway biographers for depending on fiction for biographical information), and open admissions that there are many explanations for various events—"Multiple scenarios suggest themselves, all of them plausible fictions" (113).

And yet, when the class turned to *A Moveable Feast*, most of my students placed their trust in Reynolds over Hemingway. A lack of trust in Hemingway was a natural result of such factors as his confusing preface, which provides an invitation to read the text as fiction, and the ways that some of the narrative undercuts the standard biographical details most of the class knew about some of the other writers in Paris, including Gertrude Stein, Ezra Pound, and F. Scott Fitzgerald.

As the class moved on to study autobiographies and biographies in pairs of such writers as Malcolm X (*The Autobiography of Malcolm X* and Peter Goldman's *The Death and Life of Malcolm X*), Richard Wright (*Black Boy* and Margaret Walker's *Richard Wright: Daemonic Genius*), and Gertrude Stein (*The Autobiography of Alice B. Toklas* and Linda Wagner-Martin's *Favored Strangers*), the same pattern prevailed: whichever genre we read first took precedence over whichever we read second. Although *The Autobiography of Malcolm X* is an as-told-to text, combining Malcolm

X's narrative with Alex Haley's biographical editing, the last portion of the text—in which, after his subject's death, Haley writes autobiographically about his own experiences with Malcolm and with the act of writing—did not seem to my students as important as the narrative proper. Even though Goldman's biography includes ample material on the aftermath of Malcolm X's assassination, his attempts at explaining the complicated political struggles behind that act seemed less significant to my class than Haley's stunning narrative, which captures the velocity with which Malcolm lived his final days.

Similarly, students reacted more positively to Walker's version of Wright's life than to *Black Boy*, even though Walker is better known as a novelist and her biography is presented as both a biography and a memoir. (I had wanted to use Michel Fabre's *The Unfinished Quest of Richard Wright*, but that text was not available at the time of the class.) For many of my students, the narrator of *Black Boy*, who is not always precisely congruent with the actual writer named Richard Wright, was frequently unbelievable, a figure whose exaggerations about his family life seemed sometimes to detract from the genuine racism he experienced as a child in Mississippi.

Because *The Autobiography of Alice B. Toklas* is in effect Stein's autobiography told in the form of Toklas's biography of her, it becomes more difficult to determine whether reading this text before Wagner-Martin's biography reinforces the pattern I have been describing. Stein's habit of exaggerating her own genius through Toklas's voice, coupled with the fact that the class had already read about the now romanticized spirit of the time and place, Paris in the 1920s, through auto/biographical pairings of Hemingway, resulted in a collective sense that genre mattered less than reading order, with Gertrude Stein seeming more trustworthy than her biographer and Hemingway less. Although Hemingway and Stein often contradicted each other and each biography included historical material that contradicted both writers, still whichever genre we read first trumped the other.

I had expected that reading these books in pairs would allow the class to think about the epigram that heads this essay, a quotation I had put at the top of our syllabus and talked about the first day. Lejeune's idea that the basis of biography relies on resemblance or likeness while autobiography is centered on identity seemed to suggest that biographers had an inherently more difficult task in grounding their texts. However, my class's experience suggests that sequence is an essential factor in determining which genre has captured its subject's resemblance or identity more accurately. My class seems to have suggested that responses to reading autobiography and biography in pairs is affected as much by the order in which the genres are read as by the quality of the individual life writing text.

In other words, to borrow from mathematical principles of the order of operations, the following formula applies: $A+B \neq B+A$, where A is autobiography and B biography. While mathematicians have demonstrated that this "commutative property rule for operations" does not apply to subtraction but always applies to both addition and multiplication—one can change the order of the numbers without changing the results of the operation—in teaching life writing in pairs the opposite is the case. Although my class might have also been unconsciously basing its reactions on the associative and distributive properties of operations, which have to do with grouping and sequence, the basic principle behind our responses seems to have been an unconscious tendency to accept as most convincing the first genre we read in each pair (as well as the first generic impulse of those books that combined genres).

I have described this principle here as an aid to those considering other ways of putting together a syllabus of autobiography/biography pairs, whether chronological, thematic, or some other combination.

Appendix

Auto/Biographical Pairs for Papers

Langston Hughes, *The Big Sea*, and Arnold Rampersad, *The Life of Langston Hughes*

Ellen Glasgow, *The Woman Within*, and Susan Goodman, *Ellen Glasgow: A Biography*

Eudora Welty, *One Writer's Beginnings*, and Ann Waldron, *Eudora: A Writer's Life*

Thomas Hardy, "Autobiography," and Michael Millgate, *The Life and Work of Thomas Hardy*

Edmund Gosse, *Father and Son*, and Ann Thwaite, *Edmund Gosse: A Literary Landscape*

Vladimir Nabokov, *Speak, Memory*, and Andrew Field, *Nabokov: His Life in Part*, or Brian Boyd, *Vladimir Nabokov: The Russian Years*

Confessions of Saint Augustine, and Garry Wills, *Saint Augustine*

Simone de Beauvoir, *The Prime of Life: The Autobiography of Simone de Beauvoir*, and Deirdre Bair, *Simone de Beauvoir: A Biography*

Margaret Mead, *Blackberry Winter*, and Jane Howard, *Margaret Mead: A Life*

Frederick Douglass, *Narrative of the Life of Frederick Douglass, An American Slave* or *My Bondage and My Freedom* or *Life and Times of Frederick Douglass by Frederick Douglass,* and William S. McFeely, *Frederick Douglass*

Lillian Hellman, *Pentimento: An Unfinished Woman* or *Scoundrel Time* (collected as *Three*), and Carl Rollyson, *Lillian Hellman: Her Legend and Her Legacy*, or William Wright, *Lillian Hellman: The Image, the Woman*

Isadora Duncan, *Mary Desti, The Untold Story*, and Walter Terry, *Isadora Duncan: Her Life, Her Art, Her Legacy*

Edith Wharton, *A Backward Glance*, and R. W. B. Lewis, *Edith Wharton: A Biography*

Jean-Jacques Rousseau, *The Confessions of Jean-Jacques Rousseau*, and Maurice Cranston, *Jean-Jacques: The Early Life of Jean-Jacques Rousseau*

William Wordsworth, *The Prelude*, and Kenneth Johnston, *The Hidden Wordsworth*

Sylvia Plath, *The Bell Jar*, and Janet Malcolm, *The Silent Woman*

Mahatma Gandhi, *My Experiments with Truth*, and Yogesh Chadha, *Gandhi: A Life*

Samuel Taylor Coleridge, *Biographia Literaria*, and Richard Holmes, *Coleridge: Early Visions*

Oscar Wilde, *De Profundis*, and Richard Ellmann, *Oscar Wilde*, or Peter Ackroyd, *The Last Testament of Oscar Wilde*

Rigoberta Menchú, *I, Rigoberta Menchú: An Indian Woman in Guatemala*, and David Stoll, *Rigoberta Menchú and the Story of All Poor Guatemalans*

Possible Final Exam Questions

Agreeing or disagreeing as you wish, apply the following quotation from Stanley Weintraub to Brightman's *Writing Dangerously* and Reynolds's *Hemingway: The Paris Years*: "The biographer perennially faces two paradoxes: the facts do not always add up to truth, and invention, which frequently furnishes tantalizing material for the biographer, often has its own kind of truth" (5).

Agreeing or disagreeing as you wish, apply the following quotation from Ira Nadel to Goldman's *The Death and Life of Malcolm X* and Hemenway's *Zora Neale Hurston*: "The signature of the biographer is as important to recognize as that of his subject. The former signs himself through literary means, the latter through the record of his life" (2).

Agreeing or disagreeing as you wish, apply the following quotation from Sidonie Smith to *Dust Tracks on a Road* and *The Autobiography of Alice B. Toklas*: "Autobiography becomes both the process and the product of assigning meaning to a series of experiences, after they have taken place, by means of emphasis, juxtaposition, commentary, omission" (45).

Agreeing or disagreeing as you wish, apply the following quotation from Philippe Lejeune to any autobiography/biography pair: "In biography it is resemblance that must ground identity: in autobiography it is identity that grounds resemblance. Identity is the real starting point of autobiography; resemblance, the impossible horizon of biography" (24).

Works Cited

Brightman, Carol. *Writing Dangerously: Mary McCarthy and Her World*. New York: Harvest, 1994.

Fabre, Michel. *The Unfinished Quest of Richard Wright*. New York: Morrow, 1973.

Goldman, Peter. *The Death and Life of Malcolm X*. Champaign: U of Illinois P, 1979.

Hemenway, Robert. *Zora Neale Hurston: A Literary Biography*. Champaign: U of Illinois P, 1980.

Hemingway, Ernest. *A Moveable Feast*. 1942. New York: Scribners, 1964.

Hurston, Zora Neale. *Dust Tracks on a Road*. New York: Perennial, 1996.

Lejeune, Philippe. "The Autobiographical Pact." *On Autobiography*. Ed. and fwd. Paul John Eakin. Trans. Katherine Leary. Minneapolis: U of Minnesota P, 1989. 3–30.

Malcolm X, with the assistance of Alex Haley. *The Autobiography of Malcolm X*. 1965. New York: Ballantine, 1996.

McBride, James. *The Color of Water: A Black Man's Tribute to His White Mother*. New York: Riverhead, 1996.

McCarthy, Mary. *Memories of a Catholic Girlhood*. 1957. New York: Harvest, 1972.

Millhauser, Steven. *Edwin Mullhouse: The Life and Death of an American Writer 1943–1954 by Jeffrey Cartwright*. 1972. New York: Vintage, 1996.

Nadel, Ira B. *Biography: Fiction, Fact, and Form*. New York: St. Martin's, 1984.

Ondaatje, Michael. *Coming through Slaughter*. 1976. New York: Vintage, 1996.

Reynolds, Michael. *Hemingway: The Paris Years*. New York: Norton, 1999.

Smith, Sidonie. *A Poetics of Women's Autobiography: Marginality and the Fictions of Self-Representation*. Bloomington: Indiana UP, 1987.

Spiegelman, Art. *And Here My Troubles Began*. New York: Pantheon, 1991. Vol. 2 of *Maus: A Survivor's Tale*.

——. *My Father Bleeds History*. New York: Pantheon, 1986. Vol. 1 of *Maus: A Survivor's Tale*.

Stein, Gertrude. *The Autobiography of Alice B. Toklas*. 1933. New York: Vintage, 1990.

Wagner-Martin, Linda. *Favored Strangers: Gertrude Stein and Her Family*. New Brunswick: Rutgers UP, 1995.

Walker, Margaret. *Richard Wright: Daemonic Genius*. New York: Amisted, 1993.

Weintraub, Stanley. *Biography and Truth*. Indianapolis: Bobbs, 1967.

Wright, Richard. *Black Boy*. 1945. New York: Perennial, 1998.

Craig Howes

Biography, Oral History, Autobiography: A Graduate Course

The graduate course I teach on biography, oral history, and autobiography provides an introduction to the texts, methodology, and theory of the major genres in life writing and suggests in what ways, and with what reservations, life writing can inform literary, creative, and cultural studies projects.

A few words about the University of Hawai'i at Mānoa's graduate program in English and the department's distinctive relation to life writing studies help explain some of the assumptions underlying this course. Students in our MA program must choose a concentration from one of four offered: literary studies, cultural studies–Asia/Pacific, composition and rhetoric, and creative writing. A certain number of courses must be taken in the selected area; every graduate course therefore carries one or more concentration designations. This course fulfills both the literary studies and the cultural studies–Asia/Pacific requirements; increasing interest in life writing in composition pedagogy and the burgeoning presence of creative nonfiction course offerings in writing programs have made the course popular with these students as well. English PhD candidates also enroll, as do graduate students from other departments and programs in the arts, humanities, and social sciences, whose research interests have carried them into this interdisciplinary field.

Institutionally, because the journal *Biography: An Interdisciplinary Quarterly* has been published from here since 1978 and because the Center for Biographical Research has been a distinct university entity since 1988, a long-standing commitment to life writing as a field of study has led not only to regular scheduling of this course—every other year for the past ten—but also to a substantial number of other frequently offered undergraduate and graduate courses in life writing. The course I'm describing here therefore serves as an introduction for students who will have the opportunity to pursue these studies further.

I begin the course with a brief discussion of the case against life writing as a useful endeavor or area for study. As Alison Booth remarks, even though "biographies are published and relished as never before" and though "the lives of women and minorities are being written and interpreted by increasing numbers," theorists still must ask why the genre should "suffer from a lack of legitimacy" (62–63). I identify the theoretical, historical, cultural, and disciplinary assumptions that provoke this question. The rest of the course encourages students to discover, and then practice, the kinds of responsible intellectual work in life writing that leads to publication, interpretation, and translation of life writing into other genres and media.

We map out the fields of biography and autobiography, with two sessions on oral history and other media set in the middle. The biography readings situate the genre historically and suggest something about its fortunes in other fields. Whether through interviews, field reports, or group narratives, representing the lives of others is an increasingly self-conscious and contentious practice in ethnography and, more generally, anthropology; and as the very existence of the *Journal of Narrative and Life History* (now *Narrative Inquiry*) suggests, modeled or recorded lives play a significant role in planning and counseling activities in social work, sociology, and educational theory.

We start off with a swift survey of hugely influential biographical texts. The Gospels, those four biographies that together compose the founding narrative for Christianity, raise questions about authorship, authority, subject constitution, evidence, narrative, and ideology that will reappear through the semester. Selections from Sima Qian's dynastic histories in *Records of the Historian* allow us to examine representations of the force of human agency on history; Plutarch's handling of exemplary figures, historicized parallels, arguments through contrast, and implicit social critique in such emblematic lives as Alexander, Julius Caesar, and Marc Antony establishes life writing as a practice with its own sense of history. A look at the hagiographical tradition foregrounds such concerns as imitation, repetition, allegory, and the ethical, but I also point to the genre's downplaying of such "incidental" details as location, culture, and historical moment. Three life narratives for each of three very different saints—Barbara, Stephen, and Francis of Assisi (Delaney; Thurston and Attwater)—demonstrate not only how the move from mythic to historically specific figures affects the representation of lives but also how representations of the same saint change in emphasis over time.

The following week concentrates on the legacy of Sigmund Freud, starting with his case study of the Wolf Man, then moving into essays on the relation between psychoanalysis and biography (Edel) and on the practice of psychobiography in general (Elms). The important transition here is from assertion to interrogation as the rhetorical method. Freud's assumptions have turned many biographers into detectives, searching for the secret, key, or hidden motive lying behind later behavior—the unobservable, the irrational, the unpredictable, or even the repellent. We then read Lytton Strachey, who drew on Freud's work in the deft, and at times hilarious, debunking of the great man or woman narrative in *Eminent Victorians*: a hallmark of the so-called New Biography, a site for superb examples of literary lives, and an important theoretical text. I conclude the biography section with Janet Malcolm's *The Silent Woman*, because it returns us to a highly skeptical contemporary view of life writing and to issues of ethics and intention as well. At this point the class revisits Booth's question, but from a deliberately widened cultural perspective. The impulse to record the life of an individual as an outstanding or defining historical or ethical agent can be seen as symptomatic of dominant ideology or as a Western cultural intrusion. Lives are, of course, recorded in many ways, in many places—in genealogies, in oral traditions, in written accounts after contact, and today in videos and on Web sites. But notions that history is somehow the collected biographies of great or notorious individuals or that the way to understand cultural or artistic life is through the representation of an individual's experience are problematic not only historically and geographically but also theoretically.

The oral history and other media interlude instructs students in current techniques for recording, preparing, creating, adapting, and publishing lives in a variety of media. The first of these classes is essentially a workshop. Using a guide prepared by the University of Hawai'i's Center for Oral History, we talk about interviewing, releases, editing, archiving, and the relative merits of various tape recorders and transcription machines. But I also introduce students to the discipline of oral history, distinguishing it sharply from journalism and ethnographic interviewing—at least as they have often been practiced. Human subject research and the institutional permissions required for certain kinds of writing are also discussed at this time. The second class, on video and audio documentaries, online lives, and life writing in other media, grows out of the first but raises aesthetic and ethical issues resulting from the orchestration of word, sound, and image through performance and montage. We examine a number of very recent texts, though my own work as a producer of television documentaries and as the coeditor of *Biography*, which has recently published guest-edited special issues on the biopic, online lives, biography and geography, and testimony, informs the discussion here.

The autobiography section begins with an overview of recent theoretical and critical work and then examines a few major themes through some representative texts. Over the past thirty years, studies in autobiography have produced most of the major critical and theoretical work on life writing. Stand-alone published personal narratives, letters, diaries, journals, and memoirs, as well as autoethnographies, testimonio, personal Web pages, and performance pieces have all been discussed at length. This interest in autobiography has also produced a far richer collection of overview studies and foundational texts. For this reason, I start the section with a discussion of three of the most influential and defining works available on autobiography: Philippe Lejeune's essays on the autobiographical pact; Paul John Eakin's *How Our Lives Become Stories: Making Selves*, and Sidonie Smith and Julia Watson's *Reading Autobiography: A Guide for Interpreting Life Narratives*. Lejeune's groundbreaking work offers a useful starting point for studying autobiography. The Eakin and the Smith and Watson books provide sharp, clear vocabularies for talking about autobiography's assumptions, forms, and rhetorical strategies; they point students to striking and complex primary texts for consideration; and they refer to other excellent secondary sources and commentary.

Since a comprehensive or even representative survey of autobiographical writing would be impossible to carry out in the remaining few weeks, I select three or four examples that supply major topics for debate and that have stimulated detailed and interesting responses. Because students can also take this course to fulfill one of the requirements for the University of Hawai'i's interdisciplinary certificate in cultural studies, I choose texts that force us to address the two questions asked of any instructor who offers a certificate course: How will the course address international and intercultural issues? and How will the course articulate with the politics of representation? (The answers I try to provide in class are "Constantly" and "In as many ways as possible.")

I spend a week on *I, Rigoberta Menchú: An Indian Woman in Guatemala*, because it allows us to examine issues related to transmission, ethnography, and the political, legal, and aesthetic aspects of testimonio. This genre/act assumes that the person publicly bearing witness is doing so not to record a personal experience for the ages but to speak for a community under siege. The resulting controversies provoked by *I, Rigoberta Menchú* also lead to discussion of veracity, justice, and the public functions of personal narrative. I then move to a cluster of texts that together invoke a vexed encounter between parent auto/biography, Native American life writing, and disability narrative. Michael Dorris's narratives of the life and death of his disabled son, *The Broken Cord* and "The Power of Love," prove to be extremely disturbing for many students, especially after reading G. Thomas Couser's *Recovering Bodies: Illness, Disability, and Life-Writing* and Arthur Frank's *At the Will of the Body: Reflections on Illness*. The following week, I move to Michael Ondaatje's *Running in the Family*. Although his account of Sri Lanka in the aftermath of British colonialism explores the effects of globalization on our sense of the past and his family vignettes almost create a group biography by way of memoir, I'm particularly interested here in the mixture of genres—the poetry juxtaposed with the short narratives, the disorienting segments composed almost entirely of dialogue, and the photographs, which implicitly comment on the stories and sometimes even become the occasion for the writing. Ondaatje's status as an established writer of fiction and poetry also allows us to look at the relation between life and creative writing and, ultimately, to evaluate the usefulness of the distinction.

Regardless of what texts or topics get raised in the first dozen or so weeks, at least for the foreseeable future I will end the prescheduled portion of the course with Art Spiegelman's *Maus*. The thematic reasons are almost too pat: *Maus* is a cartoonist's autobiographical account of how he gathered his father's biography, primarily through oral history interviews, and then recorded the entire process in graphic novel form. Other characteristics, however, make this work a perfect summary. The visual format allows for discussions of life writing and mixed media. The accounts of trauma—Art's father's, Art's mother's, his own—lead us into a major area of recent life writing study and to the invocation of the Holocaust, complete with its relation to cultural memory—or as Spiegelman puts it, "My Father Bleeds History."

What remains of the semester—usually three or four classes—is devoted to class presentations of the students' research projects. Since the students' own interests are so diverse—preliminary work for writing a biography, life writing as a pedagogical issue, extensions of biographical issues into cultural or rhetorical or race or gender studies, narrative theory, biographically oriented literary or film criticism, and so on—I find that class members learn a great deal about life writing simply from listening to one another. Each student gives a detailed report on a self-selected topic. Initial and final drafts of a substantial seminar paper or equivalent are also required. The other assignments relate directly to the course content. Shortly after the oral history class, all students conduct a substantial interview, transcribe the entire tape, edit the resulting text, and then prepare selections for specifically identified research purposes. (Often the final project grows out of this initial interview.) And every week, students post comments to an e-mail list about readings and topics.

Though the announced goal, to introduce students to life writing, can only barely begin in a course of this type, the interest students have shown in the field, as measured by their enrollment in related courses and by the increasing numbers of doctoral dissertations and master's theses and projects written within the field in our department and in our university, suggests that at the very least such a graduate course does get people started.

Works Cited

Booth, Alison. Rev. of *The Seductions of Biography*, ed. Mary Rhiel and David Suchoff. *Biography: An Interdisciplinary Quarterly* 21.1 (1998): 62–68.

Center for Oral History. *How to Do Oral History*. 3rd ed. Honolulu: Center for Oral History, U of Hawai'i, 2000.

Couser, G. Thomas. *Recovering Bodies: Illness, Disability, and Life-Writing*. Madison: U of Wisconsin P, 1997.

Delaney, John J. *Dictionary of Saints*. New York: Doubleday, 1980.

Dorris, Michael. *The Broken Cord*. New York: Harper, 1989.

———. "The Power of Love." *Paper Trail: Essays*. New York: Harper, 1994. 111–17.

Eakin, Paul John. *How Our Lives Become Stories: Making Selves*. Ithaca: Cornell UP, 1999.

Edel, Leon. "Psychoanalysis." 1959. *Writing Lives: Principia Biographia*. New York: Norton, 1984. 142–58.

Elms, Alan C. "The Psychologist as Biographer." *Uncovering Lives: The Uneasy Alliance of Biography and Psychology*. New York: Oxford UP, 1994. 3–18.

Frank, Arthur W. *At the Will of the Body: Reflections on Illness*. Boston: Houghton, 1991.

Freud, Sigmund. "From the History of an Infantile Neurosis" [The Wolf Man]. 1918. *Three Case Histories*. Trans. James Strachey. New York: Collier, 1963. 187–316.

Gospels: Matthew, Mark, Luke, and John. King James Version.

Lejeune, Philippe. "The Autobiographical Pact" and "The Autobiographical Pact (bis)." *On Autobiography*. Ed. and fwd. Paul John Eakin. Trans. Katherine Leary. Minneapolis: U of Minnesota P, 1989. 3–30; 119–37.

Malcolm, Janet. *The Silent Woman: Sylvia Plath and Ted Hughes*. New York: Vintage, 1993.

Menchú, Rigoberta. *I, Rigoberta Menchú: An Indian Woman in Guatemala*. Ed. Elisabeth Burgos-Debray. Trans. Ann Wright. New York: Verso, 1984.

Ondaatje, Michael. *Running in the Family*. New York: Norton, 1982.

Plutarch. *Eight Great Lives*. New York: Rhinehart, 1960.

Sima Qian (Szuma Chien). "The Life of Sima Qian" and "Lord Ping Yuan." *Records of the Historian*. Ed. and illus. Tai Chih Chung. Trans. Tang Nguok Kiong. Singapore: Asiapac, n.d. 1–17; 57–73.

——. "Lord Pingyuan and Yu Ching." *Selections from Records of the Historian*. Ed. Yang Hsien-yi and Gladys Yang. Peking: Foreign Languages Press, 1979. 128–32.

Smith, Sidonie, and Julia Watson. *Reading Autobiography: A Guide for Interpreting Life Narratives*. Minneapolis: U of Minnesota P, 2001.

Spiegelman, Art. *And Here My Troubles Began*. New York: Pantheon, 1991. Vol. 2 of *Maus: A Survivor's Tale*.

——. *My Father Bleeds History*. New York: Pantheon, 1986. Vol. 1 of *Maus: A Survivor's Tale*.

Strachey, Lytton. *Eminent Victorians*. 1918. New York: Penguin, 1990.

Thurston, Herbert, and Donald Attwater, eds. *Butler's Lives of the Saints: Complete Edition*. 4 vols. New York: Kenedy, 1963.

Cynthia Huff

A Text of Their Own:
Life Writing as an Introduction
to Undergraduate English Studies

How can collaborative group projects that use noncanonical life writing manuscripts as the lynchpin in a semester-long gateway to English studies courses help give students the needed expertise to feel confident that they can do English studies? One answer is that the pedagogy of reading and editing noncanonical life writing acquaints students with the concept of usable familiarity, which underscores the genre-based undergraduate English studies curriculum at Illinois State University. But other answers foreground central disciplinary concerns such as canonicity, the complexities of textual production and reception, and the making of meaning—all of which were an integral part of my gateway course for English studies majors and minors.

I taught the 100-level course Introduction to English Studies in spring 2003 at Illinois State University, a large, multipurpose university whose undergraduate students come almost exclusively from Illinois and contiguous states, are often first-generation college students, and frequently earn teaching certificates. English 100, a requirement for all majors and minors, is ideally taken during a student's freshman year, but commonly later, since many students don't declare their commitment to English studies until their junior year.

Usable familiarity, which is reiterated in the "Goals of the Major in English," a department text, emphasizes combining theory and praxis in the acquisition of a knowledge base in and practice of the subdisciplines of English studies, namely, literature, linguistics, and rhetoric and composition. The goals statement also indicates that transdisciplinarity, a perspectival approach, historical knowledge of language, and the ability to write about and do research not only in different genres but also in other disciplines are all integral to an English studies model. These emphases dovetail well with issues immediately raised by working with life writing manuscripts, which foreground canonicity, varied readings, audience analysis, invention, and changes in language, among other considerations. In short, reading and editing life writing manuscripts catalyzes challenges to and reintegration of disciplinary boundaries that exemplify a fusion-based English studies curriculum (see North 73, 255–57).

By taking a cultural studies approach inflected by feminism and acquainting students with current schools of thought and concepts in literary studies and other subdisciplines, I provided students with some conceptual knowledge. I assigned relevant chapters in Jonathan Culler's *Literary Theory: A Very Short Introduction* and required students to select terms discussed by Culler, illustrate their application to English studies after doing additional research, and then post the terms on a Web site glossary. This exercise allowed students to practice the theoretical work of English studies and gave them cultural capital in relevant disciplinary concepts, capital that they later used and questioned as they confronted life writing manuscripts (see Berlin 15).

Three weeks into the semester my students, divided into learning communities of five, had a burgeoning conceptual foundation with which to approach unfamiliar reading strategies and undertake the task of editing, annotating, and providing a bibliography for an excerpt of a life writing manuscript provided to them. Their initial response to reading and discussing the manuscript was telling. A usually rowdy class greeted me that day with stunned silence, the look of deer caught in the headlights, and complete disbelief that English students in a gateway course could read, much less edit and contextualize, a manuscript (inherited by me on my mother's death) written by a middle-aged, midwestern doctor about World War II that details events historically familiar to contemporary students, as well as changing conditions on the home front and in his family circle. The range of the journal's topics and students' familiarity with World War II make Walter L. Albin's journal a good introduction to reading and editing manuscripts. We spent one class period generally discussing an excerpt from the journal; another talking about possible reading strategies for manuscript journals or diaries based on an article I wrote; a third day looking at artifacts from Albin's life and family members to provide information about his personal life as referenced in the journal; and a fourth and fifth day listening to a rhetorician and a linguist explain how their archival research informed both their work and English studies. We also visited two local archives, one kept by Illinois State and the other by the county historical society, so that students could learn about additional transdisciplinary approaches to pursuing archival work and locate sources for their second life writing manuscript project. Although these activities helped allay students' fears about their competence in working with manuscripts, I still had to reassure them and prod them to let go of their deep-seated convictions that doing English studies meant only reading canonical literature.

The first exam fell in the midst of these activities. To assess how students were responding to the unfamiliarity of reading life writing manuscripts and coping with challenges to their conceptions of what constitutes an English studies curriculum, one exam question asked them to discuss how their reading strategies for the Albin manuscript, as an example of nonfiction, were or were not different from those employed in reading a novel. Generally, the answers suggested that students resisted using new reading strategies and awarding noncanonical works the status of privileged texts. Not only did many students miss the familiar narrative pattern of a beginning, middle, and end and the narrator's description of characters, but they also chafed against the additional time required to decipher handwriting and make sense of a manuscript through secondary research. Yet they pointed out their satisfaction in reading a historical document, pursuing the detective work that, as one student put it, necessitated picking up "small clues such as the use of the word *patient*" to construct Albin's profession. They were also gratified to understand the distinction between the hyperprotected cooperative principle that operates in our reading of a novel (Culler 25–26), where we afford the novelist substantial leeway because all relevance and meaning has been validated in the novel's production, and our reading of the Albin journal, where, as one student said, "we have to look *outside* the text because of references to speeches, acts of congress and public opinion."[1]

The points of pride felt by my students suggest not only the authority I wanted them to feel but also the questioning of authority I expected to be tweaked by their continued work with noncanonical life writing manuscripts (for complications of authority and life writing, see Gilmore 120–30). My students' justifications for their editing of the Albin journal point to both meanings of authority. The most obvious questioning of authority came at the level of textual construction. While some groups sought to create universal appeal by standardizing Albin's spelling, punctuation, and grammatical construction and by providing visual rhetoric through the imposition of paragraphs, others emphasized the necessity of "a loose editorial hand" to preserve the voice of "the ordinary male citizen on the home front." The latter groups realized that because a journal's genre laws are not canonical, standard grammar rules do not apply and that preserving the integrity of Albin's voice and expression brought readers closer to the experiences he was describing, while providing a case study for language use and change. Some groups pointed out that reading and editing the Albin journal gave them a sense of accomplishment.

I encouraged the collaborative groups to locate and start reading a life writing manuscript of their choice no later than the due date for the Albin manuscript activities. To underscore the integration among the collaborative group projects, reading and writing about *Jane Eyre*, and our continued perusal of Culler's book and its offshoot of glossary listings, I interspersed our concentration on these projects throughout the second half of the semester. I chose *Jane Eyre* for two reasons. First, it is a canonical fictional autobiography whose construction, voice, and place in an English studies curriculum can be easily juxtaposed to noncanonical life writing manuscripts. Second, by asking students to create meaning about the novel and to adopt a current critical practice of their own choosing, I could help them see the similarities and differences between the invention involved in that activity and the ones imbricated in editing and writing an introduction for life writing manuscripts. Students' exposure to Brontë's canonized novel and their work with life writing manuscripts let them discover firsthand "that a canon constructs value as much as it reflects value," as Catharine Stimpson wrote (266).

Although the second collaborative group life writing project built on many of the skills and issues visited in the first one—namely, editing, annotating, finding, and using appropriate secondary material and providing a bibliography and contextual background—it foregrounded authority in two important ways. Each collaborative group was asked, first, to present its project orally by organizing a panel modeled after conference presentations and, second, to write an eight-page introduction that clarified for readers the reasons for publishing the text and its possible uses. These distinguishing requirements meant that students had to consciously consider their role in creating a text, the publishing process, and the interplay between their conception of audience and the realized product: they had to situate themselves in relation to the manuscript and then resituate themselves in the context of producing a text—a crucial exercise in an English studies curriculum, according to Helene Moglen (88). That such activities are integral to English studies, its subdisciplines, and their interrelations seems apparent, not only because scholars produce texts, but also because questions of language use, rhetorical positioning, and metaphorical interplay, among other considerations, are commonplace.

The texts my students produced show their increased facility for considering multiple aspects of English studies and envisioning their interrelationships. One of the five groups dealt with a family text, the 1953 journal of an Illinois farmer. Other groups edited the 1878 journal of a Bloomington, Illinois, laborer, the early-twentieth-century diary of a local schoolteacher, the journal of a local Depression-era workingman, and the letters of a World War I soldier written to a lab-school teacher at Illinois Normal State University. Almost every college and every community has archival resources that could be used as outlined here. As hoped, the textual sophistication of editing and explanation was greater for the second collaborative project. Both the oral group presentations and the introductions to the texts indicated much greater awareness of the intricacies between editorial decisions and audience reception, the hard yet rewarding labor involved in producing a text, and the complex issues affecting canon formation. As a number of students put it, *"we've* created a text, and what it tells us is important, but I don't know if it would get taught."

But it was their responses to the final exam question that crystallized the ways in which students reconceptualized English studies as a result of their work with noncanonical life writing manuscripts. The question read:

> Cultural studies critics advocate an approach that questions canonicity and thus enables scholars to study texts other than recognized masterpieces. Using your glossary listings, *Jane Eyre* paper, and collaborative group projects as examples, show how you have followed the lead of cultural critics this semester and practiced an English studies model not bound by the canon.

Their visual response to the question was revealing, as I saw slowly spreading smiles of recognition that, yes, beginning English studies students can read, edit, and contextualize life writing manuscripts of their own choosing and that they've practiced a methodology commonly used in English studies. These are their words: "By reading, transcribing, editing and annotating these journals I was able to put the definitions of linguistics or rhetoric to work. Reading *Moby Dick* doesn't do that." "The stuff of ordinary lives did not follow the conventional literary model. Our groups had to seek and create meaning." "We played a very small part in introducing unrecognized work from outside the canon."[2] Assigning noncanonical life writing manuscripts enables students to discover central disciplinary issues in English studies and to demonstrate their power to create and interrogate meaning. As the compositionist Erika Lindemann writes, students using archival resources learn "that research involves making knowledge, interpreting artifacts and sources, solving problems raised by evidence, experiencing the excitement of discovery" (4).

Appendix

Collaborative Research Projects: Guidelines for Students

Each of you will join one of five collaborative research groups that will complete two primary research projects during the semester. For the first collaborative project, I will provide the necessary primary material. For the second project, your group will locate the primary material and all secondary sources needed to explain the significance of your research. Consider especially how this impinges on our conceptions of English studies as a discipline and the methodologies that we use to arrive at our view of English studies and its subdisciplines. Field trips to both the Illinois State University Archive and the McLean County Historical Society will help you locate possible primary material for your second project.

For each of the projects, I will ask you to transcribe onto a computer disk pages from your primary source that illustrate your editorial practice. Provide a hard copy of the transcription as well. There should be an obvious and direct correlation between how your transcription looks and the editorial guidelines you offer in your justification. You should talk about your stance as editor—why you chose to include or exclude certain material, standardize or maintain original punctuation, and explain or not explain the writer's habits as exemplified by the document's form and how your editorial stance influences a reader's perception of the text. It will be as important to consider what you chose not to do as what you decided to do and to link both to how the text might be read. You should also consider what the text's uses might be—for example, in a classroom, as a source of regional history or literature, or as a text accessible to the general reading public. This link should also exhibit a clear connection to concepts current in English studies and its subdisciplines.

The second collaborative project should feature an introduction of eight pages to the text you chose to edit. This introduction should clarify the reasons for publishing the text, its possible uses, and your editorial practices; describe significant contextual material, which might include biographical or historical information; and, of course, provide a bibliography. With your introduction, you should transcribe the portion of your manuscript that best illustrates your editorial principles and decisions. Write your introduction as though it were to be published.

Each collaborative group is responsible for presenting its text, its editorial decisions, contextual materials, and the significance of these for English studies as part of a thirty-minute panel—the standard form for the delivery of research at academic conventions.

Notes

1. For a compelling overview of the complexities and potentialities of reading and teaching life writing, see Smith and Watson.

2. All student writing used with permission.

Works Cited

Berlin, James. *Rhetorics, Poetics, and Cultures: Refiguring College English Studies.* Urbana: NCTE, 1996.

Brontë, Charlotte. *Jane Eyre.* 1847. Ed. Beth Newman. New York: St. Martin's, 1996.

Culler, Jonathan. *Literary Theory: A Very Short Introduction.* Oxford: Oxford UP, 1997.

Gilmore, Leigh. *Autobiographics: A Feminist Theory of Women's Self-Representation.* Ithaca: Cornell UP, 1994.

Huff, Cynthia. "Reading as Re-Vision: Approaches to Reading Manuscript Diaries." *Biography: An Interdisciplinary Quarterly* 23.3(2000): 504–23.

Lindemann, Erika. "Playing in the Archives: Pleasures, Perils, and Possibilities for Teaching." Conference on College Composition and Communication Meeting. Minneapolis. 12–15 Apr. 2000.

Moglen, Helene. "Crossing the Boundaries: Interdisciplinary Education at the Graduate Level." *The Future of Doctoral Studies.* Ed. Andrea Lunsford, Moglen, and James F. Slevin. New York: MLA, 1989. 84–90.

North, Stephen M. *Refiguring the Ph.D. in English Studies: Writing, Doctoral Education, and the Fusion-Based Curriculum.* Urbana: NCTE, 2000.

Smith, Sidonie, and Julia Watson. *Reading Autobiography: A Guide for Interpreting Life Narratives.* Minneapolis: U of Minnesota P, 2001.

Stimpson, Catharine R. "Feminist Criticism." *Redrawing the Boundaries: The Transformation of English and American Literary Studies.* Ed. Stephen Greenblatt and Giles Gunn. New York: MLA, 1992. 251–70.

Kristine Peleg

Teaching *Rachel Calof's Story: Jewish Homesteader on the Northern Plains*

Rachel Kahn immigrated to the United States from the Ukraine as an eighteen-year-old and married Abraham Calof. They lived on a homestead near Devils Lake, North Dakota, from 1894 until 1917, when the family moved to Saint Paul, Minnesota. In her memoir, originally written in Yiddish in 1936, she tells of the difficulties of farming, giving birth to nine children, and maintaining a Jewish home under problematic circumstances. I have traced this text from handwritten manuscript to publication, paying special attention to the translation and editing process, drawing on a new translation of the Yiddish manuscript that led to the English publication of 1995.

In a semester-long composition course based on literature, I introduce my community college students to the Calof life writing text as an interim unit designed to prepare them to write an independent research paper. Approaching academic research methods, autobiography, and archival study through this text has encouraged students to think about autobiographical text production as a dynamic field of inquiry.

About eighty percent of the students in this second composition course at Century College, White Bear Lake, Minnesota, are fulfilling the requirements of an associate of arts degree, with transfer options to other

universities and colleges. The other students are working on certificate programs such as law enforcement and nursing that require two semesters of
composition. A smaller but not insignificant component are students from
local high schools completing college courses (a postsecondary education
option). Usually highly motivated, they do not see this composition course
as their final English requirement. Most students have taken the prerequisite composition course at Century College, and the vast majority are taking this course because it is required for their program. About half are
between nineteen and twenty-two, with about one-fourth younger and
one-fourth older. Roughly fifteen percent of Century College students are
first-generation immigrants, but this advanced composition course draws a
lower percentage of ESL students than the college as a whole. Perhaps
most significant, nearly half of the students have never read an autobiography, and another fourth say they've read one but don't remember the title
or subject. The remaining fourth remember Anne Frank, Maya Angelou,
or familiar others.

We read *Rachel Calof's Story* along with other life writing and some
immigrant and western studies scholarship (Bunkers; Hampsten; Monk). I
place the Calof story within the history of the midwestern Jewish community and in relation to frontier immigrant and ethnic literature (Hansen;
Jacobson; Limerick; Payant). We discuss the translation and editing process. Since linguistic differences between the Yiddish manuscript and the
English publication are significant, I raise issues of collaboration and translation (Myerhoff). I also follow the shift in emphasis from the individual
subject to relational and contextual aspects found in recent scholarship in
autobiography theory (Eakin). Viewed in this light, I offer *Rachel Calof's
Story* as a hybrid text, integrating both oral histories and written texts to
portray a more complete picture of life on that homestead.

Jacob Calof, Rachel's son and the compiler of the English version for
publication, brings to the work a remarkably comprehensive knowledge of
her life, but the objectivity of his collaboration is problematic because he
was, indeed, her son. Recent scholarship in women's studies (Alpern;
Lensink; Temple; Wagner-Martin), western studies (Armitage; Bloom), and
immigrant literature (Muir) introduces ideas of situational context and of
the search for daily and prosaic details as part of an increasingly multifaceted
picture. Recent immigrant literature theory (Bergland) generally emphasizes
ambivalence rather than the more monolithic stance of earlier assimilationist
projects (Handlin). And an approach developed by the Personal Narratives

Group elucidates women's voices in particular, helping students consider the context, narrator-interpreter relations, and the many-layered connotations of multiauthored "truths." The status of Yiddish as an oral language is an additional factor in the layers of interpretation (Harshav).

The initial challenge of this unit is to explain the goals in ways that immediately connect it to the subsequent unit on research and autobiography. Students who make the connections show a remarkable interest in applying our discussions of author, context, point of view, manuscript transmission, translation, and editing to their own research on an autobiography they choose. Nonetheless, there is usually some confusion. Students first read Rachel Calof's text, then the preface and acknowledgments (Rikoon), epilogue (J. Calof), and accompanying articles (Rikoon, "Jewish Farm"; Jameson). They propose possible research directions into narratives, publication processes, translation issues, and voice. I supply an extensive bibliography and ask them to find two items on the list. For most students this means going into the college library, and for many, using the interlibrary loan system for the first time. Limiting them to materials inaccessible by the Internet produces stress and seems to threaten previously adequate research methods. Of course, this exercise does not help students generate their own sources, but they do need to know the scope of library and archival possibilities, and usually this knowledge is sorely lacking.

We discuss Calof's story in great detail. By probing the narrative, students discover directions, see gaps, and question issues of community, family, immigration, and heroics. They think about context and whose stories are told. They start to think about varying research issues: other family stories, changes in autobiography theory, transitions from oral to written stories, western settlement, Yiddish as an oral language. They bring in their two outside sources, and without being required to read through them in their entirety, the students make the connections to *Rachel Calof's Story* and develop possible research directions. Working with other life writing sources, including unpublished sources, is of course a possibility, but the texts that follow this unit, works such as Elinore Pruitt Stewart's *Letters of a Woman Homesteader* and the follow-up text, Susanne K. George's *Adventures of the Woman Homesteader: The Life and Letters of Elinore Pruitt Stewart* or Robert Root's *Recovering Ruth: A Biographer's Tale*, provide similar examples of texts and editing. (I've limited the use of Holocaust works and Anne Frank because students tend to get stuck at the level of news reporting and do not go on to examine the life writing as texts.)

The unit concludes with an in-class essay about an issue that interested the students concerning either text production or context. Using at least one of the texts they found in the library, they record sources in MLA format, including a works-cited listing. All these exercises prepare them for the final section of the semester, when they read and research an autobiography they've selected.

I usually show students a video of Jacob Calof talking at a community college gathering in Devils Lake, North Dakota, presenting the text as he understands it. His input is of course crucial because of the details he contributed and because he was the moving force behind getting the book published. But by then I've shared with the students some of my own work on manuscript and translation issues, leading them to greet with some healthy skepticism Calof's lack of transparency and his claims to have changed nothing from the original Yiddish manuscript. Finally, Akira Kurosawa's *Rashomon* serves as a sometimes awkward transition into the next unit. The different versions provided of the rape and murder confuse the students, who now meet any story with some degree of questioning, if not of the facts, then at least of the interpretations. An article from David Richie's book *Focus on Rashomon* provides some context.

The life writing research required in the next unit challenges most of the students. They have to choose and read an autobiography, and although I provide a list of books, I encourage them to read something that interests them. Their energy level is often electric at this stage. I've had students read and write about B-17 bombers, fishing, desegregation, and scientists; chosen authors have included Elie Wiesel, Jimmy Carter, Roger Freeman, Paul Radin, Maya Angelou, Cynthia Kaplan, C. S. Lewis, Fanny Kelly, Gustavo Perez Firmat, Louise Bogan, Lee Iacocca, Cole Younger, Terry Tempest Williams, Elizabeth Wurtzel, Ada Lois Fisher Sipuel, N. Scott Momaday, Monty Roberts, and Mel White. The students generally conduct the type of research that I've shown them: working with a sense of authenticity, looking into everything, reading the front and concluding materials, investigating thoroughly, believing in their own research inventiveness. We discuss their papers in individual conferences, and they present them to the class for peer feedback, so their work has an audience.

Despite a strong emphasis on life writing texts that deal with lesser-known subjects, students tend toward famous faces. Sometimes knowing they have to write a research paper guides the choices; better to opt for a primary text with multiple secondary sources. Some students get distracted and choose aspects of the story that are easy to research rather than relevant to a literary essay. For the most part, however, the scope and depth of the students' work surpass my expectations. There is little plagiarism and an absence of that frantic incomprehension I've seen when teaching other research units. This interim unit thus shows how one life writing text can be approached from multiple directions to teach students how to weave research into a thesis-driven, evidence-supported essay. By the time students choose an autobiography independently, they are ready to advance critical questions and have some ideas about where to find answers.

Works Cited

Alpern, Sara, Joyce Antler, Elisabeth Israels Perry, and Ingrid Winther Scobie, eds. *The Challenge of Feminist Biography: Writing the Lives of Modern American Women*. Urbana: U of Illinois P, 1992.

Armitage, Susan. "Through Women's Eyes." *The Women's West*. Ed. Armitage and Elizabeth Jameson. Norman: U of Oklahoma P, 1987. 9–18.

Bergland, Betty. "Ideology, Ethnicity, and the Gendered Subject: Reading Immigrant Women's Autobiographies." *Seeking Common Ground: Multidisciplinary Studies of Immigrant Women in the United States*. Ed. Donna Gabaccia. Westport: Praeger, 1992. 101–21.

Bloom, Lynn Z. "Utopia and Anti-utopia in Twentieth-Century Women's Frontier Autobiographies." *American Women's Autobiography: Fea(s)ts of Memory*. Ed. Margo Culley. Madison: U of Wisconsin P, 1992. 128–51.

Bunkers, Suzanne L., and Cynthia Huff. "Issues in Studying Women's Diaries: A Theoretical and Critical Introduction." *Inscribing the Daily: Critical Essays on Women's Diaries*. Ed. Bunkers and Huff. Amherst: U of Massachusetts P, 1996. 1–20.

Calof, Jacob. Epilogue. R. Calof 99–103.

Calof, Rachel. *Rachel Calof's Story: Jewish Homesteader on the Northern Plains*. Ed. J. Sanford Rikoon. Bloomington: Indiana UP, 1995.

Eakin, Paul John. *How Our Lives Become Stories: Making Selves*. Ithaca: Cornell UP, 1999.

George, Susanne K. *Adventures of the Woman Homesteader: The Life and Letters of Elinore Pruitt Stewart*. Lincoln: U of Nebraska P, 1992.

Hampsten, Elizabeth. "Editing a Woman's Diary." *Women's Personal Narratives: Essays in Criticism and Pedagogy*. Ed. Leonore Hoffmann and Margo Culley. New York: MLA, 1985. 227–36.

———. *Read This Only to Yourself: The Private Writings of Midwestern Women, 1880–1910*. Bloomington: Indiana UP, 1982.

Handlin, Oscar. *The Uprooted: The Epic Story of the Great Migrations That Made the American People*. Boston: Little, 1951.

Hansen, Karen V. "Historical Sociology and the Prism of Biography: Lillian Wineman and the Trade in Dakota Beadwork, 1893–1929." *Qualitative Sociology* 22.4 (1999): 353–68.

Harshav, Benjamin. *The Meaning of Yiddish*. Berkeley: U of California P, 1990.

Jacobson, Matthew Frye. *Whiteness of a Different Color: European Immigrants and the Alchemy of Race*. Cambridge: Harvard UP, 1998.

Jameson, Elizabeth. "Rachel Bella Calof's Life as Collective History." R. Calof 135–53.

Kurosawa, Akira, dir. *Rashomon*. Daiei, 1950.

Lensink, Judy Nolte. "Expanding the Boundaries of Criticism: The Diary as Female Autobiography." *Women's Studies* 14.1 (1987): 39–54.

Limerick, Patricia Nelson. "What on Earth Is the New Western History?" *Trails: Toward a New Western History*. Ed. Limerick, Clyde A. Milner II, and Charles E. Rankin. Lawrence: UP of Kansas, 1991. 81–88.

Monk, Janice, and Susan Hanson. "On Not Excluding Half of the Human in Human Geography." *Professional Geographer* 34.1 (1982): 11–23.

Muir, Lisa. "Rose Cohen and Bella Spewack: The Ethnic Child Speaks to You Who Never Were." *College Literature* 29.1 (2002): 123–42.

Myerhoff, Barbara. *Remembered Lives: The Work of Ritual, Storytelling, and Growing Older*. Ed. Marc Kaminsky. Ann Arbor: U of Michigan P, 1992.

Payant, Katherine B. "Introduction: Stories of the Uprooted." *The Immigrant Experience in North American Literature: Carving Out a Niche*. Ed. Payant and Toby Rose. Westport: Greenwood, 1999. xiii–xxvii.

Personal Narratives Group. *Interpreting Women's Lives: Feminist Theory and Personal Narratives*. Bloomington: Indiana UP, 1989.

Richie, David. *Focus on Rashomon*. New York: Prentice, 1972.

Rikoon, J. Sanford. Acknowledgments. R. Calof xi–xiii.

——. "Jewish Farm Settlements in America's Heartland." R. Calof 105–34.

——. Preface. R. Calof vii–ix.

Root, Robert. *Recovering Ruth: A Biographer's Tale*. Lincoln: U of Nebraska P, 2003.

Stewart, Elinore Pruitt. *Letters of a Woman Homesteader*. 1913. Boston: Houghton, 1988.

Temple, Judy Nolte. "'They Shut Me Up in Prose': A Cautionary Tale of Two Emilys." *Frontiers* 22.1 (2001): 150–73.

Wagner-Martin, Linda. *Telling Women's Lives: The New Biography*. New Brunswick: Rutgers UP, 1994.

Katrina M. Powell

Reading, Writing, Performing Life Writing: Multiple Constructions of Self

A graduate course taught at a large research university in the southern United States, Autobiography: Construct(s) of the Self examines modern and postmodern constructions of the self. Though it is offered by the English department, students with interests in communication studies, theater, creative writing, literature, and rhetoric and composition enroll. The primary goal is engagement in a deep study of the ways researchers in various disciplines use life histories. In addition, given recent epistemological shifts in relation to subjectivity and identity, the course examines how self-construction across genres—novels, memoirs, or ethnographies—is a performance: a self-conscious act calling conventions of writing and representation into question.

Postmodernism's focus on issues of identity, subjectivity, plurality, multiplicity, and relativism has famously called the unified, inherent self into question. The postmodern self is often a performance of social expectations and codes, and notions of constructed, shifting, and multidimensional selves are being explored across disciplines. Hierarchies have been flattened, and often, to some consternation, life experience has been elevated to the level of research. Life histories, life writing, and personal stories have become primary and supplemental research.

I ask students to study life writing as a way to deepen their understanding of the constructions and performance of self, which then in turn inform constructions of culture, gender, sexuality, class, ethnicity, and race. First, students read theories of autobiography, addressing issues of subjectivity, identity, and memory. Theories of performance and performativity are then introduced. Students read several primary autobiographical texts, focusing on constructions of self, and then together the students perform aspects of these texts, putting notions of performativity into action. Beginning with autobiographical texts in the literary tradition, the class moves on to works in anthropology, oral history, and rhetoric and composition to explore the uses of life history across disciplines. Students' final projects include individual research projects and autobiographical performances.

To learn about life writing theory, we examine issues of power and subjectivity (Foucault); we then discuss how postmodern concepts of power have influenced theories of identity, the body, and performance (Smith; Gilmore). We read theories about memory and narrative (Olney) and about material aspects of the body. We also discuss the power dynamics involved in the production of knowledge (Althusser), focusing on how our self-conceptions are influenced by the ways we see ourselves within certain systems of power and within social expectations and conventions, leading us to perform the self in a manner always already determined. As the gender theorist Judith Butler observes, we take on certain gestures as they suit us—as they "work" for us and our sense of who we think we are.

Performance and performativity are the next major topics (Pollock; Butler). To the students, "performance" typically suggests the performing arts (viewed as spectacle). I show how this notion has become an important critical and theoretical term in such disciplines as theater, anthropology, communication studies, literary studies, rhetoric, feminist and queer theory, and postcolonial studies. Reflecting intercultural interests and the postmodern sense of shifting selves, performance studies has emerged as a field in its own right that crosses disciplinary boundaries and resists stable definitions. Coined by J. L. Austin, "performative" refers to those aspects of a text that are overtly self-conscious about interaction with the audience or reader, who then cocontributes to meaning. Performative texts thus assume interaction with an audience, as the texts' construction reveals.

Scholars and artists of performativity examine the intertextual dimensions of texts. Performative autobiography therefore critiques its own form while displaying it to readers who use it to construct a life. Performance studies scholars tend to emphasize the transgressive nature of their subject: how a performance subverts traditional and accepted norms. As Butler has suggested, however, whether written or oral, a performance cannot be recognized as transgressive until its normative features are visible, distinctive, and analyzable. Form is recognized as both enabling and limiting. When contexts are broken down—when a man dresses as a woman, for instance—then conventions, such as those signaling femininity, are parodied and revealed as in fact conventions.

The same can be said for writing. Performative writing includes "the interplay of reader and writer in the joint production of meaning. . . . [It] uses language like paint to create what is self-evidently a *version* of what was, what is, and/or what might be" (Pollock 80). Writers learn to "perform" the particular generic conventions of a discourse, imitating the conventions they find useful and pushing the boundaries of those they find limiting. When writers perform a genre such as autobiography, they imitate the discursive characteristics of that genre while simultaneously recognizing its inability to represent their lives fully. By not simply following accepted or normative cultural codes for autobiography, performative autobiography critiques hegemonic discourse through its self-conscious treatment of the genre.

Since the concept of performativity tends to be new to English studies students, I ask a colleague in communication studies who specializes in performance theory to explain how performance and texts are examined in this discipline. I ask a performance studies graduate student to perform an autobiographical text, providing students with an example for their own performance assignment. (Students also learn about related courses offered in communication studies: Performative Writing and Autobiographical Performance.)

The primary written texts have included works by Virginia Woolf, Jeanette Winterson, Shirley Geok-lin Lim, and Zora Neale Hurston. To explore contradictions and similarities in constructs of self from the same author, we read fiction together with autobiography, critical academic essays with memoir, and ethnography with autobiographical accounts of research. And to discover the subtle distinctions between modern and postmodern concepts of self, we read Woolf first, showing, for example, how the high modernist prose of *The Waves* illustrates theories of memory and narrative explicitly explored in "A Sketch of the Past." Winterson's memoir uses fairy tales throughout the "true" account of her childhood to highlight the limitations of autobiography, while in *Art Objects*, Winterson draws on her reading and writing experiences to insist on the materiality of texts and on her belief that authors' lives are in fact irrelevant to their fiction. And in *Among the White Moon Faces*, Lim examines her conflicted and displaced self as she studies English literature, moves to and teaches in the United States, and becomes a scholar of Asian American literature. Other pairings could include Joyce Johnson's letters to Jack Kerouac together with her memoir, *Minor Characters*; Audre Lorde's biomythography *Zami* together with *The Cancer Journals*; Reinaldo Arenas's *Before Night Falls* together with *Hallucinations; or, The Ill-fated Peregrinations of Fray Servando*; and Tim O'Brien's *The Things They Carried* together with *In the Lake of the Woods*. In each text, students read closely for instances where generic and self-construction conventions are broken.

Reading life writing as performance asks students to look beyond the textual representation to ask further questions about truth, narrative, and representation in general. To understand how self, performance, text, and disciplinarity intersect, we read across genres, exploring authors' discussions of multiple identities and constructs of the self, paying particular attention to the way form drives notions of the self. Recurring questions include these: What does it mean to write the self? What does it mean to perform the self? How is a self performative? How is a text performative? What is the role of autobiography in literature? What is the role of autobiography in critical research? Is examining and writing about personal experience valid in the same way that critical or scholarly research is? What general or specific questions do various disciplines ask in relation to life writing, performance, and the self?

Once the class has discussed all the authors and their texts in the light of autobiography and performance scholarship, students perform some aspects of the authors' works. In groups of three or four, they write scripts and perform for the class important issues in the texts. The purpose of this assignment is twofold: to show how performances deepen our understanding of the texts themselves and to give students an opportunity to perform someone else's text before performing their own later in the semester.

Class sessions then shift to examining ways that life writing is used across disciplines, as primary and as supplemental research. (Pairing Hurston's anthropological texts *Mules and Men* and *Tell My Horse* with

Their Eyes Were Watching God or *Dust Tracks on a Road* can work well as a transition to this unit.) Those working in such fields as English studies, cultural studies, rhetoric and composition, and anthropology often read personal accounts and use them as scholars and teachers, and in this course, we read texts that are explicitly about such practices. In *The Vulnerable Observer*, for instance, the anthropologist Ruth Behar examines her role as researcher—how she affects the participants in her studies and vice versa. The rhetoric and composition specialists Gesa Kirsch and Joy Ritchie discuss the ethics of collecting information from research participants, urging researchers to reflect critically on their research practices by including personal accounts of their research processes—including breakdowns. The folklorist Carolyn Ware visited the class at this point to discuss her research methodology and the ethics of representing herself and her participants in her written documentation. I also introduce Eve Kosofsky Sedgwick's notion of experimental critical writing and discuss whether the academy accepts such writing and, if it does, who the writers are. We read scholarship by oral historians that addresses similar questions of representation, transcription, and narrative in their field, and we discuss graduate research projects and the degree to which newcomers can resist generic boundaries within life writing or academic discourse (Bridwell-Bowles).

Students then conduct their own research, using life writing to inform their interpretations of other texts by the same author. I encourage them to extend their existing research by including aspects of life writing theory or to imagine how their thesis or dissertation projects could incorporate theories of subjectivity, identity, and performance. (I also ask students to write with specific academic publications in mind.) Examples of the research projects (20 to 25 pages long) that students have produced in this course include the following:

Examination of the religious altars of Mexican women
Identity construction of women prostitutes in nineteenth-century frontier narratives
Identity and trauma in the slave/captivity narrative of Mary Prince
Comparative analysis of self-construction in English and Spanish versions of Helena Valero's captivity narrative
Autopsychoanalysis in Eve Kosofsky Sedgwick's *Dialogue on Love*
Art Spiegelman's *Maus* as performative text examining the Holocaust
The function of Charlayne Woodard's plays as oral history

In addition to these research projects, students write their own autobiographical pieces. This creative piece can take any form: poetry, essay, short story, novel chapter, song lyrics, painting, digital storytelling. In fact, I ask students to experiment with form and content. Depending on their approach, I also ask them to merge scholarly with personal life by making generic features visible, inviting interpretation from the audience, or reiterating notions of performativity discussed throughout the course. This assignment is based on my own workshop experience with Dorothy Allison, who suggests that it is not the fact of a life that makes a story but the way it is crafted and performed. In this way, the control over the event—in some cases trauma—lies with the writer. To accompany the creative piece, students must also write an "academic rationale," in which they theorize the choices made in their creative performances, including their thinking about form and content and how certain words and gestures reflect or resist the theories learned in the course.

Students have performed their creative autobiographical pieces in a local tavern in the presence of invited students and faculty members. Others have performed at poetry slams. Some resist the assignment (which I encourage them to do, in a critically reflective way) and the notion of speaking in front of an audience, consequently constructing pieces that include no live performance. One student created an installation piece that mimicked the religious altars she had been studying for her research project. Another sang a folk song in his native tongue, Korean. Another student prerecorded her voice in multiple layers, so that while the chaos of voiced layers played for the audience, she acted out several scenes from her life story. Regardless of the eventual form, however, all the students described in their academic rationale the purposeful choices made in constructing their ten-minute performances.

This is an intensely theoretical course, with a rigorous reading and writing schedule. From the students' innovative research projects and stunning performances, however, it is clear that they gain an enhanced understanding of the multiple and complex ways that life writing is constructed and studied across fields of inquiry.

Note

James Olney visited the class to discuss the history of autobiography studies and the development in the field he has witnessed as an autobiography scholar and teacher. The author wishes to thank Olney (and the other guest lecturers) for generously giving time to this class and contributing to its design.

Appendix

Sample Assignment: Presentation and Literary Performance

In groups you will develop and present a performance piece on one of the four authors we're discussing in depth. For the presentation, distribute a one- to two-page handout to the class, summarizing a critical research article that discusses issues of life writing in relation to the author. Provide four or five discussion questions from the article that help us discuss the author's text based on the article's perspective. While your group prepares the article for discussion, think of ways to "perform" the author's work or ideas. Your group will perform for the rest of the class your interpretation(s) of the text(s). Consider issues of form, performative and generic features, transgression, and so on as you design your script. In other words, take full creative license with this assignment while considering issues of performativity. Consider how you might "play" with form, making visible (and calling into question) the textual features of the text(s) and your (and the audience's) interaction with that text. Your performance should be fifteen minutes long, and you must turn in a written script. You must also turn in an academic rationale, which describes the various decisions you made as researchers and performers.

Works Cited

Althusser, Louis. "Ideology and Ideological State Apparatuses (Notes towards an Investigation)." *"Lenin and Philosophy" and Other Essays.* Trans. Ben Brewster. London: NLB, 1971. 121–73.

Arenas, Reinaldo. *Before Night Falls.* Trans. Dolores M. Koch. New York: Viking, 1993.

——. *Hallucinations; or, The Ill-Fated Peregrinations of Fray Servando.* Trans. Andrew Hurley. New York: Penguin, 1994.

Austin, J. L. *How to Do Things with Words.* Cambridge: Harvard UP, 1962.

Behar, Ruth. *The Vulnerable Observer: Anthropology That Breaks Your Heart.* Boston: Beacon, 1990.

Bridwell-Bowles, Lillian. "Discourse and Diversity: Experimental Writing within the Academy." *College Composition and Communication* 43 (1992): 349–68.

Butler, Judith. *Gender Trouble: Feminism and the Subversion of Identity.* New York: Routledge, 1990.

Foucault, Michel. *Michel Foucault: Beyond Structuralism and Hermeneutics.* Ed. Hubert L. Dreyfus and Raul Rabinow. Chicago: U of Chicago P, 1983.

Gilmore, Leigh. "The Mark of Autobiography: Postmodernism, Autobiography, and Genre." *Autobiography and Postmodernism.* Ed. Kathleen Ashley, Gilmore, and Gerald Peters. Amherst: U of Massachusetts P, 1994. 3–18.

——. "Technologies of Autobiography." *Autobiographics: A Feminist Theory of Women's Self-Representation.* Ithaca: Cornell UP, 1994. 65–105.

Hurston, Zora Neale. *Dust Tracks on a Road.* 1942. New York: Harper-Perennial, 1996.

——. *Mules and Men.* 1935. New York: Harper-Perennial, 1990.

——. *Tell My Horse: Voodoo and Life in Haiti and Jamaica*. 1938. New York: Harper-Perennial, 1990.

——. *Their Eyes Were Watching God*. 1937. New York: Harper-Perennial, 1998.

Johnson, Joyce. *Door Wide Open: A Beat Love Affair in Letters, 1957–1958*. New York: Viking, 2000.

——. *Minor Characters*. Boston: Houghton, 1983.

Kirsch, Gesa, and Joy Ritchie. "Beyond the Personal: Theorizing a Politics of Location in Composition Research." *College Composition and Communication* 46 (1995): 7–29.

Lim, Shirley Geok-lin. *Among the White Moon Faces: An Asian-American Memoir of Homelands*. New York: Feminist, 1996.

——. "Complications of Feminist and Ethnic Literary Theories in Asian American Literature." *Challenging Boundaries: Gender and Periodization*. Ed. Joyce W. Warren and Margaret Dickie. Athens: U of Georgia P, 2000. 107–33.

——. "English-Language Creative Writing in Hong Kong: Colonial Stereotype and Process." *Pedagogy* 1.1 (2001): 178–84.

——. "Writing out of Turn." *Profession 1999*. New York: MLA, 1999. 214–24.

Lorde, Audre. *The Cancer Journals*. San Francisco: Spinsters/Aunt Lute, 1987.

——. *Zami: A New Spelling of My Name*. Trumansburg: Crossing, 1983.

O'Brien, Tim. *In the Lake of the Woods*. Boston: Houghton, 1994.

——. *The Things They Carried*. Boston: Houghton, 1990.

Olney, James. *Memory and Narrative: The Weave of Life Writing*. Chicago: U of Chicago P, 1998.

Pollock, Della. "Performative Writing." *The Ends of Performance*. Ed. Peggy Phelan and Jill Lane. New York: New York UP, 1998. 73–103.

Sedgwick, Eve Kosofsky. "Teaching 'Experimental Critical Writing.'" 15 Aug. 1997. 8 Oct. 2004 <http://www.duke.edu/~sedgwic/prof/experim.htm>.

Smith, Sidonie. "Identity's Body." *Autobiography and Postmodernism*. Ed. Kathleen Ashley, Leigh Gilmore, and Gerald Peters. Amherst: U of Massachusetts P, 1994. 266–92.

Winterson, Jeanette. *Art Objects: Essays on Ecstasy and Effrontery*. New York: Vintage, 1995.

——. *Oranges Are Not the Only Fruit*. New York: Grove, 1985.

Woodard, Charlayne. *Pretty Fire*. New York: Plume, 1995.

Woolf, Virginia. "A Sketch of the Past." *Moments of Being*. Ed. and introd. Jeanne Schulkind. 1976. London: Harcourt, 1985. 64–159.

——. *The Waves*. 1931. London: Harcourt, 1959.

Kenneth Womack

"In My Life":
Growing Up with the Beatles
from Liverpool to Abbey Road

In an undergraduate English course entitled The Literature of the Beatles, my students and I traced various narrative-driven aspects of the Beatles' musical canon in terms of their autobiographical and cultural components. Our analysis of the Beatles' lyrics and music underscored the significant classroom potential of life writing theory and criticism as a means for interpreting nonliterary texts such as sound recordings. In many ways, the band's musical forays, from *Please Please Me* (1962) through *Abbey Road* (1969), represent the very act of life writing itself: by authoring the text of their lives through their music in the 1960s, the Beatles engaged in a self-conscious effort to tell their stories about the difficulties that come with growing up and growing older.

The Literature of the Beatles was designed as a fifteen-week, three-credit course at the upper-division undergraduate level. The class's fairly traditional student cohort included English, communications, and human development and family studies majors. Our course objectives originated from two overarching questions that characterize many scholarly and sociocultural discussions about the Beatles. The first issue involves the band's progression in a mere seven years from such adolescent-oriented love songs as "Love Me Do," "From Me to You," and "I Saw Her Standing

There" through more verbally evolved tracks such as "Norwegian Wood (This Bird Has Flown)," "A Day in the Life," and the unabashed nostalgia of *Abbey Road*'s symphonic suite that marks the zenith of their career. How do the Beatles make such an astounding lyrical and musical leap in the space of only a few years? Further, how do we account for the interpersonal factors that led to what many fans and critics alike consider to be the band's untimely breakup in August 1969?

My class attempted to answer these questions by working from the premise that the Beatles, as a created family of sorts, served as one another's fictive kin for at least a decade from the late 1950s through 1969.[1] The increasingly personal and narrative-oriented nature of their lyrical and musical textures provides us, as "readers" of the Beatles, with an intellectual foundation for understanding the group—particularly their primary songwriters, John Lennon and Paul McCartney—as life writers in the act of generating autobiographical narratives. For this reason, my class discussed a selection of readings from James Olney's *Metaphors of Self: The Meaning of Autobiography* and *Memory and Narrative: The Weave of Life-Writing*. In his valuable work on autobiography and life writing, Olney contends that understanding the human impulse for self-narrative affords us with a means for comprehending the nature of other selves, as well as our own.

In *Metaphors of Self*, Olney identifies three distinct stages of "auto-emergence"—the human inclination for recording experience through life writing exercises—including metaphor, memory, and narration, which he describes as the autobiographer's "narrative imperative" (*Memory* 1). According to Olney, the metamorphosing process allows us to comprehend the unknown by organizing, incorporating, and ultimately exploring what constitutes the known in our personal universes. Olney's second stage of auto-emergence involves the relation between personal memory and the inner worlds in which we live. Autobiographical memory concerns the ways in which life writers reflect on their memories to examine the emotional significance of the past in context with the ongoing evolution of the self. Olney's final stage of auto-emergence involves the act of narration—or the narrative imperative, which denotes the human autobiographical desire. Olney defines autobiographical weaving as a procedure in which the autobiographer constructs a self-conscious tapestry that reflects the text of his or her life by weaving back and forth among a selection of metaphors and memories; in so doing, the life writer attempts to establish a more expansive vision of the self in relation to the world of countless other selves trying to make sense of life's fragmented journey.

Olney's three stages of auto-emergence provided us with a powerful tool for creating an autobiographical map of the Beatles that accounts for their remarkable creative development as recording artists cum life writers between 1963 and 1969, a frenetic period in which they produced a dozen groundbreaking albums and recorded more than two hundred original songs. Reading the Beatles' musical evolution in terms of Olney's three stages of auto-emergence afforded us with a mechanism for understanding the band's collective progress toward selfhood. Not surprisingly, our study of the Beatles' early work found them directing rudimentary, first- and second-person gestures at their listening audience, while an analysis of their later albums underscored the band's more expansive comprehension of their various selves in terms of the universality of human experience. In contrast with their early albums, the Beatles' later efforts revealed them to be fully engaged as storytellers in the act of meaning making, the metatextual result of their auto-emergent travels. Our discussions were also guided by readings from William J. Dowlding's *Beatlesongs*, a detailed, album-by-album study of the band's output, and *The Beatles Anthology*, the group's prodigious compendium of memories about their time together.

In addition to midterm and final examinations, the course requirements were largely concerned with our creation of an autobiographical map of the Beatles. In their full-length research paper assignment, the students addressed this issue by contextualizing their analyses of the Beatles' work in terms of particular aspects of life writing theory. Their goal, of course, was to elucidate the manner in which the band members' autobiographical emergence sheds valuable light on our understanding of their development as storytellers, as well as individuated selves in their own right. Likewise, our classroom discussions principally involved the semester-long establishment of an autobiographical map that detailed the group members' early lives through their activities as recording artists during the 1960s and beyond. Olney's terminology afforded us a revelatory means of understanding both the Beatles' evolution as storytellers and its significant interrelation with a variety of self-making moments in their personal and collective histories. For the most part, we accomplished this end by conducting a chronological investigation of the Beatles' sound recordings.

We based our examination of the Beatles' first four albums—*Please Please Me* (1963), *With the Beatles* (1963), *A Hard Day's Night* (1964), and *Beatles for Sale* (1964)—on the concept of metaphor, Olney's first stage of auto-emergence. By concocting one-dimensional metaphors for narrating youthful experience, the Beatles engaged in a series of language games—verbal experiments, if nothing else—that suggest little, if any, genuine meaning. Olney's metaphorical self attempts to give shape and to construct a forum for self-expression. The metaphorical self exists, moreover, from moment to moment and announces, with sheer exuberance and a touch of narcissism, "This is my universe." It mediates between, in Olney's words, "ourselves formed and ourselves becoming" (*Metaphors* 34, 35). Early songs like "I Want to Hold Your Hand" and "She Loves You," for example, reveal the embryonic Beatles at their most lyrically guileless. Each song features a wide-eyed speaker fearlessly knocking on love's door. Without a hint of irony, Lennon and McCartney sing about a genial world in which "you'll let me hold your hand"—a place where love won't make you sad, "and you know that can't be bad." For the metaphorical self, aglow with postadolescent possibility and unflinching sincerity, love is indeed the answer—the only answer.

The Beatles' next trio of albums—*Help!* (1965), *Rubber Soul* (1965), and *Revolver* (1966)—depict the band in the act of realizing a state of interpersonal crisis before reflecting on the past in an extended musical journey across the staves of time and memory during their psychedelic years. With "In My Life," for example, Lennon deftly examines the power and inevitable failure of memory, the subject of Olney's second stage of auto-emergence. While some places and people remain vivid, others recede and disappear altogether. "Memories lose their meaning," Lennon's speaker sings, although he knows that he'll "often stop and think about them," referring, yet again, to the past's fecundating layers of character and setting. Fittingly, the song's instrumental interlude features a wistful baroque harpsichord solo by the band's brilliant producer, George Martin—the real fifth Beatle, if ever there were one. With "In My Life," Lennon recognizes his inherent narrative instinct: "That was the first time I consciously put [the] literary part of myself into the lyric," he later remembered (qtd. in Dowlding 124). For *Rubber Soul*'s "Norwegian Wood," George Harrison's sitar lines accent the flourishes of Lennon's haunting acoustic guitar. They also provide a curious palette for Lennon's confessional tale about an extramarital affair. Lennon's lyrics—far from underscoring love's everlasting possibilities—hint at something more fleeting, even unromantic: "She asked me to stay and she told me to sit anywhere / So I looked around and I noticed there wasn't a chair." Compare the words of "Norwegian Wood" with such earlier phraseology as "I ain't got nothing but love, babe / Eight days a week" (*Beatles for Sale*), and the Beatles' intellectual development becomes resoundingly clear.

The Beatles' studio years are characterized by an increasing interest in storytelling and rudimentary ethical philosophy, a narrative posture that diverts rather purposefully from the idealism of their earlier forays into the mystical land of memory. Their pursuit of a narrative imperative, Olney's third stage of auto-emergence, finds its roots in their post-touring lives, a radically different environment in which they self-consciously removed themselves from the entertainment world's high-profile treadmill in an explicit attempt to concentrate on their art. With such albums as *Sgt. Pepper's Lonely Hearts Club Band* (1967), *The Beatles* ("The White Album"; 1968), *Let It Be* (recorded in 1969; released in 1970), and *Abbey Road* (1969), the Beatles often concern themselves with the fleeting nature of human interconnection and existence, as well as with the comfort that nostalgia affords us when it acts as a balm for the aching soul. "Let It Be" and "The Long and Winding Road," for instance, devote particular attention to nostalgia's death-defying limbo, a place in which disillusionment and anguish commingle ad infinitum. While "Let It Be" counsels us to meditate on "words of wisdom" during our hours of darkness and to embrace the gentle consolation of peace, "The Long and Winding Road," in many ways, knows better. For the speaker, nostalgia's circuitous road "will never disappear." And while it always leads us back to the memories of lost friends and loved ones, the long and winding road never quite gets us there. For the song's speaker, the panacea inherent in "Let It Be" merely produces "a pool of tears" in the harsher reality lost amid the restless and unconvincing hopefulness of "The Long and Winding Road."

Life writing, Olney tells us in *Memory and Narrative*, is rarely a tidy and altogether coherent process. "What does this reverie of the artist produce but broken dreams on the one hand, a coherent body of work—sequential,

integral, and summative—on the other?" Olney asks (404). The Beatles' career as life writers is no different. Although their passage through Olney's
phases of auto-emergence may seem vaguely uneven and indeterminate at
times, from their earliest moments as recording artists through their magis-
terial efforts during their waning days together at Abbey Road studios, the
Beatles fashioned an enduring legacy based on our innately human needs
for hopefulness and reconciliation. As McCartney remarks in the final reel
of the *Beatles Anthology* documentary, "I'm really glad that most of [our]
songs dealt with love, peace, understanding. There's hardly any one of them
that says: 'Go on, kids, tell them all to sod off. Leave your parents.' It's all
very 'All You Need Is Love' or John's 'Give Peace a Chance.' There was a
good spirit behind it all, which I'm very proud of."

   As the course came to a close, my students and I concluded that the
dissolution of the Beatles, although disconcerting for legions of music
lovers, makes perfect sense when understood in an adult-developmental
context. Indeed, how many people complete the developmental tasks commonly associated with adulthood—including marriage, child rearing, and
the assumption of more expansive leadership positions in work and family
life—in the company of their childhood mates?[2] In this sense, isn't the
breakup of the Beatles more usefully understood as the result of four men
going in decidedly different directions as they approach midlife and all that
growing older entails? While the Beatles may have gone their separate ways
in the late summer of 1969, their music, as the product of an increasingly
mature sense of selfhood, leaves us with an abiding legacy of peace, wisdom, and hope. "No autobiography is completed, only ended," Jerome S.
Bruner reminds us in *Making Stories* (74). For tomorrow's generation of
listeners, the Beatles are only just getting started.

Appendix

Course Readings

Week 1: Course introduction; Beatles biographical and sociocultural introduction
Week 2: Readings from Olney's *Metaphors of Self* and *Memory and Narrative*
Week 3: *Please Please Me* (1963): "From Me to You"[3]
Week 4: *With the Beatles* (1963): "She Loves You"; "I Want to Hold Your Hand"
Week 5: *A Hard Day's Night* (1964): "I Feel Fine"
Week 6: *Beatles for Sale* (1964)
Week 7: *Help!* (1965): "We Can Work It Out"; "Day Tripper"
Week 8: *Rubber Soul* (1965): "Paperback Writer"; "Rain"

Week 9: *Revolver* (1966): "Penny Lane"; "Strawberry Fields Forever"
Week 10: *Sgt. Pepper's Lonely Hearts Club Band* (1967)
Week 11: *Magical Mystery Tour* (1967): "Lady Madonna"
Weeks 12 and 13: *The Beatles* ("The White Album"; 1968), part 1: "Hey Jude";
    part 2: "Revolution"
Week 14: *Let It Be* (recorded in 1969; released in 1970): "Don't Let Me Down"
Week 15: *Abbey Road* (1969): "The Ballad of John and Yoko"

Notes

1. In addition to denoting an absence of blood ties, the concept of fictive kin refers, in the parlance of marriage and family studies, to a group of nonrelatives who accept one another as de facto family members. As Nijole V. Benokraitis observes, such families "may be as strong or stronger and more lasting than the ties established by blood or marriage." These units "emphasize affection and mutual cooperation among people who are"—for all intents and purposes—"living together" (4). From their earliest, postboyhood days in Liverpool and their traumatic initiation into adulthood in the sex clubs and saloons of Hamburg to the simultaneously exhilarating and nerve-wracking nature of international superstardom, the Beatles shared a series of experiences that clearly challenged (yet also validated) their individual and collective senses of self at nearly every turn.

2. In an interview with *Rolling Stone* magazine's John Harris, Ringo Starr offers additional commentary on the Beatles' dissolution and its relation to life choices: "I think the reason the Beatles split up was because we were thirty, and it was, 'Hey, I got married, I've got kids, I've got a few more friends.' We didn't have the energy to put into it" (44). When asked about her own ostensible role in the band's demise, Yoko Ono suggests that they were responding to internal forces—perhaps even involving individual needs and desires related to growing up—rather than to external pressures: "I don't think you could have broken up four very strong people like them, even if you tried. So there must have been something that happened within them—not an outside force at all" (Lennon and Ono 144).

3. The Beatles recorded a number of songs for the express purpose of generating single (or 45 RPM) releases that were not included on their albums. Hence, these songs are listed separately among the course readings.

Works Cited

The Beatles. *The Beatles Anthology*. Television documentary. ABC, 1995.
——. *The Beatles Lyrics: The Songs of Lennon, McCartney, Harrison, and Starr*. Milwaukee: Leonard, 1993.
Benokraitis, Nijole V. *Marriages and Families: Changes, Choices, and Constraints*. 4th ed. Upper Saddle River: Prentice, 2001.
Bruner, Jerome S. *Making Stories: Law, Literature, Life*. New York: Farrar, 2002.
Dowlding, William J. *Beatlesongs*. New York: Simon, 1989.

Harris, John. "Ringo Solo." *Rolling Stone* 17 Apr. 2003: 43–44.

Lennon, John, and Yoko Ono. *All We Are Saying: The Last Major Interview with John Lennon and Yoko Ono*. Interview by David Sheff. New York: Griffin, 2000.

Olney, James. *Memory and Narrative: The Weave of Life-Writing*. Chicago: U of Chicago P, 1998.

———. *Metaphors of Self: The Meaning of Autobiography*. Princeton: Princeton UP, 1972.

Thomas J. D. Armbrecht

The Whole Picture:
Using Nonliterary Forms of Artistic
Production to Teach Life Writing

In *Brouillons de soi*, Philippe Lejeune states, "Un autobiographe, ce n'est pas quelqu'un qui dit la vérité sur lui-même, mais quelqu'un qui dit qu'il la dit" (125; "An autobiographer isn't someone who tells the truth about himself but rather someone who says that he does").[1] It is often difficult to get students to understand that an autobiographer is, in effect, the author of his own life. When reading autobiographical works, many people forget to distinguish between the life of the narrator and that of the author and view such texts as historical truth since they are from "the horse's mouth." Accordingly, my primary pedagogical task is to encourage students to approach autobiography as literature, instead of reading it for the biographical "truths" it contains about the author. Students must learn to apply to autobiography the same tools of literary analysis that they use for self-avowedly fictional works, such as looking at narrative structure and the use of tropes.

One effective way to reveal the textual elements of an autobiographical narrative is to read it in conjunction with an author's nonliterary works—photographs, paintings, even residences—which can serve as a sort of *mise en relief* for the literary work. Using nonliterary forms of artistic production to analyze life writing is an interdisciplinary approach that can encourage students at all levels to apply their developing critical skills to various types of

151

narratives. I first employed this strategy in a junior- and senior-level French literature class of about fifteen students who felt comfortable reading novels and excerpts of critical articles in French and who had some experience analyzing literature.

The nineteenth-century French writer Pierre Loti is an excellent example of an author of autobiographical volumes whose value as autofiction becomes more evident when read alongside the "texts" provided by his house and photographs. A painter, photographer, designer-cum-architect, and protoperformance artist whose work is well documented and available in all these genres, Loti is a particularly appropriate subject for multimedia comparisons.[2] Born in Rochefort, France, in 1851 as Julien Viaud, Loti (a pseudonym) wrote in a variety of literary genres. He was best known for his novels, which are often accounts of his travels as a French naval officer. Among his best-known works is *Aziyadé*, the story of Pierre Loti's—the character's—romantic involvement with Aziyadé, a married Turkish woman. First published anonymously in 1879, the novel was soon reissued by an author named, like the protagonist, Pierre Loti. This confused readers, who were unsure whether to view the book as truth or as fiction, as autobiography or as novel (Vercier, "Loti" 10). In *Nouveaux essais critiques*, Roland Barthes points out that the confusion is inherent in the relation of the author with this work:

> [Viaud] s'est donné, à lui, auteur, le nom de son héros. De la sorte, pris dans un réseau à trois termes, le signataire du livre est faux deux fois: le Pierre Loti qui garantit *Aziyadé* n'est nullement le Loti qui en est le héros; et ce garant (*auctor, auteur*) est lui-même truqué, l'auteur ce n'est pas Loti, c'est Viaud; tout se joue entre un homonyme et un pseudonyme; ce qui manque, ce qui est tu, ce qui est béant, c'est le nom propre, le propre du nom (le nom qui spécifie et le nom qui appropie). Où est le scripteur? (1402)

> [Viaud] has given to himself, the author, the name of his hero. So that, caught up in a network of three terms, the man who signs the book is false twice over: the Pierre Loti who guarantees *Aziyadé* is not at all the Loti who is its hero; and this guarantor (*auctor, author*) is himself fabricated, the author is not Loti but Viaud: it is all played out between a homonym and a pseudonym; what is missing, what is passed over in silence, what is wide open, is the proper name, the propriety of the name (the name which specifies and the name which appropriates). Where is the scriptor? (*New Critical Essays* 107)

This game of literary smoke and mirrors proved to be just one of many for the writer commonly known as Loti (his literary identity having eventually supplanted the other). An example is his scripting of his identity as embodied in his house, now a museum in Rochefort. During the writing of *Aziyadé*, he constructed a "salon turc," filling a room with things he had brought back from Turkey to create what he called "un petit appartement mystérieux où [il] pourrai[t] [s']enfermer pour rêver de Stamboul" (*Journal* 243; "a small mysterious room in which [he] could shut himself up to dream of Istanbul"). As photographs attest, Loti would dress as a Turk to withdraw to this room—a practice first begun when attempting to pass as a native while visiting foreign countries. This private role-playing suggests that the Turkish salon was a space where Loti could live out an alternate identity: that of the foreign Casanova he had created in *Aziyadé*.

Gaston Bachelard's critical text *La poétique de l'espace* can help students understand the relation between space and identity. Calling the house "le non-moi qui protège le moi" (24; "the non-I that protects the I" [8]), Bachelard argues that all parts of a dwelling, including its layout and contents, express the human psyche. Phenomenological in approach and fairly jargon free, his text works well in an undergraduate classroom. Reading Bachelard's first chapter, "La Maison, de la cave au grenier" ("The House, from Cellar to Garret: The Significance of the Hut"), helps students recognize that Loti shared with Bachelard a belief that "la maison est un corps d'images qui donnent à l'homme des raisons ou des illusions de stabilité" (34; "a house constitutes a body of images that give mankind proofs or illusions of stability" [17]). What better method for Loti to stabilize his own self-authored identity than by building a space in which to live it?

The *salon turc* was the first of many foreign-culture rooms constructed in Loti's house. By the time of his death, he had not only renovated the entire building but also bought the houses on either side, added them to the original dwelling, and filled them with architectural pastiches of other cultures and time periods. An Arab bedroom, a mosque, a Renaissance room, and a Gothic chamber can be viewed as part of the museum or in books by Thierry Liot, Pierre de Boisdeffre, and Gérard Teillay and Anne Crichton. A Chinese-style room and a Japanese pagoda survive only in pictures. Each room corresponds to a moment in Loti's literary oeuvre and therefore to a facet of his literary personae. He built the Arab bedroom soon after he returned from Morocco, while working on *Au Maroc* in 1884. He wrote *Madame Chrysanthème* while designing the pagoda (Liot 122–23). These rooms were not simply museums for Loti but stages for his *tableaux vivants*, which took the form of elaborate theme parties for which he and his friends disguised themselves and imitated rituals from the corresponding cultures. Photographs of these galas reveal Loti's theatrical nature and something about his creative process. As Liot remarks in *La maison Pierre Loti à Rochefort*, "Faite d'un 'mélange de luxe et de barbarie' . . . la maison de Rochefort est à l'image de son créateur, un homme introverti mais exhibitionniste, extravagant et mystérieux, recherchant les effets produits et les apparences" (13; "Built with a 'mix of luxury and barbarity' . . . the house in Rochefort is in the image of its creator, who was an introvert, extravagant and mysterious, an exhibitionist seeking to produce effects and appearances").

Loti's numerous photographs of himself reinforce the idea that he was a character in a constantly rewritten life story. The images appear together in *Pierre Loti portraits: Les fantaisies changeantes*, a remarkable book compiled and edited by Bruno Vercier. The photographs clearly indicate that Loti's idée fixe was to reinvent himself continually. We see the writer dressed in his party costumes, but also as a naval officer, a member of the Académie Française, an Egyptian pharaoh, an acrobat, and perhaps most shockingly, a corpse. Far from simply cataloging Loti's guises, however, the photographs provide what Vercier calls "l'image que Loti . . . donn[ait] de lui-même . . . moins un témoignage pour la postérité que la trace d'une interrogation incessante" (5; "the image that Loti . . . created for himself . . . is not so much a testimony for posterity's sake as the trace of an unceasing self-interrogation").

So many correspondences emerge among Loti's house, his photographic self-portraits, and events recounted in his literary works that it is useful simply to draw on his nonliterary works to illustrate his writings. Lower-level language learners can find visual clues to enhance their understanding of Loti's fairly complex literary works. (An excellent text for this purpose is Teillay and Crichton, which presents excerpts from the writings next to photographs of the related rooms.) Considering Loti's nonliterary artistic works as mere visual aids, however, ignores their significance as narratives in themselves and misses what they can bring to Loti's written corpus. To help students connect Loti's visual and textual self-representations, Hervé Guibert's *Image fantôme* supplies a useful nontheoretical exploration of the relation between photographs and the identities of photographic subject and photographer. In short, easily excerpted chapters, Guibert "reads" both photographs of himself and ones that he has taken—not for their content so much as for what they say about his (or the photographer's) powers of creation and interpretation. Guibert calls his text "une tentative de biographie par la photographie: chaque histoire individuelle se double de son histoire photographique, imagée, imaginée" (124; "an attempt at biography through photography: each individual story has a photographic, imaged, imagined double"), an idea that could also be applied to Loti's quasi biography, *Le roman d'un enfant*.

Unlike *Aziyadé*, which was not published as an autobiographical work, *Le roman d'un enfant* was assumed to be the story of Loti's childhood, even though "*roman*" suggests that it is fiction. Adding to the confusion, the protagonist is called Pierre Loti, a pseudonym for Julien Viaud. The ambiguous identity of the novel increased when it was republished in 1919 along with the first edition of *Prime jeunesse*, presented as *Le roman d'un enfant's* "*suite*" ("follow-up")—though in the second volume the name of the protagonist is Julien Viaud, while the author remains Pierre Loti.

Ideas for unraveling this sort of literary quid pro quo and for understanding its relation to Loti's other works can be found in Barthes's discussions of rhetorical tropes, featured in *Nouveaux essais critiques*, *Roland Barthes par Roland Barthes*, and other writings. An excellent example is what Barthes writes about the *anacoluthon*, "a grammatical interruption or lack of implied sequence within a sentence. That is, beginning a sentence in a way that implies a certain logical resolution, but concluding it differently than the grammar leads one to expect" (Burton). Barthes uses this term to point out places where Loti's text is interrupted. An example is a description from *Aziyadé* of an erotic dream involving the title character and Samuel, the manservant. In the midst of a description of Samuel's promise to procure some of Aziyadé's hair for his master, the narrator's dream is interrupted with the phrase, "Il plut par torrents cette nuit-là, et je fus trempé" (24; "It rained in torrents that night, and I was soaked"), which Barthes claims causes the dream to "perd[re] tout sens, même le sens du non-sens" (*Nouveaux essais* 1404; "los[e] all meaning, even the meaning of meaninglessness" [*New Critical Essays* 110]).

The best nonliterary example of a "lack of implied sequence" is perhaps the discontinuity between the exterior and interior of Loti's house (see figs. 1 and 2). Although Loti eventually combined three adjacent residences into one much larger building, he never modified the facades of either his childhood home or those he bought. From the street they still

Figure 1. La maison Pierre Loti. Photograph by Thierry Liot.

Figure 2. Le salon turc. Photograph by Thierry Liot.

seem to be three separate houses. The exterior of a house usually relays information about the size and character of the interior, but here the relation between the facade and the interior is like the relation between the two parts of an anacoluthon. An unexpected conclusion/interior interrupts the logical sequence implied by the introduction/exterior. According to Barthes, such discontinuities in Loti's writing rupture the individual meanings of both parts of the sentence. The effect in Loti's building is similar. The modest facades, which Loti himself said represented "la paix bourgeoise du vieux logis" (*Cette éternelle* 445; "the bourgeois peace of the old home") on what is now Rue Pierre Loti suggest that their occupants are just as modest. The panoply of foreign cultures within, however, suggests quite the opposite. What is the visitor to believe? Is Loti a reserved Protestant or an unrestrained hedonist? Neither: preserving the facade of his house creates a break with the asocial heterodoxy inside, thereby allowing the visitor to the house—like the reader encountering the anacoluthon—to see it as what Barthes calls "un discours presque immobile, qui pose des sens mais ne les résout pas" (*Nouveaux essais* 1405; "a practically immobile discourse, which asks for meanings, but does not resolve them" [*New Critical Essays* 111]).

Since this same lack of resolution characterizes Loti's literary depiction of his childhood and the actual event, looking for anacoluthons can also make students realize that there is no way to repair this Barthesian break. Although the facts of Loti's (or rather, of Viaud's) childhood are not entirely unrelated to those in his books, one cannot consider Loti's account of his life as more true than one of his stories. Loti even admits this, noting in *Le roman d'un enfant* that he was tempted to call the work "Journal de mes grandes tristesses inexpliquées, et des quelques gamineries d'occasion par lesquelles j'ai tenté de m'en distraire" (156; "Journal of my great, unexplained sadness, and a few casual childhood pranks with which I tried to distract myself"). Are the *gamineries* here distractions of his youth or those he experienced as an adult, while actually writing the novel? The only possible answer is both, which, while perhaps hard for students of literature to accept, is truly a literary (as opposed to a naively historical) reading of the novel.

I am not, of course, arguing against interpreting life writing texts for their historical or psychological significance. Loti's writings themselves provide many possibilities for studying representations of the exotic and of colonialism in literature and could even be used as examples of early queer writing. My approach is designed to enlarge the possibilities for students reading autobiography, to respond to difficulties that arise while teaching it, and to challenge students who respond increasingly well to nonliterary narratives.

There are many assignments that instructors can create to put this approach into practice. In classes with a creative component, students can write personal histories in which they embellish events from their lives (albeit in a realistic fashion) to create a character based on themselves. They can then share these with the class and discuss their methods and means of fictionalizing reality.

In a class whose focus is literary analysis, teachers can ask students to spot examples of anacoluthon, anapodoton, and other tropes in both the literary and nonliterary works of an author.[3] Examining a limited number of rhetorical devices will help students make connections between authors' writings and their nonliterary work.

In a similar vein, students can "read" authors' self-portraits, houses, and other nonliterary works before studying their life writing texts. Teachers can introduce students to a writer by asking them what they can infer about this author from his or her self-presentation. Students can then compare the written texts with the nonwritten ones and can revise their interpretations of the author's work accordingly. Colette invites this kind of introduction. Students can watch Jean Cocteau's and Paul Tschinkel's films of her, listen to her read her works, and examine well-known photographs of her. Instructors can then ask students to describe the author before comparing their depictions with Colette's descriptions of herself. Her inherent theatricality will undoubtedly stimulate a discussion about how she dramatizes herself visually as well as verbally.

Notes

1. All translations are my own, except for those from the published texts by Barthes and Bachelard.

2. Many other French authors—Balzac, Yourcenar, and Cocteau, to name a few—would also be good candidates. For examples of authors from other countries and literary traditions, see Lennard and Premoli-Droulers.

3. See Burton for a comprehensive listing of tropes. See Armbrecht for a detailed exploration of the relation between Loti's life writing and his house in Rochefort.

Works Cited

Armbrecht, Thomas. "The Nostalgia of Nowhere: Pierre Loti's Utopian Spaces." *Mosaic* 36.4 (2003): 81–102.

Bachelard, Gaston. *The Poetics of Space*. Trans. M. Jolas. 1969. Boston: Beacon, 1994.

——. *La poétique de l'espace*. Paris: PU de France, 1957.

Barthes, Roland. *New Critical Essays*. 1980. Trans. Richard Howard. Berkeley: U of California P, 1990.

——. *Nouveaux essais critiques*. 1972. *Œuvres complètes*. Vol. 2. Ed. Eric Marty. Paris: Seuil, 1995. 1333–416.

——. *Roland Barthes par Roland Barthes*. 1975. *Œuvres complètes*. Vol. 3. Ed. Eric Marty. Paris: Seuil, 1995. 7–252.

Boisdeffre, Pierre de. *Pierre Loti: Ses maisons*. St.-Cyr-sur-Loire: Pirot, 1996.

Burton, Gideon O. "Anacoluthon." *Silva Rhetoricae*. 8 Aug. 2006 <http://humanities.byu.edu/rhetoric/silva.htm>.

Cocteau, Jean, dir. *Colette of the Goncourt Academy and "Le Chevre de Monsieur Seguin: Lettre d'Alphonse Daudet."* 1951. New York: First Run/Icarus, 2003.

Colette. *Colette Reading* Gigi, a Section; Chéri, a Section; [and] "Flore et Pomone," a section from Gigi. Sound recording. Paris: Caedmon, 1954.

Guibert, Hervé. *Image fantôme*. Paris: Seuil, 1984.

Lejeune, Philippe. *Les Brouillons de soi*. Paris: Seuil, 1998.

Lennard, Erica, and Francesca Premoli-Droulers. *Maisons d'ecrivains*. Paris: Chêne, 1984.

Liot, Thierry. *La maison Pierre Loti à Rochefort: 1850–1923*. Poitu-Charantes: Patrimonies-Médias, 1999.

Loti, Pierre. *Au Maroc*. Paris: Calmann-Lévy, 1884.

——. *Aziyadé*. 1879. *Pierre Loti: Romans*. Paris: Presses de la Cité, 1989. 7–132.

——. *Cette éternelle nostalgie, Journal intime 1878–1911*. Ed. Bruno Vercier, Alain Quella-Villéger, et al. Paris: Table Ronde, 1997.

——. *Journal intime 1878–1881*. Vol. 1. Paris: Samuel Pierre-Loti-Viaud, 1926.

——. *Madame Chrysanthème*. Paris: Calmann-Lévy, 1887.

——. Le roman d'un enfant *suivi de* Prime jeunesse. 1890. Ed. Bruno Vercier. Paris: GF-Flammarion, 1988.

Teillay, Gérard, and Anne Crichton, eds. *La maison de Loti, ou, Le port immobile*. By Pierre Loti. Paris: Nompareille, 2000.

Tschinkel, Paul, dir. *Colette, the Arist: A Sampling of the Many Art Events, Exhibitions and Installations That Colette Has Created*. New York: Inner Tube Films, 1993.

Vercier, Bruno. "Loti l'écrivain." *Loti en son temps: Colloque de Paimpol 22–25 juillet 1993*. Rennes: PU de Rennes, 1994. 9–21.

——. *Pierre Loti portraits: Les fantaisies changeantes*. Paris: Flammarion, 2002.

Julie F. Codell

Life Writings as
New Cultural Contexts for
the Meanings of Art and Artist

Traditionally, art history courses focus on artworks, with complementary examinations of patronage, period biographies, period styles, critical reception, and aesthetic theories or movements. Although the scholarly biographical monograph has been a vital resource from the discipline's inception in academia about 135 years ago, art historians rarely incorporate artists' life writings as an analytical tool. Yet this literature offers social contexts for artists' works that can challenge and shape aesthetic interpretations with broader social and economic topics of art production, consumption, and reception and as a result can profoundly affect the hermeneutics of artworks.

Scholarly biographies of artists arose when art history became a university discipline in England in the 1870s; it was a discipline on the Continent earlier. Through these monographs, artists are simultaneously biographically recognized and canonized, the two processes being mutually interdependent. Monographs have significantly altered canons, as in the modern "discoveries" of the Pre-Raphaelites, European academic artists, Piero della Francesca, and Vermeer. Designed to replace popular artists' biographies that still flood libraries and adorn domestic coffee tables, the monograph also mystified ideas of the artist and of creativity (despite its scholarly pretensions) and avoided social, economic, and political topics. Recently many scholars criticize art history's disciplinary reliance on the monograph as a tool for explaining artistic worth. Many modern monographs often engage in psychoanalysis, treating artworks as Rorschach tests rather than as aesthetic products, ignoring the reality, often forgotten by those outside the discipline, that artists' decisions are generally motivated less by the personal than by stylistic conventions and historical resonances that dictate subject, composition, and style. Monographs often go hand in hand with exhibitions of an artist's work to create an institutionalized representation of that artist.

Many art historians suggest examining components of an artwork's production beyond the fundamental analyses of iconography and form. Art historians have adopted many poststructural methods, which may explain the interest in social history that artists' life writings can offer. Such topics as patronage, social history, semiotics, and poststructural interrogations of the artist as author have all expanded the tools art historians now use to identify art's meanings as a function, in part, of social relations. The question some art historians raise is how to use life writings in new ways in relation to a sociology of art and the artist. Art not only reflects its historical circumstances and milieu but also shapes its own social and political conditions of production and consumption. Aesthetic evaluation is not simply a pronouncement of mystifying authority but is constituted by public, historic, economic, and discursive processes.

Yet despite these changes toward more attention to cultural and social intertextuality among artworks, artists, and their historical circumstances, life writings are still largely ignored. Artists' autobiographies coordinate artists' careers with their social functions and roles in a given historical period. In their autobiographies artists reveal career strategies, private and public motives, their use of style as self-fashioning, their carefully projected gendered and national identities, and detailed economic and social relations with patrons and the public. In these texts artists produce themselves as professional identities inhabiting modern public spaces of exhibitions and press reviews (following Habermas's definition of such spaces as modern by virtue of their multiple voices and social dynamics).

Life writings offer a model of discursive and intertextual meanings for art. Autobiographies embed art in social and economic relations, in reception, and in multiple and sometimes conflicting personal, professional, and national identities. Furthermore, artists' life writings often contain a visual paratext of photos of artists' works, families, friends, studios, and other memorabilia, including drawings and sketches that expose the creative process. Interconnections between artists' texts and images vary: images sometimes endorse the text, sometimes complement it, and sometimes contradict it. Images and texts offer insight into studio practices, one of the most neglected areas of art historical study.

As Pierre Bourdieu has noted (110–11), artists' life writings participate in the very production of art. Life writings expand the study of art into the study of the relations between high and popular culture (e.g., advertisements, the press). From such studies we can begin to demystify creativity with concrete historical analyses of art's function and value, to complement or replace the explanation by "genius" with less mystical, more complex national, religious, social, and moral circumstances contributing not only to art production but also to the production of canons and artistic identities. This would also offer a critique of art history itself.

Besides Bourdieu and Michel Foucault, I use some theories that are rooted in autobiography scholarship, such as biographical recognition and self-fashioning, secondary scholarship on artists' and Victorian life writings, and the many studies of autobiographies and life writing theories. Given the tremendous popularity Victorian artists enjoyed and scholars' attention to other Victorians' life writings, it's curious that artists' life writings have been ignored in the classroom and only recently considered in scholarship. Life writing's subject is the artist as text and requires treating biographical constructions of "artist" as discursive with Victorian social, national, ideological, and ideal identities, all of which are multiple, not monolithic or consistent. Linda Nochlin argues that now "the time is ripe for a return to biography in a new sense, to biography as a history of personal making in the world, within community and society." J. R. R. Christie and Fred Orton suggest a reconsideration of multiple representations of the biographical subject "simultaneously and noncontradictorily . . . in a society, a culture, sub-culture, a country, a mode of production" (558–59). They propose balancing historicity with human agency without "over-individualized accounts of artistic creation, and reductive explanations in terms of talent or genius, or incorrigible psychoanalytic interpretations" (559). Given that we live "plural-biographically," they argue that we must excavate "explanatory systems" and institutions to understand "the conditions under which they . . . worked to produce their explanations, their expression claims, their biographies; and why" (560–61).

My course is designed to carry out this kind of excavation into explanatory systems of Victorian art and into relations between taste and artists' biographical elevation into new social and cultural agency. Victorian artists' life writings sutured them to a public becoming increasingly interested in art for various reasons: the proddings of John Ruskin, increased leisure, and associations of culture with virtue and with civic and national identities. Artists' life writings reveal the status of artists, social attitudes toward art, and functions of art in civic life.

Students must also gain a quick understanding of Victorian autobiography and some history of artists' life writings, a subgenre going back to the Italian Renaissance. Reading John Stuart Mill and Benvenuto Cellini, students can categorically identify both Victorian and artist content. Mill's is a spiritual autobiography, a type avoided by most artists, so students learn about autobiographical genres (spiritual, res gestae). Cellini's was an extremely popular model for Victorian artists; their texts' differences from his, especially their reticence about some topics, help define what is Victorian and artist in the genre.

I explore here one university course intended for upper-division students (juniors and seniors) and graduate students, all of whom have had as a prerequisite at least one course in Victorian culture. My course focuses on the Victorian artistic self and deploys life writings to illuminate the historicity of aesthetic values and the relation between aesthetics and artists' social and national roles. My students come from art history, English, humanities, history, and studio art.

Artists' autobiographies offer information often overlooked or considered déclassé. Artists proudly reveal economic and social successes, as well as topics of genealogy, family life, historical events, and conditions of artistic production and consumption. These books are filled with photographs and reproductions of studios and artworks and lists of exhibited works with patrons, exhibition dates, and sometimes prices. Such data are also included in period biographies by artists' families and friends, another life writing source virtually ignored in art history courses.

Art historians readily raid life writings for research but less often for the classroom. Life writings offer a sociology of the artist. Victorian male artists came from all classes, including rural poor (T. Sidney Cooper), and often struggled toward success, while women artist autobiographers all came from the middle and upper-middle classes and enjoyed encouragement and support from their families—support not always enjoyed by their male cohorts and certainly not enjoyed by many Victorian women. But until the 1920s most women artists did not publish their autobiographies, whereas male artists had published autobiographies since the eighteenth century. The women, like the men, were very successful, but their emergence into biographical recognition and claims to be authentic autobiographical subjects came much later, a sign of a disconnect between their artistic and biographical successes. Finally, the subjects of most Victorian life writings are artists whose reputations, high when their lives were textualized, have since fallen. This dramatic change indicates that the relation between autobiographies and taste can become inverse over time.

For many students, however, the crucial issue is still canonic recognition, or greatness. Because life writings are primary sources written by artists or their contemporaries, they help demystify notions of greatness or genius and offer an opportunity to see how art functions in a culture; how its functions historically change and what motivates these changes; how consensual, rather than absolute, aesthetic values are; how fluid artistic identities are; and how these identities and aesthetic values mutually inflect each other. One of the most stunning examples is James McNeill Whistler's version of an autobiography, *The Gentle Art of Making Enemies*, in which his identity is fused with the largely hostile critical reception of his work and his response to this reception. Another example is William Holman Hunt's *Pre-Raphaelitism and the Pre-Raphaelite Brotherhood*, in which Hunt presents his imperial and masculinized artistic identity as fused with Pre-Raphaelite Brotherhood aesthetics, eliding his aesthetics in his text with Englishness and Christian ideals.

Victorian women artists' autobiographies defy scholarly views that Victorian women autobiographers focus on their domestic lives. These women artists adamantly promoted their professional identities and downplayed the domestic plot. But women were usually absent in Victorian serialized press and book biographies of artists, indicating that their career success did not parlay into full biographical recognition, with the exception of biographical dictionaries in which they were prominent. As I discuss in *The Victorian Artist: Artists' Lifewritings in Britain, ca. 1870–1910*, life writings can thus offer a nuanced map of Victorian gendering in art and of differences among biographical genres.

The most important assignment is for students to find ways to understand the autobiography within its period history and in relation to the author's works of art. Students must find two major works given attention in the artist's autobiography ("major" means the work was promoted in the autobiography and is still recognized by scholarly attention or placement in a museum). This work is then placed in a triangulated set of discourses. The student compares current scholarly assessment of the work with the assessment by the artist-autobiographer (or, in some cases, family biographer) and with a third assessment by a Victorian critic or popular biographer. The class as a whole does this exercise, and then students reduplicate it for their final paper. In class we study popular paintings and life writings by Hubert von Herkomer, William Holman Hunt, and Elizabeth Butler. This selection introduces students to important styles (realism, Pre-Raphaelitism), media (painting and press illustration), gender issues, newspaper art criticism, and John Ruskin's criticism of Hunt and Butler.

The work of William Holman Hunt is exemplary for several reasons: his current importance as evidenced by scholarly writing about him and his work, the visibility of his works in the United Kingdom and the United States, the value of his two-volume autobiography then and now in scholarly writing for understanding the Victorian art world, and his relation to Pre-Raphaelitism, an important set of movements in both literature and art history. His painting *Finding the Savior in the Temple* was examined in the press, in a special one-work exhibition (a venue Hunt and his dealer Ernest Gambart practically invented), and in a special pamphlet by the Pre-Raphaelite critic F. G. Stephens. Considering the painting within this intertextuality exposes discourses that constitute Victorian artistic identity: the relation of aesthetics to personal character, economic venues, articulations in public spaces (autobiography, exhibition, critical review), and the differences between our own and Victorian aesthetic assessments. Other Hunt paintings can be similarly used (*The Shadow of Death*, *The Awakening Conscience*, and *The Scapegoat*), as can other artists' works such as Butler's *Quatre Bras* (also reviewed by Ruskin) and William Powell Frith's trilogy of modern-day subjects (*Derby Day*, *The Railway Station*, *Ramsgate Sands*). Much depends on what autobiographies are available or can be purchased for the class; many of the images are online on Web sites devoted to specific artists, to museum collections, or to Victorian culture.

The major assignment incorporates a number of intersecting contents: Victorian culture, painting, and autobiographies; the periodical press of the time; and the relations between images and texts in a culture in which narrativity had a high value. Students can compare and contrast their three sources and not have to generate an aesthetic or historical study of the painting to assess multiple valuations of the work and the artist. Students can also determine a relation between artworks and artists' self-fashioning that can be applied to other examples of high-profile artists (notably Jackson Pollock and Pablo Picasso). They gain familiarity with the periodical press, a major venue for art criticism, reproductions, and biographies, and have the opportunity to question asymmetries in life writing and art production related to gender and class.

Ultimately, students work in teams, depending on their selected works, and come together to determine if there are life patterns among Victorian artists and patterns of aesthetic taste or career trajectories. They can compare autobiographies to understand differences and similarities in some historical framework. We ask questions provoked by life writings that go beyond history to include theoretical topics of economics, gender, and reception.

This course matches artists' life writings to works of art, including artists' self-portraits, and can be readily tied to similar connections with Victorian literature or science. The major assignment can be applied to literature courses to explore how this triangulation reveals the status of writers and their social functions, as well as the relations between taste and the public space. John Henry Newman, John Ruskin, Margaret Oliphant, and Harriet Martineau are ideal candidates for such a critical study. Another course I teach combines the autobiographies of Victorian artists, writers, and scientists (e.g., Darwin's autobiography in relation to *The Origin of Species* and his critics). Artists' autobiographies were largely a British phenomenon, rare on the Continent, but the course could include European examples (Delacroix's journal, Bonheur's autobiography) for comparison.

Given the increasing attention to visual culture in literature departments and the sometimes naive studies of paintings by those unaware of the history of conventions and of the role of patronage, the market, and the public in the creation and production of art, it is worth considering how to incorporate more sophisticated assignments about the art world in literature courses. This course could be modified to examine concepts of modernism and artistic rebellion or avant-garde culture.

Appendix

Topics and Readings

Week 1: Portraiture traditions in painting and photography; readings from Briggs, Brilliant, Pollock, and Folkenflik.

Week 2: Issues in artists' autobiographies: an overview; readings from Smith and Watson, Christie and Orton, Bourdieu, Altick, and Jay.

Week 3: Traditions in artists' autobiographies: Renaissance Italy; readings from
Cellini, Vasari, Soussloff, Kris and Kurz, and Codell. Download biogra-
phies from <http://www.kfki.hu/~arthp/bio/c/cellini/biograph.html> and
<http://www.mega.it/eng/egui/pers/vasa.htm>.
Week 4: The modern in artists' autobiographies: France; readings from Delacroix,
Bonheur, Barlow, and McWilliam. Download biographies from
<http://www.artchive.com/ftptoc/Delacroix_ext.html> and <http://www
.bbhc.org/womenGalleries/menu2_01.cfm>.
Week 5: Victorian autobiographies: the case of John Stuart Mill; readings from
Mill, Peterson, Danahay, and Machann.
Weeks 6, 7: Autobiography, history, and national identity: William Holman
Hunt; readings from Hunt, Codell, Landow, and Pointon. Download
biography from <http://victorianweb.org/painting/whh/replete/conscience
.html>.
Weeks 8, 9: Biography, portraiture, greatness: John Everett Millais and George
Frederick Watts; readings from Millais, Watts, Funnell, Woodall, and
Shafer. Download biography from <http://www.speel.demon.co.uk/artists/
watts.htm>.
Week 10: Autobiography versus criticism: James McNeill Whistler and the National Portrait Gallery; readings from Whistler, Brilliant, Codell, and Barlow. Download biography from <http://www.ibiblio.org/wm/paint/auth/
whistler> and material from <http://www.npg.org.uk/live/history.asp>.
Week 11: Women's professional and gendered identities: Elizabeth Butler; readings
from Butler, Cheney, Borzello, and Stephenson. Download biography from
<http://www.spartacus.schoolnet.co.uk/Jbutler.htm> and Butler's paintings
from <http://www.artrenewal.org/asp/database/art.asp?aid=2191>.
Week 12: Autobiography, class and gender: Henrietta Ward; readings from Ward,
Codell, and Nunn. Download biography from <http://www.artnet.com/
library/09/0906/T090675.asp>.
Weeks 13, 14: Life writings and artists' works: autobiography theory. Choose an
autobiography and focus on how two of the artists' major works are
treated in the autobiography, in press reviews, and in one example of
scholarly writing.
Week 15: Artist as producer and consumer: Victorian biography and art historical
monograph; readings from Baldry, von Herkomer, Dafforne, Edwards,
and Gilmore. Download material from <http://www.artcyclopedia.com/
artists/von_herkomer_sir_hubert.html> and <http://www.artrenewal.org/
asp/database/art.asp?ais-882>.

Works Cited

Altick, Richard. "Writing the Life of J. J. Ridley." *Nineteenth-Century Lives: Essays
Presented to Jerome Hamilton Buckley*. Ed. Laurence S. Lockridge et al. Cam-
bridge: Cambridge UP, 1989. 26–58.
Ashley, Kathleen, Leigh Gilmore, and Gerald Peterson, eds. *Autobiography and
Postmodernism*. Amherst: U of Massachusetts P, 1994.

Baldry, A. L. *Hubert von Herkomer, R. A.: A Study and a Biography*. London: Bell, 1904.

Barlow, Paul. "The Imagined Hero as Incarnate Sign: Thomas Carlyle and the Mythology of the 'National Portrait' in Victorian Britain." *Art History* 17 (1994): 517–45.

Bonheur, Rosa. *Reminiscences of Rosa Bonheur*. Trans. Theodore Stanton. New York: Appleton, 1910.

Borzello, Frances. *Seeing Ourselves: Women's Self-Portraits*. London: Thames, 1998.

Bourdieu, Pierre. *The Field of Cultural Production*. Ed. Randal Johnson. Cambridge: Polity, 1993.

———. "The Invention of the Artist's Life." *Yale French Studies* 73 (1987): 75–103.

Briggs, Asa, ed. *A Victorian Portrait: A Record of Victorian Life and Values through Studio Photographs*. London: Harper, 1989.

Brilliant, Richard. *Portraiture*. London: Reaktion, 1991.

Butler, Elizabeth. *An Autobiography*. London: Constable, 1922.

Cellini, Benvenuto. *Autobiography*. Trans. J. A. Symonds. New York: Collier, 1937.

Cheney, L., et al, eds. *Self-Portraits by Women Painters*. Brookfield: Ashgate, 2000.

Christie, J. R. R., and Fred Orton. "Writing on a Text of the Life." *Art History* 11 (1988): 545–64.

Codell, Julie F. *The Victorian Artist: Artists' Lifewritings in Britain, ca. 1870–1910*. Cambridge: Cambridge UP, 2003.

Cooper, T. Sidney. *My Life*. London: Bentley, 1891.

Dafforne, James. "The Works of Hubert Herkomer, A.R.A." *Art Journal* n.s. 19 (1880): 109–12.

Danahay, Martin. *A Community of One: Masculine Autobiography and Autonomy in Nineteenth-Century Britain*. Albany: State U of New York P, 1993.

Delacroix, Eugène. *The Journal of Eugene Delacroix*. Trans. W. Pach. New York: Covici, 1937.

Edwards, Lee MacCormick. *Herkomer, A Victorian Artist*. Aldershot: Ashgate, 1999.

Folkenflik, Robert. "The Artist as Hero in the Eighteenth Century." *Yearbook of English Studies* 12 (1982): 91–108.

———, ed. *The Culture of Autobiography: Constructions of Self-Representation*. Stanford: Stanford UP, 1993.

Foucault, Michel. *The Order of Things: An Archaeology of the Human Sciences*. New York: Vintage, 1970.

France, Peter, and William St. Clair, eds. *Mapping Lives: The Uses of Biography*. Oxford: Oxford UP, 2002.

Funnell, Peter, et al. *Millais: Portraits*. London: Natl. Portrait Gallery, 1999.

Gilmore, Leigh. "The Mark of Autobiography." Ashley, Gilmore, and Peterson 3–18.

Habermas, Jürgen. *The Structural Transformation of the Public Sphere*. Trans. Thomas Burger. Cambridge: MIT P, 2000.

Herkomer, Hubert von. *The Autobiography of Hubert Herkomer*. London: privately printed, 1890.

Hunt, W. H. *Pre-Raphaelitism and the Pre-Raphaelite Brotherhood*. 2 vols. London: Macmillan, 1905.

Jay, Paul. "Posing: Autobiography and the Subject of Photography." Ashley, Gilmore, and Peterson 191–211.

Kris, Ernst, and Otto Kurz. *Myth, Magic, and Legend in the History of the Artist: A Historical Experiment*. New Haven: Yale UP, 1979.

Landow, George. "William Holman Hunt's 'Oriental Mania' and His Uffizi *Self-Portrait*." *Art Bulletin* 64 (1982): 646–55.

Machann, Clinton. *The Genre of Autobiography in Victorian Literature*. Ann Arbor: U of Michigan P, 1994.

McWilliam, Neil. "Art, Labour and Mass Democracy: Debates on the Status of the Artist in France around 1848." *Art History* 11 (1988): 64–87.

Mill, John Stuart. *Autobiography*. 1873. Ed. John Robson. New York: Penguin, 1990.

Millais, John Guille. *The Life and Letters of Sir John Everett Millais*. 2 vols. New York: Stokes, 1899.

Nochlin, Linda. "Whither the Field of Nineteenth-Century Art History?" *Nineteenth-Century Art Worldwide* 1.1 (2002). 8 Aug. 2006 <http://www.19thc-artworldwide.org/spring_02/articles/whither.html>.

Nunn, Pamela Garrish. "The Case History of a Woman Artist: Henrietta Ward." *Art History* 1 (1978): 293–308.

Peterson, Linda. *Victorian Autobiography: The Tradition of Self-Interpretation*. New Haven: Yale UP, 1986.

Pointon, Marcia, ed. *Pre-Raphaelites Reviewed*. Manchester: Manchester UP, 1989.

Pollock, Griselda. "Artists' Mythologies and Media Genius, Madness and Art History." *Screen* 21 (1980): 57–96.

Shafer, Elinor S. "Shaping Victorian Biography: From Anecdote to *Bildungsroman*." France and St. Clair 115–33.

Smith, Sidonie, and Julia Watson. *Reading Autobiography: A Guide for Interpreting Life Narratives*. Minneapolis: U of Minnesota P, 2001.

Soussloff, Catherine. *The Absolute Artist: The Historiography of a Concept*. Minneapolis: U of Minnesota P, 1977.

Stephens, F. G. *William Holman Hunt and His Works: A Memoir of the Artist's Life, with Descriptions of His Pictures*. London: Nisbet, 1860.

Stephenson, Andrew. "Leighton and the Shifting Repertoires of 'Masculine' Artistic Identity in the Late Victorian Period." *Frederic Leighton: Antiquity Renaissance Modernity*. Ed. Tim Barringer and Elizabeth Prettejohn. New Haven: Yale UP, 1999. 221–39.

Vasari, Giorgio. *Lives of the Artists*. Trans. G. Bull. 2 vols. New York: Penguin, 1987.

Ward, Henrietta. *Memories of Ninety Years*. London: Hutchinson, 1924.

Watts, Mary. *George Frederic Watts: The Annals of an Artist's Life*. London: Macmillan, 1912.

Whistler, James McNeill. *The Gentle Art of Making Enemies*. 1892. Introd. Alfred Werner. New York: Dover, 1967.

Woodall, Joanna. *Portraiture: Facing the Subject*. Manchester: U of Manchester P, 1997.

Frances Freeman Paden

Emblematic Sculptures: The Artwork of Felix Gonzalez-Torres in the Life Writing Classroom

Midway through a seminar on gender and autobiography, my undergraduate students consider work by Felix Gonzalez-Torres (1957–96), a Cuban-born American artist one critic has called "the finest artistic intelligence . . . in the past decade" (Baltz). Gonzalez-Torres's installations have been exhibited widely in leading museums in the United States and abroad, as well as on the streets of New York. These works mirror concerns in recent life writing because Gonzalez-Torres consistently manipulates conventional objects to represent the dismantling of authority, creates dialogue between the personal and political, alludes to bodies that do not stop at the skin (Haraway 178), reinvents "aura" (Benjamin 217–51; Bourriaud 337–41), and produces art that is performative (Butler 12–16). Experiencing Gonzalez-Torres's work has helped my students understand on a visceral level what the autobiographical text asks of them. Confronting his images gives them a new sense of the way their engagement may create and affect meaning.

Most of my students have had other gender studies courses before they come into this seminar and are eager to read works by writers conscious of autobiography as cultural practice. I usually begin with postcolonial literature by Gloria Anzaldúa, Maryse Condé, and Reinaldo Arenas. These works,

171

grounded as they are in time and place, allow students to bring their knowledge of history and politics to their reading. Within that relatively secure framework, we begin to raise more speculative questions concerning formation of identities, representation, and performativity. Lectures and readings draw on works by autobiographical theorists, as well as historians, philosophers, and cultural critics, including figures such as Walter Benjamin, Judith Butler, Michel Foucault, Joan Wallach Scott, and Michael Warner. For a working definition of autobiography, we turn to Sidonie Smith: "Autobiography becomes both the process and the product of assigning meaning to a series of experiences, after they have taken place, by means of emphasis, juxtaposition, commentary, omission" (45). As our discussions become more theoretical, some students begin to lose sight of the reader-writer dyad and forget that they are implicated in the literary work. Taking them away from the verbal and into the visual arts is a radical move that makes them pay attention to their positioning as viewers and readers. It also sets them up for theorizing subjectivity and the process of life writing.

Integrating visual arts is a pedagogical strategy I have used in two other life writing courses I teach: in my freshman seminar Imagining Gender, my students study self-portraits by Frida Kahlo; in my course Writing Women's Lives, we study Charlotte Salomon's paintings along with Mary Lowenthal Felstiner's biography *To Paint Her Life: Charlotte Salomon in the Nazi Era*. The introduction to Sidonie Smith and Julia Watson's *Interfaces* provides a helpful grounding for the instructor who wishes to move in this direction. The essays that make up Smith and Watson's collection focus on specific women artists and provide insightful commentary on the intersection between life writing and visual and performance arts.

To begin the unit on Gonzalez-Torres, I ask my students to view online materials, particularly the link to the artist's page on the Creative Time Web site (www.creativetime.org/programs/archive/2000/Torres/torres/felix_intro.html), and to browse in Gonzalez-Torres exhibition catalogs in Northwestern University's art library. I follow up with a slide lecture consisting of twenty-five to thirty images of the artist's work, as well as a few works by the minimalist and conceptual artists who influenced him. The students then divide into groups to visit the Art Institute of Chicago. I encourage them to talk among themselves and to send me e-mail reflections on their experiences as viewers. In those responses and in the class discussions that follow, the students begin to connect what they have learned in the course with their experience of the artwork.

In his photographs, sculptures, and installations, Gonzalez-Torres confronts the AIDS crisis head-on. He urges his viewers to recognize our complicity in problems that plague not only the body but also the body politic. He pushes us to question the role that institutions such as the museum, the medical establishment, and the state play in the construction of subjects—in their histories and their future possibilities. Ravishingly beautiful and provocative, his artworks seduce their viewers into responsiveness.

Gonzalez-Torres's artwork may be said to be emblematic because it "speaks." Embedded in his installations and sculptures are narratives concerning AIDS, cell counts, homoerotic desire, loss, love, and redemption. As the students interact with his work and realize that its meaning is contingent on their response, they become part of a dialogue. They also begin to see that lines of demarcation, whether separating life and death, bodies, political fiefdoms, social attitudes, or genres, are more porous and malleable than they may seem. Finally, they learn that space and time, instead of being discrete categories, may be conjoined.

At the Art Institute of Chicago my students view several of Gonzalez-Torres's works, including *"Untitled"* (*Portrait of Ross in L.A.*) (fig. 1). It is a pile of candies, brilliantly lit, that lures them into the contemporary gallery, where they find it, seemingly spilled in a corner where two white walls meet. Wrapped in six colors of cellophane over silver foil, the candies sparkle in the light beaming down from the ceiling. Their combined weight (175 pounds) matches the ideal weight of Ross Laycock, Gonzalez-Torres's lover, who died of AIDS in 1991. A sign invites the students and other viewers to take a piece of candy. Students realize that when they remove the candy, they literally diminish the representation of Ross but hold in their hands (or mouths) the possibility that Ross's self is continuous, extending not only beyond his body but also beyond the memory of those who knew him. Like Augustine's pears or Proust's madeleines, the sight of the candies fills its beholders with anticipation, moving them closer to the pleasure of the artist's remembered experience and to their own future pleasure, the promise of the next succulent bite. For some students the candy has a transubstantiating effect, suggesting communion with a vanished body and the possibility of continuity and redemption.

Gonzalez-Torres began making his candy spills in 1990, when Ross became increasingly debilitated by AIDS-related illnesses. He also made paper stacks that, like the candy spills, invite viewers to dismantle them, this time by taking a sheet of paper; according to the artist's wishes, exhibitors may

Figure 1. *"Untitled" (Portrait of Ross in L.A.)*, 1991. Candies individually wrapped in multicolored cellophane, endless supply. Ideal weight: 175 lbs. Dimensions vary with installation. ARG #GF1991–64. Installation view of "Felix Gonzalez-Torres" at Luhring Augustine Hetzler, Los Angeles, 1991. Photo: James Franklin. © The Felix Gonzalez-Torres Foundation. Courtesy of Andrea Rosen Gallery, New York.

or may not replace the objects removed from candy spills and paper stacks. Though some of my students have seen paper stacks at Chicago's Museum of Contemporary Art or the Milwaukee Art Museum, most gain access to them only in catalogs and at my slide lecture, which includes *"Untitled"* (*Loverboy*) (fig. 2). For these students, removing a sheet of paper from the stack is an imagined act.

The paper stacks help my students learn to interrogate form because the stacks draw their attention to the role that contingency and the viewer's perceptions play in determining meaning. Like minimalist art produced by Donald Judd, Anne Truitt, and others, the stacks appear unitary and hard-edged. In imitating minimalist art Gonzalez-Torres queers it; he appropriates its forms and then subverts them. As viewers approach *"Untitled"* (*Loverboy*), they find that it is not unitary but interactive, that it performs in

Figure 2. *"Untitled" (Loverboy),* 1990. Blue paper, endless copies. 7½ in. at ideal height × 29 × 23 in. Installation view of "Felix Gonzalez-Torres" at Andrea Rosen Gallery, New York, 1990. Photo: Peter Muscato. © The Felix Gonzalez-Torres Foundation. Courtesy of Andrea Rosen Gallery, New York.

response to touch. I point out to the students that the stack, like autobiography (and gender), is inherently performative, that the reiterative practice of dispersal produces meaning (Butler 2; Smith and Watson 9).

If we substitute *writer* for viewer and *memory* for stack, the parallels to life writing become palpable. Though we may consciously store images in memory, our efforts at recall teach us that memory is never reliable, that it exists in a state of constant flux. Like viewers who remove a sheet of paper from the stack, wondering what they will do with it and whether or not museum guards will object, writers must decide what to do with the recollections they find in memory. They must consider the truth value of those memories and recognize the possible consequences of using their recollections. Imagining themselves interacting with the paper stacks helps my students understand that the raw material of life writing comes from a continually changing matrix of remembered objects and experiences and that neither reader nor writer has access to an essential or unrealized memory.

In 1992 Gonzalez-Torres photographed his empty bed, with indentations left by two heads on the pillows, and in collaboration with the

Museum of Modern Art installed the image on billboards in twenty-four locations above the streets of New York City. The rumpled bed "allude[s] to libidinal desire while remaining intentionally elusive" (Spector 72). Like the candy spills, it depicts not only loss but also the possibility of moving on, suggesting that "something substantial can be made from the outline left after the body has disappeared" (Phelan 3). The bed is captured in black-and-white photography, a medium that signals both the absence of the original object and the presence of an infinite possibility for renewal (Barthes 80; Adams xv). The installation teaches my students the power of omission and juxtaposition, both key terms in Smith's definition of autobiography.

For spectators on the street below, the photograph of the bed is remote; its context, a busy urban landscape instead of the usual white museum wall, distracts the viewer. The image requires an effort, a deliberate involvement on the part of its viewers, if it is to be understood. Its presence suggests both desire and loss; it asserts public responsibility for the freedom to sleep and to love. For Gonzalez-Torres, the making of the photograph recalled the very recent death of his lover, as well as the 1986 case of *Bowers versus Hardwick*, when "the Supreme Court determined that the zone of privacy . . . does not encompass a private individual's right to engage in certain sexual acts." Gonzalez-Torres represents the bed as a "legislated and socially contested zone" (Umland). Readers of autobiography will see parallels to the intersection of violence, history, and personal narrative in Assia Djebar's *Fantasia* or Michelle Cliff's *Abeng*.

Gonzalez-Torres seeks to activate the space that separates art from its viewers. He encourages us to disrupt the stacks of paper, to take and eat the candies in the spills. With the billboards he challenges spectators, despite the distractions of the urban environment, to respond to an image that is both remote and intimate. In a fourth work, *"Untitled" (Blood)*, Gonzalez-Torres engages the whole body, setting it in motion. He strings red and white beads in narrow rows and hangs them like a screen across a passageway. The screen not only suggests blood tests and white cell counts but also alludes to the doorway of his grandmother's house in Puerto Rico. The mobility of the strands and the light filtering through them from behind encourage the spectator to push the beads aside and walk through. While representing cells that die and nostalgia for the past, the strings of beads "foreground the body, *your* body . . . moving through them" (Spector 171).

My students and I imagine walking through the screen, understanding that when we do so, we become engaged physically and personally in the installation. Extending that insight to the reading of autobiography, we consider that when we read, the "I" touches us, thus reversing Arthur Rimbaud's depersonalizing claim, "Je est un autre" (270), "I is an other," and changing it to "An other is I," or more colloquially, "Another is me." The shift in positioning, whether it occurs in artwork or in a verbal text, transforms the subject into a complement that, while not identical, reiterates it. The grammar of engagement ("Je est") is no longer strained. The instructor may hope that those who take a walk, even an imaginary one, through *"Untitled" (Blood)* will gain a deeper grasp of intersubjectivity. They will understand better that the narrative "I" is performative and that readers are complicit in the process of autobiography.

Leaving the emblematic sculptures of Gonzalez-Torres, my students and I pick up Michelle Citron's *Home Movies and Other Necessary Fictions*, a work that combines visual art with narrative and theory with personal experience. As we watch Citron turn the camera on herself as subject, refusing to bring any scene to closure, we reflect on our experience with Gonzalez-Torres. Like him, Citron not only makes room for readers and viewers in her work but also demands their participation. After we read *Home Movies*, my course culminates with Cliff's fictionalized memoir *Abeng*, where we see an adolescent Clare struggle with the politics of location that she encounters in colonial Jamaica. As my students watch her run her hand across the faded, torn wallpaper in the home of her white ancestors, they respond with empathy. Felix Gonzalez-Torres has helped them understand what it means to finger your own history, to see redemption in loss, to find your voice, and to be heard.

Note

For their inspiration and insight, I am grateful to Kristine Thompson and Emily Hagenmaier. Special thanks to Michelle Reyes of the Andrea Rosen Gallery.

Works Cited

Adams, Timothy Dow. *Light Writing and Life Writing: Photography in Autobiography*. Chapel Hill: U of North Carolina P, 2000.

Anzaldúa, Gloria. *Borderlands / La Frontera: The New Mestiza*. 2nd ed. San Francisco: Aunt Lute, 1999.

Arenas, Reinaldo. *Before Night Falls*. Trans. Dolores M. Koch. New York: Penguin, 1993.

Baltz, Lewis. "(sans titre)." *L'architecture d'aujourd'hui* Sept. 1996: 12–15. Creative Time, 2000. 14 June 2007 <http://www.creativetime.org/programs/archive/2000/Torres/torres/baltz.html>.

Barthes, Roland. *Camera Lucida: Reflections on Photography*. Trans. Richard Howard. New York: Hill, 1981.

Benjamin, Walter. *Illuminations*. Ed. Hannah Arendt. Trans. Harry Zohn. New York: Schocken, 1969.

Bourriaud, Nicolas. "Coexistence and Availability: The Theoretical Legacy of Felix Gonzalez-Torres." *Il Dono / The Gift: Generous Offerings / Threatened Hospitality*. Milan: Charta, 2001. 329–43.

Butler, Judith. *Bodies That Matter: The Discursive Limits of "Sex."* New York: Routledge, 1993.

Citron, Michelle. *Home Movies and Other Necessary Fictions*. Minneapolis: U of Minnesota P, 1999.

Cliff, Michelle. *Abeng: A Novel*. Trumansburg: Crossing, 1984.

Condé, Maryse. *Tales from the Heart: True Stories from My Childhood*. Trans. Richard Philcox. New York: Soho, 2001.

Djebar, Assia. *Fantasia: An Algerian Cavalcade*. Trans. Dorothy S. Blair. London: Quartet, 1985.

Felstiner, Mary Lowenthal. *To Paint Her Life: Charlotte Salomon in the Nazi Era*. Berkeley: U of California P, 1997.

Foucault, Michel. *The History of Sexuality: An Introduction*. Trans. Robert Hurley. New York: Vintage-Random, 1978.

Gonzalez-Torres, Felix. "Interview by Tim Rollins." *Felix Gonzalez-Torres*. New York: Art Resources Transfer, 1993. 5–31.

——. *"Untitled."* 1991. Projects 34: Felix Gonzalez-Torres. Exhibition. Museum of Modern Art, New York. 1992.

——. *"Untitled" (Blood)*. 1992. Private collection.

——. *"Untitled" (Loverboy)*. 1990. Collection of Andrea Rosen, New York.

——. *"Untitled" (Portrait of Ross in L.A.)*. 1991. Collection of Howard Stone and Donna Stone. Art Inst. of Chicago.

Haraway, Donna. *Simians, Cyborgs, and Women: The Reinvention of Nature*. New York: Routledge, 1991.

Phelan, Peggy. *Mourning Sex: Performing Public Memories*. London: Routledge, 1997.

Rimbaud, Arthur. "À Paul Demeny." 15 May 1871. *Œuvres complètes . . . [by] Arthur Rimbaud*. Edited and annotated by Rolland de Renéville and Jules Mouquet. Paris: Gallimard, 1963. 269–74.

Scott, Joan W. "Experience." *Women, Autobiography, Theory: A Reader*. Ed. Sidonie Smith and Julia Watson. Madison: U of Wisconsin P, 1999. 57–71.

Smith, Sidonie. *A Poetics of Women's Autobiography: Marginality and the Fictions of Self-Representation*. Bloomington: Indiana UP, 1987.

Smith, Sidonie, and Julia Watson, eds. *Interfaces: Women, Autobiography, Image, Performance*. Ann Arbor: U of Michigan P, 2002.

Spector, Nancy. *Felix Gonzalez-Torres*. Xunta de Galicia: Centro Galego de Arte Contemporanea, 1995.

Umland, Anne. "MoMA Projects 34 Essay." New York: Museum of Modern Art, 1992. Creative Time Past Projects, 2000. 14 June 2007 <http://www.creativetime.org/programs/archive/2000/Torres/torres/umland.html>.

Warner, Michael. *The Trouble with Normal: Sex, Politics, and the Ethics of a Queer Life*. Cambridge: Harvard UP, 2000.

Miriam Fuchs

A Graduate Seminar in Life Writing: Posing and Composing Lives

Preliminaries: First Class

Students are listening to excerpts from "Visits with Joseph Cornell." This CD records "interviews" conducted at the Whitney Museum of American Art in 2001 with Cornell, the New York artist known for his collages and shadow box constructions. The CD begins as one of the researchers explains the purpose and the unconventional methods used to carry out the interviews. Next, students hear "Cornell" patiently responding to many questions on both his art and his life. A few students smile. Most of them, though, look mystified.

Apparently, the problem with these 2001 interviews isn't that Cornell died in 1972. The researchers are well aware of the unusual circumstances, and they begin the recording by citing persons who made the interviews possible: experts that included trance mediums and spiritual intermediaries. No, we're told, the problem instead was Cornell himself. As they explain in the liner notes (beautifully designed to evoke Cornell's methods and materials), the researchers had to go back repeatedly to Cornell's diaries and source materials because the exchanges were more difficult than they expected. They attribute the difficulty to the problem of separating "the mediums' factual errors, their personal biases, and our own fantasies from the Cornell spirit's actual communications (and miscommunications)." In other words, it was Cornell's famous reticence, not the particular circumstances of his death, that made the interviews so challenging.

My students struggle to understand. After all, they are in a graduate seminar that presumes an advanced level of seriousness and sophistication, and I've told them the interviews illustrate the theoretical underpinnings of the course. They realize that every component of the Cornell interviews is professionally handled. Every detail is well explained. But the "contact zone," set against what they already know about encounters that involve disparate geographical, spatial, and temporal spaces (Pratt 6–7), presents new difficulties.

Before asking students to record their impressions, I offer background: the mediums and researchers can all be found on the Internet. A discussion with Anne Walsh and Chris Kubrick, the principal researchers of the project, is also on the Internet, and I distribute copies. So is the abstract of their 2003 presentation at the Centennial Reevaluation of Joseph Cornell, held at the University of Essex. I ask one person to read from the handout where the two researchers talk about their "fieldwork":

> Q: Have people tried to talk you out of this?
> A: Yes, actually. Mostly on the grounds of it being a dangerous pursuit that should not be taken lightly. . . . [But] we take the whole project very seriously, we're careful, and we work with trained professionals. It's still a little nerve-wracking sometimes, but it really feels like work that should be done. . . . [and earlier] Of course, as the project's gone on, it seems both more real and more unreal.

Students write for a few minutes. Watching them, I consider how the interviews with Cornell are a perfect example of Philippe Lejeune's "anti-Pact" in operation: a "dizzying game of lucidity around all the presuppositions of autobiographical [or biographical] discourse—so dizzying that it ends up giving the reader the illusion that it is not doing what it nevertheless is doing" (131). I wonder how the students are balancing the (fairly) lucid dialogue with their own ideas of evidence and testimony. In "The Autobiographical Pact (bis)," Lejeune cites Barthes's remark "in the field of the subject there is no referent" in order to rebut it strongly. And soon I'll recite that rebuttal: "We *indeed know* all this; we are not so dumb, but, once this precaution has been taken, we go on as if we did not know it. . . . In spite of the fact that autobiography [or other forms of life narrative] is impossible, this in no way prevents it from existing" (131–32).

Concepts and Outline of the Seminar

I've lingered over the previous exercise because it effectively dramatizes the trap of referentiality or, better yet, authors' or interviewers' professed efforts toward referentiality and our predictable response: we believe, at least until we feel compelled to do otherwise. Students recognize the tenuous grounding of *Visits with Joseph Cornell,* yet they remain wondrously open minded:

> I have to admit that I really think some *parts* of the dialogue are convincing.
>
> Some of it *must* have taken place.
>
> *Some* of the remarks do explain his work and really do refer to those boxes I've seen in museums. So maybe sections of it are legitimate? What do I mean by legitimate, anyway? I don't believe in . . . *Were those seances?*

The possibility that sincerity can be posed seems odd to most of these graduate students. But skeptical or accepting, everyone comments on the multiple elements of dialogue, the number of speakers, the mixing of autobiography, testimony, biography, and art criticism. Nearly everyone notices that Cornell is evoked through noises almost as much as through his answers. We examine the functions of the poser or poseur and the dynamic of aural impressions (including interferences) with the environment (unfamiliar, and maybe impossible, spaces). I bring up the phenomenon of sound art and posit applications to collaborative narrative and interviews.

The syllabus is designed as a collage of the seminar's content, with statements by Gertrude Stein, Andrei Codrescu, Norman Bryson, and others. Rosalind Krauss's remark, from *The Originality of the Avant-Garde and Other Modernist Myths,* is useful for introducing the power of multiple poses:

> For it is doubling that produces the formal rhythm of spacing—the two-step that banishes the unitary condition of the moment, that creates *within* the moment an experience of fission. For it is doubling that elicits the notion that to an original has been added its copy. The double is the

simulacrum, the second, the representative of the original. It comes after the first, and in this following, it can only exist as figure, or image.
But in being seen in conjunction with the original, the double destroys
the pure singularity of the first. Through duplication, it opens the original to the effect of difference, of deferral, of one-thing-after-another, or
within another: of multiples burgeoning within the same. (109)

It doesn't matter if we all agree that doubling texts and images banishes the
unitary or if fission leads to reintegration or if technology has made origi-
nals and copies obsolete. My goal is that students leave the first class session questioning the expectations they came in with.

The emphasis on multiple discourses and channels of delivery and reception runs through the term. The contradictions are worth investigating
because students have trouble putting aside beliefs about biography and
autobiography that they have held all their lives. If they haven't taken our
graduate course in biography or haven't been undergraduates at the University of Hawai'i, this may be their first life writing course. (Courses on
disability narratives, women's life writing, ethnic life writing, contemporary life writing, family narratives, the academic memoir, creative nonfiction, autobiographical writing, and crisis and catastrophe narratives have
been offered.) Most of the MA and PhD candidates' area of concentration
is creative writing, the rest choosing composition/rhetoric, literary studies,
or cultural studies in Asia/Pacific. Almost everyone, even the creative writing students, holds to traditional notions of biography and autobiography.

For the remainder of the semester, students study life writing and life
imaging, finding ways that autobiographical and biographical representations resemble, infuse, or, depending on perspective and position, infect
the other. They look carefully at what these ideas suggest in historical and
cultural terms and at the repercussions of applying their own criteria to
transcultural works. Instructional units are groupings rather than discrete
genres. These units encourage arguments on genre to take place as a consequence of discussions, not because genre boundaries are the controlling
norms. I choose units from the following: videographic texts (Hatoum);
political texts (Lili'uokalani's *Hawaii's Story*); quilt texts (Ringgold; Kalinowski; Deborah Willis's photo texts); archival texts (Hurston's *Dust
Tracks on a Road*; Lipton's *Alias Olympia*; Maechler's *The Wilkomirski Affair*); culinary texts (De Silva's *In Memory's Kitchen*); bio-drama texts (Bennett's *Lady in the Van*); mixed-genre texts (Banti's *Artemisia*; Momaday's
The Names); artifact texts (Sophie Calle's work); bio-autobio-historical

texts (Stein's *Autobiography of Alice B. Toklas*), fraudulent texts (Wilko-mirski's *Fragments*); evolving texts (Allende's *Paula*), and future texts (Beckett's *Not-I*). The groups overlap and are arbitrary in some ways, but they call attention to multiple authorship and collaboration, composition, mediums, subjects, voices, languages, rhetorical poses, narrational modes, photographs, digital imagery, paintings, visual images, and landscapes. They point to the tensions we will investigate between expansiveness and limitations on how lives and subjects are constituted. They lead to debate on the role of parody. We will ask how one reads or views representational parody and how to recognize it. We will consider the nature of evidence and the limitations of believability. And we'll ask whether in doubling text and image, photographs become analogous to literary portraits and a photo series to literary chapters. Is the textual framing of images comparable to embedded genres? Where and why do visual components subvert the graphic text?

Readings, Viewings, and Discussions

The early weeks include an overview of life writing scholarship of the past thirty years. With the library's e-reserve facility, students access and print out assigned essays for their course reader. Selections from James Olney's *Autobiography: Essays Theoretical and Critical* contrast with more recent selections from Paul John Eakin's writings and Sidonie Smith and Julia Watson's *Women, Autobiography, Theory* and *Interfaces*. Additional readings are by Linda Haverty Rugg, Susanna Egan, Timothy Dow Adams, Leigh Gilmore, Lawrence Langer, Norman Bryson, John Rodden (on interviews), and Shoshana Felman and Dori Laub (on interviews and trauma).

Mona Hatoum's videographic *Measures of Distance* is the transition to the rest of the course, for it allows students to apply theoretical ideas to a half-hour film that skillfully uses text, calligraphy, sound, visual, and linguistic frames. Hatoum, now based in London, was born in Lebanon to exiled Palestinians. She conducted the interview in *Measures of Distance* while visiting her parents and her childhood home. In the shower and just partially concealed by the curtain, her mother is shown answering Hatoum's questions. Multiple overlays create a progression of sound and visual texts, with Arabic script from her mother's letters (presumably) partly blocking what we see, as Hatoum (presumably) reads selected translations (again, presumably). Elements of contradiction and uncertainty found in the other primary selections are all here. They elude our attempts to measure them and offer a rich contact zone as distancing as it is intimate. And the parallels of this "documentary" to the Cornell "interview" extend students' understanding of the limitations of evidence.

Hawaii's Story by Hawaii's Queen, by Lili'uokalani, who was the last indigenous monarch before United States annexation, continues the theme of exile. Students read the book as an evolving political text whose narrator assembles a series of poses. The autobiographical protagonist is properly Victorian for the author's turn-of-the-century American readers. She modulates into an articulate young woman, who comments on political battles that led to the overthrow of Hawaiian rule. For the author, though, in the midst of writing, the postoverthrow crisis is suddenly the catastrophe of imminent annexation. With the United States Congress in debate, the author alters the style and heightens emotions; we can trace how the narrator serves less as a framing device for the protagonist than as the enunciating site for strong rhetorical poses. The evolution from bildungsroman to argument against annexation sheds light on American imperialism. The last stage to evolve is the appendix, which is a rich library of government documents, photographs, letters, newspaper articles, and Hawaiian genealogies. The whole volume is a significant addition to life writing bibliographies. It can be studied along with Noenoe Silva's "Kanaka Maoli Resistance to Annexation" and *Aloha Betrayed* and Caren Kaplan's "Resisting Autobiography." My own works on Lili'uokalani's diaries and other writings would be useful as well.

Studying the quilt that Lili'uokalani began while imprisoned and that she embroidered with details of her abdication leads to a unit on quilt texts. Through print media and Web sites, we view Faith Ringgold's story quilts and the autobiographical video that explains their familial and African American contexts. Work by Deborah Willis also brings out issues of race and gender, while Andrea Kalinowski's biohistorical quilts evoke the history of immigration and religion. These digital quilt designs center on manuscript pages from journals by Jewish women who homesteaded in the American West. The challenge in this unit is not the assemblage of materials but the inaccessibility of art that leaves the public domain for private purchase. Aside from temporary exhibits, the only access to such materials is indirect or virtual.

This topic opens up the discussion to merchandising. Students become aware of how life texts can be packaged into commercial objects. They read Joanne Karpinski's "Artifacts and Life Writing" and think about classifications of art. They are often puzzled at the distinctions between an original and limited editions, lithographs, artists' books, posters, calendars, slides, videos, and assorted kitsch. Discussion may shift to geographic sites and architecture that must serve many constituencies at the same time. Pearl Harbor and a memorial in Waikiki to World War I usually come up. Over the years the memorial has been alternately refurbished and neglected depending on shifts in public sentiment and local politics. Its location in the most commercially valuable area of Hawai'i is undoubtedly a factor. At this point I expect students to be making other connections that will yield ideas for final research projects. If students are especially interested in life writing and geography, they go to the *Encyclopedia of Life Writing* (Jolly) for related entries. They also find suggestions in the archive of the International Autobiography and Biography Association's electronic discussion list, in Smith and Watson's collection *Getting a Life*, and in the Winter 2002 issue of *Biography*, which focuses on the relationship of biography to geography. Essays by Sarah Ann Wider and Ellen Percy Kraly and by Jennifer Lloyd deal with objects and artifacts rather than art.

Interacting text and visual imagery is further developed in the unit on mixed-genre texts. Roland Barthes's *Camera Lucida* impresses some students as being opaque, but they gradually understand the mix of theory, autobiography, biography, and photographs. Since they are young enough to know the most up-to-date technologies, they tend to critique his analysis and often use *Camera Lucida* and *Roland Barthes by Roland Barthes* in their final projects.

Allende's *Paula* too can be taught in the mixed-genre unit for blending letters and journal entries in present and retrospective narratives. It is also an evolving text that uses history and legend. But the choice of genre depends on the progress of Allende's seriously ill daughter. Two narratives unfold simultaneously. One centers on Paula, who is in a comatose state, and the other, triggered by changes in the medical condition, tells stories of ancestors and immediate family. The epistolary frame is a performance enacting the mother's wish that Paula is somehow receiving the text, and it's clear the narrative will be aborted when she emerges from the coma. Yet because historical and fantastic materials coalesce, students recognize that the only certainty is Paula's death, and this realization triggers debate on the relations between ethics and privacy. Students' opinions on biography and vulnerability (see Couser) and life writing and appropriation (see Fuchs, *Text*) may differ, but ethics remains central to their dialogue.

The Wilkomirski case also fits into various units—mixed-genre, archival, and fraudulent texts—and to broader discussions of posing and composing. In some ways, Binjamin Wilkomirski's *Fragments* no longer exists, since it is the short, final chapter in Stefan Maechler's archival *The Wilkomirski Affair: A Study in Biographical Truth*. By the final weeks of the seminar, students are commenting on the sequencing, wording, and tone of chapter titles. They notice that *Fragments* comes after fourteen other sections. Together, we trace directions of the Wilkomirski affair, of the events and repercussions in the context of Paul de Man's statement that life afterward may indeed be determined by what is recollected in the autobiography. Students observe ways that this remark applies to both authors. If the chapters of the discredited Holocaust memoir will be available for as long as Maechler's book is available, then Maechler's work will be around for just as long as the public is interested in Wilkomirski. It is a symbiosis worth exploring.

Contemporary events and what goes in and out of print have led to changes in the syllabus. My 2000 seminar included Cindy Sherman's film stills, Mary Lowenthal Felstiner's *To Paint Her Life: Charlotte Salomon in the Nazi Era*, selections from Salomon's *Charlotte: Life? or Theatre? An Autobiographical Play*, and Vladimir Nabokov's *Speak Memory*. My 2004 seminar concentrated on selections described in this essay. H.D.'s *The Gift*, Theresa Hak Kyung Cha's *Dictée*, parts of Amia Lieblich's *Conversations with Dvora*, Saira Shah's *Storyteller's Daughter*, Art Spiegelman's *Maus*, and Marjane Satrapi's *Persepolis* are likely choices for the next seminar.

Incidentally, interviews with the much photographed nineteenth-century Countess of Castiglione and with the twentieth-century painter Yves Klein are available for sale along with the CD *Visits with Joseph Cornell*. The researchers say there may be more on the way. After all, it's a series.

Works Cited

Adams, Timothy Dow. *Light Writing and Life Writing: Photography in Autobiography*. Chapel Hill: U of North Carolina P, 1999.

Allende, Isabel. *Paula*. Trans. Margaret Sayers Peden. New York: Harper, 1994.

Banti, Anna. *Artemisia*. Trans. Shirley D'Ardia Caracciolo. Lincoln: U of Nebraska P, 1988.

Barthes, Roland. *Camera Lucida: Reflections on Photography*. Trans. Richard Howard. New York: Hill, 1981.

——. *Roland Barthes by Roland Barthes*. Trans. Richard Howard. New York: Noonday, 1989.

Beckett, Samuel. *Not-I*. London: Faber, 1973.

Bennett, Alan. *The Lady in the Van*. London: Faber, 2000.

Bryson, Norman. "The Gaze in the Expanded Field." *Vision and Visuality: Discussions in Contemporary Culture*. Ed. Hal Foster. New York: New, 1990. 87–113.

Cha, Theresa Hak Kyung. 1995. *Dictée*. Berkeley: U of California P, 2001.

Codrescu, Andrei. "Adding to My Life." *Autobiography and Postmodernism*. Ed. Kathleen Ashley, Leigh Gilmore, and Gerald Peters. Amherst: U of Massachusetts P, 1994. 21–30.

Couser, G. Thomas. *Vulnerable Subjects: Ethics and Life Writing*. Ithaca: Cornell UP, 2003.

de Man, Paul. "Autobiography as De-facement." *MLN* 94 (1979): 919–30.

De Silva, Cara, ed. *In Memory's Kitchen: A Legacy from the Women of Terezín*. Trans. Bianca Steiner Brown. Northvale: Aronson, 1996.

Eakin, Paul John. *Fictions in Autobiography: Studies in the Art of Self-Invention*. Princeton: Princeton UP, 1985.

——. *How Our Lives Become Stories: Making Selves*. Ithaca: Cornell UP, 1999.

——. *Touching the World: Reference in Autobiography*. Princeton: Princeton UP, 1992.

Egan, Susanna. *Mirror Talk: Genres of Crisis in Contemporary Autobiography*. Chapel Hill: U of North Carolina P, 1999.

Felman, Shoshana, and Dori Laub. *Testimony: Crises of Witnessing in Literature, Psychoanalysis, and History*. New York: Routledge, 1992.

Felstiner, Mary Lowenthal. *To Paint Her Life: Charlotte Salomon in the Nazi Era*. New York: Harper, 1994.

Fuchs, Miriam. "Autobiography as Political Discourse: Lili'uokalani's *Hawaii's Story by Hawaii's Queen*." Fuchs, *Text* 29–77.

——. "The Diaries of Queen Lili'uokalani." *Profession 95*. New York: MLA, 1995. 38–40.

——. *The Text Is Myself: Women's Life Writing and Catastrophe*. Madison: U of Wisconsin P, 2004.

Gilmore, Leigh. *The Limits of Autobiography: Trauma and Testimony*. Ithaca: Cornell UP, 2001.

Hatoum, Mona. *Measures of Distance*. Prod. Western Front Video. New York: Women Make Movies, 1988.

H.D. *The Gift*. Introd. Perdita Schaffner. New York: New Directions, 1982.

Hurston, Zora Neale. 1942. *Dust Tracks on a Road: An Autobiography*. New York: Perennial, 1996.

Jolly, Margaretta, ed. *The Encyclopedia of Life Writing*. 2 vols. London: Fitzroy Dearborn, 2001.

Kalinowski, Andrea. *Stories Untold: Jewish Pioneer Women, 1850–1910*. Santa Fe: U of New Mexico Museum P, 2002.

Kaplan, Caren. "Resisting Autobiography: Out-Law Genres and Transnational Feminist Subjects." Smith and Watson, *De/Colonizing* 115–38.

Karpinski, Joanne B. "Artifacts and Life Writing." Jolly 1: 55–57.

Krauss, Rosalind E. *The Originality of the Avant-Garde and Other Modernist Myths.* Cambridge: MIT P, 1985.

Langer, Lawrence L. *Holocaust Testimonies: The Ruins of Memory.* New Haven: Yale UP, 1991.

Lejeune, Philippe. "The Autobiographical Pact (bis)." *On Autobiography.* Ed. and fwd. Paul John Eakin. Trans. Katherine Leary. Minneapolis: U of Minnesota P, 1989. 119–37.

Lieblich, Amia. *Conversations with Dvora: An Experimental Biography of the First Modern Hebrew Woman Writer.* Ed. Chana Kronfeld and Naomi Seidman. Trans. Naomi Seidman. Berkeley: U of California P, 1997.

Liliʻuokalani. *Hawaii's Story by Hawaii's Queen.* 1898. Honolulu: Mutual, 1982.

Lipton, Eunice. *Alias Olympia: A Woman's Search for Manet's Notorious Model and Her Own Desire.* New York: Scribner's, 1992.

Lloyd, Jennifer F. "Collective Memory, Commemoration, Memory, and History; or, William O'Brien, the Bible Christians, and Me." *Biography: An Interdisciplinary Quarterly* 25.1 (2002): 46–57.

Maechler, Stefan. *The Wilkomirski Affair: A Study in Biographical Truth, Including the Text of* Fragments. Trans. John E. Woods. New York: Schocken, 2001.

Momaday, N. Scott. *The Names.* New York: Harper, 1976.

Nabokov, Vladimir. *Speak, Memory: An Autobiography Revisited.* New York: Vintage, 1989.

Olney, James, ed. *Autobiography: Essays Theoretical and Critical.* Princeton: Princeton UP, 1980.

Pratt, Mary Louise. *Imperial Eyes: Travel Writing and Transculturation.* New York: Routledge, 1992.

Ringgold, Faith, perf. *The Last Story Quilt.* Written and dir. David Irving. Prod. Linda Freeman. Chappaqua: L & S Video, 1998.

Rodden, John. *Performing the Literary Interview: How Writers Craft Their Public Selves.* Lincoln: U of Nebraska P, 2001.

Rugg, Linda Haverty. *Picturing Ourselves: Photography and Autobiography.* Chicago: U of Chicago P, 1997.

Salomon, Charlotte. *Charlotte: Life? or Theatre? An Autobiographical Play.* Trans. Leila Vennewitz. Amsterdam: Jewish Historical Museum / Charlotte Salomon Foundation, 1998.

Satrapi, Marjane. *Persepolis: The Story of a Childhood.* New York: Pantheon, 2003.

Shah, Saira. *Storyteller's Daughter.* New York: Knopf, 2003.

Sherman, Cindy. *Untitled Film Stills.* Munich: Schirmer, 1998.

Silva, Noenoe K. *Aloha Betrayed: Native Hawaiian Resistance to American Colonialism.* Durham: Duke UP, 2004.

——. "Kanaka Maoli Resistance to Annexation." *ʻŌiwi: A Native Hawaiian Journal* (1998): 40–71.

Smith, Sidonie, and Julia Watson, eds. *De/Colonizing the Subject: The Politics of Gender in Women's Autobiography.* Minneapolis: U of Minnesota P, 1992.

——, eds. *Getting a Life: Everyday Uses of Autobiography.* Minneapolis: U of Minnesota P, 1996.

——. *Interfaces: Women, Autobiography, Images, Performance*. Ann Arbor: U of Michigan P, 2002.

——. *Women, Autobiography, Theory: A Reader*. Madison: U of Wisconsin P, 1998.

Spiegelman, Art. *And Here My Troubles Began*. New York: Pantheon, 1991. Vol. 2 of *Maus: A Survivor's Tale*.

——. *My Father Bleeds History*. New York: Pantheon, 1986 Vol. 1 of *Maus: A Survivor's Tale*.

Stein, Gertude. 1933. *The Autobiography of Alice B. Toklas*. New York: Vintage, 1990.

Visits With Joseph Cornell. Prod. Anne Walsh and Chris Kubrick. Archive, 2004.

Walsh, Anne, and Chris Kubrick. Abstract. "Public Programme." 29 Aug. 2003. 18 Jan. 2007 <http://www.essex.ac.uk/sos/public%20programme.htm>.

——. "Art after Death." *Life and Death*. Spec. issue of *LOG Illustrated* 14 (2001). 18 Jan. 2007 <http://www.physicsroom.org.nz/log/archive/14/artafterdeath>.

Wider, Sarah Ann, and Ellen Percy Kraly. "The Contour of Unknown Lives: Mapping Women's Experience in the Adirondacks." *Biography: An Interdisciplinary Quarterly* 25.1 (2002): 1–24.

Wilkomirski, Binjamin. *Fragments*. Maechler 375–496.

Additional Resources for Teaching Life Writing Texts: Generic Approaches

Coe, Richard. *When the Grass Was Taller: Autobiography and the Experience of Childhood*. New Haven: Yale UP, 1984.

Danahay, Martin A., ed. *Reevaluating the Boundaries of Autobiography: Theory, Practice, Pedagogy*. Spec. issue of *CEA Critic* 57.3 (1995).

Eakin, Paul John, ed. *The Ethics of Life Writing*. Ithaca: Cornell UP, 2004.

Epstein, William H., ed. *Contesting the Subject: Essays in the Postmodern Theory and Practice of Biography and Biographical Criticism*. West LaFayette: Purdue UP, 1991.

——. *Recognizing Biography*. Philadelphia: U of Pennsylvania P, 1987.

Hamilton, Nigel. *Biography: A Brief History*. Cambridge, Harvard UP, 2007.

Hirsch, Marianne. *Family Frames: Photography, Narrative, and Postmemory*. Cambridge: Harvard UP, 1997.

Jay, Paul. *Being in the Text: Self-Representation from Wordsworth to Roland Barthes*. Ithaca: Cornell UP, 1984.

Kadar, Marlene, ed. *Essays on Life Writing: From Genre to Critical Practice*. Toronto: U of Toronto P, 1992.

Lane, Jim. *The Autobiographical Documentary in America*. Madison: U of Wisconsin P, 2002.

Lejeune, Philippe, and Catherine Bogaert. *Un journal à soi: Histoire d'une pratique*. Paris: Editions Textuel, 2003.

Marcus, Laura. *Auto/biographical Discourses: Theory, Criticism, Practice*. Manchester: Manchester UP, 1994.

McAdams, Dan P., and Richard L. Ochberg, eds. *Psychobiography and Life Narratives*. Durham: Duke UP, 1989.

Nadel, Ira Bruce. *Biography: Fiction, Fact, and Form*. New York: St. Martin's, 1984.

Nussbaum, Felicity A. *The Autobiographical Subject*. 2nd ed. Baltimore: Johns Hopkins UP, 1995.

Parke, Catherine N. *Biography: Writing Lives*. New York: Twayne, 1996.

Rhiel, Mary, and David Suchoff, eds. *The Seductions of Biography*. New York: Routledge, 1996.

Roberts, Brian. *Biographical Research*. Buckingham: Open UP, 2002.

Rugg, Linda Haverty. *Picturing Ourselves: Photography and Autobiography*. Chicago: U of Chicago P, 1997.

Schultz, William Todd, ed. *Handbook of Psychobiography*. New York: Oxford UP, 2005.

Smith, Sidonie, and Kay Schaffer, eds. *Human Rights and Narrated Lives: The Ethics of Recognition*. New York: Palgrave, 2004.

Swindells, Julia. *The Uses of Autobiography*. London: Taylor, 1995.

Part II

Cultural Approaches

Michael W. Young

The Many Voices of Creation: Early American and Canadian Life Writing

When teaching the life writing of early explorers and thinkers such as John Smith and Benjamin Franklin, who helped expand the American frontier west, we in the United States often ignore similar stories from those who opened up the land to our north. In fact, for well over a hundred years, these explorers' dreams, fears, politics, hardships, and rewards were completely entwined. Studied individually or in parallel, the early life writing from what became the United States and Canada can teach us much about ourselves and our many cultures and especially about a common theme of the time: creation, whether self-creation, the re-creation of others, or the creation of a nation.

There are three obvious ways of organizing this material. There is certainly enough material for two individual courses, each devoted to one country's early life writing. I have also experimented with combining the two traditions, running them along sets of parallel tracks, each track having the theme of creation as its destination, and showing how these traditions contributed to North America's search for its identity.

One kind of undergraduate course on early American life writing is the typical American literature survey class, covering the time from the explorers up to the Civil War. An opening text I use is John Smith's *General*

History of Virginia, New England, and the Summer Isles (1624). The contrast between an early section, where Smith often refers to himself in the seemingly objective third person as Captain Smith, and a later section on New England, where he consistently praises himself, provides students with clear lessons in comparison and interpretation. Of course, the book's best-known part is Smith's revisionist adventure with Powhatan and Pocahontas, and it is entertaining and instructive for students to compare this version, the one that made Smith famous, with other historical accounts of Pocahontas's life—and even with the Disney animated movie—to make students understand the fluidity of both history and literature.

A good counterpoint to Smith's grandiose vision is *A Narrative of the Captivity of Mrs. Mary Rowlandson* (1676). Captivity stories were popular in their time, and, like Smith's twisted version, they helped shape European and settlers' understanding of the native people. Often these stories tell of great savagery by their captors, as Rowlandson's tale does, but her *Narrative* also depicts the Indians' orderly society. After weeks of reading letters and journals, my students appreciate her work because it is structured as if there were a plot and because there are main characters: Mary, King Philip, his wife, Mary's children, and John Hoar. The students come to see that Mary's nearly constant references to the Bible signify her trust in a divine order, a faith that helps lead eventually to freedom.

That belief system is then a good transition to a very different, eminently canonical work: Benjamin Franklin's *Autobiography*. The beginning of the first section, which speaks reverently of God and Franklin's debt to the Almighty, also gives a compelling look into the average colonist's life. Because Franklin was the youngest son in an obscure family with seventeen children, his chances for success were slim, but his constant hard work and reliance on self-education helped define later generations' belief in a self-created individual. As he presents his evidence, especially in the book's second section, he also shows his sense of humor. Writing in a different tone, he explains how he tried to perfect himself through his page of virtues. I use a document camera—a gadget Franklin would have loved—to project the sample page on a screen, and I have my students work together through his densely packed prose. In this way, they replicate the ironically earnest pursuit of perfection by a man who preached an intemperate mode of ambition.

Franklin's *Autobiography* is a cornerstone for much of the literary, political, and philosophical writing that followed. The Declaration of Independence is built on the premise that a community of self-created individuals may choose its form of rule and its leaders. It is, in effect, a self-created government, and, through Thomas Jefferson's autobiographical writing, students can see how much further Jefferson had wished to push that argument in his draft of the declaration. Again, the document camera allows easy visual comparisons of the texts. I then use Ralph Waldo Emerson's essay "Self-Reliance" to show the continuing call for the creation of an independent self and Henry David Thoreau's *Walden* to show a literal search for personal discovery. Finally Frederick Douglass's *Narrative* of his life, through its powerful condemnation of slavery and Franklinesque story of ambition despite society's obstacles, combines with the earlier texts to affirm a belief in what may be, not just what is, for individuals and for the nation.

If the class creates lists of similarities and differences between Franklin's and Douglass's lives, the dynamics of their experiences quickly become evident. Another useful lesson for novice readers is to show that despite the parallels that may be drawn among these four influential and overlapping Americans' lives and philosophies, their writing styles—word choice, tone, rhetorical structure, first-person voice—are very different. Still, their works all support a new belief in what may be.

A course on Canadian life writing could follow a similar sequence, starting, for instance, with the writings of Samuel de Champlain, whose works were among the first books to introduce the New World to Europe. *Des sauvages* (1603), *Les voyages de la Nouvell France* (1632), and his other works were translated from French into other languages soon after their first publication. Champlain describes in detail the land, climate, and native people, and, compared with the dramatic Smith, his work can come across as overly concrete and dry—still very much a captain's log. But he was an explorer, not a novelist. Historical maps of North America are excellent resources during these lessons, and many history texts and Web sites show what lands were under the rule of various indigenous or colonial nations.

While the Jesuits were not the only order of missionary priests in the New World, they sent back to France and published to great acclaim volumes of the *Jesuit Relations* every year from 1632 to 1672, fixing additional images of the New World for generations. These amazing collections contain letters and reports from the missionaries as they spread out over New France—an area that today extends from the Maritime (or Atlantic) provinces of Canada through the Great Lakes and down the Mississippi River—and provide some of the most complete colonial records of life, culture, politics, and early anthropological study. At the outset of studying these letters and reports, one strategy is to ask the class to identify the cultural stereotypes of native people—especially the established ones shown in older popular culture—and then to compare them with the *Relations'* descriptions that contributed to the formation of many of them.

The first great author and editor of the *Relations* is Father Paul Le Jeune, whose stories of surviving the harsh winters and of learning about, and then beginning the conversion of, the Algonquin-Montagnais people helped fire the French imagination. Another writer well suited for a course in early Canadian life writing is Father Jean de Brébeuf, whose particular mission was befriending and converting the Hurons. This mission began in 1629, and Father de Brébeuf soon wrote detailed accounts of Huron creation myths, ceremonial dances, politics, and belief in the power of dreams. (He was tortured and killed during a war with the Iroquois in 1649 and later canonized.)

Not all of the articles in the *Relations*, however, show respect for the Indians, since the priests often write despairingly of native cultures and morality, reinforcing stereotypes. The *Relations* also tells of the long negotiations that led to peace in New France but that created allegiances that played a bloody part in the French and Indian Wars. In addition, the *Relations* contains exploration stories by Louis Joliet and the missionary Jacques Marquette, as they traveled down the Mississippi River.

Even after the *Relations* was discontinued, stories like that of Kateri Tekakwitha, a member of the Mohawk, were published as examples of Catholicism thriving in the wilderness and especially of what was considered to be a saintly life for a woman. Together, these tales created an understanding of the New World for its conquerors as dangerous, exotic, and idyllic.

Any course in Canadian life writing has to consider tales of the great arctic explorers trying to find the fabled Northwest Passage. Considering the differences in media, they were as famous and lionized in their day as astronauts were in the 1960s and 1970s. One of the first was Samuel Hearne, who published his exploits in *Journey from Prince of Wales Fort in Hudson's Bay to the Northern Ocean* (1795), a story credited with being the inspiration for Coleridge's *The Rime of the Ancient Mariner*. Then came Alexander Mackenzie's *Voyages from Montreal on the River St. Laurence: Through the Continent of North America to the Frozen and Pacific Oceans in the Years 1789 and 1793* (1801). Mackenzie was the first explorer to cross the entire continent, and his readers ranged from Napoléon to Lewis and

Clark. But the most romantic, in an almost gothic way, are the stories by and about John Franklin. His *Narrative of a Journey to the Polar Sea* (1823) describes one of his early expeditions, and his fame and standing continued to grow even after his last expedition, in 1847, which took his life. To this day, no trace of him has been found.

Like the United States, Canada has writers of the frontier who dealt with harsh terrain, their fear of indigenous peoples (the First Nations), and the quest to complete a transcontinental railroad. A major difference, which students come to understand, is that Canada was a cluster of British colonies until 1867, when Confederation created the Dominion of Canada. As a result, many Canadian frontier writers show strong signs of writing for British readers. Among the most famous are the Strickland sisters: Catherine Parr (C. P.) Traill and Susanna Moodie. Traill's *Backwoods of Canada: Being Letters from the Wife of an Emigrant Officer* (1836) and Moodie's *Roughing It in the Bush* (1852) and *Letters of Love and Duty: The Correspondence of Susanna and John Moodie* are keystones in the formation of Canadian letters. Moodie's style shows a greater desire to be literary—some of her poetry on colonial life for women is reminiscent of Anne Bradstreet's—while Traill wrote her many works in a more straightforward style. Both writers told of the hard work of adapting to the new land, but at the same time—echoing Franklin—they recognized the success that hard work and opportunity can bring. The second subtitle of Traill's book is telling: *Illustrative of Domestic Economy in British America.*

All the American literature mentioned here, as well as life writing by William Bradford, Olaudah Equiano, and many others, and excerpts from Champlain's journals are available in the *Norton Anthology of American Literature*, sixth edition, package 1 (vols. A and B). The other Canadian work has been regularly reprinted in many places, including online. Two recent paperbacks, *Jesuit Relations* and *The Journals of Alexander Mackenzie: Exploring across Canada in 1789 and 1793*, provide excellent texts. The new *Relations* book is both a translation and a manageable set of excerpts from the huge yearly editions. An instructor may also wish to use recent creative responses to these texts, such as Farley Mowat's *Coppermine Journey*, spun from Samuel Hearne's journals, or Margaret Atwood's *The Journals of Susanna Moodie*, a set of poems written in Moodie's voice. An excellent one-volume reference is W. H. New's *A History of Canadian Literature.*

As more and more classrooms are outfitted with computers and projection systems, the Internet can play an important role in teaching this kind of course. The *American Memory* collection of pictures, maps, and manu-scripts is available from the Library of Congress at http://memory.loc.gov. The National Library of Canada and the National Archive of Canada are accessible through the Web site www.nlc-bnc.ca, and elaborate sites may also be found at the Digital Library of Canada (www.collectionscanada.ca), which includes links to sites like online exhibitions. Links to copies of man-uscripts of the Stricklands and the *Images Canada* collection are especially helpful.

The writers mentioned here can be usefully studied to show how cre-ating their successes, philosophies, and even freedom led them to become role models for one another and for subsequent generations. By creating for the rest of the world what had been unknown, each writer is a revolu-tionary of sorts, challenging the status quo while contributing to North America's creation of its identities. These writers' allegiances were not to France or England, to Canada or America, to North or South, but to the New, and sharing their works can preserve part of that spirit.

Works Cited

American Memory. Library of Congress. 10 Aug. 2006 <http://memory.loc.gov>.

Atwood, Margaret. *The Journals of Susanna Moodie*. Toronto: Oxford UP, 1970.

The Jesuit Relations: Natives and Missionaries in Seventeenth-Century North America. Ed. and introd. Allan Greer. Boston: Bedford–St. Martin's, 2000.

Mackenzie, Alexander. *The Journals of Alexander Mackenzie: Exploring across Canada in 1789 and 1793*. Santa Barbara: Narrative, 2001.

Mowat, Farley. *Coppermine Journey: An Account of a Great Adventure. Selected from the Journals of Samuel Hearne*. 1958. Boston: Little, 1990.

New, W. H. *A History of Canadian Literature*. Montreal: McGill-Queen's UP, 2003.

Norton Anthology of American Literature. Ed. Nina Baym. 6th ed. Package 1: vols. A and B. New York: Norton, 2003.

Kathleen Boardman

Experiencing Collaborative Autobiography

Although scholars and critics of life writing are more or less comfortable with the concept of collaborative autobiography, undergraduates often find this type of memoir troubling and confusing—a challenge to their assumptions about truth and autonomy. Expecting autobiography to be simply "a narrative of a person's life, written by himself" (Cox 145), they soon must confront a disorienting array of cowritten, ghostwritten, as-told-to, and other collaborative texts. The resulting sense of dissonance provides a good starting point for an exploration of key issues, not only for collaborative autobiography, but also for life writing in general. Therefore a unit specifically addressing collaborative autobiography appears in any course I teach that deals with memoir.

This unit, which includes two or three collaboratively produced texts, plays an important role in two upper-division undergraduate capstone courses I teach.[1] American Autobiography, an English course, explores memory, truth telling, textual ownership, self-representation, genre and form, and cultural identity. To discuss collaboration, I have paired *Black Elk Speaks* with *The Narrative of the Life of Mrs. Mary Jemison* (Seaver) or *The Autobiography of Malcolm X* with *Mourning Dove: A Salishan Autobiography* or John Edgar Wideman's *Brothers and Keepers*. I have not yet included a ghostwritten celebrity memoir on the required reading list, but students often draw on their own experience of reading such memoirs of pop culture figures.

Team-taught and cross-listed in Anthropology and English, the second course, Native and European American Literature, includes a substantial unit entitled "Whose Story Is It, Anyway?" Here we deal with non-Indian authors' uses of traditional Indian stories and Indian personae, with ethnographic practice, and with as-told-to autobiographies. *Black Elk Speaks* is usually a good choice because of the wealth of commentary available on the methods and ethics of the production of this text. We have paired it with Ruth M. Underhill and Maria Chona's *Papago Woman* and with Mary Ellicott Arnold's and Mabel Reed's *In the Land of the Grasshopper Song*.

In both courses, students develop their critical reading of collaborative texts by focusing on the circumstances and ethics of textual production. Evidence for our discussions appears within and outside the texts, in historical records and author or eyewitness commentaries. Students' own experience of doing as-told-to life writing also helps them understand *what happened* when a certain text was produced and *what happens* when a subject and a writer collaborate on a life story.

Students are most familiar with ghostwritten celebrity memoirs, in which "the subjects typically outrank writers in wealth and clout" (Couser, "Making" 40), and the final product obliterates the interview questions and conversations that allowed the writer to gather material, turning the two voices into one. This would have happened in Malcolm X's *Autobiography*, except that in the extensive epilogue, the writer Alex Haley makes himself visible. Not only does he describe the interview process, but he also discusses his strategies for persuading Malcolm to speak openly on certain topics and recalls occasions when the collaboration threatened to break down. And in both the autobiography and epilogue, Haley includes Malcolm's comments on the process—his noting, for example, how difficult it is to represent a self that seems always to be changing.

Examples of ethnographic autobiography, which G. Thomas Couser places at the other end of the continuum from celebrity memoir because the power balance is reversed ("Making" 40), introduce students to issues of cross-cultural collaboration—or, as Arthur Krupat terms it, "original bicultural composite composition" (31). When Nicholas Black Elk told John Neihardt about his life, Black Elk's son translated the Lakota into English,

Neihardt's daughter took shorthand, and Neihardt himself (as he later asserted) selected the stories that would go into the book and wrote the beginning and ending. Claiming a common ground of spirituality with his subject, Neihardt was confident that he had represented Black Elk correctly. A few decades later, the release of the interview transcripts led to a split decision on the authenticity of *Black Elk Speaks*. The Lakota activist Vine Deloria wrote a complimentary introduction to the new edition, but Couser was more critical in "Black Elk Speaks with Forked Tongue."

Underhill's introduction to *Papago Woman: The Autobiography of Maria Chona* explains how Underhill met Chona and gathered her stories with the help of translators. She includes a brief memoir of her own, describing her stay at Chona's village and her efforts to learn the language. Despite the challenges of translation, Underhill (like Neihardt) insists that "the wording expresses Chona's thought as accurately as may be" but adds immediately that the arrangement of material is not Chona's, acknowledging that the autobiography "has elaboration and emphasis at some points where she [Chona] would not have placed them, and it stops short where she would have found repetition comfortable. It is an Indian story told to satisfy whites rather than Indians" (33). But Chona may also have exercised some editorial control by withholding information from this collaboration. In one description of a ceremony, for instance, she declares cryptically, "The song is very short because we understand so much" (51).

In such examples students can see that, while the writers may not have *made up* the details of the story, they have *made* the story by shaping and arranging details in ways that seem natural to them, but perhaps not so to the subjects. The process is still more complicated than it might appear, for writers cannot simply appropriate whatever they want from the subjects, because the subjects have ideas—and silences—of their own.

Another interesting case is *Mourning Dove: A Salishan Autobiography*. Mourning Dove saw herself as a cultural broker, with the task of bringing traditional Salishan culture and mainstream European American culture together. She actively sought editorial help with both language and form and was explicit about aiming to produce a story that would appeal to whites. She left her manuscript with someone who seemed enthusiastic about reworking it, and, according to the editor, Jay Miller, she "undoubtedly hoped for a speedy revision" (xxxii). Nevertheless, only after her death was her autobiography revised and edited—by several different people, with the collaboration of her family. Thus, although Mourning Dove was no more able to review the final result than Chona was, the result is in keeping with her original stated intentions.

I do not ask my students (mostly nonmajors) to read great amounts of criticism; however, once we have talked about the ways that the collaborative autobiographies have been written, I ask them to evaluate the explanatory power of critical statements like these:

> Collaboration blurs in a disturbing way the question of responsibility, and even damages the notion of identity. The model and the writer both tend to believe that they are the principal, if not the only, "author" of the text. . . . [I]t is true that the "life" in question belongs to both of them—but perhaps also, for the same reason, belongs neither to one nor to the other. Would not the literary and social form of the life story, which preexisted their undertaking, be the "author" to both of them? (Lejeune 192)

> The roles of a coaxer in assembling a life narrative can be more coercive than collaborative. . . . In giving thematic shape to the narrative by virtue of decisions about what is included or excluded, a coaxer can subordinate the narrator's modes and choices of storytelling to another idea of how a life story should read and how its subject should speak appropriately. (Smith and Watson 55)

> Unlike Indian biographies, Indian autobiographies require contact with living Indians, for it is the central convention of autobiography that the subject speaks for himself. And it is in its presentation of an Indian voice not as vanished and silent, but as still living and able to be heard, that the oppositional potential of Indian autobiography resides. (Krupat 35)

Awareness of how collaborative life writing is produced and of the ethical issues involved often leads students to condemn misrepresentations, appropriation, ambiguous ethical choices, and other "errors" they locate in the texts. Some become cynical about the value of any collaborative life writing if they feel they cannot separate subject from writer, or they become judgmental of anyone who would engage in such ethically ambiguous writing practices. Other students prefer that we all just "get over it," read the text on the page, and be happy. These positions can serve as starting points for pushing on to more dynamic conversations that recognize both the oppositional potential and interlocking understandings represented by collaborative texts. Task-oriented collaborative projects help students break out of prefabricated either-or positions, because they let students approach the genre not only from the outside (as readers) but also from the inside (as writers and subjects).

We began one such project by evaluating the editorial options taken in the texts already studied. Some writers were "self-conscious editors," who made self-referential statements at various points, while others opted to be "absent editors," invisible in the text. Working as partners over a period of three weeks, students tried out some of the techniques. After the writing partners interviewed each other, each student produced a draft of a fragment of the partner's autobiography. The subjects commented on the manuscripts, and each student produced a revised as-told-to or ghost-written autobiographical essay—and a written response to the whole project, reflecting on the questions raised. These responses show some interesting shifts in perspective. As readers, students had been preoccupied with accuracy and access to facts. As writers and subjects, however, they became more interested in issues of authorship, in workable modes of collaboration, and in equitable representation of the other, posing questions about how to negotiate style and voice, how to balance the writer's wish for coherence against the subject's preference for privacy, and so on.

Many students begin this collaborative project assuming that they will only be transcribing their partner's words, but they quickly find themselves entangled in questions of voice, style, and ownership. For example, one student reported feeling like a fake because he was writing a story he didn't see as his own. Another observed that, despite his intention to report his partner's story just as he heard it, he had nevertheless interpreted her words, utilized his own style of writing, and ultimately (in the judgment of both collaborators) failed to convey his partner's story as she would have presented it. In this way, for some students, a sense of the difficulty and subtlety of this writing process replaced their earlier naive acceptance or easy condemnation of collaborative autobiography.

Students doing such an exercise also experience some of the problems and insights familiar to subjects of collaborative life writing. One student provided a powerful example of the impact of differences in cultural background and individual interests. For him, the most important story to tell was of the time he broke both legs at the age of thirteen. His writing partner, however, was less interested in this experience than in the details of his American childhood because her Mexican upbringing had been quite different.

Another student commented on the importance of physical and cultural context to the meaning of anyone's life story—observing that the solo autobiographer, but not necessarily the as-told-to collaborator, would have rich experience of these contexts. She concluded that anyone who wished to do a good job of ghostwriting her autobiography would need to do three things: spend time with her, interview the people who were close to her, and take note of her reaction to the ghostwriter's own cultural environment. Although she granted that collaborative autobiography would always, inevitably, involve some fictionalizing, she also maintained that the ghostwriter or collaborator might be able to reveal important truths to the person whose life was being written. This insight came out of her own cultural tradition, which viewed ghosts as carriers of important messages.

When transcripts and alternative accounts are available, students can use questions like the following to trace the dynamics and ethics of collaboration: Who initiated the project? Who has control of which facets? Who looked at the final product? Who organized the material? Who edited the work? Who developed and who asked the questions? Whose style and whose language predominated, and at what stages of the project? What strategies did autobiographical subjects use to circumvent editorial management? For some texts on our class reading list, the answers to many of these questions are not available. But students currently working on their own collaborative life writing can answer all these questions about their own projects.

Although the special issues of collaborative autobiography have their own unit in the course, I do not leave them there. Many problems arising in our discussions of ghostwriting, cowriting, and bicultural collaborations reappear in the more typical forms of solo autobiography. For example, collaborative life stories upset some deeply held commonsense notions about the nature of autobiography as "the life of the subject, written by himself," for in them the "I" is always written by someone else. But as Lejeune observes, "Autobiography by people who do not write throws light on autobiography written by those who do: the imitation reveals the secrets of fabrication and functioning of the 'natural' product" (186). Many single-author autobiographies also involve interviews with family members, advice from fellow writers, and negotiations with editors. Ethical issues dealing with ownership abound in solo texts as well. Far from being merely a special case or even a marginal subgenre, collaborative writing can be central to an understanding of life writing.

Note

1. Students at my university must take two capstone courses in their senior year—at least one of them outside their major. A course is approved as a capstone offering if it meets five criteria: it builds on basic ideas or concepts students have learned in their lower-division general studies (core) courses; it is integrative and, if possible, interdisciplinary; it deals at some point with ethical issues; it includes a strong discussion component and promotes critical thinking; and it requires a substantial amount of writing. Thus most of the students in the courses I describe are not English majors, but they expect to do a good deal of reading, writing, and discussing; they also know they will be expected to make connections between the materials in the course and some of the key issues in their own major fields of study.

Works Cited

Arnold, Mary Ellicott, and Mabel Reed. *In the Land of the Grasshopper Song.* 1957. Lincoln: U of Nebraska P, 1980.

Black Elk. *Black Elk Speaks: Being the Life Story of a Holy Man of the Ogalala Sioux as Told to John G. Neihardt.* New York: Morrow, 1932.

Couser, G. Thomas. "Black Elk Speaks with Forked Tongue." *Studies in Autobiography.* Ed. James Olney. Oxford: Oxford UP, 1988. 73–88.

———. "Making, Taking, and Faking Lives: Voice and Vulnerability in Collaborative Life Writing." *Vulnerable Subjects: Ethics and Life Writing.* Ithaca: Cornell UP, 2004. 34–55.

Cox, James M. "Autobiography and America." *Aspects of Narrative: Selected Papers from the English Institute.* Ed. J. Hillis Miller. New York: Columbia UP, 1971. 143–72.

Deloria, Vine, Jr. Introduction. *Black Elk Speaks: Being the Life Story of a Holy Man of the Ogalala Sioux as Told through John G. Neihardt (Flaming Rainbow).* Lincoln: U of Nebraska P, 1961. xi–xiv.

Krupat, Arnold. *For Those Who Come After: A Study of Native American Autobiography.* Berkeley: U of California P, 1985.

Lejeune, Philippe. *On Autobiography.* Ed. and fwd. Paul John Eakin. Trans. Katherine Leary. Minneapolis: U of Minnesota P, 1989.

Malcolm X, with the assistance of Alex Haley. *The Autobiography of Malcolm X.* New York: Grove, 1965.

Mourning Dove (Christine Quintasket). *Mourning Dove: A Salishan Autobiography.* Ed. Jay Miller. Lincoln: U of Nebraska P, 1990.

Seaver, James E., ed. *A Narrative of the Life of Mrs. Mary Jemison.* Ed. and introd. June Namias. Norman: U of Oklahoma P, 1992.

Smith, Sidonie, and Julia Watson. *Reading Autobiography: A Guide for Interpreting Life Narratives.* Minneapolis: U of Minnesota P, 2001.

Underhill, Ruth M. *Papago Woman: The Autobiography of Maria Chona.* 1936. Prospect Heights: Waveland, 1985.

Wideman, John Edgar. *Brothers and Keepers.* New York: Holt, Rinehart, 1984.

Richard Freadman

Teaching Contemporary
Australian Autobiography

Academic subjects are often shaped by passion, pressure, and happenstance. If they have been on offer for more than a few years, they tend to have complex histories of adjustment to changing societal circumstances and shifting patterns of institutional need. All this applies to La Trobe University's English 2/3 GUA: Growing Up in Australia.

In any given year, La Trobe's English program offers a set of single-semester life writing units: often a first-year creative nonfiction course, GUA, and two other second- and third-year subjects—one on writing creative nonfiction, another an academic course on postcoloniality or indigeneity. Most years there's a fourth-year honors academic unit on biography and autobiography. While our students cannot take a submajor or a niche degree in life writing, they can follow a loosely structured sequence of courses in the area. Quite a number proceed to graduate (in Australian parlance, postgraduate) life writing studies.

GUA, which can be taken either as a first- or a second-year course, has been on the books for eleven years. Nowadays it attracts an enrollment of 125 students. In the early days GUA (then GRO) focused on the growing-up experience in fictional autobiography and novels, as well as on autobiography proper. In Australia, growing-up stories have been perennial favorites, the Australian tradition being heavily inflected by Romantic myths of bush innocence and adult moral decline. But the publication in 1966 of Hal Porter's *The Watcher on the Cast-Iron Balcony: An Australian Autobiography* heightened interest in the genre as an art form that could provide more sophisticated representations of childhood. In the 1980s several anthologies appeared, and 1990 saw the advent of Joy Hooton's landmark study *Stories of Herself When Young: Autobiographies of Childhood by Australian Women*.

Such was the situation in which my colleague David Tacey, an Australianist with deep interests in archetypal psychology, established English GRO in 1993. I gratefully inherited the course in 1996 and set about refocusing it, but without changing its title. Why refocus? My personal research interests played a part, and I was also thinking about the course's place in what was becoming a more structured set of La Trobe life writing options: with other life writing offerings coming into being, a general introduction to Australian autobiography that restricted itself to autobiography proper seemed desirable, and after departmental approval, that is what GRO became. We retained the title because it had proven student appeal and still gave a fair impression of the orientation of course texts. (GRO eventually became GUA to satisfy new handbook nomenclature requirements.)

While my own preferences played their part, the changes arose principally from cultural pressures. GUA needed to reflect shifts in progressive Australian consciousness: greater openness to multiculturalism, more urgent concern with indigeneity and the stories Aboriginal Australians were publishing in significant numbers in the 1980s, an increasing tendency to link Australian republicanism to a more nuanced critique of postcoloniality, and greater openness about gender and sexuality. Though these shifts were apparent in the media and in social movements, they were even more evident in the unprecedented numbers of autobiographies being published. Patrick White's classic *Flaws in the Glass: A Self-Portrait* had already provided a powerful template for new-wave autobiographical writing. It featured acerbic, if idiosyncratic, postcolonial critique, feistily unapologetic openness about his homosexuality, and the literary sophistication of a great novelist. Sally Morgan's *My Place* was another pathfinding text and the first of many significant works of indigenous autobiography that have appeared since—generally through the estranging world of white commercial publishing.

Developments in literary and cultural theory have also heavily influenced GUA's history. Indeed, the subject's emergence in 1993 reflected a departmental decision to diversify its syllabi, giving greater representation to noncanonical texts and to theory itself. GUA needed—and wanted—to reflect these developments. Additionally there were the usual challenges of content coverage. Could this fourteen-week course featuring five prescribed texts adequately reflect standard themes in the Australian autobiographical tradition: bush and city; convict stories; the settler experience; childhood; place and space; race, ethnicity, and migration; problems of belief; expatriate stories; gender; Romantic individualism, class, and egalitarianism? Clearly not. And never mind the less standard themes. The best we could do was select main texts with care and provide plenty of survey-style follow-up: introductory synoptic lectures, anthologies, essays, book-length studies.

The GUA course description currently reads thus:

> In the subject students will focus on autobiographies by Australians from diverse backgrounds: an indigenous Australian woman; two major male novelists; a gay poet from a legendary sporting family; an adopted woman who discovers the identity of her famous and tragic biological mother. Issues include: the family; how "mainstream" Australian values and myths influence the development of the individual; how these values and myths interact with attitudes and beliefs held by Australian minority groups; the meanings of "elsewhere" for those who grow up in Australia; parent-child relations; indigeneity; sexuality and gender ideology; disability; and life-writing in a multi-cultural society.

The course tries to satisfy several requirements. It promotes detailed engagements with particular texts—we retain with pride the department's earlier emphasis on subtle close reading. It presents course texts in their wider historical and social context but cautions against reductive accounts of the text-context relation; and it endeavors to acquaint students with autobiography and its surrounding secondary literature. In some years, we also run workshops for those keen to write autobiography.

What is the subject's methodological orientation? The best answer to that question is pluralism—in text selection and in theoretical and critical approaches. We say—and I think we are true to our word—that in assessing student work, we will value all approaches equally (provided, of course, that they exhibit appropriate ethical sensitivity on social issues). Is such pluralism really just a front for a humanism that eschews the commitments required by identity politics? Insofar as no one set of identity claims structures the subject, yes; but lectures and seminars air identity claims of various kinds, and most student essays are deeply sympathetic to such claims. Does my humanism—a position openly espoused in my work on theory and autobiography—pervade the subject? Well, yes: we tend to treat autobiographers as agents, albeit ideologically constrained ones, and their texts as acts of substantial, albeit ideologically mediated, representation and self-expression. But there is no denying the situatedness of texts, nor is there any desire to suppress counterhumanist perspectives. Sidonie Smith and Julia Watson's *Reading Autobiography* is recommended reading; the postgraduate tutors are encouraged to do it their way, and often theirs is the way of identity politics. In planning lectures we also try to air various perspectives, including those from other disciplines. (A lecture on motherhood in Australia, for example, is given by a feminist from the sociology department.)

In order of study, the current GUA texts are David Malouf's *12 Edmondstone Street*, Susanne Chick's *Searching for Charmian*, Roberta Sykes's *Snake Cradle*, Peter Rose's *Rose Boys*, and White's *Flaws in the Glass*. The list aspires to broadly representative coverage and to stylistic diversity. Though the figure of the other threads its way through the texts and seminar and lecture discussions, we want seminar groups to pursue the topics that most interest them. It's impossible to capture the diversity of class discussion, but the following are some text-specific samples.

We start with Malouf because he is so deeply interested in the conditions of autobiographical possibility: the nature of memory; the ways of the imagination; the shaping power of place, space, and ideology—including ideology's imprint on the body. Malouf isn't introspective, but he conjures up an almost magical, miniaturized childhood world, infused by an essentially sanguine metaphysic of separation and reconnection. The other here is a childhood self with whom he craves reunion. His sanguinity resides in the conviction that "the world is full of odd, undisclosed connections" (51).

Chick encounters the other when she learns in adulthood that her biological mother was the celebrated Australian bohemian novelist Charmian Clift. The discovery is both empowering and disturbing, for Clift had killed herself at the age of forty-six. Chick's account of her search for Charmian centers on the problems of identity. The book's central metaphor for identity formation—a necklace that incorporates new pieces, thereby changing its overall design (348)—provides an important course theme, as does Chick's juxtaposition of bohemian expatriate life and the still sometimes sleepy security of postwar Australian suburbia.

Sykes also uses autobiography to probe riddles of identity, not least because her mother refused to reveal the identity of her father. It seems likely that he was African American and that her "white" mother, who exhibits nascent racist attitudes, had aboriginal blood. Sykes's preoccupation with "terrible secrets" (68) and haunting silence is typical of much Australian indigenous autobiography. Though not one of the Stolen Generation who were forcibly removed from their families by white authorities, she shares the terrors and perplexities associated with lost histories, occluded personal identities. Like most indigenous autobiographers, Sykes addresses her audience through the displacing protocols of white commercial publishing, with its commitments to Western conceptions of autobiographical narrative. She writes in a plain style common in indigenous autobiography—a momentous choice given her advanced tertiary education (an MA from Harvard). Sykes figures personal identity in deeply relational and symbolic terms: an identification with snakes symbolizes and helps structure her identity. There is no more horrific example of racial othering and its associated viciousness in Australian autobiography than her description of the pack rape she suffered at the age of seventeen.

Rose Boys tracks the lives of two brothers born into one of Australia's great football dynasties. Robert, the elder, is a brilliant athlete; Peter, the author, is gay and a poet—a sort of dynastic other. When a car accident renders Robert quadriplegic, wrenching him from the "virile nirvana" (24) of Australian masculinity, he finds himself in the stigmatized no-man's-land of profound disability. Thus do the life trajectories of brothers "so close yet so incongruous meet improbably in this shifting text" (27). Peter seeks the fullest possible recognition of the narrative's subject, Robert, but the text is also deeply introspective. *Rose Boys* is perhaps best termed a relational memoir.

The lacerating gay critic of middle-class Australian mores and the archetypally fierce, self-loathing writer-genius, White is the other embodied—a figure of fear and awe for the culture to which he returned after many years abroad. Refusing consistent chronology, *Flaws in the Glass* works through poetically charged vignettes, wild emotional swings, and symbols that veer between prophetic and bathetic. The other here is the land and its absent god, who summon White, a sort of Job of slops. Feeding the dogs on his New South Wales farm, White slips and finds himself lying "where I had fallen, half-blinded by rain, under a pale sky, cursing through watery lips a God in whom I did not believe" (144). White's avowedly "fragmented character" (32) again focuses course discussion on identity issues, and his ambiguous title, which asks whether this autobiography's flaws lie in its author-subject or in the representational medium itself, brings us back, at the end, to questions of language, genre, and representation.

Give me a second semester for GUA and I'll give you a tighter, better-integrated, more capacious course. But for all its present "flaws," the current subject is a pleasure to teach.

Works Cited

Chick, Susanne. *Searching for Charmian: The Daughter Charmian Clift Gave Away Discovers the Mother She Never Knew*. Melbourne: Macmillan, 1994.

Freadman, Richard. *Threads of Life: Autobiography and the Will*. Chicago: U of Chicago P, 2001.

Freadman, Richard, and Seumus Miller. *Rethinking Theory: A Critique of Contemporary Literary Theory and an Alternative Account*. Cambridge: Cambridge UP, 1992.

Hooton, Joy. *Stories of Herself When Young: Autobiographies of Childhood by Australian Women*. Melbourne: Oxford UP, 1990.

Malouf, David. *12 Edmondstone Street*. Melbourne: Penguin, 1986.

Morgan, Sally. *My Place*. Perth: Fremantle Arts Centre, 1987.

Porter, Hal. *The Watcher on the Cast-Iron Balcony: An Australian Autobiography*. London: Faber, 1966.

Rose, Peter. *Rose Boys*. Sydney: Allen, 2001.

Smith, Sidonie, and Julia Watson. *Reading Autobiography: A Guide for Interpreting Life Narratives*. Minneapolis: U of Minnesota P, 2001.

Sykes, Roberta. *Snake Cradle*. Sydney: Allen, 1997.

White, Patrick. *Flaws in the Glass*. London: Penguin, 1983.

Gillian Whitlock and Kate Douglas

Located Subjects

In *Teaching Literature*, Elaine Showalter argues that the genres of literary study contain their own guidelines for classroom method and practice. Our genre is autobiography, taught at a time and in a place of extraordinary opportunity for undergraduate classroom practice. We acknowledge the importance and necessity of taking up a genre as Showalter suggests, but we make two critical additions—pedagogy and location—because the practice of teaching in a particular historical and cultural location is crucial to what we do with literary genres, and so too is how we think about effective learning.

Pedagogy

We share an implicit theory of teaching. Recently in Australia there has been an increasing emphasis on the formal training of teachers in higher education, and each of us has been awarded an accredited Certificate in Higher Education. Although we completed these programs at different universities and at opposite ends of the career cycle, we have both been trained into thinking about pedagogy in terms of specific paradigms and strategies that promote certain concepts of good learning. To rephrase

214

this autobiographically and precisely: we have been trained into a particular discipline of professional practice that draws heavily on the constructivist approach of researchers such as Paul Ramsden and John Biggs. Thus we share student-centered learning as an approach. Rather than concentrate on the lecture, we design courses by focusing on what the students will do, with a view to incorporating diverse sources, resources, and activities. Lectures are important as a way of performing our passionate commitment to the subject, but not to transmit key content. If we want students to grasp a significant idea or concept (such as interpellation or reader positioning or testimony), it is best done in practice—theirs. All course activities—from aims to methods to assessment—are aligned to the idea that good learning happens when students generate ideas, analyze readings, and "own" the course. There is nothing implicit in our strategies: we repeatedly tell the students the reasons we've designed the course the way we have.

An ongoing portfolio ensures that all work completed during the course (from major essays to lecture notes to in-class reflective writing pieces) counts toward student assessment, and students are constantly engaged in practical work. They are encouraged to connect all the learning activities they complete, but, most important, they are required to reflect on everything they hear, read, and say during the course. The portfolio is a formative assessment piece: students share their portfolio work with one another and with their tutor, gaining feedback that markedly affects subsequent work. They also bring different types of autobiographical texts to class during the semester (newspaper or magazine clippings, books, television clips, photographs, and other personal items—anything relevant to the topic we are covering that week) and apply autobiographical theory and concepts to critical readings of this primary material. Thus the students' choices and reflections significantly influence the development of the courses.

The two undergraduate courses we taught in 2002–03 at the University of Queensland in Brisbane (Postcolonialism and Australian Lives) brought together a diverse cohort: some in their second year and recently out of high school, some mature-age students, some doing a literature major, and others doing a few subjects in English as part of a degree in psychology or engineering or law. There also were many study-abroad students from North America and Europe, studying for six or twelve months in a place they often think of as exotic. It was therefore essential to

think about how such a diverse group of people might be constructed autobiographically as national subjects—or not. (The presence of overseas
students was a bonus, allowing for some comparative thinking.) To take
these students forward into a terrain where we wanted them to begin to
feel uncertain and critical about the self was the challenge that our pedagogy had to address and the reason the courses proved to be a pleasure to
teach, producing unexpected and rich insights into autobiography for the
students and for us.

Student diversity could have made pitching the course content difficult. While some students were ready for a sophisticated discussion of the
significance of Paul Keating's new biography, other students had never
heard of the ex–prime minister. Two strategies addressed this problem
through learning activities and assessment design. We ensured that ample
time was available during lecture and tutorial discussions for explaining
and exploring people and events brought up during these discussions.
Though most course assignments were self-contained and manageable,
students were asked to bring in extra content, and study-abroad students
often found this material baffling. Interactive lectures encouraged students
to ask questions about content or make connections between different issues raised. When the lecturer or a student mentioned a name or event not
previously discussed, we quickly gauged the students' familiarity. One positive outcome of this strategy was that the Australian students commonly
took the lead in explaining this new material, creating an empowering,
student-centered dynamic that encouraged the sorts of reflections about
subjectivity that we had hoped the students would undertake.

We also addressed student diversity by designing open assessments.
Though tasks had clear criteria and learning objectives attached, students
could choose their primary and secondary texts from a wide range of options. Most students found this approach empowering because it allowed
them to write on issues that they had a personal interest or investment in.

Genre

In these times "autobiography" has become "life narrative"—a profusion
of styles and subjects across print and electronic media. It is no accident
that in an appendix to *Reading Autobiography*, a guide to the discipline,
Sidonie Smith and Julia Watson set out "fifty-two genres of life narrative,"
ranging from "Apology" to "Witnessing." They emphasize that these

generic modes mutate, and new possibilities emerge as an ongoing process of innovation in ways of representing the self. This dynamic way of thinking about autobiography emphasizes the cultural locations of both writers and readers. Time, place, belief system, and social position are critical determinants in the production and circulation of life narrative. What Smith and Watson say of writers is equally true for readers of these genres:

> [A]s subjects of historically and culturally specific understandings of memory, experience, identity and embodiment, and agency, they both reproduce the various ways in which they have been culturally read and critique the limits of those cultural modes of self-narrating. (183)

Here is the challenge and the gift of teaching our genre (or genres) now: to set out to engage with life narratives in ways for undergraduate students to think about themselves as subjects, possessing agency, and yet also as interpellated into dominant discourses. We aren't at all modest in our claims for teaching autobiography: we think it is one of the most important and useful courses our undergraduates can take, because it causes them to think about themselves as a historically and culturally specific self (understood variously in different theoretical paradigms) in a place and time (contemporary Australia). Though we hope we infect them with the desire to undertake more traditional studies in autobiographical writing—much can be learned from Jean-Jacques Rousseau, Augustine, Gertrude Stein, and Patrick White—in this course our task is to make students think self-consciously about the autobiographical text, broadly conceived.

We try to get students thinking about the self in practical ways. Our course Postcolonialism, for example, immerses the students in short primary texts for the first four weeks. Gathered in the course dossier, the readings are drawn from journals, letters, and other texts produced during the British colonization of Australia, Canada, and South Africa in the late eighteenth and early nineteenth centuries.[1] Students read these pieces with an eye for how the writer is constructing a sense of self in the circumstances of colonization. (Smith and Watson's "Tool Kit: Twenty Strategies for Reading Life Narratives" is an excellent guide for this task.) By induction, students see how these colonizing subjects positioned themselves as civilized, alien, estranged, British, English, or authoritative by drawing on different discourses that were available to them in that place and time: Romanticism, Enlightenment concepts of reason and civility, the categorization of the noble savage and the primitive, ideas about the scientific and the poetic, masculinity and femininity. We work at two levels. First, these texts clearly show students how the narrating "I" is constructed historically, discursively, variously, and always with a view to the reader. Second, during class discussion we speculate about how different theories of subjectivity might lead to particular insights. This is a second-year subject, and theory is approached cautiously, but these texts are rich resources for feminist, psychoanalytic, and Foucauldian analyses in particular. Most important, this approach allows students to engage with the past—with sights, sounds, and perspectives that are unexpected and authentic. From Mary Ann Parker, for instance, students learn that cultured women of the eighteenth century might set sail around the world and from the deck of the ship at Sierra Leone see the terrible sights of indentured laborers being shipped around the world: convicts on their way to Botany Bay and enslaved Africans en route to the Caribbean.

In Australian Lives the emphasis is on contemporary genres of autobiography and on the range of ways contemporary Australians represent themselves and are represented by others. We study various nonfictional, life narrative forms—from autobiography and reality television to documentary and blogs. Some of the issues we consider are contemporary life narration in Australia, indigenous lives, young Australians, traumatic lives, sporting autobiographies, online and visual lives, and travel narratives. The central question is how have Australian identities been formed and re-formed through these various forms of self and life representation? Since in Australia, life narrative is dynamic and shifting fast, the course design is ready to embrace important events that occur during the semester. For example, when the iconic country and western singer Slim Dusty died midway through the semester, we set aside time to critique the newspaper obituaries; and we also looked at the media's reportage of Jana Pittman's world-championship-winning run in the four hundred meters, evaluating the representation of sporting lives through a gendered comparison of cricketers' life narratives and the media coverage of Pittman.

Location

Location, a vital component of our courses, allows us, more than anything else, to tap into tasks and issues that students regard as meaningful in their everyday lives but that need analysis at a high conceptual level. Location also allows us to build on prior knowledge. We show our students that they are suspended in an ocean of life narrative, which flows around them in media of all kinds and in and through them as they make sense of their own selves. The notions that they have plural selves and are themselves narrating subjects in place and time are two of the most powerful ideas they take away from the course.

Life narrative has been especially powerful in thinking about Australia. Debates about land rights, personal rights, governance, generational change, and reconciliation have been hot topics for a decade now, and life narrative has been at the heart of these debates. The idea of whiteness as a racialized identity comes into play here, and for students in the course Postcolonialism, this issue links back to those early constructions of self by explorers and settlers that initiated the long and ongoing anxieties of settler colonialism.

Steve Waugh's Cap

Location breathes life into the autobiographical body of our courses. Although our pedagogy dethrones the charismatic lecturer, it transfers the energy and engagement traditionally delivered in the lecture into other risky acts. If Australian Lives is to really work, it must be open to happenstance. We need to be ready to go with the flow. Hence the subtitle of this last section: "Steve Waugh's Cap." During the second semester of 2003, the media latched onto the fact that the Australian cricket captain had worn the same cap throughout his representative career and that it now needed careful strategic repair. Unraveling the cap as metaphor and synecdoche, we showed how it was put to work on behalf of various national, sexual, and gendered identities that are constantly renewed. Suggesting how the cap can link an individual subject with agency and to a national institution at one and the same time is our work in Australian Lives.

Recently in the Australian version of the reality television series *Big Brother*, a contestant ejected from the house changed the game, coming into the arena but refusing to speak, holding instead a sign protesting current refugee policy in Australia. Like Steve Waugh's cap, the contestant's action is happenstance but also an opportunity to bring genre, location, and pedagogy into contact—to get out the "tool kit" and to begin to ask, How does this challenge a narrative of identity?

Note

1. For example: "The Instructions to Captain Cook for His First Voyage, July 1768"; "Captain Cook at Botany Bay, April 1770"; "Captain Cook Sums up His Impressions of New Holland, August 1770"; Watkin Tench from *A Complete Account of the Settlement at Port Jackson in New South Wales*; Thomas Watling, "Letters from an Exile"; Elizabeth Macarthur, "Letters"; George Vancouver from *Voyage of Discovery to the North Pacific Ocean*; Samuel Hearne from *A Journey from Prince of Wales' Fort in Hudson Bay*; Susanna Moodie from *Roughing It in the Bush*; Catharine Parr Traill from *The Backwoods of Canada*; J. W. D. Moodie from *Ten Years in South Africa*; and Mary Ann Parker from *A Voyage around the World*.

Works Cited

Clark, Manning, ed. *Sources of Australian History*. Melbourne: Oxford UP, 1982.

Cook, James. "Captain Cook at Botany Bay, April 1770." Clark 40–48.

———. "Captain Cook Sums Up His Impressions of New Holland, August 1770." Clark 48–55.

Hearne, Samuel. *A Journey from Prince of Wales' Fort in Hudson Bay to the Northern Ocean*. 1795. New York: Da Capo, 1968.

"The Instructions to Captain Cook for His First Voyage, July 1768." Clark 35–40.

Macarthur, Elizabeth. "Letters." *Colonial Voices: Letters, Diaries, Journalism, and Other Accounts of Nineteenth-Century Australia*. Ed. Elizabeth Webby. St. Lucia: U of Queensland P, 1989. 95–99.

Moodie, J. W. D. *Ten Years in South Africa*. London: Bentley, 1835.

Moodie, Susanna. *Roughing It in the Bush*. 1839. Ottawa: Carleton UP, 1988. 26 Feb. 2007 < http://digital.library.upenn.edu/women/moodie/roughing/roughing .html >.

Parker, Mary Ann. *A Voyage around the World*. 1795. Sydney: Hordern, 1992.

Parr Traill, Catherine. *The Backwoods of Canada*. 1836. Toronto: New Canadian Lib., 1989. 26 Feb. 2007 < http://www.gutenberg.org/etext/13559 >.

Showalter, Elaine. *Teaching Literature*. Oxford: Blackwell, 2003.

Smith, Sidonie, and Julia Watson. "Fifty-Two Genres of Life Narrative." Smith and Watson, *Reading* 183–207.

———. *Reading Autobiography: A Guide for Interpreting Life Narratives*. Minneapolis: U of Minnesota P, 2001.

———. "Tool Kit: Twenty Strategies for Reading Life Narratives." Smith and Watson, *Reading* 165–79.

Tench, Watkin. *A Complete Account of the Settlement at Port Jackson in New South Wales*. 1793. Melbourne: Text Publishing, 1996.

Vancouver, George. *Voyage of Discovery to the North Pacific Ocean*. 1798. London: Hakluyt Soc., 1984.

Watling, Thomas. "Letters from an Exile." *Colonial Voices: Letters, Diaries, Journalism and Other Accounts of Nineteenth Century Australia*. Ed. Elizabeth Webby. St. Lucia: U of Queensland P, 1989. 11–19.

Judith Lütge Coullie

Life Writing in
the New South Africa

The campus of what was the University of Durban-Westville overlooks, in the distance, the Indian Ocean.[1] The view is an apt one because under apartheid the university was designated for exclusive use by those of Indian descent. By the mid-1980s, responding to student activism, the university had abandoned racial exclusivism. In the last few years before its merging with the University of Natal, in 2004, the student body comprised mostly Africans, followed closely by Indians and then by small numbers of coloreds and whites. A "historically disadvantaged institution," the university was seldom the first choice of high achievers, and many students were economically and educationally disadvantaged.[2] Perhaps unexpectedly, the university considered this situation a matter of pride and policy: it was our mission to provide access to higher education for apartheid's most wronged.

Students' ability levels diverged widely, and even now, more than a decade after the attainment of a nonracial, democratic state, apartheid's hierarchization of educational resources still resonates. Moreover, in English-language institutions such as this one, many black students are further disadvantaged since, in addition to being the products of inferior schooling, they are not mother-tongue speakers of English. Their advantage, however, lies in their multilingualism—most speak at least two African languages, English, and some Afrikaans—and its attendant multicultural fluency. They absorb hegemonic white culture through their schooling and the mass media, while Indian, white, and colored students often have only superficial knowledge of African cultures.

The course that is the subject of this essay, Self-Representation: Theory and Practice, set out to capitalize on diversity. It sought to empower learners to meet the challenges of the "new" South Africa by providing the means (creative and theoretical) to interrogate identity and the implication of history and culture in self, life, and text. Informed by poststructuralist (notably Foucauldian) and postcolonial theory, it fostered the "capacity to discover the historical links between certain modes of self-understanding and modes of domination, and to resist the ways in which we have already been classified and identified by dominant discourses" (Sawicki 186).

The students, of all races, some full- and some part-timers, ranged in age and disciplinary backgrounds.[3] Some had little or no English studies in their undergraduate degree.[4] The course sought to circumvent these obstacles by using, as the starting point for each week's theoretical discussion, the students' own efforts at self-representation (of all genres, undeniably the most accommodating). Ideas were refined and extended through readings of prescribed (principally South African) life writing texts and key theory texts, ideally to advance students' theoretical insights along with their attempts at life writing.

This was a postgraduate semester-long module, conducted chiefly through dialogue rather than lecture. Exchange was aided by the fact that classes were small, averaging six students.[5] The objectives were as follows:

> to develop awareness of, and respect for, the rich cultural diversity in South Africa through writing, reading, and discussion of the cultural implications of identity and of forms of life writing

> to encourage critical thinking about students' own identity formation, about the roles of race, ethnicity, gender, and class

> to increase students' reading capital and sense of South African history by introducing them to a range of Western-style prose narrative and indigenous nonnarrative oral auto/biographical texts

> to introduce the complexities of life writing through practice and through theoretical and critical readings reflecting current debates in South Africa and internationally

to improve students' writing skills (creative and academic) by means of weekly auto/biographical exercises, a research (theory) essay, and a book review[6]

The course ran for three years and was adapted each year to accommodate vagaries of the calendar and variances in class composition. The outline given here thus represents an aggregation rather than an exact description of any one year's offering. The basic pattern, though, was the same. Each week students wrote short auto/biographical pieces. Sometimes work was read out in class. Usually, however, because of pressures of time and because the material may have been too personal, students commented on the ways in which they responded to specific problems that the writing assignment forced them to tackle—issues such as self-knowledge, style, definitions of truth, and the (conscious or unconscious) implication of cultural practices in all of these. Topics were intentionally interlinked, appearing for emphasis in several guises. We then turned to the prescribed theoretical and creative readings.

I begin the course by outlining the forms and functions of self-representational practices of South Africans during and after apartheid, contrasting prose narrative print autobiographies with vernacular oral, performance texts (*izibongo* in isiZulu). Non-Africans are rarely familiar with this genre, so I provide some (translated, printed) samples and ask black students to share their knowledge with the class. I explain that *izibongo* function primarily as oral IDs, naming and identifying the subject; they are nonnarrative and densely allusive, relying on audiences who are part of the subject's community (and would thus understand the allusions), thereby cementing community ties. As oral texts they are not fixed, but they usually have a stable core. They blur the distinction between autobiography and biography: *izibongo* are performed by the subject as well as by members of the community (to "recognize" or hail the subject), and performers may adjust the performance text.

The class investigates the role of *izibongo* during apartheid (1948–94) and afterward, along with the functions of print autobiographies and biographies. We debate the reasons for the high proportion of published auto/biographical texts banned by the apartheid government.[7] We then consider how the function of life writing may have changed in the "new" South Africa.

Readings for the next class include my survey of apartheid and postapartheid life writing ("Apartheid") and essays by Georges Gusdorf and by James Olney ("Autobiography"). Over the next week students keep a journal.

Self-Knowledge

The class begins with comments on the journal exercises. In writing their autobiographical pieces, what had students found pleasurable or difficult? What was the role of the reader? What impact did the knowledge that the lecturer would be reading these entries have on the writing? In what ways was the form constraining or enabling? How did the strict time structure compare with *izibongo*, which do not quantify time? We then turn to the main topic for the day's class: Were there experiences that could not be explained? Did others with whom the students interacted present to them views of themselves that seemed strange or mistaken? What assessments might family members or friends add to one's self-portrait? (In this regard, we consider the auto/biographical nature of *izibongo*.)

Students are encouraged to raise questions about the readings. What seemed to be the most important aspects (strengths, weaknesses, cultural biases) of the essays? Readings for the next week include the first two chapters of the autobiography of the Soweto gangster Godfrey Moloi and two essays that focus on theoretical models for the reading of South African autobiography: my own "'Not Quite Fiction'" and M. J. Daymond's response to it, and Olney's "Some Versions of Memory." Each student must also find a review of a recently published South African auto/biographical text. The writing assignment focuses on the limits of memory, illustrated by an experience that they know others remember differently.

Truth and Memory

We talk about how notions of truth vary in changed cultural and generic contexts. What relation between truth and confession is posited in the auto/biographies students have encountered or written? What is the role of confession in *izibongo*? What variances can be discerned between apartheid autobiography (which often foregrounds the life lived rather than the autobiographical subject) and postapartheid autobiography (which is often more confessional)? When is self the source of truth about the self? What is the nature of this truth, and how is it affected by the limits of memory? When is verifiable (communal) truth indispensable, and are the demands of biography and autobiography genre-specific? Of what relevance are the poststructuralist positions I articulate in "'Not Quite Fiction'" and the concerns raised by Daymond?

Students are asked to identify the key features of their sample book reviews. Ideas are pooled and used as guidelines for their own reviews of new publications.

Working with a family member or acquaintance, preferably someone who is semiliterate, students will act as scribes or collaborators in the composition of an autobiographical piece (with the other person as subject). They must also choose their topics for the theory essay.

Readings for the next class include Mpho 'M'atsepo Nthunya's *Singing Away the Hunger* and essays on the politics of collaborative autobiography by Carole Boyce Davies and Anne E. Goldman.

Collaborative Autobiography and Biography

Students share their collaborative projects with classmates and relate the difficulties or successes. What kind of knowledges and skills did each person bring to the project? In Nthunya's text, what are the features of the collaboration between Nthunya and K. Limakatso Kendall? I mention other collaborative life writing texts by South Africans, autobiographies and biographies (and we talk about the differences), and relate these to the issues raised by Davies and Goldman.

Prescribed readings (for the next two classes) are selections from the autobiographies of Bloke Modisane (published in the early days of apartheid) and Sarah Penny (published three decades later as negotiations for transition to democracy were under way); the recommended reading is Roger Rosenblatt's "Black Autobiography." The writing assignment examines racial identity.

The Racialized Self

Students discuss what their life writing reveals about their feelings on what race meant during apartheid and what it means to them in democratic

South Africa.[8] (Postapartheid South Africa has not entirely overcome the old obsession with racial classification: declaration of race and gender is de rigueur so that affirmative action can be implemented.) We talk about the effect of race on social interactions and lifestyle and about Modisane's agonized confession that being black dehumanized him (contrasting this account with Moloi's self-portrait). We exchange views on Penny's account of whiteness: how the nonracial, nonsexist tenets of liberalism crumble in the face of others' insistence that skin color matters.

The writing assignment focuses on gendered experiences. Students are to read Modisane and Penny again, this time examining the authors' treatment of gender. Frantz Fanon's gender-specific analysis of race in *Black Skin* is required reading; Mary G. Mason's "The Other Voice" is recommended.

The Gendered Self

Discussion addresses what gender identity means to students and how they depict it in their life writing. How and when is gender identity shaped? How does gender intersect with ethnicity and culture and with race—for students and for Modisane, Fanon, and Penny? Does gender influence genre? Sometimes? Always? How? We evaluate Mason's argument about a gender distinction in prose narrative autobiography and consider too the significance of gender in praise poetry (*izibongo*).

For the next class, students compose a short biographical sketch. They are to read extracts from Lyndall Gordon's *Shared Lives* and Ruth Hoberman's encyclopedia entry on biography. They also reread my " 'Not Quite Fiction' " essay for the implications of poststructuralist theory for biography.

Authority in Auto/Biography and Izibongo

Discussion centers on authority and responsibility in biography. How are these defined for the writer, subject, and reader? We reflect on the ways in which, seeking to write biographies of her best friends, Gordon smudges the distinctions between biography and autobiography. What are the ethical implications of this blurring? What is the significance of the gender of narrating and narrated subjects in Gordon's narrative? Concerning the politics of biography, which lives are worthy of being recorded, and who should record them? What are the class's thoughts on Gordon's account of the lives of women who achieved no fame or exceptional accomplishment? Who did students choose to write about and why?

We relate these questions to self-representational output during and after apartheid, suggesting reasons for the virtual absence, during apartheid, of pro-apartheid autobiography, while a number of laudatory biographies of key government figures were published. We look into the role, during apartheid, of the *izibongo* of prominent black South Africans, which were largely or wholly composed by professional bards and thus more akin to biography than autobiography. The praises of figures like the Zulu king Shaka often served to remind the oppressed of proud traditions and heroes and to inspire them to rededicate themselves to the anti-apartheid struggle. We compare the relations between *izibongo* and history and between biography and history, in terms of both generic distinction and the ways in which historical change affects biography.

What insights emanating from Hoberman's survey and from my essay on poststructuralist theory seem to be pertinent to biography, and how might these insights influence any biographical projects the students may embark on?

Reading for the next class is Liz Gunner and Mafika Gwala's introduction to *Musho!* and a sample of some of the poems, as well as Noleen Turner's essay on contemporary praises of urban Zulu women. Using the *izibongo* as models, the students' life writing assignment is to compose—with or without the input of family members—their own praises.

Narrative and Nonnarrative Forms

We watch a video recording of an *imbongi* (a praise poet) performing praises. We talk about his performance style and what has been learned from the work of Gunner and Gwala and Turner. Students discuss their own *izibongo* compositions and the role of memory in oral literature and in print and its effect on form; the contrasting notions of selfhood—both sacred and profane—in *izibongo*, since traditionally through this medium one communicates with the living as well as the ancestors, versus largely or wholly secular conceptions in prose autobiography; and the role of the audience or readers, especially the intimate involvement of the community in both composing and performing *izibongo* versus the individualism of autobiography.

I summarize key points from my essay "(Dis)Locating Selves" on the implications of the growing move among black South Africans from *izibongo* to prose narrative autobiography.

As preparation for the next class, we talk about some of the issues about which students feel strongly—poverty, rape, HIV and AIDS, crime, and so on. We discuss how life writing can raise awareness and how one might expect readers to respond to testimony. The writing exercise concerns the narration of issue-based experiences to achieve sociopolitical impact.

Readings for the next class include selections from life writing that respond to the Truth and Reconciliation Commission (Krog; Tutu; and Gobodo-Madikizela), as well as testimony from those who are HIV-positive (Fox and Wulfson).

Life Writing as Political Act

Students review their issue-based or polemical life writing: How could it be more effective? Is life writing the best genre? What other options are there? How do classmates, as auditors, respond? How does the testimony of victims and perpetrators of gross human rights abuses affect auditors like Antjie Krog, Desmond Tutu, and Pumla Gobodo-Madikizela (as evidenced in their life writing)? What, in general terms, have been the effects of Truth and Reconciliation Commission testimony on South Africans? We appraise the relevance of Gillian Whitlock's essay on Stolen Generations testimony in Australia.

Readings for the next class include Hayden White's seminal essay on narrative as a noninnocent mode for referring to reality and chapters on narrators and narration in Shlomith Rimmon-Kenan and in Steven Cohan and Linda Shires. For the writing exercise, students narrate one particular experience in the first, second, and third persons.

Narrative

I introduce the fundamental concepts of narratology, honing in on narration and narrators. I invite comments on the effects that shifts in grammatical person have on the narration of an event. By way of illustration or contrast, I read excepts from Jay McInerney's *Bright Lights, Big City* and J. M. Coetzee's *Boyhood* and *Youth* (longer passages of which students read over the next week). Other readings include chapters from Rimmon-Kenan and from Cohan and Shires on focalization, implied readers, and tone, as well as the first eighty or so pages of Dave Eggers's *A Heartbreaking Work*. In their writing, students should narrate an experience that clearly distinguishes focalizer from narrator.

Points of View and Readers

Turning to Coetzee's texts, we interrogate the effects of third-person narration on the "autobiographical pact" (Lejeune). We contrast narrators and focalizers in Coetzee with those in Eggers and other autobiographies. What effects can be achieved by shifts in focalization? How effective were the students' writing experiments, and how could they be made more effective? What kind of relationships can be established with readers? How do implied readers influence the narrative?

Final drafts of reviews must be completed this week.

Students read their reviews, and we revisit key issues raised during the seminar series. Students evaluate the course.[9]

My sense is that the course enabled conscientious students not only to glimpse their potential as life writers and scholars but also to confront, in uniquely personal ways, their place in South Africa's history. The qualifier "conscientious" is necessary, however. The course failed to achieve this objective for those students who did not attend all the classes; their grasp of the theoretical issues floundered. Those (usually the same students) who did not do all the readings also failed to benefit much. Moreover, for a few students, limited English abilities and lack of training in literary interpretation were debilitating: they could not understand the theoretical and critical readings and lacked the skill or confidence to contribute to class discussion on anything more than a very basic level. On balance, however, it seems to me that most students, and I, their facilitator, left the course having discerned new ways of understanding ourselves and one another, thinking of "difference as a resource rather than a threat. . . . Of course, this [meant] discovering what we have in common as well" (Sawicki 187).

Notes

1. The University of Durban-Westville merged with the University of Natal, intended for whites, to become the multicampus University of KwaZulu-Natal. This

essay describes the University of Durban-Westville, at which the course described in this essay was offered.

2. The government-funded National Research Foundation recognized the need to promote research in these disadvantaged institutions and through bursaries made it possible for many of our students to fund their studies. The "disadvantaged" student profile affected teaching in other ways as well. Because few students were likely to purchase prescribed texts, the books had to be placed in the reserve room of the library. This arrangement was somewhat limiting, because students with full-time jobs claimed that they lacked the time to do the readings. It also meant that newer texts might not be available.

3. About half of my students were in their twenties but some were older, and there were even two in their midfifties (both white females). Because about half were studying part-time (usually they were full-time teachers), I had to limit the amount of reading I could assign. Variations in skill levels were often extreme. The entry requirement (60% aggregate in the final year of the undergraduate degree) was not a reliable indicator of English literary skills or knowledge of literary theory, since standards varied from one university to another and from one discipline to another.

4. The course was offered under the auspices of the Centre for the Study of South African Literature and Languages (which no longer exists), not the English department, and thus students may have had undergraduate degrees in isiZulu or education.

. 5. At South African universities, the BA is a three-year degree. The BEd, which some students had, is a four-year degree. The BEd students would thus go straight into the master's program. This course was considered postgraduate because it was offered to both honors and master's students.

6. Honors students were required to write a final exam (the exam representing 50% of the total mark), but not the master's students, from whom I expected more extensive written assignments. All writing exercises were handed in at the end of each class and graded as part of a "continuous assessment mark." Students' specific problems were addressed in private consultation. I revised the most promising book reviews for publication, which was especially encouraging for the students.

7. Most notable was the apartheid state's desire to suppress testimony by activists of all races and by the oppressed—who were ostensibly receiving separate but equal treatment. The suppression of information in South Africa was thus not confined to political matters; the Nationalist government also sought to keep people of different races separate from one another (hence the word *apartheid*) and to ensure that the common humanity of "non-White" South Africans did not enter the white electorate's imaginary.

8. One student, a Jewish woman, surprisingly wrote about how her whiteness had come to acquire far more significance in postapartheid South Africa than it had during apartheid, when to her, a supporter of the then-banned Communist Party, a person's race was less important than ideological commitment, while most decisive

of all for whether she was prejudiced for or against someone was their identity as Jew or gentile.

9. This was a formal evaluation, conducted by the university's Quality Assurance Office. Evaluations were very positive.

Works Cited

Coetzee, J. M. *Boyhood: Scenes from Provincial Life*. London: Secker, 1997.

———. *Youth*. London: Secker, 2002.

Cohan, Steven, and Linda Shires. *Telling Stories: A Theoretical Analysis of Narrative Fiction*. New York: Routledge, 1988.

Coullie, Judith Lütge. "Apartheid and Post-apartheid Life Writing." Jolly 1: 42–44.

———. "(Dis)Locating Selves: *Izibongo* and Narrative Autobiography in South Africa." *Oral Literature and Performance in Southern Africa*. Ed. Duncan Brown. Oxford: Currey; Cape Town: Philip; Athens: Ohio UP, 1999. 61–89.

———. "'Not Quite Fiction': The Challenges of Poststructuralism to the Reading of Contemporary South African Autobiography." *Current Writing* 3.1 (1991): 1–23.

Davies, Carole Boyce. "Collaboration and the Ordering Imperative in Life-Story Production." *De/Colonizing the Subject: The Politics of Gender in Women's Autobiography*. Ed. Sidonie Smith and Julia Watson. Minneapolis: U of Minnesota P, 1992. 3–19.

Daymond, M. J. "On Retaining and Recognising Changes in the Genre 'Autobiography.'" *Current Writing* 3.1 (1991): 31–41.

Eggers, Dave. *A Heartbreaking Work of Staggering Genius*. London: Picador-Macmillan, 2000.

Fanon, Frantz. *Black Skin, White Masks*. Trans. Charles Lam Markmann. New York: Grove Weidenfeld, 1967.

Fox, Susan [interviews], and Gisèle Wulfson [photographs]. *Living Openly: HIV-Positive South Africans Tell Their Stories*. Pretoria: Beyond Awareness Campaign, HIV/AIDS and STD Directorate, Dept. of Health, 2000.

Gobodo-Madikizela, Pumla. *A Human Being Died That Night: A Story of Forgiveness*. Claremont: Philip–New Africa, 2003.

Goldman, Anne E. "Is That What She Said? The Politics of Collaborative Autobiography." *Cultural Critique* 23 (1993): 177–204.

Gordon, Lyndall. *Shared Lives*. Cape Town: Philip, 1992.

Gunner, Liz, and Mafika Gwala, trans. and eds. *Musho! Zulu Popular Praises*. 1991. Johannesburg: Witwatersrand UP, 1994.

Gusdorf, Georges. "Conditions and Limits of Autobiography." Olney, *Autobiography* 28–48.

Hoberman, Ruth. "Biography: General Survey." *Encyclopedia of Life Writing: Autobiographical and Biographical Forms*. Ed. Margaretta Jolly. Vol. 1. London: Fitzroy, 2001. 109–12.

Krog, Antjie. *Country of My Skull*. Johannesburg: Random, 1998.

Lejeune, Philippe. "The Autobiographical Pact (bis)." *On Autobiography*. Ed. and fwd. Paul John Eakin. Trans. Katherine Leary. Minneapolis: U of Minnesota P, 1989. 119–37.

Mason, Mary G. "The Other Voice: Autobiographies of Women Writers." Olney, *Autobiography* 207–35.

McInerney, Jay. *Bright Lights, Big City*. New York: Vintage-Random, 1984.

Modisane, Bloke [William B.]. *Blame Me on History*. 1963. Craighall: Ad Donker, 1986.

Moloi, Godfrey. *My Life: Volume One*. Johannesburg: Ravan, 1987.

Nthunya, Mpho 'M'atsepo. *Singing Away the Hunger: Stories of a Life in Lesotho*. Ed. K. Limakatso Kendall. Pietermaritzburg: U of Natal P, 1996.

Olney, James. "Autobiography and the Cultural Moment: A Thematic, Historical, and Bibliographical Introduction." Olney, *Autobiography* 3–27.

——, ed. *Autobiography: Essays Theoretical and Critical*. Princeton: Princeton UP, 1980.

——. "Some Versions of Memory / Some Versions of *Bios*: The Ontology of Autobiography." Olney, *Autobiography* 236–67.

Penny, Sarah. *The Whiteness of Bones*. Johannesburg: Penguin, 1997.

Rimmon-Kenan, Shlomith. *Narrative Fiction: Contemporary Poetics*. London: Methuen, 1983.

Rosenblatt, Roger. "Black Autobiography: Life as the Death Weapon." Olney, *Autobiography* 169–80.

Sawicki, Jana. "Identity Politics and Sexual Freedom: Foucault and Feminism." *Feminism and Foucault: Reflections on Resistance*. Ed. Irene Diamond and Lee Quinby. Boston: Northwestern UP, 1988. 177–91.

Smith, Sidonie, and Julia Watson. *Reading Autobiography: A Guide for Interpreting Life Narratives*. Minneapolis: U of Minnesota P, 2001.

Turner, Noleen. "Censure and Social Comment in the *Izihasho* of Urban Zulu Women." *AlterNation* 2.2 (1995): 55–73.

Tutu, Desmond Mpilo. *No Future without Forgiveness*. Johannesburg: Rider, 1999.

White, Hayden. "The Value of Narrativity in the Representation of Reality." *Critical Inquiry* 7.4 (1980): 1–25.

Whitlock, Gillian. "In the Second Person: Narrative Transactions in Stolen Generations Testimony." *Biography: An Interdisciplinary Quarterly* 24.1 (2001): 197–214.

Julia Clancy-Smith

An Undergraduate and Graduate Colloquium in Social History and Biography in the Modern Middle East and North Africa

In his fictionalized autobiography, *The Pillar of Salt*, written in 1955, the Tunisian writer Albert Memmi observes, "How blind I was to what I really am, how naive it was of me to hope to overcome the fundamental rift in me, the contradiction that is the very basis of my life" (x). Memmi is emblematic of generations of North African and Middle Eastern writers who have grappled with problems of identity—and who continue to do so.

The Literatures of Identity in the Modern Middle East and North Africa, circa 1880–Present is an upper-division undergraduate and graduate course aimed at advanced history majors and MA students in a variety of disciplines. It addresses the history of identities in the modern Middle East and North Africa through indigenous literatures, particularly personal narratives or life stories. Intellectuals, writers, and activists from a range of religious, sociocultural, and ethnic backgrounds speak about themselves and their societies in multiple voices and in combined genres, such as memoirs, diaries, and semiautobiographical fiction. Through the biographies of these writers and their literary production, we explore the various ways that gender, social class, ethnicity or race, generation, and religious affiliation intersect in both stable and unstable combinations throughout the life span of our authors. As important, we use their writings, combined with other media, such as images and photographs, films, and music, as a lens to understand the major forces in modern Middle Eastern and North African history—imperialism, colonialism, nationalism, changing gender norms, migration, education, knowledge—that shape and are shaped by identities. Finally, we consider the theoretical and methodological relations among history, historiography, and literature, particularly biography and life narratives.

The assumption underlying the course is that students can best grasp the region's social history—the multifarious daily as well as large-scale, even global, forces that forge individual and collective destinies—through a close reading of life stories. In addition, since the Middle East and its peoples have been demonized by the West for centuries, it is especially challenging to confront and critically examine the layers of prejudices deposited by orientalist cultural stereotypes, European imperial tropes, and the CIA version of Islam and Muslims. I have found that unraveling and interpreting an individual's life trajectory is a compelling strategy for dispelling the demons long associated with the Middle East, largely because of its strategic location and resources.

I introduced this course into the University of Virginia's history seminars for freshmen in 1987. I did so because of the somewhat impoverished state of teaching materials then available in standard history textbooks. At that time, the history of the Middle East and North Africa was not about people and certainly not about the individual—or at least not about nonelites. Rather it tended toward discussions of impersonal, large-scale historical processes that effaced human agency and flattened out ethnographic texture, thus concealing similarities as well as differences in worldviews and lived experience. My syllabus was largely determined by the relatively small number of works in translation from Arabic, Turkish, Hebrew, or Persian available for course use. Since that time, the range of life narratives written by Middle Eastern writers and available in English translation has expanded dramatically—for example, the social biographies found in Edmund Burke III's *Struggle and Survival* and Elizabeth Warnock Fernea's *Remembering Childhood in the Middle East*. In consequence, the course has gone through a number of permutations that reflect contemporary political events; the expansion of new theoretical fields, such as gender studies (Kandiyoti); and the increased availability of images, including important photographic archives, such as the nineteenth-century Bonfils collection of Near Eastern portrait and landscape photos in the University of

Pennsylvania Museum (see Haller). The explosion of documentary films and other videographic media, many devoted to life stories—the Algerian film *Rachida*, for instance—during the past decade has also greatly enriched the fund of pedagogical materials.

The readings discussed below were selected not only to reflect literary diversity, contradictory voices, and historical breadth but also to encourage the students to problematize the kinds of binaries that emerge from writers such as Edward Said and Frantz Fanon. This is not to suggest that systems of domination, like colonialism, do not construct political and racial binaries but rather to explore what historical conditions converge to produce binaries and how these conditions shape life narratives. The readings illustrate perspectives that have probed the ambiguous, untidy, unstable, and contingent in constructions of identity in specific places and in specific time periods.

We begin by formulating the big questions that we will wrestle with throughout the semester: What is identity, how is it constructed, and why is it important historically? Once we have conceptualized identity as bundles of social meanings constantly in flux, we can ask, What factors cause specific identities to shift or come to the foreground in a personal account? Who is a Middle Eastern or North African writer, and what sociopolitical positions have literati assumed, or been assigned, in the region's cultures and states Is a person who is born there but educated in Europe or the United States from the region? Why is cultural authenticity important in terms of an author's legitimacy and political positioning? Should we view these writers and their literary production from a regional geographic perspective or an ethnolinguistic perspective—as Arabs or Persians, for example? This last question leads us into the issue of how language, authenticity, and translation relate to identity, particularly since the Middle East has been, and still is, deeply marked by multilingualism and cosmopolitanism. The complex connections among nation-states, nationalism, and postcolonial programs to suppress ethnolinguistic minorities and cultures need to be explored because in the older order of things, elites were frequently educated in several languages, and ordinary people often operated in linguistically complex situations.

These considerations open up questions of translation. Is the Ottoman Turkish writer Halidé Edib (1884–1964), who composed her personal memoirs in English (*House with Wisteria*) and not in her maternal language, Turkish, a Middle Eastern writer? How did belated translation from Arabic into English alter the meanings expressed in the memoirs of the Egyptian feminist Huda Sharaawi (1879–1947), whose life story was composed sometime before 1947 but only published, as *Harem Years*, in 1987? A related problem is that of audience, both intended and unintended. Some of our autobiographies—Fadhma Amrouche's *My Life Story* and Sharaawi's *Harem Years*—were not intended for publication when written. I ask the students to consider the effect that the intended audience might exert on a particular life story and how that effect might be factored into evaluations of its historical documentary value. We juxtapose these works with Edib's *House*, which clearly aimed at an intended audience— the Americans and British in the post–World War I era when the newly independent Republic of Turkey sought international legitimacy. Now the students can address the issue of why a Turkish woman wrote an ostensibly personal memoir in English; they also perceive the different poses assumed by the narrator as she recounts her early childhood and married years, yet later assumes the guise of an indigenous historian explaining recent events to her Anglo-British readers.

Once some of the big questions have been laid out, I complicate the readings by playing off life narratives against conventional biographies of the authors, using a systematically comparative approach; I also provide a history of how each work came to be—a sort of biography of the memoir itself, or "geography of biography," as Miriam Fuchs puts it (iv). I find that dense, vivid ethnographic portraits—reinforced by visual materials— of the place, space, and time that produced both writers and works encourage students to follow the authors around on their daily rounds. By conjuring up a particular society or culture at specific historical junctures, students can intellectually experience the social worlds framing the autobiographies. Once again, this approach undermines commonly held but unexamined assumptions, such as that all women in the Middle East have always and everywhere been suppressed or that Jews and Muslims have always been fighting. That Memmi (1920–), Tunisia's foremost francophone novelist and philosopher of racism, grew up in a Tunis that was home to complex, socially differentiated Jewish communities, some European, others Arab in origin, does much to dispel the notion of a monolithic Middle East.

Reading more or less in chronological order, we begin with Istanbul and the late Ottoman Empire as portrayed in the works by Edib and Sharaawi. I do this in part because our final reading, *Baghdad Diaries*, by

Nuha al-Radi (1941–2004), offers a provocative parallel to the question of how war, violence, and state formation influence life stories. Edib's memoir signals the end of an ancient imperial culture, a culture that deeply configured identities. Al-Radi's diary entries, composed during two deadly episodes of American imperialism, 1991 and 2003, give voice to a secular Middle Eastern nationalism that emerged after World War I from the ashes of the defeated Ottoman Empire but that is currently shifting rapidly because of neoimperialism. The themes of war, colonial violence, and racism are echoed in the works by Memmi and Amrouche, as well as by the Moroccan writer Leila Abouzeid (1950–) in her *Return to Childhood*. Memmi and Amrouche, however, originally from the lowest rungs of the colonial pecking order, invite students to consider how gender, social class, and minority status determined by ethnicity—Memmi is from a Berber Arab Jewish family, and Amrouche is an Algerian Berber—shape individual and collective destinies during great upheavals. While Abouzeid is middle-class and educated, her stance as both writer and translator presents new opportunities to rethink questions of translation, identity, and political positions. Raised in the postcolonial era and capable of writing in French, Abouzeid deliberately composed her fiction and autobiography in Arabic as an act of defiant nationalism; for her autobiography, she elected to translate it herself into English.

Some of our most passionate exchanges involve gendered representations of one culture by another; above all, how colonized women's bodies have been visually portrayed, eroticized, and "offered up for view" to the colonizer, as discussed by me ("Visit," "Islam") and Rana Kabbani. In class I juxtapose Malek Alloula's disturbing French colonial photographs of purportedly Algerian women in *The Colonial Harem* with Edib's narrative of life in elite harems, with Amrouche's depiction of peasant women's daily struggle for subsistence, and with the biographies on my Web site documentary teaching module, "Imperialism in North Africa." Why and how female bodies, sexuality, and matters of intimacy are recast as matters of state—as justifications for colonialism and military interventions—brings us to our final reading and to closure. We trace the increasing attention paid to the Middle Eastern or the Muslim woman by the United States media since 1991. Al-Radi's daily log of the indescribable sufferings imposed on Iraq's people constitutes at the same time a movingly personal record of musings on her own identities. A secular Muslim, an artist educated in Europe, and a woman from a family that had been pro-Western for generations, al-Radi wonders how democratic nations claiming moral superiority can drop the equivalent of several Hiroshimas' worth of bombs and uranium weapons on innocent civilians. Had al-Radi lived, she might have produced another memoir that traced how her identity as Western and secular came apart after 1991. Such a memoir was not to be—she died of cancer in 2004, one of the many casualties of the New American empire and its weapons of mass destruction.

Works Cited

Abouzeid, Leila. *Return to Childhood*. Austin: U of Texas P, 1998.

Alloula, Malek. *The Colonial Harem*. Trans. Myrna Godzich and Wlad Godzich. Manchester: Manchester UP, 1986.

Amrouche, Fadhma. *My Life Story: The Autobiography of a Berber Woman*. Trans. Dorothy Blair. New Brunswick: Rutgers UP, 1989.

Burke, Edmund, III, ed. *Struggle and Survival in the Modern Middle East*. 1993. Rev. ed. Berkeley: U of California P, 2006.

Clancy-Smith, Julia. "Albert Memmi and *The Pillar of Salt*." *African Literature and Its Times*. Ed. Joyce Moss. Los Angeles: Thomson/Gale, 2000. 337–46.

——. "Imperialism in North Africa (18th–20th c.)." Center for History and New Media Project, George Mason University. *Women in World History*. <http://chnm.gmu.edu/wwh/lessons/lesson9/lesson9.php?s=0>.

——. "Islam, Gender, and Identities in the Making of French Algeria, 1830–1962." *Domesticating the Empire: Languages of Gender, Race, and Family Life in French and Dutch Colonialism, 1830–1962*. Ed. Clancy-Smith and Frances Gouda. Charlottesville: UP of Virginia, 1998. 154–74.

——. "A Visit to a Tunisian Harem." *Journal of Maghrebi Studies* 1–2.1 (1993): 43–49.

Edib, Halidé. *House with Wisteria: Memoirs*. 1926. Introd. Sibel Erol. Charlottesville: Leopolis, 2003.

Fernea, Elizabeth Warnock. *Remembering Childhood in the Middle East: Memoirs from a Century of Change*. Austin: U of Texas P, 2002.

Fuchs, Miriam. "Autobiography and Geography: Introduction." *Biography: An Interdisciplinary Quarterly* 25.1 (2002): iv–ix.

Haller, Douglas M. Introduction. *In Arab Lands: The Bonfils Collection of the University of Pennsylvania Museum*. Cairo: Amer. U in Cairo P, 2000. 11–27.

Kabbani, Rana. *Europe's Myths of the Orient*. Bloomington: Indiana UP, 1986.

Kandiyoti, Deniz. *Gendering the Middle East: Emerging Perspectives*. Syracuse: Syracuse UP, 1996.

Memmi, Albert. *The Pillar of Salt*. Trans. Edouard Roditi. Boston: Beacon, 1991.

Rachida. Dir. Yamina Bachir-Chouikh. First Run Icarus Films, 2002.

al-Radi, Nuha. *Baghdad Diaries: A Woman's Chronicle of War and Exile*. New York: Vintage, 2003.

Sharaawi, Huda. *Harem Years: The Memoirs of an Egyptian Feminist*. Trans. and introd. Margot Badron. New York: Feminist, 1986.

Sandra Chait and Ghirmai Negash

Teaching Multicultural Life-History Writing Texts through Technology's Third Space: Reflections on a University of Washington– University of Asmara Collaboration

In spring quarter, 2002, Ghirmai Negash (then teaching Eritrean languages and literature at the University of Asmara, Eritrea) and Sandra Chait (then teaching comparative literature at the University of Washington) collaborated on a pedagogical experiment to teach ethnographic life-history writing through Internet exchanges between students in the partner countries.[1] Funded by the William and Flora Hewlett Foundation, Chait sought to explore with Ghirmai the role the Internet could play in preparing their students to be culturally competent biographers. In particular, the two instructors hoped to train students in the skills and understanding necessary to participate in Eritrea's World Bank–funded national cultural recovery project CARP (Cultural Assets Rehabilitation Program), which was then planning to collect and document the oral histories, as well as the music, literature, and architecture, of Eritrea's nine ethnic groups. Ghirmai and Chait titled their ten-week-long qualitative methods course Writing Multicultural Life Histories in Communities in Transition: Africa and the USA. Developed by Chait, with input from Ghirmai and help from Chait's research assistant, Alex Baron, the course was designed to teach students cross-cultural life-history writing skills both in the field and on the Internet. It was divided structurally into four sections:

Interviewing, which included preparing questions, taking notes, taping and filming, and conducting dyadic and group interviews

Refining interviewing skills, which explored issues of empathy, transference and countertransference, and romance

Writing the life story: analysis and interpretation, in which students learned how to identify pattern or meaning in their storytelling partners' lives; to deal with the narrative variants and active forgetting; and to recognize national, ethnic, religious, class, and gender slants

Checklist, which dealt with authenticity and coherence, ethical and moral concerns, and the use of interpreters

A University of Washington computer engineering graduate student, Bart Niswonger, designed the course Web site (http://depts.washington .edu/poa/courses/hum498). It included Chait's lesson plans, full text readings, and a private e-mail site that allowed for bidirectional life-history interviewing. Ghirmai and Chait chose the simple e-mail structure rather than the more ambitious chat rooms and bulletin boards originally envisaged, because technological capacity and the eleven-hour time difference made a synchronous interactive site unviable.

Much of the course was conducted in this virtual space, which allowed students to share their cultural knowledge and thus enrich the basic field research skills learned in the classroom. Each student was allotted a conversational partner from the other university, and, over the ten-week period, the partners interviewed each other at least once a week. Chait provided a list of general topics to cover the different stages of the interviewee's life so that by the end of the term students would have sufficient material to write up a brief (twelve-page) life history. The rest of the class time was spent discussing the online lessons and illustrating them in practicums.

The student body on the Eritrean side consisted of graduate and senior students taking courses in the new Department of Eritrean Languages and Literature. Two-thirds were men, one-third women, and the group's ethnicity was predominantly Tigrinya. All identified themselves as upperclass, and most as religious. On the American side, the students were first- to fourth-year undergraduates; one was a graduate student. Gender broke evenly, but great variety in religious beliefs prevailed. Most students considered themselves middle-class, and the rest, blue-collar. Anomalies appeared on both sides. One University of Washington student, an American man of Eritrean descent, spoke a certain amount of Tigrinya and was familiar enough with the culture to assume the role of insider. Similarly, three local Seattle Eritrean American correspondents, and Ghirmai himself, participated in the program on the Eritrean side to provide everyone with a partner.

Life-History Teaching Texts

In selecting texts for teaching life-history writing in English through the Internet to students in a developing country, Chait paid attention to two criteria. First, although English is the medium of instruction at the University of Asmara, students read English as their second or third language and therefore need relatively straightforward texts. At the same time, required texts have to be challenging enough to keep American students engaged. (Although students at the University of Washington acquired a few words of Tigrinya, they could not read or correspond in that language or in Arabic.) Second, as in most developing countries, the University of Asmara's campus library stocked few up-to-date scholarly works in English. To accommodate this lack of access, Chait placed all readings online. (Since the site functioned only for members of the two classes and for a given period of ten weeks, the use of such material fell within copyright guidelines.) Even with the texts made available, however, the Eritrean students had difficulty keeping up with the reading because of their time-limited access to the Internet and the Eritrean service provider's erratic service. Since legibility of the online readings was not always optimum, long articles that strained the eyes had to be avoided. On the whole, however, the online readings proved relatively successful in circumventing the problem of unequal access to textual knowledge.

The Life Story Interview, by Robert Atkinson, proved the most valuable text for online multicultural instruction because of its breadth of material and its straightforward description of the steps involved in life-history interviewing and writing. Covering virtually every aspect of the process, the book also features a sample life history. *Current Biography* issues provided additional instructive case histories. Brief and topical, they appealed to student tastes, Eminem and Condoleezza Rice being popular choices. Chait had hoped these case histories would help students in the two countries explore problems inherent in multicultural interviewing and lead to the mutual brainstorming of solutions, but once again, the Eritreans' limited Internet access proved a stumbling block. Ultimately, Internet priority had to be given to acquiring life-history material, so that the final texts could be completed in the ten-week period.

Herbert Rubin and Irene Rubin's *Qualitative Interviewing: The Art of Hearing Data* supplemented Atkinson, as did L. L. Langness and Gelya Frank's *Lives: An Anthropological Approach to Biography*, which proved particularly helpful on such topics as professional responsibility and ethical and moral concerns. Other standard life-history texts especially valuable for developed- developing-world interaction included Kent A. Ono's "Change as a Cultural Variable in Cross-Cultural Communication Research." The danger of an African version of Edward Said's *Orientalism*, an issue that concerned both Chait and Ghirmai, lurks in many cross-cultural communication efforts, and students must be apprised constantly of the inevitability of change. The phrase "Communities in Transition" in the course title was designed to alert both sides to the fact that their societies were not static but always in process, although despite post-9/11 events, the Americans struggled to see their country as being in transition.

Also valuable for cross-cultural communication was Amanda Coffey's *The Ethnographic Self: Fieldwork and the Reproduction of Identity*. This text stressed an aspect of the relation, whether in the field or online, that sometimes is overlooked—that in the process of finding out about the other person and his or her culture, one learns even more about oneself. Perceiving how one is viewed by the other stimulates self-examination, about both oneself and one's country. To further this effect, Chait gave students a three-step project in which their selves were assessed from their own perspectives, from the perspectives of their costudents, and finally as perceived in the virtual space. The result opened the eyes of many students, who had assumed an essential self. On the other hand, the new awareness of a versatile self afforded certain freedoms and suggested opportunities for self-reconstruction. In the course evaluations, a number of students mentioned the insight into themselves as a valuable class experience.

Chait devoted class discussion to empathy, sympathy, transference, and countertransference in the interviewing process. Though unable to find a text perfectly matched to the transcultural virtual reality relationships developing between the two lots of students, Chait drew on Mikhail Bakhtin's notion of architectonics to explore the way one acquires one's sense of one's self from the reflections of it seen through the eyes of others. Bakhtin's blurring of distinctions between biography and autobiography also helped convince students that they not only played an integral part in acquiring the life stories but also existed themselves in the others' texts that they wrote. Romance too was an inevitable presence. On the Web site, students had posted photographs of themselves, and it was no coincidence that the most photogenic students were contacted and paired off first. Romantic undercurrents transcended cultural barriers; private e-mail accounts suddenly popped up and were offered for further conversation. (Coffey's chapter 6, "Romancing the Field," proved helpful in negotiating this challenge.)

In addition to reading life-history texts, students read on their own for historical and cultural representations of their conversational partners' country. Chait compiled for the American students a reading list of Eritrean fiction and nonfiction available at the campus library. Classroom visits by Eritrean speakers, a scheduled Eritrean history test, interaction with Eritrean Americans, and a class visit to an Eritrean restaurant increased the students' knowledge. A similar list of United States texts was given to the Enitrean students, but availability posed a problem. As a result, the students had unequal degrees of exposure to the others' country, although the Eritrean group had the advantage of CNN and in fact knew a great deal more about the United States than the Americans did about the Horn of Africa.

In preparing class, Chait drew on theoretical texts in psychology, psycholinguistics, and semiotics. While students were not required to study such texts themselves, summaries of the specific arguments, made relevant to their multicultural situation, helped them read beyond the lines. Roland Barthes's *The Semiotic Challenge* oriented students toward identifying cultural embeddedness in their partners' stories—whether ethnic, political, religious, class, or gender-driven—and also toward identifying it in themselves and their texts. Bakhtin's dialogism taught students how to recognize heteroglossial strands in the supposedly unitary voices of their interviewees. And Jacques Lacan's *Écrits* gave insight into the division of the self, alerting students to the *objet petit a* that sometimes lurked in the text and to which they might—or might not—need to respond.

While no specific postcolonial theoretical texts were assigned, Eritrea's colonial past under Italy and England was central to student discussion. Chait introduced concepts such as center/periphery, Manichaean allegory, master-slave narrative, neocolonialism, borderlands, contact zones, autoethnographic texts, and sameness/difference. Most often, these references arose spontaneously in response to specific circumstances, but a postcolonial reader and relevant papers containing these terms would be valuable assets to understanding individual and communal behavior.

Student Texts

While all these texts honed the life-history writing skills that the students developed, their correspondences themselves became the texts that elevated class learning.[2] Cultural competence in the other's social, religious, and historical background had been one of the pedagogical goals, but the student texts went further, providing an on-the-spot, incremental acquisition of connection and understanding. As mediums of learning, these texts shifted student knowledge toward a deeper, intercultural consciousness and a more intimate appreciation of the conversational partner, thus creating a relationship rather than merely a knowledge transaction. The texts could serve this purpose because the Web site provided a virtual home where students could express themselves relatively freely. Although Ghirmai and Chait had access to students' correspondence, the students had been assured that the design of the Web site precluded others from reading their mail. (One intruder from Asmara did attempt to check into the program but could not lurk beyond the set text of the Web site.) Given the political unrest in Eritrea and the danger to students, confidentiality was a high priority, and Chait's students were instructed to use the utmost sensitivity and discretion in political discussion with their correspondents. The University of Washington donated two laptops to provide Ghirmai's students with more readily available computer access.

In the relatively safe harbor of the course Web site, then, students found a third space where they could speak. Despite the time difference and server erraticism on the Eritrean side, the conversations continued, each text containing appropriate questions, follow-ups, and probes to move the life story further. In effect, the conversations were three-way, the instructors serving as silent onlookers who followed the interview and response process and then commented on their own students' work. Chait responded directly through the site, identifying problems in the content, nature, or tone of the questioning; suggesting alternate approaches; and generally helping forward the student's life-history project. In this way, the emerging student life stories became pedagogical texts in themselves. Following instructor guidelines, conversational partners also conducted peer

reviews of each week's interview, evaluating each life-story writing install-
ment for accuracy, clarity, the organization of material, and so on.

Two additional developments emerged in this third space that proved
particularly conducive to the flow of life-story narrative. First, the conversations of the two learning communities converged. The early life texts
started off formally, but as the conversations continued, students found
points of contact. As with students anywhere, this common territory included love, romance, and dreams for the future, but, unexpectedly, it also
contained intimate expressions of loss, inadequacy, pain, and betrayal.
When one partner made an admission of this kind, it often elicited a similar soul-baring account in the other. Couched in the particularities of the
culture, such intimacies were assimilated effortlessly alongside the affective
discourse. Since a local Eritrean American had prepared the Seattle students to expect reticence at a personal level from their Eritrean partners,
this openness came as a surprise, especially since the Americans had
planned to hold back on their own loquaciousness and to start off more
formally. As expectations were recalibrated, however, the conversations
found their level, moving between sameness and difference. Whereas self-
consciousness might have hindered personal disclosure in a face-to-face
conversation, in this third space a degree of anonymity prevailed, as if the
students were talking not of themselves but of other objectivized persons.
Since Eritrean culture historically emphasizes the community rather than
the individual, personal reflection rarely surfaces in conversation. For some
Eritreans, therefore, these online conversations, and the life histories written about them, represented the first time they had seen themselves and
their life experiences as coherent wholes. Because students had been instructed to search for patterns and to find the organizing principles in the
stories, they offered their counterparts images, even *imagos*, of themselves
that they had consciously or unconsciously projected.

The second helpful development was that, in providing a third space
for textual production, one neither Eritrean nor American, the Internet to
some degree liberated students from the unequal power relationship represented by each country's stance toward the other. As postcolonialist scholars,
Ghirmai and Chait were intimately aware of the pitfalls of developed- and
developing-nation collaboration and tried their utmost to maintain equal
learning experiences for the students and for themselves. Limitations on
technological, financial, and informational access inevitably handicapped
their best intentions; nevertheless, in this virtual storytelling place, the

re-created textual self emerged on a relatively even playing field. Cut loose from such perceived dichotomies as black/white, rich/poor, First World / Third World, the narrative I appeared in the electronic space as equal with the narrative other. As new online versions of the other emerged and students revisioned their correspondents, they began to query existing texts about the other and to interact more critically with their own life-history texts, which they now saw as situated.

Electronic texts add a new strand of writing to the life-history genre, a strand that can elicit from multicultural conversational partners an openness and directness not easily obtained in traditional encounters. Further, the addition of this electronic thread in the dialogic space provides the instructor with varied and productive pedagogical opportunities. Added to standard instructional and theoretical texts, student texts created in the third space provide teachers with continuing access and thus the chance to instruct and guide the emergent life-history writer. While initially development of an online course plus a real-time lesson plan may seem like double duty, repeated use and adaptation of the online structure eventually render it time- and cost-effective. With some modifications, the Web site can also be adapted by instructors from fields and disciplines outside the English department and with universities in other countries.

Reflections on the University of Asmara Participation

Sandra Chait's portion of this article describes and analyzes our educational experiment in life-history writing through electronic space, conducted between students of Asmara University and the University of Washington. I focus on the experience of the Eritrean participants, detailing some of the real problems, challenges, and gains but also reviewing the experiment critically, with the benefit of hindsight. I begin by briefly comparing traditional and modern modes of life-history telling, which I use later in analyzing the performance of the Asmara University students that takes into account Eritrean cultural and linguistic reality.

First-person written narrative, or autobiography, refers to socially and culturally constructed accounts of men and women, as ascribed to and projected by them, on the basis of their gender, ethnicity, class, and professional and ideological stances. If successful, the genre provides storytellers with considerable advantages, enabling the chroniclers to generate in their own voices information about themselves and their lived experiences—and to do so, as Edward Said remarked in the introduction to his memoir, without being too bothered about "others"; it gives the narrator sole responsibility "[f]or what I recall and see, not individuals in the past who could not have known what effect they might have on me" (*Out of Place* xii–xiii). Once constructed, such narratives can also help correct wrong views about the writers and their communities at large. That is why there has recently been an enormous proliferation of autobiographical works from members of minority ethnic groups, marginalized persons, women, exiles, refugees, and displaced persons in the West and elsewhere. But writing one's autobiography has its pitfalls. Once fixed in print, the written text becomes an artifact in the public domain, one that is open to reader interpretations, which can lead to all kinds of (unintended) social and political sanctions against the subject. Though widely practiced now, historically this form of writing is regarded as a Western invention (see Lejeune).

Oral history, on the other hand, is traditionally perceived as a mode of telling and preserving that is transmitted orally rather than through writing. Because of the "technologizing of the word," oral history has assumed a "secondary" role in the West, while it still remains the "primary" mode in Third World countries where the rate of literacy is low (Ong 1–3). But apart from their historical and geographic associations, written autobiography and oral history also differ in a number of methodological and stylistic ways, and these differences determine and affect their production and consumption. Drawing on readings of autobiographical texts by postcolonial and other writers and on my engagement with Eritrean oral and written literatures over the past few years (Negash), I offer a quick list of the most visible differences.

Written autobiographies are constructed by an active and conscious nurturing of the maker; oral deliveries depend on casual, more intimate, and spontaneous methods.

By being fixed in print, the written autobiography evokes an authoritative air; oral history is more flexible and always open for feedback, even for corrections and additions from listeners.

Oral rendition communicates with verbal (language) as well as nonverbal (physical gestures) signs; the written narrative typically tends to use cultivated and conventional discourse techniques.

Because the primary source of oral history and literature is memory, oral stories are almost always communicated in bits of information and thus often look incomplete, fragmentary. Written autobiographies generally create the impression of having an organized structure and wholeness—a beginning, middle, and end. This alleged authenticity and orderliness is reinforced by the often claimed use of private and public documents, as well as the soul-searching periods undergone by their authors, though these sources too are largely shaped by memory.

Finally, and more important, written narratives are meant to be read as more private accounts of individuals, while oral histories claim or want to be received as collective histories and dwell less on personal matters in any depth.

In Eritrea, oral history has been used since time immemorial. Storytellers and oral historians have depended on firsthand observation and heard evidence to communicate information and preserve culture. In addition to enacting their artistic roles, male and female oral poets have been instrumental in shaping the society's perception of itself and its history. But Eritrean society and culture today is at a crossroads of tradition and modernity, as a result of the combined effects of increased local literacy, globalization, and cultural transformation campaigns instigated by the liberation movement during the armed struggle (1961–91) and after independence.

Such critical discriminations between the traditional oral form of history and written life history and contemporary Eritrea's obviously changing culture are very important for understanding the background and the perspectives of the students of Asmara University who participated in ethnographic life-history writing through the Internet. Growing up in Eritrea, they were conditioned by direct and indirect knowledge and the influence of traditional storytelling. Yet coming from the disciplines of history, literature, and anthropology, they also had considerable knowledge of other cultures and of the kind of writing expected of them to communicate effectively with their American counterparts. Concretely, what this means is that the students' representations of themselves were informed by an amalgam of two concepts and norms of writing: one indigenous and almost intuitive, reflecting their home culture, and the other acquired and cosmopolitan, dictated by the more instant demands of the print and electronic age. Though there were of course clear instances of cultural code switching on both sides of the equation, those by the Asmara University students were especially perceptible in situations where they felt that their experiences or expectations seemed to diverge from those of the American students. Some adjustment and fine-tuning strategies were thus necessary to maintain effective communication—which may explain the hesitancy in the beginning and the communicative directness and intimacy toward the end of the program.

Two other factors affected, for better or worse, the students' positioning and style of writing. One is language. All the participating students of Asmara University were bilingual or multilingual, speaking Tigrinya as their first or second language. They were fluent in English, the language of their education, but when they had to write in it, two tendencies became apparent: at one extreme, to produce abstract and less emotional writing and, at the other, to produce narratives that read as a translated version of their first language. Though often done unwittingly, eventually the latter inclination seemed to work better and also proved easier to do. As became clear to us in the process, it was easier because, as Said assures us, "everyone lives life in a given language; everyone's experiences therefore are had, absorbed and recalled in that language" (*Out of Place* xi). The second factor was of my own doing. Though I had wanted to act more as a facilitator than as a participant, I also frankly discussed with the students beforehand the implications writing public or semipublic histories (such as we had designed) could have on their lives, following more or less the analysis I put in the opening passages of this piece. Thus one can say that the input of the Asmara University students was predicated on a complex web of factors and immediate (my intervention) and long-term (culture, history, their training, and language) influences, some of which must have been liberating, and others impeding.

It is necessary to mention one more practical element that affected our work during the exchange. The students of Asmara University were all highly computer-literate and made continued effort to be up-to-date with the University of Washington students, but because of the slow and failing Internet provisions in Eritrea, we had to put up with frustrations and temporary disappointments. It was only when we realized that online communication was not doable and moved to more conventional uses of the Internet that we participated fairly actively.

What was most satisfying in the whole experience was to see that in the end feelings, including love and friendship, were pouring out between the partner students. Interestingly, as one student told me, some had even exchanged their private e-mails to continue the fun outside the common cyberspace created, so as not to let the teachers and other students feel embarrassment. My initial interest was focused on the success of the project in itself, but as it turned out, one of the important things this experience teaches and reconfirms at a pedagogical level is that there is always a more complex and a more human hidden story behind every formalized, shared life story—as indeed the continued interchanges of the privately corresponding students clearly show.

Notes

1. Surnames, as we know them in the West, do not exist in Eritrea. Eritrean names are composed of a given name followed by the given name of one's father. Thus in this article reference to Ghirmai Negash is to Ghirmai (and not to Negash). Although our original intention was to conduct parallel classroom instruction, this plan did not materialize on a consistent basis. Difficulties with computer and textual access in Eritrea and institutional responsibilities limited the time and involvement Ghirmai and his students could devote to the course project. For similar reasons, although we planned this essay as a joint effort, our descriptions of class activities, projects, and discussions apply to each of our classrooms alone. The first three sections, by Sandra Chait, focus on the University of Washington participation; the final section, by Ghirmai Negash, describes the University of Asmara participation.

2. Quotes from student texts have not been used in this essay as it was not possible to obtain permission from all the students involved. Nevertheless, we would like to take this opportunity to express our sincere thanks to all members of the spring 2002 class in Seattle and Asmara.

Works Cited

Atkinson, Robert. *The Life Story Interview*. Qualitative Research Methods Series 44. London: Sage, 1998.

Bakhtin, Mikhail. *The Dialogic Imagination: Four Essays by M. M. Bakhtin*. Ed. Michael Holquist. Trans. Caryl Emerson and Michael Holquist. 1981. Austin: U of Texas P, 1992.

Barthes, Roland. *The Semiotic Challenge*. Trans. Richard Howard. New York: Hill, 1988.

Brislin, Richard W., Kenneth Cushner, Craig Cherrie, and Michaelani Yong. *Intercultural Interactions: A Practical Guide*. Cross-Cultural Research and Methodology Series 9. London: Sage, 1986.

Coffey, Amanda. *The Ethnographic Self: Fieldwork and the Representation of Identity*. Thousand Oaks: Sage, 1999.

Jameson, Fredric. *The Political Unconscious: Narrative as a Socially Symbolic Act*. Ithaca: Cornell UP, 1981.

Lacan, Jacques. *Écrits: A Selection*. Trans. Alan Sheridan. New York: Norton, 1977.

Langness, L. L., and Gelya Frank. *Lives: An Anthropological Approach to Biography*. Novato: Chandler, 1981.

Lejeune, Philippe. *Le Pacte autobiographique*. Paris: Seuil, 1975.

Negash, Ghirmai. *A History of Tigrinya Literature in Eritrea: The Oral and the Written (1890–1991)*. CNWS 75. Leiden: Universiteit Leiden, 1999.

Ong, Walter. *Orality and Literacy: The Technologizing of the Word*. 1982. London: Routledge, 1993.

Ono, Kent A. "Change as a Cultural Variable in Cross-Cultural Communication Research." *Communication and Identity across Cultures*. Ed. Dolores V. Tanno and Alberto Gonzalez. London: Sage, 1998.

Rubin, Hubert J., and Irene S. Rubin. *Qualitative Interviewing: The Art of Hearing Data*. Thousand Oaks: Sage, 1995.

Said, Edward W. *Orientalism*. New York: Vintage, 1979.

———. *Out of Place: A Memoir*. New York: Knopf, 1999.

Ethnographic and Autoethnographic Approaches

Daniel Heath Justice

No Indian Is an Island: On the Ethics of Teaching Indigenous Life Writing Texts

The latter half of the nineteenth century is an instructive period to begin this brief reflection on the ethical teaching of Indigenous life writing. It is in this era that the individual life stories of Indigenous peoples as racially coded stereotypes became particularly popular among Euro-Western readers, as an aggressive militarized campaign of United States imperialism and cultural nationalism led to the slaughter of Lakotas at Wounded Knee Creek in South Dakota, the decimation of the Métis resistance in present-day Manitoba, and the overthrow of the Hawaiian monarchy for the benefit of a small group of United States missionaries and plantation owners, just to mention some of the most striking attacks. At the same time, feverishly obsessed ethnologists, assuming that Indigenous peoples were destined to vanish before the onslaught of white civilization, collected (often through deception and outright theft) both human burial remains and various expressions of material and oral culture, which were then consigned to museums—away from the very Indigenous peoples to whom those bodies and materials were of deep cultural and spiritual significance. Finally, an increased fascination in Euro-Western popular culture with the image of the vanishing native, given vitality by Henry Wadsworth Longfellow's "Song of Hiawatha" (1855), led to an ostensible mourning for the supposed fading of the culturally generic noble savage with a nostalgia drawn from the willful denial of the brutality of Euro-American colonialism.

Why do I begin here? Indigenous lives didn't begin or end with the nineteenth century, and Indigenous communities were and continue to be vibrant, adaptive, and expressive despite unrelenting oppression by the dominant nation-states in this hemisphere. It could be argued that starting this inquiry with the nineteenth century replicates some of the most intransigent problems that accompany Native studies, particularly the overwhelming emphasis on Native communities after Euro-Western colonization—as though Native America came into being only after Columbus began his reign of terror in 1492 or as though Indians were only historical artifacts relegated to the past.

Despite these risks, I bring attention to this period because it illuminates the origins and endurance of some of the greatest challenges to teaching Indigenous life writing. As colonialism of this period denied the living realities of Native peoples through armed force, economic deprivation, and geographic displacement and enclosure, it simultaneously celebrated the assumed erasure of Indians in both scientific and popular discourse, as each elegy to the vanishing noble savage simply embedded this mentality more firmly in the Euro-Western mind. "The Noble Savage," as Robert F. Berkhofer, Jr., notes, "is really a nineteenth-century fashion" that drew from many social, intellectual, and artistic influences (88), and the representations of Indians emerging from this time became the blueprint for many of the stereotypes and expectations that mainstream readers still bring to texts by and about Native peoples.

Indigenous literatures—from life writing to traditional orature, fiction, poetry, nonfiction, sermons, treaties, wampum belts, winter counts, totem poles, paintings, birch-bark documents, and so on—are often a challenge to teach, primarily because of the disconnect between the contexts of most students' subject positions and those of the texts, authors, and communities being encountered. The challenge is particularly acute with Indigenous life writing, as the privileged and generally invisible individualism that permeates most mainstream auto/biography often clashes with the kinship ethos defining tribal communities across the world. Life writing in most Native contexts is understood as being about the individual as part *of* a community, not apart *from* it. The singularity of "life writing" is its plurality. The story isn't just about the individual Indigenous subject but extends to the web of relationships and contexts defining that subject's place in the world—what the Seneca social worker Terry L. Cross calls a "relational world view." If "to form a relationship with somebody you have to become a part of their context" (149), this relationship between self and context, individual and community, gives us insight into the most meaningful values of Indigenous life writing.

The teaching of Indigenous life stories across North America introduces students to many different kinds of texts, including direct, fictionalized, and fraudulent autobiographies, biographies, and as-told-to or, as the Crow Creek Sioux scholar Elizabeth Cook-Lynn dubs it, "informant-based" narratives, where "the essential focus is America's dilemma, not questions about who the Indian thinks he/she is in tribal America" (122–23). Such texts often become little more than an ethnographic inquiry—an attempt to understand the supposedly mysterious and inscrutable nature of the objectified Indian. The most popular and enduring texts among non-Natives have often been those that draw most explicitly from those three historical threads of influence from the nineteenth century that entwined around the idea of the inevitable disappearance of Indigenous peoples. Some are the romanticized as-told-to narratives of "an old Indian person who, for whatever reason, turns, not to other Indians, but to a good-hearted white writer to preserve his or her sacred knowledge" (Deloria 174), such as John G. Neihardt's account of a Lakota holy man's life and visions, *Black Elk Speaks* (1932), and John Fire Lame Deer's *Lame Deer, Seeker of Visions* (with Richard Erdoes), both staples of New Age fascination since the 1970s. Fraudulent autobiographical works by Archie Belaney (better known as Grey Owl), Sylvester Long (a.k.a. Chief Buffalo Child Long Lance), and the notorious Forrest (Asa) Carter share a deep fatalism about Indigenous continuity, and their popularity among the mainstream public during various eras reveals much about the anti-Indian sentiment at the root of even those "mediated" texts purporting to celebrate the lives of Native people. In each of these texts, there is no Native future. Living Indians are artifacts and museum pieces, meaningful only as memory.

My teaching approach to all Indigenous literatures is heavily context-based, and it privileges Indian lives told by Indian people themselves. Following the examples of the literary scholars Craig S. Womack (Muskogee Creek/Cherokee), Robert Allen Warrior (Osage), Jace Weaver (Cherokee), and Cook-Lynn, I believe land, history, politics, community, and cultural contexts matter. We can't understand the literature of the People in ways meaningful or respectful to their living realities without engaging with the social and cultural understandings that inform that literature. Since Indigenous writers consistently affirm their relationships to a particular community, the significance of those ties to their aesthetic expressions and the values, history, and concerns of that community should be of central importance to any thoughtful inquiry.

Sensitivity to context is especially important when we approach the highly contested category of Indigenous life writing. Many Indigenous scholars, writers, and communities challenge the supposed ethnographic transparency of Indigenous life writing as participating in individualistic, Euro-Western traditions that often privilege the solitary self at the expense of the People and the rights and responsibilities embedded in the practice of kinship (see esp. Cook-Lynn 119–31). Other Native people, however, view life writing as a site of decolonization that humanizes and challenges the often invisible processes of oppression (see Owens 151–66), and while outlining these positions in detail is beyond the scope of this essay, it is an important concern for teaching Indigenous life writing, because the sociopolitical status of Indigenous peoples is different from that of other groups, especially in the Americas. Native people aren't just representatives of another ethnicity. Politically, legally, and culturally, they are distinct tribal nations whose sovereignty is, in large part, maintained through spiritual and social ties to specific land, community, and kin networks. Indigenous life stories are as much, if not more, about the People as about the individual, and our approach must neither erase the writer's personal voice and vision nor displace the writer's self from these larger contexts. Indeed, an individual's life story reveals a necessary human dimension of the struggles against the forces of assimilation and Indian hating. At its best, then, the self-in-community gives voice to the community, not simply to the self.

For these reasons, life writing is always a component of my Indigenous literature courses but never the exclusive focus, since singular attention to that form inevitably runs the risk of privileging individualism over community, no matter how much the material addresses relevant historical, cultural, and political contexts. When I teach life writing, the works I select are those that highlight those contexts. Maria Campbell's autobiography, *Halfbreed*, can't be understood without understanding the history of the Métis people in Saskatchewan and western Canada; and the Métis poet Gregory Scofield's poetic biography of his mother and aunt, *I Knew Two Métis Women*, is emptied of much of its meaning if the reader is unfamiliar with Métis history, the concerns of contemporary urban Natives, and the particular struggles of Aboriginal women in Canada during the latter half of the twentieth century. The cowritten autobiography of the former principal chief of the Cherokee Nation, *Mankiller: A Chief and Her People*, explicitly weaves Wilma Mankiller's personal story with those of her family and the larger Cherokee national body, as does the Quiche Mayan activist Rigoberta Menchú's compelling *I, Rigoberta Menchú*, which gives witness to her people's resistance to the Guatemalan government's killing squads in the 1970s and 1980s. Although the latter book has been challenged by academics such as David Stoll and Dinesh D'Souza for its assumption of a collective perspective in its politicized narrative account, a number of others, including Cook-Lynn, Arturo Arias, and Greg Grandin have vigorously defended Menchú's work, charging her critics with misunderstanding (or misrepresenting) Indigenous narrative conventions that emphasize the collective I over the individual I. This misunderstanding is one of the most important challenges in teaching Indigenous life writing, since it's far too easy in class to fall back on established individualist Euro-Western conventions, to the detriment of the entire educational experience. Because teaching is an ethical practice and intellectual exercise, we must firmly root Native voices at the center of analysis, for to do otherwise is to prepare the fertile soil for a harvest of ignorance, misrepresentation, and the active silencing of Indian voices.

Because I include Indigenous life writing to emphasize the enduring presence and vitality of Native communities today, in the face of enduring stereotypes and metaphors of erasure, the texts we read tend to be contemporary, drawing from the growing body of literature by Native writers speaking their own truths and those of their various peoples. On occasion I'll teach something older—the nineteenth-century autobiography of Lili'uokalani, the monarch of Hawai'i who was deposed with the help of the United States in 1893, is a particularly moving account of the Hawaiian people's struggle to remain sovereign despite a corrupt and brutal imperialist regime—but I generally leave these texts to my upper-level courses for those students already fully aware of the endurance of Indigenous peoples today. It's also important to note that before the red power movement of the 1960s and 1970s, much life writing by Indians is permeated with despair and pessimism that can readily reinforce the nineteenth-century stereotypes about the vanishing native. I don't advocate censoring these voices—indeed, they speak to the realities of many Indigenous people of that time (and ours) and deserve attention too—but I do believe that these texts provide challenges that require particular sensitivity to the larger contexts in which they exist. For example, *Indian Boyhood* and *From the Deep Woods to Civilization*, by Charles Alexander Eastman (Santee Sioux), are richly layered chronicles of his early years, but their embrace of much of the era's assimilationist rhetoric can, when read out of historical context and without an eye toward today's vibrant Indian presence, solidify deeply rooted cultural biases that are already difficult to dislodge.

Native people have never had much use for Euro-Western borders, especially those imposed across land and on symbolic or physical bodies. Indigenous life writing crosses genres as well as historical and cultural boundaries, and much of the most powerful life writing comes in the form of poetry. Take the work of the Menominee poet Chrystos, who confronts the reader with the sensual, passionate, and pain-filled chronicle of her ongoing life story as a queer, working-class Indian woman, while also giving voice to the silenced stories of those others who share her world. Her poetry breaks definitions of life writing wide open, freeing her to speak with a searing honesty that is often missing from more conventional autobiographical narratives. The list of contemporary Native poets whose work travels the narrative contours of their lives is as diverse as it is impressive, including Beth Brant (Mohawk), Joy Harjo (Mvskoke), Haunani-Kay Trask (Hawaiian), Gregory Scofield (Métis), Simon J. Ortiz (Acoma Pueblo), Carroll Arnett/Gogisgi (Cherokee, deceased), Wendy Rose (Hopi/Miwok), Esther Belin (Navajo), and Deborah Miranda (Esselen/Chumash). While in dominant cultures poetry tends toward overtly personalized expression, the most compelling Indigenous poets consistently commit their individual voices to community concerns—Brant writes of Two-Spirit / Queer Natives and their necessary place in their tribal nations, Trask responds to the effects of the ongoing colonization of Hawai'i, and Belin comments on the struggles and possibilities of urban Indian lives—in ways largely foreign to the still-influential nineteenth-century decadent aesthetic of art for art's sake.

I teach Indigenous literatures at the University of Toronto, the largest university in Canada and one of the largest in North America, with a combined student body of about seventy thousand. Of the ten thousand–plus faculty and staff members on campus, I'm one of a handful of tenure-track Indigenous professors; there are only a few hundred self-identified Aboriginal students here, although there are an estimated fifty thousand Aboriginal people in Toronto, a city with a population of four million human beings. The large majority of students in Aboriginal studies and Aboriginal literature courses are non-Native. These statistics tell me a few things. The first is that a lot of students go through the higher education system, and most of them aren't Native. The second is that the classes my Native colleagues, non-Native allies, and I teach might be the only significant contact that many students have with the cultural, intellectual, political, and artistic concerns of over a thousand culturally and politically distinct Indigenous nations in the United States and Canada alone, not to mention the thousands of others elsewhere in this hemisphere and around the world. The enrollment statistics also show me that there's a hunger among students, regardless of their heritage or background, for truthful education about Indigenous peoples.

It's often a struggle to try to make up for a lifetime of miseducation in a term or a year, but it's a worthy challenge. Teaching Indigenous life writing gives living voice to the realities of contemporary Native peoples, but only when done with respect for the contexts and values that define Indigenousness today. Whether we present a single text taught in a non–Native studies course or multiple Indigenous voices on the syllabus, it's the relation of the writer, text, community, and contexts that make engagement with Indigenous life writing meaningful. These texts present us with an ethical choice that challenges the notion of Indians as artifacts of a vanished age and places students in conversation with different ways of being and of understanding self and community.

Gloria Bird (Spokane) reminds us that "writing remains more than a catharsis; at its liberating best, it is a political act. Through writing we can undo the damaging stereotypes that are continually perpetuated about Native peoples. We can rewrite our history, and we can mobilize our future" (30). As teachers, we are writers, too—active participants in social narratives that have an enduring impact. What our students encounter in the classroom—both text and context—will be written into the stories that give meaning to their lives, but not all meaning is healthy, or honest. It's not enough simply to teach about the life of an individual Indigenous writer and expect that we've done our part in sensitizing students to Native concerns. The self outside of community is, in the end, simply more of the noble savage writ large, the Indian without a tribe, the last of the Mohicans disappearing with the sunset. It is as *peoples* that we endure, and those are the life stories that matter the most.

Works Cited

Arias, Arturo, "After the Rigoberta Menchú Controversy: Lessons Learned about the Nature of Subalternity and the Specifics of the Indigenous Subject." *MLN* 117.2 (2002): 481–505.

Berkhofer, Robert F., Jr. *The White Man's Indian: Images of the American Indian from Columbus to the Present.* New York: Vintage, 1978.

Belin, Esther. *From the Belly of My Beauty: Poems.* Tucson: U of Arizona P, 1999.

Bird, Gloria. "Breaking the Silence: Writing as 'Witness.'" *Speaking for the Generations: Native Writers on Writing.* Ed. Simon J. Ortiz. Tucson: U of Arizona P, 1998. 26–48.

Brant, Beth. *Writing as Witness: Essay and Talk.* Toronto: Women's Press, 1994.

Campbell, Maria. *Halfbreed.* 1973. Lincoln: U of Nebraska P, 1982.

Cook-Lynn, Elizabeth. "American Indian Intellectualism and the New Indian Story." *Natives and Academics: Researching and Writing about American Indians.* Ed. Devon A. Mihesuah. Lincoln: U of Nebraska P, 1998. 111–38.

Cross, Terry L. "Understanding Family Resiliency from a Relational World View." *Resiliency in Native American and Immigrant Families.* Ed. Hamilton I. McCubbin. Thousand Oaks: Sage, 1998. 143–57.

Deloria, Philip J. *Playing Indian.* New Haven: Yale UP, 1998.

D'Souza, Dinesh. *Illiberal Education: The Politics of Race and Sex on Campus.* New York: Free, 1991.

Eastman, Charles Alexander. *From the Deep Woods to Civilization: Chapters in the Autobiography of an Indian.* 1916. Lincoln: U of Nebraska P, 1977.

———. *Indian Boyhood.* 1902. Mineola: Dover, 1968.

Grandin, Greg, and Francisco Goldman. "Bitter Fruit for Rigoberta." *Nation* 8 Feb. 1999: 25–28.

Lili'uokalani. *Hawaii's Story by Hawaii's Queen.* 1898. Honolulu: Mutual, 1982.

Mankiller, Wilma, and Michael Wallis. *Mankiller: A Chief and Her People.* New York: St. Martin's, 1993.

Menchú, Rigoberta. *I, Rigoberta Menchú: An Indian Woman in Guatemala.* Ed. Elisabeth Burgos-Debray. Trans. Ann Wright. New York: Verso, 1984.

Owens, Louis. *Mixedblood Messages: Literature, Film, Family, Place.* Norman: U of Oklahoma P, 1998.

Scofield, Gregory. *I Knew Two Métis Women.* Vancouver, Polestar, 1999.

Stoll, David. *Rigoberta Menchú and the Story of All Poor Guatemalans.* New York: Harper, 1998.

Trask, Haunani-Kay. *From a Native Daughter: Colonialism and Sovereignty in Hawai'i.* Rev. ed. Honolulu: U of Hawaii P, 1997.

Joycelyn K. Moody

Women, Race, Reading, and Feeling: Postmemory in Undergraduate Studies of Slave Narratives

> *Our masters always tried to hide*
> *Book learning from our eyes;*
> *Knowledge didn't agree with slavery—*
> *'Twould make us all too wise.*
>
> —Frances E. W. Harper, "Learning to Read" (1872)

I once considered it my duty to write pedagogical essays about African American literature. I thought, If—as the demographics indicate—white folk are the teachers and white folk are the students, but black folk are the subject, it might as well be me who teaches the teachers. No more. Given that my current research projects and classroom teaching focus on African Americans as learners, teachers, and scholars; unpack black encounters in fundamentally white classrooms; and analyze black negotiations of white higher education, this essay does not advise white professors about how to teach African American literature to white students. Instead it offers some strategies for instructing black (women) students as they study enslaved women's narratives in ethnically diverse college classrooms.[1] Because black women students are desperately outnumbered in most courses in African American literature in state and research universities, and even more in small, private liberal arts colleges, they do not get the critical pedagogical consideration that they deserve, suffering instead the status quo of their marginalized lives.[2] Even if a black feminist scholar—like me—directs their professors' teaching of African American literature, they will be neglected. No more.

I first planned to explain how I circumnavigate the extreme sentimentality white women students tend to bring to their study of antebellum slave narratives. In preparation, I read Laura Wexler's essay "Seeing Sentiment: Photography, Race, and the Innocent Eye," a penetrating analysis of whites' readings of nineteenth-century photographs of black women servants and slaves with white infants.[3] Wexler sharply admonishes a sentimental denial and political resistance that she exposes in contemporary feminist literary criticism and cultural theory: "although feminism sees photographs, the question has become, frankly, just what is it that feminism sees" (252) and to what "has [it] so far refused to attend" (251). A similar sentimental cultural resistance cum blind(ing) racism flourishes in my classrooms. I want to extend Wexler's useful theorizing to the positions of pity and pathos that my white students apparently expect their African American women classmates to occupy. For without the thoughtful intervention of conscientious professors, black women students risk being read through lenses no less objectifying than those embodied in their enslaved forebears' narratives, which form the central subject of the course.

Wexler's characterization of early photography as a form of "domestic self-representation [that] worked by staging affect, or imaging relation— literally *seeing sentiment* as a way of organizing family life" (255)—is useful to me in contemplating race and gender dynamics that sometimes emerge when I teach antebellum slave narratives.[4] My white women students often unwittingly organize and even hierarchize the class population sentimentally, apparently to reduce their own discomfiture with the key tropes of narratives of chattel slavery—backbreaking labor, racial subjugation, physical violence, psychosexual sadism, and ruptured kinships—and yet at the same time to reify their self-conceptualizations as sympathetic and decent, true women. The results of these efforts can be to leave African American women students on the margins of a course in which their ancestors form the primary subject. I mean this image quite literally: winter 2003, most of my black students congregated in one corner of the classroom, at the tip of the semicircle of student desks, closest to the lectern-table. At the opposite tip of the arc, two more black students sat among whites.

Wexler borrows from the sociologist Patricia Hill Collins the term "outsider within" to identify blacks on the periphery of antebellum formal family portraits—photographs of slaveholding whites (258–59). For Hill Collins, this term designates "the social position of the black woman domestic worker in white families" (qtd. in Wexler 273n21); for me, it suggests the positionality of black women in the white academy. The autobiographical opening of Brenda M. Greene's "Remembering as Resistance in the Literature of Women of Color" describes her traumatic schoolgirl feelings during the stage that racial identity formation theorists call *encounter*: "This duality and alienation began to manifest themselves when I entered primary school, the real world of school" (97).[5] Although at college Greene found community and guidance among "other black students who had had similar experiences" (or what racial identity formation theorists call African American *immersion/emersion*; see Tatum 55–56, 75–77, 80–82), it is as coeditor of and contributor to *Rethinking American Literature* that she articulates not only the *internalization/commitment* (see Tatum 55–56, 76) that marks African American adult maturity but also the confusion of her girlhood: "as an African American woman in higher education, I do not see myself represented in America's perception of itself" (97).[6]

So this essay asks, What are the particular needs and challenges of African American women students who take (my) courses in United States antebellum slave narratives?[7] What might African American women gain by studying enslaved women's narratives alongside white women in majority white institutions? What acts of subversion must they engage to avoid being regarded by their peers (and professors) as native informants, especially on academic terrain they entered precisely to learn what they did not know?

To theorize answers to these questions, I confess I draw on subjective perceptions rather than empirical data—in part because, as a poststructuralist critic, I affirm the textuality and the constructedness of history. If, as Fredric Jameson says, "History is what hurts" (qtd. in Peterson 1), then I reconstruct my experiences with teaching the sorrowful history of chattel slavery in the United States to demonstrate that for black students, "it has become painfully difficult to articulate [i.e., to remember, to study alongside whites] counterhistories that do not share [the] values" of "mainstream American history" (Peterson 1). My twenty years of college classroom teaching validate Njoki Nathani Wane's contention that "[f]or many years, African American students have stood on the periphery of educational success. Traditional educational methods have often proved inadequate, necessitating the examination of alternative school models" (548). Specifically, African Americans engaged in studies of chattel slavery seem to me to experience what Marianne Hirsch has called "post-memory." Hirsch applies this term to post-Holocaust Jews whose lives are "dominated by memories of what preceded" their births ("Family Pictures" 8). So too are my students, as descendants of slaves, deeply connected to a horrific past they did not endure but nonetheless embody, remember, and sustain. Like the Holocaust photographs Hirsch analyzes, the narratives my students read combine the documentary with the aesthetic:

> They hold up the "having-been-there" of the victim and the victimizer, of the horror. They remove doubt, they can be thrown in the face of revisionists. In contrast, the aesthetic is said to produce agency, control, structure, and therefore distance from the real, a distance which could leave space for doubt. ("Family Pictures" 10)

Exploring this paradox is my greatest challenge in teaching slave narratives, for as a subgenre of autobiography, they deploy distinct sets of rhetorical conventions that students must be taught how to read. As Lindon Barrett contends, students "expect to engage through their experiences of reading [slave] narratives singularly representative or authentic experiences of 'blackness' and 'enslavement,' and these expectations are problematic because they diminish intriguing textual negotiations undertaken by the narrators as well as the powerful sociopolitical imperatives overdetermining racial categorization" (31). Moreover, United States antebellum slave narratives often deploy tropes of sentimentality and sympathy that invoke students' own sentimental responses to the vexed legacies of slavery.[8]

I strive to establish the difference between sympathy and empathy—the former manifest as pity and condescension, the latter consisting of "cognitive, affective, and behavioral components" that, when interacting with cultures alien to one's own, yield the assumption of a perspective that privileges those alien cultures or that yields action taken "on behalf or in service to other's needs" (McAllister and Irvine 433). United States antebellum slave narratives written in the mid–nineteenth century served didactic functions in the struggle for abolition. One lesson they collectively aimed to teach was, of course, that grief or sympathy was a right response to the dehumanizations of chattel slavery. As social psychologists have shown, however, when the response to great injury remains only grief, sympathetic persons fall into either depression or apathy rather than move toward the healthier responses of empathy and action. To move from grief to empathy requires the proverbial combination of head and heart; that is, such transition requires an emotionally intelligent excavation of slave narratives as sites of human debasement and moral defiance.

As I work to effect this transition, I find that black and white women students, though for different reasons, have difficulty understanding the phenomena of African American subversion and "signifyin(g)" (Gates). Nonblack students seem to fear a loss of control over their relationships with their African American classmates or, worse, with the black woman professor who will evaluate their course performance. For blacks, unpacking these rhetorical strategies conversely includes an anxiety about self-revelation and about my ability to manage power relations in the classroom. Black women students experience complicated feelings of guilt, pain, shame, pride, anger, and relief (there but for the grace of God . . .) when studying slave narratives—fears intensified by studying slavery alongside whites and increased further when the professor is another African American woman. Black students also fear a loss of control over their nonblack classmates' ignorant or insensitive attitudes toward blacks; they seem to fear disclosing their own deployment of subversion for survival as well as to fear validating the racist myth that blacks are natural prevaricators and therefore untrustworthy, immoral, and unscrupulous.

A brief assignment usually suggests the range of emotions brought to studies of slavery. At the beginning and at the end of the course, I ask students to write a one- to two-page self-assessment. The first essay states their expectations, goals, and hopes for our explorations of African American literature, life, and cultures. In the final self-assessment, students reflect on an aspect of their course work—perhaps an analysis of problems and challenges along the way—and describe resolutions they devised, provide a diagnostic overview of what their writing for the course reveals about their individual academic strengths, and conclude with a critical discussion of ideas they pursued about African American literature or people. Whatever its focus, this essay allows students to reconsider and participate in the evaluation of their course performance. While I have been amazed at the resistance of some white students to these assignments, many black women students have welcomed both introspective essays as a kind of safe dialogue with me—or rather a monologue, since an implicit rule is that I neither grade the essays nor talk back to them.

One major assignment recently elucidated for me some of the critical needs of black women students. I close with a brief discussion of this assignment, to reinforce my perception of the urgency with which instructors must heed African American voices in college classrooms. (As Wane warns, "[T]he negation of African American perspectives is one of the root causes of the perpetuation of inequities and disadvantages facing African American educators and students" [550].) This library research project required students to find, read, assess, and review a scholarly article that addressed a critical course issue. From the provided list of topics, several African American women students selected sexual violence against enslaved women and in turn Edward E. Baptist's "'Cuffy,' 'Fancy Maids,' and 'One-Eyed Men': Rape, Commodification, and the Domestic Slave Trade in the United States." While the title arguably reveals Baptist's condemnation of sexual violence within chattel slavery, these black students discounted his critique of historians of nineteenth-century slavery who "have focused their attentions on explaining slaveholders' paternalist defenses of their planter institution" (1620). Pushing past the apologies of these earlier historians, Baptist uncompromisingly exposes sexual perversions not as merely among slavery's atrocities but as so integral to them that the peculiar institution was itself a sexual fetish for some slave traders (1622–23). Baptist's anger, however, was lost on my students, each of whom denounced his succinct declaration that "[r]esistance is not the subject of this essay" (1623). Clearly, their own experiences with race, gender, sex, and perhaps class oppression led them to misread the article as insufficiently critical of sexual violence against enslaved women. From their perspectives and in their value systems, when the rape of black women is the issue, disregarding resistance negates both the discussion and the discussants. Furthermore, decentering resistance in this context can only produce irresponsible scholarship.

So they failed a decisive component of the assignment. On their papers and by e-mail, I asked each student to meet with me so that I could reiterate in person the extensive critique I had written on her paper. Two did come (separately), and I explained further the significant difference between explicit protest literature in African American literary traditions and a scholarly analysis thoroughly researched and couched in academic language. While affirming the value of ethically responsible scholarship, I explained how academic language as political activism can go a long way toward confronting immoral systems and arguing for social change.

Several aspects of this experience are significant. For one, my students clearly mistrusted Baptist as (they presumed) a straight, white, male academic who seemed to support the violence against slaves that he researched. To an extent, his very topic, and his relation to it, condemned him. Moreover, my students seemed to read themselves in and as the rape victims and thus saw both themselves and their ancestors as violated by powerful men. Their misapprehension of Baptist's thesis ensued from a lack of critical distance from the topic, from their profound lack of experience with reading scholarly articles (which I designed the assignment to begin to correct), and from their internalization of enslaved women—their foremothers—as *me–not me* and their self-perception among "sympathetic" white peers as object and subject. Also instructive for conscientious teachers is the students' apparent assumption that protest against rape and other forms of sexual violence against enslaved women should take only one discursive form in academic writing and their insinuation that no one who is not a black woman can function as the political ally of black women. I had effective and mutually satisfying conversations about their misinterpretation[9]—perhaps because I ensured their safety with my affirmations about the various functions and forms academic writing can take, with my positive comments about other aspects of their article reviews, or with my phenotype—that is, with my race and gender identities.[10]

Initially, I wanted to explore in this essay my pedagogical goals of having students desert their persistent need for a simplistic historical truth in the study of slavery and of supplanting it with more sophisticated questions about authorship, authority, reality, and authenticity. Instead, I have explained ways I teach performative elements of slave narratives, as part of my effort to get all students "to see the conscious nature of our constructions. . . . That very constructedness is among the chief constituents of slave narrative testimony that we want to bear in mind in our examinations of the narratives" (McBride 8, 9). Specifically, I have tried to articulate the importance of centering and strategizing to resolve some of the reading and feeling experiences of African American women students in their study of enslaved women's narratives.

Notes

For very helpful comments on early drafts of this essay, I am grateful to Angela Ginorio, Susan Glenn, Karen M. Gourd, Lorraine J. Martínez, Caroline Chung Simpson, and Shirley J. Yee.

1. By "black" I refer to persons who identify themselves as descending from Africans (as well as, perhaps, from additional racial or ethnic groups). I also refer to persons judged by others as black on the basis of complexion or phenotype. And I refer to persons whose cultural origins or values conform to conventional African American cultural values. Moreover, as Njoki Nathani Wane notes, "Black communities are increasingly composed of a complex fabric of different cultures, customs, and ethnicities, particularly in large urban centers" (552).

2. Gretchen McAllister and Jacqueline Jordan Irvine report that even a majority of African American women instructors involved in a research study of shifting paradigms in cultural transformation, ethnic diversity, and student-centered education—instructors who teach in "high-poverty, predominantly African American schools"—ultimately "seemed to focus on their teaching of non-African American children. Most of their examples . . . regarding their practice revolved around children from cultures that were different from their own despite the emphasis in lectures and readings on African Americans and schooling" (441). While McAllister and Irvine speculate that this disparity is due perhaps to the study's explicit concentration on "different cultural backgrounds" or to the "cognitive dissonance" that can occur from interaction with cultural communities other than one's own (442), I am arguing that neglect of the educational needs of blacks, even by black women, is conventional and normative vis-à-vis pedagogies, epistemologies, and research foci in the white academy.

3. It is important to note that the portraits Wexler scrutinizes—part of the George Cook Collection at the Valentine Museum in Richmond, Virginia—antedate abolition though taken "circa 1865" (254), not only because the black "nursemaids" they depict are significantly either still bound or yet subject to bondage, but also because of paradigm shifts in both photography and literature, namely, the rise of realism, after abolition.

4. In my courses on slave narratives, I use photographs, such as Sojourner Truth's *cartes de visites*, reproduced in Nell I. Painter's *Sojourner Truth*. I select images that I hope will stimulate discussions of the power of nineteenth-century visual imagery, the relative absence of photographs of black folk in nineteenth-century America, and acts of subversive self-representation in nineteenth-century portraits. Truth and Harriet Tubman are perhaps the most famous black women of the nineteenth-century United States precisely because extant photographic images of them accompany their heroic legends. Also helpful are Jeanne Moutoussamy-Ashe's *Viewfinders: Black Women Photographers*, Deborah Willis's *Picturing Us* as well as her *The Black Female Body* (coauthored with Carla Williams), and Kathleen Thompson and Hilary Mac Austin's *The Face of Our Past*, to illustrate the power of the photographic image as icon, performance, or retribution.

5. Stages of African American racial identity development are discussed, for example, by Beverly Daniel Tatum throughout *"Why Are All the Black Kids Sitting Together in the Cafeteria?" and Other Conversations About Race*. She provides an overview on 18–28.

6. See Tatum for fuller discussion of the stages of African American racial identity.

7. La Flamme articulates many of the challenges that women of color graduate students face in predominantly white institutions.

8. For fuller discussions of these terms and their antebellum connotations, see Barnes; Hartman; and Samuels.

9. According to McAllister and Irvine, "the research literature confirms that empathy and caring are linked with achievement, particularly for culturally diverse students"—the latter phrase probably intended to connote nonwhite students.

10. I think another black woman student was more wary not only of my professional authority but also of her own performativity and "self"-representation, and so she did not talk with me as I requested. This student's paper overall was weaker than the other women's; the misreading of Baptist's thesis was not its only problem.

Works Cited

Baptist, Edward E. "'Cuffy,' 'Fancy Maids,' and 'One-Eyed Men': Rape, Commodification, and the Domestic Slave Trade in the United States." *American Historical Review* 106 (2001): 1619–51.

Barnes, Elizabeth. *States of Sympathy: Seduction and Democracy in the American Novel*. New York: Columbia UP, 1997.

Barrett, Lindon. "The Experiences of Slave Narratives: Reading against Authenticity." *Approaches to Teaching* Narrative of the Life of Frederick Douglass. Ed. James C. Hall. New York: MLA, 1999. 31–41.

Gates, Henry Louis, Jr. *The Signifying Monkey: A Theory of Afro-American Literary Criticism*. New York: Oxford, 1988.

Greene, Brenda M. "Remembering as Resistance in the Literature of Women of Color." *Rethinking American Literature*. Ed. Lil Brannon and Greene. Urbana: NCTE, 1997. 97–114.

Hartman, Saidiya. *Scenes of Subjection: Terror, Slavery, and Self-Making in Nineteenth-Century America*. New York: Oxford UP, 1997.

Hirsch, Marianne. *Family Frames: Photography, Narrative, and Post-memory*. Cambridge: Harvard UP, 1997.

———. "Family Pictures: *Maus*, Mourning, and Postmemory." *Discourse* 15 (1992–93): 3–29.

Jacobs, Harriet. *Incidents in the Life of a Slave Girl, Written by Herself*. 1861. Ed. Valerie Smith. New York: Oxford UP, 1988.

La Flamme, Michelle. "An 'Uppity' Memoir and Some 'Cheeky' Tips: On What It Is Like for Me to Be a Woman of Colour at a University Whose Structure Is

Still Predominantly White and Eurocentric in Its Focus." *Thirdspace* 3.1 (2003). <http://www.thirdspace.ca>.

McAllister, Gretchen, and Jacqueline Jordan Irvine. "The Role of Empathy in Teaching Culturally Diverse Students: A Qualitative Study of Teachers' Beliefs." *Journal of Teacher Education* 53 (2002): 433–44.

McBride, Dwight A. *Impossible Witnesses: Truth, Abolitionism, and Slave Testimony.* New York: New York UP, 2001.

Moutoussamy-Ashe, Jeanne. *Viewfinders: Black Women Photographers.* New York: Writers, 1993.

Painter, Nell I. *Sojourner Truth: A Life, a Symbol.* New York: Norton, 1996.

Peterson, Nancy J. *Against Amnesia: Contemporary Women Writers and the Crises of Historical Memory.* Philadelphia: U of Pennsylvania P, 2001.

Samuels, Shirley, ed. *The Culture of Sentiment: Race, Gender, and Sentimentality in Nineteenth-Century America.* New York: Oxford UP, 1992.

Tatum, Beverly Daniel. *"Why Are All the Black Kids Sitting Together in the Cafeteria?" and Other Conversations about Race.* Rev. ed. New York: Basic, 1999.

Thompson, Kathleen, and Hilary Mac Austin, eds. *The Face of Our Past: Images of Black Women from Colonial America to the Present.* Bloomington: Indiana UP, 1999.

Wane, Njoki Nathani. Rev. of *African-Centered Schooling in Theory and Practice*, ed. Diane S. Pollard and Cheryl S. Ajirotutu. *Urban Education* 37 (2002): 548–57.

Wexler, Laura. "Seeing Sentiment: Photography, Race, and the Innocent Eye." *The Familial Gaze.* Ed. Marianne Hirsch. Hanover: UP of New England, 1999. 248–70.

Willis, Deborah, ed. *Picturing Us: African American Identity in Photography.* New York: New, 1994.

Willis, Deborah, and Carla Williams. *The Black Female Body: A Photographic History.* Philadelphia: Temple UP, 2002.

Sarah Brophy

Olaudah Equiano and the Concept of Culture

Arguments abound regarding the correct way to frame Olaudah Equiano's narrative for students. In a debate that appeared in *Eighteenth-Century Studies* in 2001, Adam Potkay takes issue with what he sees as the tendency of postcolonial criticism to privilege evidence of resistance; he insinuates that critics manufacture evidence of Equiano's resistance to acculturation and claims that contemporary criticism neither pays enough attention to rhetorical conventions nor will admit that Equiano was a wholehearted Christian ("History" 602). In the same issue, Srinivas Aravamudan and Roxann Wheeler each take Potkay to task for his argument that students be made to attend foremost to Equiano's mastery of rhetoric, arguing that this move depoliticizes the text. All three essays turn on questions of culture, though none fully names conflicting ideas of culture as the underlying source of contention. Potkay implicitly defends capital-C culture (culture as offering a universal model for identity) against reformulations of *culture as cultures,* which unmoor the concept from the Anglo-European tradition and rearticulate it to address questions of social justice, history, and identity formation. I suggest that, by stepping outside the framework of literary studies while remaining attentive to historical context, rhetorical strategy, narrative structure, and figurative language, we—teachers as well as students—can work toward a better grasp of what was at stake for Equiano in publishing this text and take the discussion of culture a step further by considering the conceptual challenges that the narrative poses to us, its legatees.

I teach *The Interesting Narrative of the Life of Olaudah Equiano* in a second-year course in cultural studies entitled Concepts of Culture and in a second-year American literature survey.[1] This early slave narrative (first published in 1789) plays an innovative historicizing role in a cultural studies curriculum; in turn, the experience of teaching this work in a course that explicitly engages the term *culture* has prompted me to rethink my approach to teaching the text in literary studies.

Following Raymond Williams's essay "Culture," the Concepts of Culture course maps out in the first few classes the contradictory meanings of culture, pointing to its early modern roots in the idea of tending natural growth, its associations with the cultivation of human character, and its dominant meaning for nineteenth- and early- to mid-twentieth-century critics: the arts considered as the source of Matthew Arnold's "sweetness and light" (Williams 90–91). I also outline the simultaneous emergence of the anthropological sense of a culture as a whole way of life and the growing awareness of a multiplicity of world cultures—a shift in meaning that Terry Eagleton argues gave rise to the characteristic postmodern use of the term *culture* to refer to group identities and allegiances of all kinds (43–44). The primary intent of the course is metacritical and historical; students trace debates about the concept of culture from the Enlightenment to the present. Since the course is cross-listed in several programs, the students come to the material with diverse backgrounds, including cultural studies, communication studies, postcolonial studies, English and American literature, comparative literature, and peace studies. I supplement the philosophical readings (which extend from Hume to Jameson) with autobiography and fiction written in the first person, because such texts stage for students a central concern of the course: the way various ideas of culture combine to constitute our working concepts (and the ideology) of the individual.

Students are most interested in two aspects of the text: Equiano's account of his early life in West Africa and his struggles to acquire literacy and gain his freedom. We begin here. I have students work in groups on a close analysis of the first chapter—an account of Equiano's early life and captivity—in terms of its content, purpose, tone, and sense of audience.

I encourage them to reflect on the narrative's strategy of relativizing Anglo-European culture by contrasting it with what is, by the narrator's admission (Equiano refers us to Anthony Benezet's history of Guinea and Thomas Clarkson's travelogue as his sources), a fictionalized and idealized account of African cultures (see Costanzo's notes 1 on p. 47 and 1–3 on p. 59). Working from the students' observations, I point out that Equiano anticipates the development of an anthropological sense of "cultures in the plural," as ways of life (Herder, qtd. in Williams 91); unlike a late-nineteenth- or early- to mid-twentieth-century anthropologist, however, he resists the typical hierarchizing that posits literate, technologically developed societies as most evolved and oral cultures as melancholy vestiges of a vanished past. He insists on a definition of the arts that includes music, dance, and oral poetry in addition to literature (48), and he collapses temporal distinctions by aligning the Eboe of Benin with the ancient Hebrews (55). Equiano's slyly serious attribution of cannibalistic appetites to the first white men that he encounters (70) also undoes progressivist accounts of culture by highlighting the ironic gap between the slave traders' claims to civility and the barbarism of their trading practices, which in their consumption of human beings are more than metaphorically cannibalistic (see Sussman, who argues that abolitionist references to cannibalism mobilize a form of "paranoid reversal" that brings into question European assumptions of cultural and moral superiority [116]).

Troubled by the fictionalization, some students raise questions about the text's reliability. I encourage them to consider how some of the most obviously invented aspects of the text play the most crucial roles in mapping out and potentially challenging the exclusion of displaced and racialized people from the matrix constituted by Western manners, customs, religion, and literacy. To take one example, we explore the significance of the trope of the "talking book," identified by Henry Louis Gates, Jr., as a central recurring trope in slave narratives (65). Fictionalized or not, the scene demonstrates several things: Equiano's youthful eagerness for knowledge, his exclusion from anything but a haphazard education, and the mystification in which the white world cloaks itself and its technologies. Including such details allows Equiano to testify to psychological truths and aspects of self-transformation that are not strictly possible to document. This is certainly the case later in the narrative, when—making the trope a reality—the Bible speaks to him, promising access to cultural knowledge and power. For who can hope to document a conversion experience, to verify its empirical truth (205–06)?

On the other hand, Equiano constructs himself as an exceptionally fortunate and gifted person—"a particular favorite of Heaven," as he says—who manages to survive the violent gulf between cultures in the era of the slave trade and to make his way to and through London, the metropolitan center of the Black Atlantic (45). His growing Calvinistic belief in predestination is interwoven with his struggle to survive by his wits and his success as a trader in his own right, a success that eventually allows Equiano to buy his manumission. Through a combination of heaven's favor, occasional opportunities to better his education and resources, and his own "dexterity," Equiano survives innumerable battles and begins to gain recognition and a measure of privilege, prosperity, and friendship among his fellows (105). As my students point out, a writer like E. D. Hirsch might applaud Equiano's mastery of the culture's common vocabulary and his application of this "cultural literacy" to economic ends, and certainly Equiano subscribes to a belief in individual transcendence that is strikingly similar to the emphasis on "personal merit" in Hirsch's neoconservative formulation of culture (12).

In the context of my American literature survey course, Equiano's mobility serves to make a nuanced transition from eighteenth- to nineteenth-century materials. Taught alongside Phyllis Wheatley's poetry and before Harriet Jacobs's *Incidents in the Life of a Slave Girl*, the story of Equiano encourages students to see the discourses of slavery and emancipation as historically changing and contingent; indeed, the relative fluidity of his world sharply and often surprisingly contrasts with the rigidity of the slave code and slave space in nineteenth-century America. Studying *The Interesting Narrative* also helps students grasp the differences that gender and religious discourse make to power relations and the formation of identity in the context of slavery. Unlike Wheatley or Jacobs and unlike the women slaves against whose plights Equiano measures his relative autonomy (for example, the woman who is forced to wear the "iron muzzle" [77–78]), he has the leeway to imagine himself as a Christian, literate, British subject by virtue of his exemplification of *Homo economicus*.

But something much more complicated is at work in the text than aspirations to acceptance, wealth, freedom, and integration. At several points, Equiano extends his discussion beyond the realms of economics and literacy to engage the notion of culture itself. He passionately denounces the asymmetries and inequities in the imperial economy and the concepts of culture that undergird it:

> When you make men slaves you deprive them of half their virtue, you
> set them in your own conduct an example of fraud, rapine, and cruelty,
> and compel them to live with you in a state of war; and yet you com-
> plain that they are not honest or faithful! You stupify them with stripes,
> and think it necessary to keep them in a state of ignorance; and yet you
> assert that they are incapable of learning; that their minds are a barren
> soil or moor, that culture would be lost on them. (127–28)

Derived from agriculture, through an analogy that links tending natural
growth and tending human development, the metaphors animating the
concept of culture function here in a creative, albeit problematic, way. For
Equiano, the minds of slaves are only "barren" because they are excluded
from culture; and commerce, when justly conducted, has an inherently cul-
tivating impact on individuals and nations. Significantly, the passage concludes with a quotation from book 2 of *Paradise Lost*, which not only
displays Equiano's mastery of the English language and its literature but
indirectly threatens insurrection by asking, in Milton's words, "and what
peace can we return? / But to our power hostility and hate" (128).
Equiano's gloss on the passage draws attention again to his belief that
commerce can be a morally invigorating force, not least because it is a vehicle for personal cultivation and prosperity. On the basis of necessary
links among commerce, individual freedom, and individual and societal
cultivation (where freedom and the right to engage in trade on one's own
behalf are really one and the same), Equiano proposes that rebellion can be
circumvented and the whole society strengthened by owners' "changing
your conduct, and treating your slaves as men" (128). He is thoroughly invested in a commercial ideology even as he seeks to criticize some prevailing assumptions about culture.

When situated as a self-conscious, strategic intervention in debates
about culture and the individual, Equiano's narrative effects a powerful
critical shift in both students' and teachers' understanding of culture's
complicated historical provenance. As a focal point of the unit on the Enlightenment in Concepts of Culture, Equiano's text opens up a conversation about the shifting dimensions and uses of ideas of cultivation,
commerce, self-development, and abolition in the late eighteenth century.
Introducing students to *The Interesting Narrative* in an American literature
survey helps, moreover, to generate a sense of slavery's discourses and material effects as historically variable. In both courses (and arguably, too, in
courses on eighteenth-century literature or transatlantic Romanticism),

staging Equiano's multifaceted and ambivalent engagement with culture prevents classroom discussions from becoming unproductively mired in questions of factual authenticity; facilitates a critical engagement with the text's broader rhetorical strategies, ideological investments, and historical significance; and sets the stage for an interrogation of culture and individualism in the courses' larger trajectories.

Note

1. The works-cited listing offers two editions of *The Interesting Narrative*. One, Vincent Carretta's, is an accessible and meticulous edition that has helpful notes and reprints·a number of Equiano's other writings. The other, edited by Angelo Costanzo, is also excellent and contains excerpts from abolition debates, including anti- and pro-slavery tracts. Page numbers for quotations from *The Interesting Narrative* in my essay are from the Costanzo edition.

Works Cited

Aravamudan, Srinivas. "Equiano Lite." *Eighteenth-Century Studies* 34 (2001): 615–19.

——. *Tropicopolitans: Colonialism and Agency, 1688–1804*. Durham: Duke UP, 1999.

Eagleton, Terry. *The Idea of Culture*. Oxford: Blackwell, 2000.

Equiano, Olaudah. *The Interesting Narrative of the Life of Olaudah Equiano*. Ed. Angelo Costanzo. Peterborough: Broadview, 2001.

——. *Olaudah Equiano:* The Interesting Narrative *and Other Writings*. Ed. Vincent Carretta. New York: Penguin, 2003.

Gates, Henry Louis, Jr. *The Signifying Monkey: A Theory of African-American Literary Criticism*. Oxford: Oxford UP, 1988.

Hirsch, E. D. *Cultural Literacy: What Every American Needs to Know*. Boston: Houghton, 1987.

Potkay, Adam. "History, Oratory, and God in Equiano's *Interesting Narrative*." *Eighteenth-Century Studies* 34 (2001): 601–14.

——. "Olaudah Equiano and the Art of Spiritual Autobiography." *Eighteenth-Century Studies* 27 (1994): 677–93.

Sussman, Charlotte. *Consuming Anxieties: Consumer Protest, Gender, and British Slavery, 1713–1833*. Stanford: Stanford UP, 2000.

Wheeler, Roxann. "Domesticating Equiano's *Interesting Narrative*." *Eighteenth-Century Studies* 34 (2001): 620–24.

Williams, Raymond. "Culture." *Keywords: A Vocabulary of Culture and Society*. Oxford: Oxford UP, 1983. 87–93.

Recommended Works on Equiano and Culture

Andrews, William L. *To Tell a Free Story: The First Century of Afro-American Autobiography*. Urbana: U of Illinois P, 1986.

Baker, Houston A. *Blues, Ideology, and Afro-American Literature*. Chicago: U of Chicago P, 1984.

Caldwell, Tanya. "'Talking Too Much English': Languages of Economics and Politics in Equiano's *The Interesting Narrative*." *Early American Literature* 34 (1999): 263–80.

Carey, Brycchan. *Olaudah Equiano, or Gustavus Vassa, the African*. June 2000. 7 Nov. 2006 <http://www.brycchancarey.com/equiano/index.htm>.

Carretta, Vincent. "Olaudah Equiano or Gustavus Vassa? New Light on an Eighteenth-Century Question of Identity." *Slavery and Abolition* 20.3 (1999): 96–105.

Chinosole. "'Tryin' to Get Over: Narrative Posture in Equiano's Autobiography." *The Art of the Slave Narrative*. Ed. John Sekora and Darwin T. Turner. Macomb: Western Illinois U, 1982. 45–54.

Elrod, Eileen Razzari. "Moses and the Egyptian: Religious Authority in Olaudah Equiano's *Interesting Narrative*." *African American Review* 35 (2001): 409–25.

Gilroy, Paul. *The Black Atlantic: Modernity and Double Consciousness*. Cambridge: Harvard UP, 1993.

Hofkosh, Sonia. "Tradition and *The Interesting Narrative*: Capitalism, Abolition, and the Romantic Individual." *Romanticism, Race, and Imperial Culture, 1780–1834*. Ed. Alan Richardson and Hofkosh. Bloomington: Indiana UP, 1996. 330–44.

Ogude, S. E. "Facts into Fiction: Equiano's Narrative Reconsidered." *Research in African Literatures* 13.1 (1982): 31–43.

A Son of Africa. Dir. Alick Riley. Aimamage Productions. BBC, 1995. 28 minutes.

Thomas, Helen. *Romanticism and Slave Narratives: Transatlantic Testimonies*. Cambridge: Cambridge UP, 2000.

Iulia-Karin Patrut

Eastern European Oral Narratives of the *Walled-Up Wife* and Their Retelling in Recent Life Writing Texts

One of the first challenges in any course on oral narratives and life writing texts is establishing the multiple links between these two forms of storytelling, both of which are closely related to personal and cultural identity. Since life writing is necessarily determined by assumptions about personal identity (Schürmann-Zeggel 71), constructing a specific life story requires outlining identity using cultural and language coordinates (Grider). To what extent, however, does the writing subject construct not only individual but also cultural identity? And how can we identify those circumstances that suggest the recurring use of patterns, motifs, and conflicts (McAdams)?

Literature and Multiculturalism is a semester course offered to advanced graduate students in cultural studies at the University of Lüneburg. A seven-lesson unit on life writing texts and oral narrative is part of this interdisciplinary seminar. The students—numbering about twenty-five—are generally highly motivated, often meeting between lessons to prepare discussions and presentations. They come from heterogeneous social backgrounds and can read and discuss in German and English. In one course, a student from the former Yugoslavia who was familiar with the oral narrative we analyzed made a short presentation about her experience with this motif, greatly enriching our discussions. I generally use oral narratives from Eastern Europe, in particular the widespread narrative of the *Walled-Up Wife*, since it is considered constitutive for cultural and individual identity in several Eastern European countries, including Romania, Greece, and the former Yugoslavia. This essay describes a typical, recent seminar.

Most of the students were familiar with questions regarding personal and cultural identity, but the multiple interconnections among oral narratives, life writing texts, and identity were completely new to them. During my introduction to the unit, I therefore pointed out the importance of oral narratives for discussing life writing texts from cultures that often define their identity through references to oral traditions. Since we were working on Eastern European texts, we had to acknowledge that numerous long-standing genres of verbal art still exist, sharing common ground with literary constructions of life experiences (Niles).

This short introduction was followed by a comparison of the impact of oral narratives on life writing texts in Germany and Romania. Students then turned to the oral narrative of the *Walled-Up Wife*, interpreting and analyzing its interactions with several contemporary life writing texts, including some autobiographical essays by Romanian students. This case study of the *Walled-Up Wife* consolidated and deepened the themes explained during the first sessions, while making students more sensitive to the concrete problems that occur when dealing with texts from unfamiliar cultures.

My German students were particularly interested in the long tradition of Romanian approaches to literary studies, which recognize the high aesthetic value of oral narratives and very often discuss oral genres such as epics, ballads, and legends when reflecting on literary theory. These oral narratives also often serve as reference points in Romanian analyses of modern novels and short stories.

One of the first classroom exercises was to draw up a chart comparing the role of oral narratives in the history of Romanian and German literature, paying particular attention to life writing texts. For the Romanian component, students became familiar with such oral narratives as the *Walled-Up Wife* or *Master Manole* and *Miorita*—in their original form (Mohanu) as well as in English translations (Levitchi). The course reader also included excerpts from works on Romanian literary history that focused on the interactions between oral narratives and written forms of literature (e.g., Behring 13–38). As for the German component, students could rely on their knowledge of literary history and theory.

In general, the students concluded that for German literature oral traditions were much less relevant. Only during the Romantic period (1795–1830) did oral genres receive close attention. Johann Gottfried Herder (*Stimmen der Völker in Liedern*), Achim von Arnim and Clemens Brentano (*Des Knaben Wunderhorn*), and Jakob Grimm (*Kinder- und Hausmärchen*) pled for their thorough examination. But generally, studies of oral genres were regarded as constituting a particular field that was not part of the central axis of literature studies.[1]

Drawing on a chart that we organized around five variants elaborated in small groups, the students proceeded with individual research. At the beginning of the next session, they presented the reasons they considered a certain autobiographical or biographical novel, journal, or other life writing text to be linked to one of the oral narratives being studied. Mihail Sadoveanu's novel *Baltagul* and Lucian Blaga's play *Master Manole* are two of the examples cited.

We developed criteria to distinguish between affirmative and distancing types of references to the oral narratives. I asked the students to what extent a life writing text critically tied to an oral narrative could still be classified as a work on identity that is indebted to verbal genres. We decided to debate this question in our final discussion of the *Walled-Up Wife*.

The Romanian version of the *Walled-Up Wife*, an oral ballad also entitled *Master Manole* or the *Monastery of Arges*, proved helpful in fulfilling the main pedagogical objective of enabling students to conduct their own analyses of the interconnections between individual and cultural identity, life writing texts and oral narratives. The selected version had to be of high aesthetic value and also generally considered constitutive of cultural identity in its area of distribution. Since I wanted students to expand their study to other Eastern European countries where this narrative is widespread, I acquainted them with Alan Dundes's volume *The Walled-Up Wife* and with information on the story known in Greece as *The Bridge of Arta* and in the former Yugoslavia as *The Building of Skadar*. Several untitled versions appear in Albania, Bulgaria, Hungary, and Turkey, and oral narratives with a similar plot exist even in India: *Seven Brothers and Their Sister* (Campbell and Bompas 17–21)[2] and *Keregehara* (Dundes 121–25).

All these *Walled-Up Wife* narratives are named after impressive architectural monuments or important buildings that still exist today—for example, the beautiful monastery on the Arges River in Romania. Almost every day at the Arges Monastery, built between 1512 and 1517, visiting pupils are told the story of *Master Manole* or the *Monastery of Arges* as if it were true, positioning the real monastery as evidence of the existence of the narrative's protagonists. A red inscription on the monastery wall still indicates the place where Ana, the mason's wife, is supposed to be immured. In this, Master Manole and Ana become a part of every generation's life experience.

The important buildings or other forms of construction in the Eastern European *Walled-Up Wife* narratives had to be erected by well-known master masons. An unusual obstacle occurs: everything they build during the day collapses overnight. In a dream, the leading mason is told to immure the first female relative—wife, daughter, or sister—reaching the building site, and he and the other nine masters swear to do so. The leading master's wife arrives first at the place, having surmounted hindrances such as a storm or a flood. The leading master, who seems to love his wife, hesitates, but then, claiming it is just for fun, he entices her into the foundation pit and immures her despite her pleas. The finished building is of unique beauty, and the masters are praised for their work.

In the Romanian ballad variants, a prince asks the masters to build a monastery; after they have started, he threatens them with immolation if they fail to finish. When the work is completed, the prince comes and orders the ladders to be removed. The nine masons cannot descend from the roof and die, some in a failed attempt to fly. Then, on hearing the mourning of his wife Ana, Manole, the leading mason, loses his mind, jumps from the roof, and dies.

In what follows, I refer to one of the most popular versions of the ballad, collected in 1852 (*Master Manole*, Levitchi 405–29). The first pedagogical challenge was to convince students not to consider the ballad as evidence of cultural primitivism or rawness. We then had to work out why the depicted violence and power relations did not necessarily affirm the status quo. A theoretical excursus elucidated ways of recognizing identity concepts that refer to unfamiliar cultural contexts. We discussed Sabina Ispas's reflections on cultural identity, ethnography, and folklore; the final chapter, written in English, was particularly valuable; it was successfully presented by three students as an introduction to the next session. Ispas proposes that widespread oral narratives are emblems for marking the processes of constructing identity, pointing to the high frequency of references to the *Walled-Up Wife* narrative as proof of this function ("The Sung Story").

The narrative's concentrated, powerful form, emblematic character, and ambivalence allow it to serve as both instrument and material for exploring representations of individual and cultural identity. We also discussed Mircea Eliade's mythic reading of the narrative. His theoretical premises are complex, and in an open discussion, I made sure that the students understood the parallels Eliade draws between the concept of axis mundi and the monastery. While acknowledging the power of his discussion, some students argued that his approach should not exclude different interpretative paths.

After two sessions on the ballad's content and questions of cultural identity, the students divided into groups to study apparent contradictions[3] and ambivalent moments not explained by their first interpretations. Their observations—the basis for their individual interpretations—included:

1. Although the masons were experienced and skillful—"nine worthy craftsmen . . . with Manole ten, the highest in fame" (405)—the walls collapsed: "at night came to nought, crumbled down like rot!" (409).
2. Manole seems to love his wife, Ana, for he tries to impede her from reaching the building site: "when he saw her yonder / his heart burst asunder; / he knelt down like dead / and weeping he prayed, / 'Send, o Lord, the rain . . .'" (415). But he still walls her up, although she implores him to stop: "Manole, Manole, / good master Manole! / Have done with your jest / 'tis not for the best" (421).
3. Manole seems to be both good-natured and cruel. Except for one line expressing compassion for the dying master—"Poor, poor Manole" (427)—the students found no text elements suggesting an unambiguous interpretation of Manole's character.
4. Although the prince obviously oppresses and menaces them, the masters never speak about this power structure that profoundly affects them.

We then proceed to contemporary life writing texts recently published in Ion Talos's anthology of original text versions. Talos collected written and oral life writing texts obviously connected to the oral narrative. I translated three texts from Romanian into German, all of them dealing with young daughters who had been walled up in a house or a tunnel that could not have been erected without this sacrifice. We focused on the story of a villager employed in building a railway tunnel that collapsed again and again. He took his young daughter to work with him, she died in the tunnel, and the work could be finished (texts 3 and 4 [446]; text 9 [447] is suitable for similar classroom use). This example shows how real-life accidents can conform to the narrative patterns of the *Walled-Up Wife* and can then become translated into new life writing texts clearly influenced by oral traditions.

We spent the last two sessions analyzing fifteen autobiographical essays by Romanian students that drew on some aspects of *Master Manole*. The students had been asked in a composition class to write three-page fictional autobiographical essays. They had been dealing with oral narratives but were not explicitly asked to link them to their fictional autobiographical essays. To distinguish different ways of understanding the narrative that could have influenced the Romanian students' essays, I referred to the unit on poststructuralism in *Literary Theory* (Rivkin and Ryan), an anthology students had worked with in earlier courses. Nine essays articulated identity concepts that echoed the character of Manole. Social pressure or concepts of faith were seen as legitimizing the necessity of sacrifice. Situations such as leaving or disappointing somebody were recast as sacrifices. Most interpretations occluded the murderous violence against the hardworking woman who reaches the building site first. The evasion of power dynamics and the failure to challenge the semantic sphere of the mythic concept of sacrifice helped suppress the plot's violence, without changing the narrative's main structure. Three essays reflected a critical attitude, but also a high awareness of the narrative's explanatory potential. Interpreting the narrative as tragic and therefore a negative example, these students revised it by trying to avoid sacrifice in their texts, preferring to find compromises. Since this plot is gendered in ways that invite the use of theoretical approaches based on gender and power structure analysis, I asked the students to write a one-page essay on these issues. (Some students also presented the ballad for discussion in a parallel course on gender studies and literature.)

By seeking to understand the different junctions between oral traditions and such constructions of identity and between reading and writing practices, the students came to perform multiple levels of analysis and interpretation of life writing texts. We discussed primarily the life writing texts of Romanian students and texts from the Talos collection; all of them transfer plots from the oral narrative *Master Manole* to their own lives. The non-Romanian students especially at first had difficulty finding causes for the positive reference to a plot that ends in a catastrophe. It was unthinkable for most of them to lend the plot an exemplary character or to take the plot as a model for the interpretation of their own lives, as the tunnel builder in the texts collected by Talos had done. This relation led immediately to the core of our problem, namely, the nature of possible links between oral narratives and the manner in which a person's own biography is interpreted or structured, retrospectively or prospectively. We therefore discussed which criteria an oral narrative had to fulfill for the students to consider it identity building. The answers ranged from complete rejection of existing narratives to concrete suggestions of models that had become objects of legend, like Joan of Arc as Saint Joan. We took this as a basis for discussing legends and myths and their being received into the academic canon.

With this in mind, especially some of the German students remembered the earlier critical analysis at school of the heroes of the *Nibelungenlied* such as Siegfried or Hagen, who were not only judged by their individual positive features such as courage or strength but also criticized for their propensity for violence. Two of the students had already suggested in their essays that those narratives considered decisive for national identity should be thoroughly analyzed but should not simply be taken as a model or template for their own experiences.

During the last, summarizing session, I addressed this relation, asking again about the dangers of unreflected identification between some oral narratives and students' own life stories. I again pointed to the approximately twenty contemporary examples that Talos cites. In the passages he quotes from the oral life stories, building sacrifices on the model of the narrative of the *Walled-Up Wife* are connected to actual deaths (449–53). The students then discussed the life writing texts of the Romanian students in which there were no actual deaths but legitimate sacrifices. As in the narrative, for example, it was right to sacrifice a holiday and a family gathering to do volunteer work organizing a weekend for senior citizens.

The students noted critically that oral narratives are, first of all, like all literary texts, ambiguous. The historical tradition of the *Walled-Up Wife* contains ambiguities and contradictions that became apparent during the seminar. Thus it creates problems when the idea of necessary sacrifice is used unreflectively as the standard for judging one's own biography. The Romanian students present supported this criticism, noting that the narrative functioned as elegy into the nineteenth century and was thus not viewed exclusively as instructions for life.

Finally, and this is the second aspect that we found, it is often only a simplified formula that is internalized as the alleged message and norm of the narrative. In the *Walled-Up Wife*, this formula, also found in Romanian schoolbooks (e.g., Toma 107–10), is that every cultural achievement demands great sacrifice. Actually this interpretation of the narrative dates from the nineteenth century, when heroic models were sought for Romanian nation building and willingness to sacrifice was a welcome norm. The Romanian students especially had evidently internalized this norm and in their essays tended to see a very strong correlation in their own life stories between outstanding individual achievement and willingness to sacrifice, once the correlation of the narrative was invoked.

Naturally, we did not critique that correlation openly during the seminar. What was more important was realizing the potential for relating oral narratives, especially when they function as building blocks for cultural identity, to the interpretation of one's own life story in autobiographical retrospectives and to developing a feeling for the ambiguity and potential multifunctionality of both narratives like the *Walled-up Wife* and one's own life story.

Notes

1. Important new impulses for the study of oral literature came from the German *Volkskunde* in the 1970s, particularly as a result of the Hermann Bausinger school.

2. In Indian narratives such as *Seven Brothers and Their Sister*, it is a water source or tank that often requires a sacrifice of a female relative; usually three, seven, or nine brothers sacrifice their sister; and in the end, she manages to escape and marry a wealthy husband, while the brothers understand that they have done wrong.

3. Thanks to Jörn Stückrath for suggesting that I use in my own seminar this method, which he developed at the Institute for German Language, Literature and Pedagogy, in Lüneburg.

Works Cited

Arnim, Achim von, and Clemens Brentano. *Des Knaben Wunderhorn: Vollständige Ausgabe nach der Erstausgabe.* 1806, 1808. Ed. Willi A. Koch. Düsseldorf: Artemis, 2001.

Behring, Eva. *Rumänische Literaturgeschichte von den Anfängen bis zur Gegenwart.* Konstanz: UP of Konstanz, 1994.

Blaga, Lucian. *Mesterul Manole.* 1927. Ed. Florea Firan and Constantin M. Popa. Craiova: Macedonski, 1992. 72–124.

Campbell, G. A., and Cecil Henry Bompas. "Three Santal Tales." Dundes 13–26.

Dundes, Alan, ed. *The Walled-Up Wife: A Casebook.* Madison: U of Wisconsin P, 1996.

Eliade, Mircea. "Master Manole and the Monastery of Arges." Dundes 71–94.

Grider, Sylvia. "Passed Down from Generation to Generation: Folklore and Teaching." *Journal of American Folklore* 108 (1995): 178–85.

Grimm, Jakob. *Kinder- und Hausmärchen.* 1837. Ed. Heinz Rölleke. Stuttgart: Reclam, 1997.

Herder, Johann Gottfried. *Stimmen der Völker in Liedern: Volkslieder.* 1778, 1779. Ed. Heinz Rölleke. Stuttgart: Reclam, 1975.

Ispas, Sabina. *Povestea Cantata: Studii de Etnografie si Folclor.* Bucharest: Viitorul Romanesc, 2001.

——. "The Sung Story." *Povestea* 182–98.

Levitchi, Leon, ed. *Romanian Popular Ballads.* Bucharest: Minerva, 1980.

McAdams, Dan. "Self and Story." *Perspectives in Personality: A Research Annual.* Ed. Abigail J. Stewart, Joseph M. Healy, and Dan Ozer. London: Kingsley, 1991. 133–59.

Mohanu, Constantin, ed. *Miorita. Mesterul Manole. Balade Populare Romanesti.* Bucharest: Minerva, 1998.

Niles, John D. *Homo Narrans: The Poetics and Anthropology of Oral Literature.* Philadelphia: U of Pennsylvania P, 1999.

Rivkin, Julia, and Michael Ryan, eds. *Literary Theory: An Anthology.* Malden: Blackwell, 1998.

Sadoveanu, Mihail. *Baltagul.* Ed. Ion Marinescu and Done Stan. Bucharest: Grammar, 2000.

Schürmann-Zeggel, Heinz. *Life Writing: Literarische Identitätskonstruktion in schwarzaustralischen Autobiographien und Lebensgeschichten.* Bern: Lang, 1999.

Talos, Ion. *Mesterul Manole: Contributie la studiul unei teme de folclor european.* Bucharest: Grai si Suflet–Cultura Nationala, 1997.

Toma, Marin. *Limba Româna. Lecturi literare. Manual pentru clasa a VII-a.* Bucharest: Didactica si Pedagogica, 1996.

Joanne Karpinski

Discerning Diversity in American Lives

The spiritual tradition founded by Ignatius of Loyola encourages students at Jesuit universities to explore the question, How ought we to live? In a Jesuit educational climate, imaginative and critical discernment is supposed to move beyond a narrow religious focus to permeate the core curriculum without stifling full and free intellectual inquiry. To accomplish this goal, Regis University requires all undergraduates to complete thirty-nine credit hours in core studies, featuring four seminars intended to provide students with an "integrative intellectual experience" grounded in the liberal arts ("Mission Statement" 16).

Though individual seminars emanate from various academic disciplines, the program as a whole is organized and sequenced by broad conceptual themes. The freshman seminar encourages students to move beyond their personal experiences to understand community and culture in a more inclusive and sophisticated way. To this end, the seminar includes community outreach and service learning as desiderata, thus emulating the Jesuit ethic that links spiritual exercises to problem solving in the world. Despite the declining numbers of Jesuits active on campus, this ethic continues to influence pedagogy at Regis.

Faculties at any institution that requires significant credit hours out-side the major wrestle with the lack of enthusiasm manifested by students in these apparently irrelevant general education courses. Faculty mem-bers at Regis who don't happen to be Jesuits—and women can't ever happen to be Jesuits—face particular challenges in constructing courses that "promote the formation of conscience and character" while teaching an academic discipline ("Undergraduate Core"). Teaching life writing helps minimize student disaffection by providing significant opportuni-ties for personal discernment that connect the individual to the broader community.

The cheerful narcissism of middle-class nineteen-year-olds frequently leads them to regard experiences outside their own narrow range as boring—or worse, invalid. Literary experience in particular suffers from this judgment to the extent that it is fictional (i.e., made-up). Life writing cannot be dismissed as a consequence of these insular criteria because it yields statements of witness, not mere stories. Examining choices and their consequences in other lives encourages students to discern the parameters of a just existence. Moving from the philosophical to the pedagogical di-mension, the study of life writing offers the students a smoother contin-uum between reading and their own writing and brings into the foreground the reverberations of race, gender, and social class on individ-ual lives.

I've found that social class, in particular, is nearly invisible to my stu-dents. Regis College was founded in 1880 to create an entrée for the chil-dren of Catholic immigrants into the economic and social leadership echelon of mainstream American culture. This American dream goal was so effectively accomplished that today the students at Regis come from a predominantly middle-class background. The study of life writing helps bring the issue of class into focus for them.

To create a more specific and personal locus for the broad themes of the seminar, I selected readings on the writers' experiences with food. Since this is an aspect of others' lives that all my students have necessarily shared and since few young adults are utterly indifferent to it, the topic encouraged class participation. The sequence of discussions led the students from the sensory, descriptive dimension of the writing with which they felt comfort-able and competent to discuss across the frontiers of economic and semiotic analysis. As Ruth Reichl points out in *Tender at the Bone*, "food could be a way of making sense of the world. . . . If you watched people as they ate, you could find out who they were" (back cover copy). In practical terms, the seminar service project of planning and providing food service to an after-school study-skills program at an inner-city middle school bridged the gap between issues raised in the texts and my students' personal experience. It opened their eyes to the economic and social complexity of the neighborhood that surrounds their campus enclave and gave them an experiential focus for analytic writing that helped overcome the deadly passivity that frequently characterizes students' research-based writing.

In the opening chapter of *The Apprentice: My Life in the Kitchen*, Jacques Pepin describes the wartime experience of being evacuated from his family apartment in an industrial town to work as a cowherd on a farm, where he would be safe from bombing and where finding food for him would not be a problem. These heavy parental considerations are visible to him only in retrospect, however; his six-year-old imagination is so fascinated by the fact that the farm wife spoons the evening porridge directly into hollows carved into the wooden tabletop that he does not notice when his mother quietly slips away. The dual narrative consciousness at work in young "Tati's" recollection not only reflects the distance between the child and the adult self but also models the distance between the biographical subject and the reader. The transition from estrangement to delight in the unfamiliar invited an empathetic response from students potentially indifferent to a life lived outside the dimensions of their experience. In other words, it encouraged them to invest in what Philippe Lejeune calls "the autobiographical pact" (14).

The first writing assignment for the seminar asked students to describe a cuisine experience that was personally significant to them. Writing in the first person reduced their reliance on the passive voice, but passives promptly cropped up as they tried to move from description to explication. Before they revised this assignment, we discussed grammar as a system of ethics that links the performer of an action to its consequences. Two passages from Helen Fremont's *After Long Silence* emphasize this connection. In the first excerpt, the author and her sister attempt to confront their mother about their shocking discovery that they are not the middle-class Catholic girls they thought they were but rather the children of Holocaust survivors. Refusing to engage with them, the mother concentrates on preparing a traditionally overabundant American Thanksgiving dinner. "Enough with the past! Enjoy today! Think about tomorrow!" the mother paradoxically exclaims (23), as she stuffs a turkey that celebrates America's origin but that for her represents the break she made with her European Jewish heritage. That this break is more wrenching than she will admit to her daughters is made evident in the verbs Fremont uses to describe her activity: she "muscle[s]" (19) the twenty-two-pound turkey onto the carving board and "breaks it up" by "twisting its bones" and "exposing its pink breasts" (20). In the second excerpt, a flashback to the mother's young adult life in the Warsaw ghetto, she and her sister use their good looks and skill with languages to get jobs in the German sector; to further her pretense, the mother buys a defiantly nonkosher sausage to bring home.

This use of food as a metonymy for family relations also appears in *Tender at the Bone*, where the mother's haphazard, thrift-driven efforts at creating meals represent her inner turmoil, her ambivalence about motherhood, and her dysfunctional relationship with her daughter. Meanwhile Reichl attempts to compensate for the disorder of her childhood by becoming an accomplished cook, because she feels that "food represents power" (74). A whole complex of social values attached to food appears in Anne Moody's *Coming of Age in Mississippi*, where the author illustrates the distance between her own class status and that of her childhood employer when she compares the meals she helps prepare for the white household with those she is able to cook in her own home:

> She taught me what a balanced meal was and how to set a table and how to cook foods we never ate at home. . . . I enjoyed learning these things, not that they were ever helpful at our house. For instance, we never set a table because we never had but one fork or spoon each; we didn't have knives and didn't need them because we never had meat. (45)

For Richard Rodriguez, food becomes entirely metaphorical: the increasing inability of the successfully assimilating Rodriguez children to converse with their parents at the family table provides the governing image of *The Hunger of Memory*. As an adult, Rodriguez goes to holiday dinners at which the only words uttered by his father are those of the grace before meals and from which his mother constantly gets up because "something [meaningful communication] is always missing from the table" (192).

I next asked the students to revise their initial essay by establishing a social context for their personal narratives about food. How do the preparation, presentation, and consumption of food reflect larger value systems? How do attitudes toward certain foods connect to overall values—are they consistent or contradictory? How can food be used as a metaphor in their expanded pieces of life writing? One student's personal essay about ordering her first espresso in a coffee bar grew into an investigation of how the fair trade coffee movement would affect growers, producers, and consumers. The drink that had opened a new, "adult" dimension of experience thus became a vehicle for exploring the world of economics and politics. Another student expanded her recollection of an Italian Christmas dinner into a reflection on the consequences that a new wave of ethnic immigration was having on her community's family businesses. Because the students had become personally invested in the research they undertook, their writing retained more energy and focus than I have found in other freshman-level research writing. Finally, the personal focus minimized the likelihood of wholesale plagiarism in the finished product.

Meanwhile, we began to plan our service learning project. I hoped that our reading had to some degree prepared my students to address empathetically the needs of the primarily Hispanic schoolchildren they would be serving. Lively discussions ensued about creating a nutritious menu that kids would actually like to eat. The students reminisced about their own food preferences at age twelve—had they included anything healthy? Somebody introduced the need for a vegetarian alternative. Finally, the class settled on lasagna (two pans with meat, one meatless), green salad, fruit salad, and brownies. They created a shopping list based on what they believed to be appropriate ingredients and quantities. One group volunteered to shop, another to cook, and another to transport and serve. Everything was accounted for, they believed.

The educational component of this enterprise began at the grocery store. The items the shopping team selected were fifty-five dollars over the budget that the dean's office had allotted. Now my students found themselves in exactly the same predicament faced weekly by the parents of their young clients. First they traded in all their name-brand items for generics. Still short of funds, they considered eliminating the meat but felt that would undermine their nutritional mission. Reluctantly, they cut the meat purchase in half and reverted to ground beef rather than Italian sausage. They decided they could do without tomatoes in the salad since the lasagna sauce was already red. Finally, they reshelved the ice cream they had planned for dessert, realizing that it would have been difficult to transport anyway.

Next the cooking team discovered that they had forgotten to reserve the well-equipped student center kitchen, so they would have to make do with the minimal facilities in the dorm kitchenette. How to cook and serve for twenty with only one pot? We were back in Mississippi with Ann Moody. The team split up, the girls doing food prep while the boys went off to scavenge equipment, but nobody besides myself seemed to notice a gender issue in this division of labor. Lasagna pans and brownie bakers were improvised from aluminum foil, salads were mixed in plastic laundry basins, and (amazingly) the results got to school on time. Luckily, cleaning up afterward wasn't nearly as chaotic as after one of the parties Reichl writes about.

Not long afterward, the class got a thank-you note from the students and their teacher. After they had all eaten as much as they could, they had sent the leftovers home with kids whose families weren't otherwise going to have much for supper. Remarkably, we learned that we were the only group who had offered a full meal to the program; neighborhood businesses had sent cookies or leftover pizza. As my students wondered if this was due to institutional indifference or to the school's being largely Hispanic, I could see that students were shifting perspective from potentially patronizing observers to empathetic participants in their young clients' situations.

Will they be able to bring this empathy to the subjects of literary texts in future reading? Perhaps not consistently, but the combination of the autobiographical pact and direct experience seems to have given them a more thorough preparation for this task. Further, autobiographical investment in the research topic produced a more energized and focused approach to analytic writing. Ultimately, I hope that this concentrated reflection on other lives contributed to the never-ending process of discernment concerning how we ought to live. That characterizes education in the Jesuit tradition.

Works Cited

Fremont, Helen. *After Long Silence: A Memoir*. New York: Delacorte, 1999.

Lejeune, Philippe. *On Autobiography*. Ed. and fwd. Paul John Eakin. Trans. Katherine Leary. Minneapolis: U of Minnesota P, 1989.

"Mission Statement." *Regis University Bulletin 2002–2003*. 16.

Moody, Anne. *Coming of Age in Mississippi*. New York: Dell-Random, 1968.

Pepin, Jacques. *The Apprentice: My Life in the Kitchen*. Boston: Houghton, 2003.

Reichl, Ruth. *Tender at the Bone: Growing Up at the Table*. New York: Broadway, 1999.

Rodriguez, Richard. *The Hunger of Memory: The Education of Richard Rodriguez*. New York: Bantam, 1982.

"Undergraduate Core Educational Experience." *Regis University Bulletin 2002–2003*. 21.

Jeraldine R. Kraver

Reading and Writing Ethnography

As a topic and a task, ethnography is an increasingly important component in all the classes I teach for preservice teachers. I am not alone: for many teacher-researchers, the qualitative analysis associated with ethnography is *the* method for studying classroom situations. One need only look to the work of Shirley Brice Heath, Mina Shaughnessy, Mike Rose, or Jonathan Kozol to see how education research benefits from ethnographic study. The concept of teacher as researcher encourages teachers to see themselves as researchers in their classrooms, schools, and communities, thereby promoting the kind of reflective teaching that problematizes issues in education and examines them critically.

Long before recent discussions, Louise Rosenblatt suggested the value of ethnographic research for students at all levels and across disciplines. In her timeless work *Literature as Exploration*, Rosenblatt describes the transaction between the reader and the literary text:

> The reader approaches the text with a certain purpose, certain expectations or hypotheses. . . . Meaning emerges as the reader carries on a give-and-take with the signs on the page. . . . [T]he meaning made of the early words influences what comes to mind and is selected for the succeeding signs. But if these do not fit with the meaning developed

thus far, the reader may revise it to assimilate the new words or may start all over again with different expectations. (27)

Within this transaction, Rosenblatt accounts for the "social origins and social effects" of both reader and text. For Rosenblatt, literature encourages readers to explore the experiences of others and to develop "the capacity to sympathize or to identify with" the unfamiliar (37), a capacity exemplifying "the multiple nature of the human being, his potentialities for many more selves and kinds of experiences than any one being could express" (40).

This transaction is not unlike the one between the ethnographer and the cultural text.[1] Reading ethnographies encourages students to explore the experiences of others, and conducting localized ethnographic research compels them to revaluate their surroundings. No longer concerned exclusively with the faraway or the exotic, contemporary ethnography examines "the near, the more familiar and the modern" (Damen 57). If traditional anthropology seeks to make the strange familiar, the goal of local ethnography is to make the familiar strange, encouraging students to consider with a more critical eye the multiple cultures that surround and define their own patterns of behavior.

Ethnographies and autoethnographies are easily incorporated into courses across the discipline of English.[2] I have integrated them into American literature courses—from broad surveys to period courses—and into courses in ethnic literatures. They are central texts in courses in women's or gender studies. In writing courses (first-year or advanced) and in teacher-education courses on literature and on writing, the reading and writing of ethnographies are central to my course content. As presented here, the curriculum may appear bifurcated—students first read and then write. However, in the same way that literacy experts well understand the connection between the processes of reading and writing, so too are the experiences of reading ethnographies and then conducting ethnographic research inseparable.

Reading Ethnographies

Students begin by reading a selection of ethnographies or autoethnographies, starting with shorter and more traditional examples like Horace Miner's 1956 parodic classic, "Body Rituals among the Nacerima," or excerpts from Margaret Mead's familiar *Coming of Age in Samoa*. Students then progress to longer narratives, selected to coincide with the course content.[3] Mike Rose's *Lives on the Boundary* works well in a composition methods course, and Pat Conroy's *The Water Is Wide* fits in literature methods. Sarah Winnemucca Hopkins's *Life among the Piutes* suits an American literature survey course, just as Zora Neale Hurston's *Mules and Men* does a course on American women writers or Tomas Rivera's *And the Earth Did Not Devour Him* does a course on Chicano literature. In women's studies, Barbara Ehrenreich's *Nickel and Dimed* is a compelling contemporary example of the genre. These texts are read alongside theoretical essays by practitioners such as Mead, Ruth Behar, James Clifford, Clifford Geertz, George Marcus, Mary Louise Pratt, or Renato Rosaldo about the role of ethnography and the position of the ethnographer.

How one integrates secondary materials and approaches the shifting notions of ethnography and culture depend on the discipline, the goals of a particular course, and the capabilities of the students. Teachers must choose for themselves the theoretical issues they raise, such as the contested codes and representations composing a given culture; the distinctions between writing about, against, or among cultures; ethnography's blurring the boundary between art and science; the "ethnographic gaze"; or the dilemma of generalizing from the experiences of an individual or a group. Because most of my students are preservice secondary English teachers and because I am trying to create activist and critical pedagogues, I approach ethnography as writing emerging from what Mary Louise Pratt describes as "the contact zone": those "social spaces where cultures meet, clash, and grapple with each other, often in contexts of highly asymmetrical relations of power, such as colonialism, slavery, or their aftermaths as they are lived out in many parts of the world today" (518).

In our formal readings, students encounter voices previously unheard, marginalized, or silenced. They recognize two key points: that consciousness resides in language and that language is social. In *Literature and Lives: A Response-Based, Cultural Studies Approach to Teaching English*, Allen Carey-Webb neatly summarizes this perspective: "If you believe you are what you eat (in a cultural sense), then examining culture carefully is part and parcel of understanding oneself." Studying not just literature but the various "texts" composing culture reveals the "scripts, codes, and institutions—the discourses—that constitute us" (135). For teachers (or teacher-candidates), whose world is often prescribed by embedded traditions and systems of meaning, understanding the cultural codes and recognizing the instability of the institutionalized truths of education nurture a healthy skepticism, readying them to create classrooms that foster inquiry and activism in students.

At the same time that students are reading ethnographic texts and theoretical essays about the genre and practice, they delve into ethnographic research,[4] scrutinizing the texts we have been reading for their methodology—specific techniques, forms, and conclusions. Students try to identify how an ethnographer collects information and to imagine what they would have done in the same situation. They attend to how authors present data and observations, thereby positioning themselves within the text. Do writers rely on exposition or narration? Is the tone subjective and reflective or objective and scientific? Such close analysis requires students to imagine how the intended audience shapes the ethnographer's choices.

Considering the relationships among ethnographer, informants, and audience brings students to the notion of authorial voice. Close reading, especially set against the tradition of the seeming objectivity of quantitative research, shows students the power authors possess in depicting another culture. As John Van Maanen describes in *Tales of the Field*:

> The narrative and rhetorical conventions assumed by a writer also shape ethnography. Ways of personal expression, choice of metaphor, figurative allusions, semantics, decorative phrasing or plain speaking, textual organization, and so on all work to structure a cultural portrait in particular ways. (5)

In short, the ethnographer creates the observed culture through the language used to craft the ethnography. As students realize this, they begin to understand the magnitude of their responsibilities as ethnographers and authors.

Writing Ethnographies

How can teachers incorporate into classes a methodology largely the domain of researchers who spend months or years among their subjects of study? James Spradley and David McCurdy in *The Cultural Experience* and Paul Kutsche in *Field Ethnography* propose microethnographies that study a "cultural scene": a "geographic or symbolic place where two or more people repeatedly share activities that lead to shared understandings" (Kutsche 85). Students need go no further than mom-and-pop stores, street gangs, playgrounds, convents, hospital wards, or junkyards to find subjects for their ethnographic study assignment (Kutsche 85): to attend to what the members of a culture do, not only in their actions or behaviors, but in what they believe, think, understand, or feel about what they do.[5]

Before asking students to choose a cultural scene, I establish some broadly stated (and flexible) goals, including describing and interpreting the cultural life of the observed group, articulating how members of the group see themselves and their world in relation to the larger community, contextualizing observations by understanding the group within the larger context of the community, and comparing their observations with those of more traditional research sources[6] or with the student-ethnographer's own preconceptions.

Students should not select a cultural scene with which they are intimately involved, because some degree of ethnographic distance is generally needed to gain perspective on the scene or group.[7] Teachers must decide whether to limit students to on- or off-campus cultural scenes, on the basis in part of whether the student-ethnographers have ready and easy access to the scenes and whether the group members are willing to be studied. Among the school-based cultural scenes my students have studied are the marching band, the computer labs, the campus theater, various athletic teams, the cafeteria, and the school's health service. Off-campus studies have taken students to a church-affiliated soup kitchen, a gasoline service station, an XXX-rated bookshop located on the interstate, a public swimming pool, and a Little League ball field.[8]

As literature teachers well know, the lives of individuals are primarily told through stories. Thus the ethnographies that students submit take the form of a narrative constructed from the lives of the observed and the observer. When developing their narratives, students attend to a number of primary sources. Material gleaned from observations and interviews may be supplemented by artifacts, including documents, newsletters, bylaws, items produced by those being observed, implements—in effect, anything within the observed scene that speaks to the experience of the participants. Students also of course rely on their own field notes, journals, and interviews.

To sharpen their skills in observation and analysis, students begin with three shorter observations that they integrate into their final ethnography. The first asks them to map their cultural scene, the second addresses the private language employed by the cultural group, and the third focuses on nonverbal communication.[9] If ethnography is a smaller course component, then one, two, or all three of these assignments can be the extent of student research.

Constructing the Ethnographic Account

The final step in this ethnography project is constructing a narrative that synthesizes and interprets the collected data.[10] Although students might find the amount of material they have collected intimidating, I suggest they approach their ethnographic research as they would the research on a more traditional text. For example, students might look for common themes running through the gathered materials, as Ruth Benedict does in her classic 1934 study *Patterns of Culture*. Choosing key terms, significant items, or particular behaviors may also help define the cultural scene. Kutsche suggests organizing data by narrative sequence: students narrate a scene or moment and then apply their research to that narrative to introduce or develop their observations. During what amounts to a prewriting phase, students return to their journals and review the questions raised by their observations and reflections. They might ask why what they saw did or did not correspond to conventional notions about the group. As Kutsche advises, "[L]ook yet again at your own likes and dislikes, your relations with your informants, your motives for choosing the particular scene, your reactions to it" (99). The goal is some kind of organizing idea—what in the writing classroom we might call a thesis statement, a focus statement, or a main point.[11]

Particularly appealing about ethnography at this stage is the connection between the author and the text. Kutsche explains to his students that the final ethnography "will be you as well as they or, to use the jargon of the trade, will be Self as well as Other. It will be, whether you intend it to be or not, a dialogue between yourself and your informants" (99). Showing students that, despite the quasi-scientific nature of the project, their responses are integral to the tale they tell prepares them to engage more personally in the writing.

After identifying a focus, students must choose from the variety of approaches available for presenting the results of their fieldwork (in earlier discussions, we've identified a working audience for the presentation). Van Maanen catalogs the multiple rhetorical and narrative ethnographic conventions around the key questions of what one wants to tell and to whom one wants to tell it. Tales told by ethnographers can be realist, confessional, or impressionistic. Each method has its own organization, and each employs the familiar patterns of development (narration, description, causal analysis) in slightly different ways.

In any course, ethnography challenges students' relation to knowledge and research. In the collection *Students as Researchers of Culture and Language in Their Own Communities*, David Bloome and Ann Egan-Robertson question the benefits of traditional library research:

> Research that is bounded by classroom and library walls, in which students are expected to reproduce the knowledge printed in authoritative texts, is little more than legitimized plagiarism. Inquiry that is designed so that students find the knowledge or insight predetermined by their teachers is little more than a teaching trick. (xii)

Although less contemptuous of traditional research, I too am concerned that developing original insights using the works of others is a difficult task, especially for novice writers whose labors often result in specious citations or uninspired book reports. (I have taught this class encouraging students to conduct traditional background research and discouraging them from doing so, and I have discovered benefits and limitations in both approaches.) Ethnography allows students to engage in "the generation of new knowledge and the production of new texts through which the new knowledge is shared" (Bloome and Egan-Robertson xii). Reading and writing ethnographies changes students' relation to writing—their own and that of others. As they write about their discoveries and the knowledge they have generated, students come to understand writing more as a tool for sharing observations than as a set of seemingly arbitrary rules or steps. But the value of ethnography in the classroom goes beyond teaching research and writing skills. In her work with underachieving and marginalized students, Carmen I. Mercado discovered that, more than competency in language arts, students who conduct ethnographic research learn "to use language to become self-directed learners," adding that adolescents in particular "gain new understandings of 'possible selves'—what they would like to become, could become, or are afraid of becoming—which serve as a link between cognition and motivation" (71). Ethnography projects also force teachers and students to reconsider both the nature of learning and their roles as learners. As Marceline Torres explains, envisioning students as researchers means "seeing students as young people who have important questions and concerns about the world in which they live, and who are energetic about understanding and addressing that world." In response, teachers must devise curricula that treat learning "as inquiry and action rather than a set of discrete skills to be drilled and then forgotten" (59).

Any successful ethnography project will make students realize that research does not begin or end with the library and the traditional research essay. Examining issues that spark interest based on genuine questions, supplementing traditional investigation with more engaging methods, and creating documents that present the results of research in ways that serve the subject of study, the audience, and the writer-researchers themselves constitute research of a high order. Very few projects engage students on as many levels as ethnography does.

Notes

1. Here I use the word *text* in its more contemporary and broader sense, as the signs and codes that compose a signifying structure.

2. Regardless of the course, students and I begin from a congenial definition of ethnography as a systematic narrative about a particular cultural group and as a method for learning about a group of people by observing aspects of the group dynamic. In autoethnography, the author recognizes himself or herself as a part of the cultural group being studied. These definitions are refined as students discuss the texts we read in class.

3. An all-inclusive text intended as "a full introduction to reading, writing, and research" (x), Bonnie Stone Sunstein and Elizabeth Chiseri-Strater's *Fieldworking: Reading and Writing Research* is excellent for writing courses (first-year, advanced, or research-based); however, as teachers become more comfortable with ethnographic methods, they might choose to develop courses around their own reading and writing assignments.

4. Although most of the practical texts for teaching ethnographic method, including Spradley and McCurdy; Kutsche; and LeCompte and Schensul, are directed toward students in the social sciences, many offer accessible instruction on ethnographic method, sample professional as well as student ethnographies, general assignments, and valuable supporting materials that can be adapted to nearly any classroom or discipline.

5. Volume 1 of LeCompte and Schensul's *Ethnographer's Toolkit* can be useful for discussing with students exactly what is meant by culture, as can discussing the classroom as a cultural scene. As students are introduced to the various tasks associated with their projects, the classroom can serve as a familiar example for prepractice as they describe, identify, and analyze this shared space.

6. In some classes, I ask students to compare the results of their study with other professional or published observations of the cultural group. This component works particularly well with preservice teachers because the classroom has been the subject of such extensive research.

7. For more on the ethnographer as a member of the observed community, see Spradley and McCurdy and Hymes, Cazden, and John. The writer, ethnographer, and folklorist Norma Elía Cantú has coined the portmanteau "auto-bioethnography" (xi) to describe her studies of life on the Texas-Mexico border, a community she knows intimately. At the University of Northern Colorado, preservice teachers spend four semesters in practicums at local partner schools, and I ask the students to use their partner school as a site for their ethnographic research, placing the preservice teachers in the position of autobioethnographers.

8. It is helpful to brainstorm a list of possible cultural scenes. The following questions can help inspire students: What hobbies, extracurricular activities, or sports do I find interesting or would I like to learn more about? From what kinds of experiences or groups have I been sheltered because of my upbringing? How can I get to the places I need to observe? Will there be people to interview? Given the time frame for this project, is the scene I am contemplating too much or too little? What skills or knowledge will I need to understand what I am observing?

9. On the basis of a series of field assignments designed by Paul Kutsche, these smaller assignments also provide multiple opportunities for assessing and evaluating students' development as ethnographers and writers.

10. The options for presenting the results of this kind of research are limitless. Ethnographic reports regularly cross generic boundaries; they can be self-narratives, fiction, even performance. Here, my focus is the more traditional written report; however, I encourage teachers, especially working in collaboration with colleagues from other disciplines, to experiment with presentation methods and encourage students to find their own voices in presenting the results of their research.

11. Although I have not addressed the role of writing groups here, it is at this stage that peer work is vital. An important component of each of the smaller tasks, as students help one another through the writing and revision process, group work is especially helpful as students prepare to interview their informants, since peers can help shape questions and identify areas for clarification.

Works Cited

Behar, Ruth. *Vulnerable Observer: Anthropology That Breaks Your Heart*. Boston: Beacon, 1996.

Benedict, Ruth. *Patterns of Culture*. New York: Houghton, 1934.

Cantú, Norma Elia. *Canícula: Snapshots of a Girlhood on la Frontera*. Albuquerque: U of New Mexico P, 1995.

Carey-Webb, Allen. *Literature and Lives: A Response-Based, Cultural Studies Approach to Teaching English*. Urbana: NCTE, 2001.

Clifford, James, and George E. Marcus, eds. *Writing Culture: The Poetics and Politics of Ethnography*. Berkeley: U of California P, 1986.

Conroy, Pat. *The Water Is Wide*. New York: Bantam, 1987.

Damen, Louise. *Culture Learning: The Fifth Dimension in the Language Classroom*. Reading: Addison, 1987.

Egan-Robertson, Ann, and David Bloome, eds. *Students as Researchers of Culture and Language in Their Own Communities*. Cresskill: Hampton, 1998.

Ehrenreich, Barbara. *Nickel and Dimed: On (Not) Getting By in America*. New York: Owl–Henry Holt, 2002.

Geertz, Clifford. *Works and Lives: The Anthropologist as Author*. Stanford: Stanford UP, 1990.

Heath, Shirley Brice. *Ways with Words: Language, Life, and Work in Communities and Classrooms*. New York: Cambridge UP, 1983.

Hopkins, Sarah Winnemucca. *Life among the Piutes: Their Wrongs and Claims*. 1883. Reno: U of Nevada P, 1994.

Hurston, Zora Neale. *Mules and Men*. Philadelphia: Lippincott, 1935.

Hymes, Dell, Courtney B. Cazden, and Vera P. John, eds. *Functions of Language in the Classroom*. New York: Teachers Coll., 1972.

Kozol, Jonathan. *Rachel and Her Children: Homeless Families in America*. New York: Crown, 1988.

Kutsche, Paul. *Field Ethnography: A Manual for Doing Cultural Anthropology*. Upper Saddle River: Prentice, 1998.

LeCompte, Margaret D., and Jean J. Schensul, eds. *The Ethnographer's Toolkit*. 7 vols. Walnut Creek: Alta Mira, 1999.

Marcus, George. *Ethnography through Thick and Thin*. Princeton: Princeton UP, 1998.

Mead, Margaret. *Coming of Age in Samoa*. New York: Morrow, 1923.

Mercado, Carmen I. "When Young People from Marginalized Communities Enter the World of Ethnographic Research: Scribing, Planning, Reflecting, and Sharing." Egan-Robertson and Bloome 69–93.

Miner, Horace. "Body Rituals among the Nacirema." 1956. *The Nacirema: Readings on American Culture*. Ed. James P. Spradley and Michael A. Rynkiewich. Boston: Little, 1975. 10–13.

Pratt, Mary Louise. "Arts of the Contact Zone." *Ways of Reading*. 5th ed. Ed. David Bartholomae and Anthony Petroksky. New York: Bedford–St. Martin's, 1999. 517–34.

Rivera, Tomas. *And the Earth Did Not Devour Him*. Salt Lake City: Sagebrush, 1999.

Rose, Mike. *Lives on the Boundary: A Moving Account of the Struggles and Achievements of America's Educational Underclass*. New York: Penguin, 1990.

Rosenblatt, Louise M. *Literature as Exploration*. 5th Ed. New York: MLA, 1996.

Rosaldo, Renato. *Culture and Truth: The Remaking of Social Anthropology*. Rev. ed. Boston: Beacon, 1993.

Shaughnessy, Mina. *Errors and Expectations: A Guide for the Teacher of Basic Writing*. New York: Oxford UP, 1977.

Spradley, James P., and David W. McCurdy. *The Cultural Experience: Ethnography in Complex Society*. Palo Alto: SRA, 1972.

Stone Sunstein, Bonnie, and Elizabeth Chiseri-Strater. *Fieldworking: Reading and Writing Research*. New York: Bedford, 2002.

Torres, Marceline. "Celebrations and Letters Home: Research as an Ongoing Conversation among Students, Parents, and Teacher." Egan-Robertson and Bloome 59–68.

Van Maanen, John. *Tales of the Field: On Writing Ethnography*. Chicago: U of Chicago P, 1988.

Gail Y. Okawa

Close Encounters: (Re)Teaching Ethnic Autobiography as Autoethnography

A veteran teacher, I have worked with students in rural Virginia, urban and rural Japan, Honolulu, Seattle, and currently Youngstown, Ohio, a region automobile manufacturers refer to as the heartland of America. The ironies in this path are many—a Japanese American English teacher in the tobacco country of once colonial Virginia, for instance. But none has been as pronounced as teaching in America's heartland, where ethnic and racial stereotypes are so entrenched and unexamined that students worry they will not understand me or they find it odd that I teach English at all.

Hired in 1994 for a new position in the Youngstown State University English Department designed to focus on issues of multicultural diversity, I have drawn on my previous sociolingistic work and engagement with cultural, rhetorical, literary, and literacy issues of importance to Americans of color to raise awareness and expand narrow attitudes about language and race. Long familiar with the liberatory power of narrative and life writing, I have consistently used autobiographical writings, both published and student generated, to highlight and unpack contradictions and conflicts in my classrooms—in students, among students, and between students and me.[1]

In this essay, I briefly explore the teaching of ethnic autobiography—works from American Indian, African American, Latino/a, and Asian and

Pacific American traditions—as a faculty member of color in a public, regional, urban university in the Midwest. In particular, I examine the process of curriculum revision, discussing changes to my syllabus and my evolving antiracist pedagogy, shaped in part by the significant resistance to the material I encountered in one undergraduate class.

When I arrived in Youngstown in the mid-1990s, having worked with high school students and traditional and nontraditional college students for over twenty years, I was confident I could adapt to most students. And yet, though a third-generation American like many of my students, I was born in Hawai'i and in some respects had entered a foreign culture in the Rust Belt, where flourishing steel mills once drew immigrants by the thousands from northern, then southern and eastern Europe. My students are largely the descendants of those immigrants—although I have the occasional African American or Puerto Rican student—and of a blue-collar, steel-town culture that is provincial, pragmatic, job-oriented, and racially divided. The closing or abandonment of many steel mills in the late 1970s led to white flight, causing what Sherry Linkon and Bill Mullen call "de facto segregation" (28) between white suburban or rural and black urban communities.

During my second year, I offered American Life Stories: Ethnic Autobiographical Writing, a four-credit course on the quarter system, catalogued under the heading English 780 American Genres. After teaching a challenging but successful graduate class in minority discourse the previous year,[2] I was asked to prepare a version of this course for English majors and chose to focus on multicultural life writing. Although some of the more mature, nontraditional students seemed to have a positive experience in this first round of English 780, I was hardly satisfied with the overall results.

To give students a broad exposure to writers of color, I had assigned such texts as Mary Crow Dog's *Lakota Woman*, Maya Angelou's *I Know Why the Caged Bird Sings*, Piri Thomas's *Down These Mean Streets*, Carlos Bulosan's *America Is in the Heart*, Maxine Hong Kingston's *Woman Warrior*, and Henry Louis Gates, Jr.'s, anthology *Bearing Witness*. I had naively thought I could teach this class with a pedagogy similar to what I had used in the graduate class, where I served as a relatively nonprescriptive facilitator. Discussion necessarily involved racial issues, and significant resistance arose to some of the texts ("This should be called 'Race 780'!" was written in one student's dialogue journal as a more explicit protest). Unlike many of my graduate students, some undergraduates were uncomfortable with what they saw as too close an encounter with the perspectives of people of color like Mary Crow Dog, Malcolm X, Eldridge Cleaver, and Piri Thomas, and they recoiled from the suspicion and anger directed at white Americans in these writings. Unprepared to work through their initial discomfort, they tired quickly of being held responsible for the ills of "those people" and grew more and more defensive.

I found myself having relatively little patience with or sympathy for what appeared to be the students' dogged, unexamined—or "home-conditioned" (Linkon and Mullen 28)—racism. My considerable teaching experience did not prepare me for the hostile silences in discussions of race and cultural difference. As a teacher, in some ways, I had to start all over again, following Paulo Freire's advice to reconsider continually the interactions between teachers and students in our "quest for mutual humanization" (62).

When I taught English 780 again, I encountered a considerably different response. Reflective writing and teaching during the four intervening years—along with reading hundreds of student autobiographies written for classes in language, literature, and composition—had enabled me to learn a great deal about my students' backgrounds, lives, prejudices, problems, and aspirations. Many were as much victims of their inherited racial prejudices as their targets were. To give my students ways of moving beyond their ethnocentricity, I had to do more than present autobiographies by people of color as examples of the genre per se. The students needed assistance in examining the sources and nature of their ethnocentricity. That guidance was my job.

Harking back to Graywolf Press usage,[3] I began to see the goal as "multi-cultural literacy" and to develop a more deliberate antiracist theory and pedagogy to assist students in seeing the perspectives of writers from cultural, linguistic, and class backgrounds different from their own—with empathy, as Patricia Hill Collins would have us do. I agree with Sidonie Smith that "the excluded and colorful have used autobiography as a means of 'talking back'" (20)—of gaining agency where we once had none, of making ourselves autoethnographic agents rather than ethnographic objects. In 1990, I listened eagerly to Mary Louise Pratt define the "autoethnographic text" as one "in which people undertake to describe themselves in ways that engage with representations others have made of them" (35). Some time later I came across Françoise Lionnet's discussion of autoethnography in relation to Zora Neale Hurston: "the defining of one's subjective ethnicity as mediated through language, history, and ethnographical analysis" (99). This term delineated a social and political dimension of the genre essential to any study of life writing by Americans of color living in a racially constructed society.

When designing my second syllabus for English 780, now titled Multicultural Autobiographical Writing, and for subsequent courses in multicultural literature and discourse, I set my goals as developing students' awareness of writing by writers of color and giving students the tools to respect that writing, to understand the autoethnographic impulse, to cope with conflicts, and to develop antiracist views if they chose to. I decided not to bury my intentions in institutional objectivity and neutrality but rather to state them clearly, starting with the course description:

> In this course, we will explore multicultural autobiographical writing. Our purpose will be two-fold: 1) to become familiar with the genre of American autobiography from various cultural perspectives and experiences (including yours; our course reading will focus on writers from American Indian, African American, Latino, and Asian/Pacific American backgrounds); and 2) to develop multicultural literacy—to read *about* people from different cultures and *from* their points of view (not necessarily the same as our own). To do this, we will work together to: develop an awareness of the criteria and dynamics of the genre through our reading, as well as the importance of narrative and reflection in personal experience; learn how such factors as culture, history, identity, power, etc., influence individual and group situations and influence perspectives; learn how these situations and perspectives lead writers to represent their lives and critique their society differently; and identify, define, and understand our personal cultural views and ethnocentricity.

Such a framework allowed me to provide students with theoretical tools: Pratt's "contact zone" metaphor[4] and Abdul JanMohamed and David Lloyd's concepts of damage and collective subjectivity describe terrains or environments of contention and minority responses to it, while Ellen Messer-Davidow's perspectivism (qtd. in Ling 152) and Donna Haraway's concept of feminist objectivity as situated knowledge and embodied vision validate the particularity of one perspective against another. I also offered another metaphor, developed through my own experience, which I call bifocality of difference: "seeing one's cultural self up close as well as from afar, the way others may" ("Removing Masks" 126). Such concepts provided lenses for better understanding of the texts and of the students' responses to them. Their surprise at the hostility of Mary Crow Dog, for example, led students to explore those facets of her damaged life that provided the basis for her "embodied vision" and to discuss stereotypes and assumptions that many people have about American Indian texts. In this way students came to appreciate how the way she constructs her self and her experiences as a Lakota woman counters stereotypes of Indian women.

To encourage multilayered reading, I reduced the number of texts for this ten-week course from six books plus readings to four: *Lakota Woman*, the anthology *Bearing Witness*, Monica Sone's *Nisei Daughter*, and Thomas's *Down These Mean Streets*. This decision gave us more time to discuss the complexities of each work. Though the assignments differed somewhat, students in both versions of English 780 kept a weekly dialogue journal in which they responded to class readings and discussions and wrote a cultural autobiography to give them a baseline text for their own lives. For their final projects, they had the option of writing autobiographical literary criticism modeled on the essays in *The Intimate Critique: Autobiographical Literary Criticism* (Freedman, Frey, and Zauhar).

Rather than assume the role of an objectified, neutralized teacher as I had in the previous version, I confronted students' assumptions about me as a Japanese American, making the teacher, as well as the students themselves and their attitudes, texts of the course. When reading student journals, I was surprised and gratified to find that this candidness played a significant role in their learning. Here are one writer's remarks:

> I think that the class thus far has been pretty interesting and full of irresolute questions that inevitably heighten one's awareness levels. However, I have felt that Dr. Okawa has tried to stay as neutral as possible, [so] as to be a good facilitator for the class to harbor its own opinions and ways to deal with the problems that arise discussing the issues. I felt that she had been almost too removed in a personal way. Then she told us of her theory about bifocality . . . [and] how she had discovered race [through] her accident in Virginia. . . . It wasn't until Dr. Okawa shared her story with us that I actually understood why she devoted her life to helping to educate some of the masses about these topics. I found it even more amazing that she thought it was a goal not solely to focus on what it means to be an Asian American, but to explore all

facets of multiculturalism. I feel more kindred with her now that she has been more open. I think before, I felt like a formality was obstructing me from more earnest communication, but now I feel like a confidant, an intimacy has been shared.[5]

In a recent graduate course titled Teaching Multicultural Autobiography, I took explicitness a step further, transforming an assumed, unarticulated, antiracist pedagogical goal into a clearly and overtly stated purpose: "to develop *multicultural literacy*—reading, viewing, understanding, interpreting, and analyzing discourse from these various cultural, social, linguistic, and historical perspectives by way of an antiracist pedagogy." Although course projects and assignments remained largely the same, the shift in my pedagogy between classes had a positive effect on the students' receptivity—on their encountering, negotiating, and absorbing difficult material. Writing their own cultural autobiographies was a kind of autoethnographic act for each of them as well, an act of self-discovery and self-recovery in the light of cultural and social class issues endemic to the region. Thus autoethnography takes on charged meanings in this context for all concerned—authors, instructor, and the students themselves.

Notes

1. In "From 'Bad Attitudes' to Linguistic Pluralism," for example, I discuss how having students write their language autobiographies in an introductory sociolinguistics course for preservice teachers raises awareness of linguistic origins, behaviors, and attitudes and gives students choices for encountering linguistic issues.

2. I describe and analyze this course in some detail in "Removing Masks."

3. Rick Simonson and Scott Walker produced *The Graywolf Annual Five: Multi-cultural Literacy* in response to E. D. Hirsch's exclusionary *Cultural Literacy*.

4. Pratt defines contact zones as "social spaces where cultures meet, clash, and grapple with each other, often in contexts of highly asymmetrical relations of power, such as colonialism, slavery, or their aftermaths as they are lived out in many parts of the world today" (34).

5. Quoted with permission.

Works Cited

Angelou, Maya. *I Know Why the Caged Bird Sings*. 1969. New York: Bantam-Random, 1993.

Bulosan, Carlos. *America Is in the Heart: A Personal History*. Seattle: U of Washington P, 1979.

Collins, Patricia Hill. *Black Feminist Thought: Knowledge, Consciousness, and the Politics of Empowerment*. New York: Routledge, 1991.

Crow Dog, Mary. *Lakota Woman*. New York: HarperPerennial, 1990.

Freedman, Diane P., Olivia Frey, and Frances Murphy Zauhar, eds. *The Intimate Critique: Autobiographical Literary Criticism*. Durham: Duke UP, 1993.

Freire, Paulo. *Pedagogy of the Oppressed*. Trans. M. B. Ramos. New York: Continuum, 1970.

Gates, Henry Louis, Jr., ed. *Bearing Witness: Selections from African-American Autobiography in the Twentieth Century*. New York: Pantheon, 1991.

Haraway, Donna J. *Simians, Cyborgs, and Women: The Reinvention of Nature*. London: Free Association, 1991.

Hirsch, E. D., Jr. *Cultural Literacy: What Every American Needs to Know*. Boston: Houghton, 1987.

JanMohamed, Abdul R., and David Lloyd. "Introduction: Toward a Theory of Minority Discourse: What Is to Be Done?" *The Nature and Context of Minority Discourse*. Ed. JanMohamed and Lloyd. New York: Oxford UP, 1990. 1–16.

Kingston, Maxine Hong. *The Woman Warrior: Memoirs of a Girlhood among Ghosts*. 1976. New York: Vintage-Random, 1977.

Ling, Amy. "I'm Here: An Asian American Woman's Response." *New Literary History* 19 (1987): 151–60.

Linkon, Sherry, and Bill Mullen. "Gender, Race, and Place: Teaching Working-Class Students in Youngstown." *Radical Teacher* 46 (1995): 27–32.

Lionnet, Françoise. *Autobiographical Voices: Race, Gender, Self-Portraiture*. Ithaca: Cornell UP, 1989.

Okawa, Gail Y. "From 'Bad Attitudes' to Linguistic Pluralism: Developing Reflective Language Policy among Preservice Teachers." *Language Ideologies: Critical Perspectives on the Official English Movement*. Ed. R. Gonzalez. Urbana: NCTE, 2000. 276–96.

——. "Removing Masks: Confronting Graceful Evasion and Bad Habits in a Graduate English Class." *Race, Rhetoric and Composition*. Ed. Keith Gilyard. Portsmouth: Heinemann–Boynton-Cook, 1999. 124–43.

Pratt, Mary Louise. "Arts of the Contact Zone." *Profession 91*. New York: MLA, 1991. 33–40.

Simonson, Rick, and Scott Walker, eds. *The Graywolf Annual Five: Multi-cultural Literacy: Opening the American Mind*. St. Paul: Graywolf, 1988.

Smith, Sidonie. *Subjectivity, Identity, and the Body: Women's Autobiographical Practices in the Twentieth Century*. Bloomington: Indiana UP, 1993.

Sone, Monica. *Nisei Daughter*. Seattle: U of Washington P, 1998.

Thomas, Piri. *Down These Mean Streets*. 1995. New York: Vintage, 1997.

Arturo Arias

Teaching Testimonio:
A New, Ex-Centric Design Emerges

Some critics have asked why we should bother studying written texts at all in this day and age. In my own teaching and research, I discuss the processes that create and sustain literary values and the ethical and political implications of aesthetic and critical practices, and I speculate on their possible consequences. For these reasons, I have never had any problem linking textuality, meaning all written texts, with social issues or political perspectives. Thus, even though I have gained some recognition as a scholar of testimonio, I believe that those texts ought to be taught within a broader sociopolitical context and compared with written documents of different genres. In this, I differ from some theorists of testimonio, who argued in the mid-1990s that we no longer needed to study "highbrow" Latin American literature and tried to make a valid point for its dismissal in favor of texts produced by subaltern subjects.[1] Perhaps a more serious issue raised since the late 1980s was that, with the supposed end of nation formation in the world, the study of literature no longer fulfilled the function of forging, framing, and sustaining national identities, the raison d'être for the formation of literary canons in the first place. In this context, replacing literary studies with cultural studies—with the understanding that the latter addressed the specific practices of powerless people, subalterns—seemed to make perfect sense.

I would argue that a dismissive attitude toward a broad range of texts is especially problematic for the study of areas of the world that have been marginalized, as Central America, my region of origin, has been. Because little documentation exists about everyday life there, discarding an entire category of documents from the overall archive in favor of others would be a wasteful luxury. What is more, the substitution of testimonios alone for literary texts could also risk essentializing the former, simplifying complex social processes and relations, and fetishizing their subaltern subjects.

The importance of textuality for representing peripheral societies has not significantly declined in many marginal areas of the world, although cinema and other visual media have now displaced the centrality that the novel occupied in the nineteenth century in cosmopolitan centers. In Central America, however, cinema and other visual media production are in their infancy. The images that people in the region see on television, in the movie theater, or on the Internet rarely represent their own reality, and they also have limited means for projecting their personal vision onto the worldwide screen. For this reason, textuality's ability to give heteroglossic representations of a people and to assert their identities, experiences, and histories remains of primary importance if they are to become visible and "crawl into the place of the 'human'" (Spivak 23). The interactions between the United States and the Central American nations and societies it has dominated (and invaded, aiding in the slaughter of their best and brightest) since the early twentieth century can best be examined through a study of the region's textual production, which can frame and contextualize those neocolonial forms of subjugation that result from expanding multinational and globalized capitalism. Central American nations have been intimately tied to the United States economy and society since the formation of banana republics. The relation was resignified in the cold war period, when Central America was viewed as the backyard through which Communist influences could creep. The resulting foreign policy meant an end to democracy and, ironically, the beginning of a period marked by guerrilla revolutions, the repercussions of which were felt in the Middle East (the Iran-Contra affair), Mexico, and the United States, flooded in the 1980s by waves of Central American exiles fleeing brutal military repression. Central America continues to be significant on the United States horizon, especially since the Central American Free Trade Agreement was implemented in July 2005.

The wide variety of narratives produced in the region has been particularly adept at recording the shifting relations that have existed fleetingly in

the spaces between these seemingly polar geopolitical sites, where a multiplicity of peoples and cultures have flowed. The scope of testimonio is much
narrower, and it is for this reason that, in my classes, I stress narrative textuality, which encompasses all genres (novel, short story, testimonio, essay,
and even some variants of poetry). I feel strongly that it is only in this context that students can come to terms with a complex reality that is unfamiliar
to them and with an understanding of genre that enables them to better
comprehend the controversy surrounding the fictionality of testimonio.

I often propose to my students that they should pay closer attention to
the words of texts, whether written by Central Americans themselves or
first spoken and then transcribed by others (testimonios). This gesture is
not just a rhetorical indulgence. One cannot understand others without
taking their words seriously, without listening. Only after this first step can
a dialogue evolve (or, in the worst-case scenario, a *différend*, in the Lyotar-
dian sense), one that overcomes an insular identity and leads to a crucial relation between ethics and politics.[2] It is a process that implies the
breakdown of provincialism. Teaching testimonio means helping students
to understand and accept the words of others and to see them rooted in a
particular discursive site (in relation to translocality), to accept the words
of others both as their property in the process of naming themselves
(which allows those "othered" subjects to be the rightful "owners" of their
subjectivity) and as an enunciative strategy for the sake of gaining agency
(as a linkage of subjectivity).

As must be clear by now, I teach testimonios in a regional, Central
American context. Usually, I teach them in the context of a course with a
broader theme, such as Women's Texts in Latino and Latin American Culture. In such a course, I might include historical novels, like the Dominican
American Julia Alvarez's *In the Time of the Butterflies* and the Mexican
American Sandra Cisneros's *Caramelo*. To these, I might add Claribel Alegría's book of poetry *Luisa in Realityland* (which she labels a novel and
which is truly written in both poetry and prose but structured as a book of
poetry) about her experience growing up in El Salvador and joining the revolution late in life; Gioconda Belli's memoir of her years as a Sandinista mil-
itant and government functionary in her country of origin, Nicaragua,
titled *The Country under My Skin: A Memoir of Love and War*; and a couple
of testimonios, such as *Child of the Dark: The Diary of Carolina Maria de Jesus*, the story of an Afro-Brazilian who wrote about her slum-dwelling days
in Rio de Janeiro in the 1960s, and *I, Rigoberta Menchú* (Burgos-Debray),

the famous testimonio of a Guatemalan Maya woman and her participation in the Committee for Peasant Unity. Usually I add a text about a Latin American–Latina woman's lesbian experience, such as Carla Trujillo's *What Night Brings*. The idea is to discover the ways by which Latin American women of different classes, races, and sexual orientations forge and assert their identities in the context of a struggle for political, economic, and social equality. The texts I choose, therefore, provide a broad range of narrative strategies for producing, circulating, and defending identities, in the context of other discourses (legal, religious, political, scientific, anthropological, literary) that seek or have sought to negate them.

Most of the students in my classes at the University of Redlands tend to be wealthy, white Americans (with a smattering of Latinos) whose parents consider the University of California system too radical or impersonal for their children. Most of them know little of Latin America, beyond tourist spots like Cancún or the bars across the nearby border with Tijuana. These observations only address their fairly homogeneous background and understanding of United States history, not their intellectual curiosity, their capabilities, or their politics, which range from extremely progressive to strongly conservative. For such students, my course opens up a vast, unimagined world. Beneath the myth of California as an interethnic globalized state, they encounter a collection of ethnic and class ghettoes and people with a different historical relation to their homeland.

They also discover a new way of interacting with texts. When dealing with testimonios in particular, students first have to address the name itself and how it intersects with other genres, particularly its seeming equivalent in English, "testimony." Without yet delving into the myriad debates about the topic dating from the 1980s, I explain the nature of testimony itself, how it is a subject's response to interrogation, and I ask them to consider the power dynamic involved in that speech act. Then I ask them to imagine how they would respond to interrogation in the following conditions: they do not speak the language in which the questions have been formulated; they do not know the consequences of their reply; the interrogators do not understand their language; and the interrogators are in a position of authority in relation to them. How could they construct a response that not only would not incriminate them but would actually allow them to exercise the same level of authority as that of their interrogators or, minimally, as that of people testifying in the same language as the interrogators? This question allows me to explain the testimonio within the

terms of what Aníbal Quijano and Walter Mignolo have called "the coloniality of power."[3] Javier Sanjinés summarizes their position as

> a pattern whose specific axes are: a) the existence and continual produc-
> tion of identities based on the notion of race; b) the hierarchized rela-
> tion of inequality between "European" and "non-European" identities,
> and the domination of the former over the latter; and c) the construc-
> tion of mechanisms of social domination designed to preserve this his-
> torical foundation of social classification. (191n1)

The testimonio clearly fits within this paradigm: it is a response to the
power structures of a dominant European culture, transcribed from the
often rich oral discourse (occasionally in a foreign tongue) of dominated
racialized subjects into the conventional written language of the dominant
culture. By leading students through this exercise, I help them distinguish
between the testimony that they themselves might provide to a judge or
jury in their own hometown and the testimonial text of a subaltern subject
who is routinely denied legal protection for reasons of class, ethnicity, or
gender. This critical difference is often obfuscated by critics who appeal to
United States students' belief in the universal respect for human rights and
who are shocked to find that many national governments around the world
either deny those rights to their citizens or refuse to protect the rights of
subgroups of their population.

Students often tend to see written testimonios rather unproblematically as representations of the voices of nonwriters (occasionally, yet not
always, illiterate) positioned in the interstices of modernity and coloniality, without considering the mediating role of publishers, editors, or com-
pilers, usually Western academics, as in the case of the anthropologist
Elisabeth Burgos-Debray, who edited Rigoberta Menchú's testimonio
from the cassette recordings, changing the order of the narrative and
"cleaning up the language" to remove the ungrammaticalities from the
Spanish produced by the nonnative indigenous speaker. Such mediation
between the *testimoniante* and the Western audience, problematic in itself
because of the introduction of Western protocols of language and reading,
further complicates the testimonio as a hybrid response to the coloniality
of power. Students can now see hybridity—the end result of mixing the
voice of the non-Western and often anti-Western subaltern speaker whose
first language is not Western with that of the Western academic mediating
the speech act—as manifest proof of power-knowledge relations related to

the colonial construction of indigenous Latin Americans by white, Western Europeans. Coloniality, students find, is not a historical category pertaining to the past; rather, it is constitutive of the present, a fundamental component of present-day modernity that permits a small number of citizens (mostly descendants of white European immigrants) to enjoy the benefits of human rights and globalization, while the great majority of people in their own country (mostly descendants of African slaves or indigenous peoples) toil in obscurity as if they were still living in colonial times, lacking most privileges of modernity, from political enfranchisement to literacy, not to speak of material goods that might be taken for granted in the First World and among the small number of elites who benefit in their own countries from the coloniality of power.

Teaching testimonio implies making a connection with the lived experience of those who, while being our chronological contemporaries, still live under conditions commonly associated with the seventeenth or eighteenth centuries. It enables students to appreciate the comparison between the lived experience of "the higher-ups" with the "longings of the common folk." It also makes it easier to explain the revolutionary experiences in Latin America to students taught to believe that all forms of revolt are wrong, antipatriotic, treasonous, or even contrary to God's designs. Students understand at a gut level the kind of resentment that drives individuals to revolutionary participation; they understand how coloniality is responsible for racial discrimination and economic disparity that feed into revolutionary aspirations. The connection can be made at a personal, instinctive level, not just at an aesthetic or conceptual one. This point is important, since even Spanish literature students cannot often make sense of traditional literary production in Latin America without first understanding the region's revolutionary concerns, from the revolutions for independence in the 1800s to those of Central America in the 1980s. Testimonios make it easier for students to understand how there can be two Mexicos, two Guatemalas, or two Brazils, consisting on the one hand of the globalized elite employing a familiar Western rationality to invoke modernity as its goal and on the other of the dispossessed, who dream of revenge in their respective non-Western languages because of the centuries of being plundered by the Western-looking elite (often, with United States or European help). As Sanjinés states, "[W]hen the dominated rise in violent insurrection they do not create a rational confrontation of points of view, but the untidy and grotesque affirmation of violence" (4–5). He goes on to create a notion, *viscerality*, which he uses as a bodily metaphor to help explain "how indigenous subalternity has resisted giving up its identity to rationalist Western discourse" (5). We could very well state here that reading testimonio is understanding viscerality. It is an exploration of the different uses of memory and narration in bearing witness to human rights abuses, but it is also a way of experiencing the emotions, anger, frustration, or dreams of revenge that these abuses generate among its victims.

At the same time, to avoid the narrow confines of testimonio alone, the genre comparison enables me to examine other types of narratives that denounce violations of human rights or attempt to register viscerality, be it in the construct of fiction or in other written expressions of the witnessing self (autobiography, memoirs, letter collections, and so on). Exploring how all these are situated within their particular historical context, comparing the similarities and the differences they present regarding their structure, use of language, as well as their specific differences or ambiguities in political and social concerns, makes it easier to present the overall scope of a nation, a region, or a continent, in crisis and transition, without simplifying or stereotyping the latter terms or reducing understanding to abstract conceptions.

Teaching testimonios alongside texts from other genres written by subjects who come from the same region but who are not necessarily subaltern also helps students resist the impulse to fetishize the indigenous or African American subject as the sole victim of the coloniality of power. That is, they find a similar critique of colonialism and neocolonialism elsewhere, and they find that not only Europe but also the United States has perpetuated these unequal, racialized relations. It helps them understand the ironies of immigrant policies, trade agreements, and United States foreign policy toward democratically elected leaders in Latin America.

By reading a variety of texts, students understand the specific historical circumstances of the areas they are studying and learn to compare historical and literary documents. They engage with these texts without assimilating them entirely to their own experience, because they are attempting to grasp meanings that are not their own and they are learning to negotiate their differences with the voices from the text, which makes this process a perfect example of Bakhtinian dialogism. All this is relevant to their everyday life, even though, or specifically because, it is not reduced to the narrow confines of the United States. Students begin to appreciate how particular areas of the world that have been shaped by United States foreign and economic policies see those processes, without falling into the traditional binaries of capitalism/socialism, patriotism/antipatriotism, and the like. Finally, though no less important, by exploring the relation between documentary and fictional representations of reality, students learn to better assess the virtues and limitations of aesthetic values, while problematizing their understanding of ethics and solidarity.

Notes

1. "Highbrow" literature is the accepted canon of Latin American literature, codified in the 1960s by Enrique Anderson Imbert at Harvard and Emir Ramírez Monegal at Yale.

2. Spivak has mentioned this, most recently in *Death of a Discipline* (30), as a crucial element for both Derrida and herself.

3. Quijano created the concept in Spanish in his article "Colonialidad del poder, cultura y conocimiento en América Latina" (1997). Mignolo reconceptualized it in *Local Histories / Global Designs* (2000). I subsequently quote Sanjinés's description because of its brevity and succinctness.

Works Cited

Alegría, Claribel. *Luisa in Realityland*. Trans. Darwin J. Flakoll. Willimantic: Curbstone, 1987.

Alvarez, Julia. *In the Time of the Butterflies*. New York: Plume, 1995.

Belli, Gioconda. *The Country under My Skin: A Memoir of Love and War*. Trans. Kristina Cordero. New York: Anchor, 2003.

Burgos-Debray, Elisabeth, ed. and introd. *I, Rigoberta Menchú: An Indian Woman in Guatemala*. Trans. Ann Wright. London: Verso, 1984.

Cisneros, Sandra. *Caramelo*. New York: Vintage, 2003.

Jesus, Carolina Maria de. *Child of the Dark: The Diary of Carolina Maria de Jesus*. Trans. David St. Clair. New York: Signet, 2003.

Lyotard, Jean-François. *The Differend*. Trans. George Van Den Abbeele. Minneapolis: U of Minnesota P, 1988.

Mignolo, Walter. *Local Histories / Global Designs: Coloniality, Subaltern Knowledges, and Border Thinking*. Princeton: Princeton UP, 2000.

Quijano, Aníbal. "Colonialidad del poder, cultura y conocimiento en América Latina." *Anuario Mariateguiano* 9 (1997): 113–21.

Sanjinés, Javier. Mestizaje *Upside-Down: Aesthetic Politics in Modern Bolivia*. Pittsburgh: U of Pittsburgh P, 2004.

Spivak, Gayatri Chakravorty. *Death of a Discipline*. New York: Columbia UP, 2003.

Swanson, Philip, ed. *The Companion to Latin American Studies*. London: Arnold, 2003.

Trujillo, Carla. *What Night Brings*. Willimantic: Curbstone, 2003.

Gendered and Sexual Orientation Approaches

Susannah B. Mintz

Anxiety of Choice: Teaching Contemporary Women's Autobiography

This brief essay—in a way that seems unnervingly similar to the syllabi I compose at the start of every semester—is fraught with indecision. As Annie Dillard has written of autobiography itself, "what to put in and what to leave out?" ("To Fashion" 143). The possibilities overwhelm any conceivable semester-long course, and it is only by steeling oneself to the thrum of all that cannot be included that one proceeds with the task of selection. What follows, then, is a necessarily particular and peculiar offering, one possible version of how to introduce students to the rich array of recent autobiographies by women. My approach is general: I suggest ways of sequencing and pairing texts that can easily be adapted depending on student need or course parameters. The framework outlined here has been the basis of courses from first-year expository writing classes all the way to graduate-level seminars, taught at both small liberal arts colleges and a large, urban university with a highly diverse student body. In structuring the plan below, I envision an introductory-level literature course that presumes some facility with literary interpretation but no prior intensive study of autobiography.

One of the most difficult tasks in teaching autobiographical writing to students relatively unfamiliar with the genre is overcoming their expectations about truth. The fictive status of self-writing can be elusive for readers taught to approach autobiography and memoir as real life. Texts by women that specifically foreground issues of racial conflict, disability, motherhood, sexuality, and physical or emotional trauma can compound that representational conflict by seeming to demand readers' admiration for their triumphs or sympathy for their distress. What gets lost in such an exchange is the fundamentally performative and revisionary work that women's autobiography often undertakes as a way of defining a marginalized self apart from the narrative structures available in patriarchal, racist, or ableist cultures. My goal in a course devoted to women's autobiography is to dislocate students from the habit of attending to the life, rather than the text, and thereby to examine the various rhetorical and formal strategies that women have employed to broaden the field of possible stories of gendered identity and experience.

On the first day of class, I ask students to define autobiography. This simple question invariably produces such answers as "a person's perspective on his life," "the story of a person's life told by that person," or "a person's thoughts and feelings about what happened to her." Pairing this type of naive response with a parsing of autobiography's three key components (auto, bio, graphy) helps bring into view the kinds of assumptions that inform our collective approach to personal narrative—what counts as a self, which experiences constitute a life worth narrating, who has access to the technologies of writing and publishing, and so on. I have found that students come quickly to appreciate the limitations of collapsing the author of the text into the persona who speaks therein, of demanding that life writing stick to the facts, or of presuming autobiography to be a chronological tale that starts with birth and catalogs major life events. Teasing out these multiple complexities even provisionally frames our ensuing project as the interpretation of the "how" of the text, rather than the summation of "what happened."

I might then turn to a short piece such as Dillard's "To Fashion a Text." Whether or not the course includes *An American Childhood* (the memoir Dillard describes writing), this accessible essay introduces several terms fundamental to the study of autobiography. Because it emphasizes the idea that life writing "cannibaliz[es]" and "replaces" rather than dutifully adheres to memory (156), Dillard's essay can usefully guide a conversation about what it means to fashion or invent a textual identity. The autobiographer's specifically writerly choices are captured in Dillard's question of "what to put in and what to leave out," a phrase that serves throughout the semester as a reminder to students that life writing actively shapes a self. Dillard's breezy and conversational style offers a way into trickier theoretical issues, shifting students' conception of autobiography from a sibling of documentary or testimonial toward a more fictive and open-ended genre.

Newly attuned to the notion of life writing as a deliberately crafted and thus potentially liberatory form, we can approach the work of early English female autobiographers to explore their tentative but also frequently defiant and subversive tactics. The fifteenth-century *Book of Margery Kempe* and Margaret Cavendish's 1656 *A True Relation of My Birth, Breeding and Life* produce autobiographical selves that conform to but also resist conventional modes of narrative structure as well as gendered behavior. Both Kempe and Cavendish were denigrated as mad and therefore tend simultaneously to exaggerate and apologize for the urgency with which they tell their stories. Both create singular voices that alternately capitulate to the prerogatives of the male authorities giving them legitimacy—for Kempe, the scribes to whom she dictated her experiences and, more crucially, the God whose visitations ostensibly initiate her narrative; for Cavendish, her aristocratic husband and father—and defy those relationships by presenting themselves as atypical individuals. While starting with these writers in a contemporary life writing course may seem to force an awkward leap across centuries, my sense is that the historical distance facilitates students' ability to examine the constellation of problems confronting women who seek to author themselves: cultural stereotypes about women's bodies or intellect, social or theological injunctions against women's writing, and so on. Though certainly embedded in their own eras' gender, class, and religious paradigms, Kempe and Cavendish also establish an important context for the oppositional stance—still a matter of some daring—taken by many women today.

From here, I proceed to a series of segments that juxtapose primary texts having some thematic focus in common, to call attention to rhetorical and textual differences and thus emphasize representational rather than real lives. One way to begin is with narratives that put some pressure on the transparency not just of the normatively white male subject of autobiography but of American ethnocentrism as well. I have paired, for instance, Anchee Min's *Red Azalea* with Gelareh Asayesh's *Saffron Sky: A Life between Iran and America. Red Azalea*, which primarily concerns Min's childhood during the Chinese Cultural Revolution and her participation in the propagandist operas of Madame Mao, ends where *Saffron Sky* begins, with the author's immigration to the United States. While Min narrates that dislocation as the lifesaving culmination of years of struggle against the evacuating effects of Communist ideology, the Iranian Asayesh (who moved with her family to North Carolina as a teenager) presents bicultural identity as a source of friction. Much of her book describes the attempt to reclaim an Iranian heritage despite American suspicion of Islamic Iran and of her own newfound Americanness.[1] Though their styles and conclusions differ, both authors detail their efforts to define sexual and gender identity in more empowering terms than those available within the authoritarian regimes of their native countries. At the same time, both invite a Western audience to become more careful readers of the exoticized as well as putatively oppressed woman of color. These are challenging texts, requiring historical awareness and sensitivity to the nuances of multicultural subject positions, but my students have responded enthusiastically to their lyrical, provocative descriptions of the individual woman's thick enmeshment in networks of family, ethnicity, and state.[2]

We delve more fully into body issues by turning next to autobiographies of disability—and again, the sheer number of choices can be daunting. Nancy Mairs is one of the most popularly recognized authors of disability narrative; her essay collections (in particular *Plaintext, Carnal Acts,* and *Waist-High in the World*) combine the intimate, conversational voice of the meditative essay with sophisticated explorations of the tensions as well as affinities between feminist and disability theory. Mairs appeals to readers with her disarming openness about depression, suicide attempts, extramarital affairs, and the unpredictable effects of multiple sclerosis, but, perhaps most important, she also employs that confessional style to break "the rules of polite discourse" that impede expression of a woman's bodily—sexual as well as disabled—experience (*Carnal Acts* 54). A similar concern to flout traditional notions of appropriate material for life writing impels Eli Clare's *Exile and Pride*, a less familiar and far more politicized text in which disability (Clare has cerebral palsy) and queerness become the provisional markers of a radically indefinable identity.[3] Like Mairs, Clare interweaves bodily specifics with a discussion of the social construction of disability, but she is less inclined to assert a stable, unified I. *Exile and Pride* is not a linear narrative but a deliberately unsteady accumulation of positions that sets a queer, disabled, "not-girl-not-boy" (130) self against reductive definitions of all types—cultural norms of gender, sexuality, and health—and the pat assertions of liberal environmentalists no less than the logging corporations that sustain Clare's rural Oregon hometown. Together, Mairs and Clare present a serious challenge to typical expectations of the autobiographical self. Neither is a secure, knowable person with a chronological story; neither culminates her tales of physical and emotional trauma by acquiescing to the tug of narrative resolution.

Texts that explicitly disrupt the conventions of form provide a neat segue from these stories of disruptive gendered corporeality. For some readers, the alternative and hybrid structures of Diane Glancy's *Claiming Breath* and Toi Derricotte's *The Black Notebooks* might rule them out from the category of autobiography altogether. Glancy's slight text (just 115 pages) is part diary, part prose poem. She writes into her prose the slash that indicates line breaks in quoted poetry, uses ampersands, and in several entries makes up a nonsense language that nearly sounds like some form of dialect. Such textual effects serve as both visual and aural protest against boundaries—between Glancy's Native American and white backgrounds, between husbands and wives, mothers and children, poetry and prose. Glancy claims openly that she "want[s] to do it in a new way" (4), and her book attests to that desire to stay in motion, breaking free at the level of punctuation and individual words from the confinements of gender and race. Her style is akin to Derricotte's in *The Black Notebooks*, a testament to twenty years spent coming to terms with passing in white America. Derricotte joins diary entries, brief meditations, poetry, quoted passages from earlier journals, and excerpts from a book written by her mother to manifest the sense of interior fragmentation produced by racism, as well as her belief that selfhood derives from the layered and often conflictual influences of family and community, individual and collective pasts, and the friction between bodies and cultural narrative. Derricotte presents her text as a wrenching act of breaking the silence of internalized racism. Like Glancy, she uses language to refuse categorical definitions of identity and to "invent" a sense of being at home in self, body, group, and place (19).[4]

From these instances of self-representational experiment, I like to close the course with works that both court and resist the autobiographical pact.[5] Such first-person novels as Jamaica Kincaid's *Autobiography of My Mother* and Jeanette Winterson's *Oranges Are Not the Only Fruit* are not strictly autobiographies; each rejects the genre's legalistic and confessional antecedents. Nonetheless, both authors engage what Leigh Gilmore has described as the "weirder expansiveness" of autobiography in order to tell a certain truth about identity (9). Set on the West Indian island of Dominica, Kincaid's novel follows the life of Xuela Richardson, who shares her last name with her author (Kincaid was born Elaine Potter Richardson). Through Xuela, daughter of a Scots African father and a mother who dies in childbirth, Kincaid tells an insistently self-referential story while simultaneously refusing to speak as a properly submissive colonial subject. Scenes of bold autoeroticism, extramarital sex, self-induced abortion, and Xuela's pleasure in her own bodily odors literally place the matter of self-creation into a woman's own hands. Kincaid writes selfhood as a return to an autonomous female body, a reclamation of the absent mother/country whose name, face, language, vegetation, foods, and culture have disappeared under the impositions of colonialism.

Winterson's *Oranges* (set in an industrial English town) follows a similar trajectory, directly opposing the truth-telling status of an evangelical upbringing and thus refusing to articulate an identity recognizable from within the limits of patriarchal religious law. The novel rewrites fairy tales and invents its own myths to insist on identity as textual and to undermine the authority of such other cultural stories as the Old Testament (which lends the novel's chapters their ironic titles). When the character Jeanette falls in love with a succession of young women, her relationship with her Pentecostal mother undergoes radical rupture, as Jeanette is first exorcised and then banished from the community. Like Kincaid, Winterson thus suggests that a woman's identity is bound up with sexual self-definition and with a process of separation from coercive and reductive ideological scripts—which mothers may metaphorically succumb to through death or may rigidly, uncritically reproduce. For both Kincaid and Winterson, the self-representational enterprise necessarily interrogates the transparency of inscribing "I am," revealing the myriad pressures and investments that motivate and endorse such a statement. To end the course here is thus to spotlight what each of the autobiographers has in some way pointed out: that identity may be in large part a textual invention but that the body also matters; that life writing may capitulate to, but also subversively revise, a culture's conventional tale of womanhood.

In sometimes subtle, sometimes explicit terms, all the texts mentioned here argue that writing down the story of self can be life-sustaining in the truest sense. Derricotte and Mairs are most adamant about just how profound an impact writing one's autobiography may have. "I have to write," Mairs avows at the end of the collection *Plaintext*. "If I avoid that mandate,

I wind up trying to kill myself. It's as simple as that" (104). Derricotte similarly claims of compiling *The Black Notebooks* that "I did it to save my life," for "[i]t was language that saved my life" (15, 22). In less overt but no less poignant ways, each of these authors names writing itself as a kind of lifeline. By working through difficult memories; by attending to the complex interplay of personal with social, historical, and literary forces; by bearing witness to the pain of marginalized communities; and by reveling in their own linguistic inventiveness, these writers announce that the old stories of women's lives (and even many of the so-called new ones) do not suffice. My hope is that this brief excursion into the ways in which women have narrated their experience will encourage students to embark on a fuller investigation of the field.

Notes

1. Another possibility here is *Reading* Lolita *in Tehran: A Memoir in Books*, by Azar Nafisi, in which she recounts organizing a women's reading group with some of her former university students and describes their clandestine meetings to discuss Western literature. Part literary scholarship, part manifesto for women's independence and intellect, this text could neatly complement Min's use of opera to explore politically sensitive material.

2. I prefer *Red Azalea* to Maxine Hong Kingston's *The Woman Warrior: Memoirs of a Girlhood among Ghosts*, if only because it is less familiar to students. I would also recommend Shirley Geok-Lin Lim's *Among the White Moon Faces: An Asian-American Memoir of Homelands*, though Lim's book overtly incorporates feminist and poststructuralist theory and may be difficult for undergraduates. A different pairing altogether, one that has worked well in introductory courses, is Mary Crow Dog's *Lakota Woman* with *Borderlands / La Frontera*, by Gloria Anzaldúa, two texts that emphasize the often competing allegiances that women of color may experience as they navigate gender, ethnic, cultural, and geographic borders in America.

3. A second very successful pairing includes Lucy Grealy and Georgina Kleege. I have found Grealy's *Autobiography of a Face* to be enormously popular with students; this memoir of childhood cancer and over thirty reconstructive surgeries in the ensuing years depicts the psychological disablement of facial scarring and raises challenging questions about the construction of beauty in American culture. Grealy's text works well against Kleege's *Sight Unseen*, a collection of essays that examines the primacy of vision in Western culture. From different places, but leading to similar conclusions, both texts ask what happens when a woman doesn't look normal—or normally.

4. One could substitute Abigail Thomas's *Safekeeping*, a collection of extremely brief vignettes (many no longer than a few sentences) that simply accumulate into a record of sorts, piling up to indicate the shape of a life with three

children, three marriages, a divorce, one husband's death, poverty, sexual freedom in the late 1960s, and so forth. Less risky than Glancy's or Derricotte's stories, *Safekeeping* nonetheless offers an intriguing alternative to a linear narrative that pretends to continuity; its many parts aim instead for the fleeting shards of memory, longing, dreams.

    5. To frame the course according to life stages, one might begin with a memoir of girlhood and youth, such as Dillard's *An American Childhood* or Mary Karr's *The Liar's Club*, and end with a narrative about aging, such as May Sarton's final journal, *At Eighty-Two*. This approach has the advantage of highlighting aspects of women's lives that are often left out of popular representations.

Works Cited

Anzaldúa, Gloria. *Borderlands / La Frontera*. 2nd ed. San Francisco: Aunt Lute, 1999.

Asayesh, Gelareh. *Saffron Sky: A Life between Iran and America*. Boston: Beacon, 2000.

Cavendish, Margaret. *A True Relation of My Birth, Breeding and Life. Paper Bodies: A Margaret Cavendish Reader*. Ed. Sylvia C. Bowerbank and Sara Heller Mendelson. Calgary: Broadview, 2000. 41–63.

Clare, Eli. *Exile and Pride*. Cambridge: South End, 1999.

Crow Dog, Mary. *Lakota Woman*. New York: HarperPerennial, 1990.

Derricotte, Toi. *The Black Notebooks*. New York: Norton, 1999.

Dillard, Annie. *An American Childhood*. New York: HarperPerennial, 1988.

———. "To Fashion a Text." *Inventing the Truth: The Art and Craft of Memoir*. Ed. William Zinsser. New York: Mariner, 1998. 141–61.

Gilmore, Leigh. *The Limits of Autobiography: Trauma and Testimony*. Ithaca: Cornell UP, 2001.

Glancy, Diane. *Claiming Breath*. Lincoln: U of Nebraska P, 1996.

Grealy, Lucy. *Autobiography of a Face*. New York: Harper, 2000.

Karr, Mary. *The Liar's Club*. New York: Penguin, 1998.

Kempe, Margery. *The Book of Margery Kempe*. Ed. Barry Windeatt. New York: Penguin-Longman, 2000.

Kincaid, Jamaica. *Autobiography of My Mother*. New York: Farrar, 1996.

Kingston, Maxine Hong. 1976. *The Woman Warrior: Memoirs of a Girlhood among Ghosts*. New York: Vintage, 1989.

Kleege, Georgina. *Sight Unseen*. New Haven: Yale UP, 1999.

Lim, Shirley Geok-Lin. *Among the White Moon Faces: An Asian-American Memoir of Homelands*. New York: Feminist, 1998.

Mairs, Nancy. *Carnal Acts*. Boston: Beacon, 1996.

———. *Plaintext*. Tucson: U of Arizona P, 1986.

———. *Waist-High in the World: A Life among the Nondisabled*. Boston: Beacon, 1997.

Min, Anchee. *Red Azalea*. New York: Pantheon, 1994.

Nafisi, Azar. *Reading* Lolita *in Tehran: A Memoir in Books*. New York: Random, 2003.

Sarton, May. *At Eighty-Two: A Journal.* New York: Norton, 1997.

Thomas, Abigail. *Safekeeping: Some True Stories from a Life.* New York: Anchor, 2000.

Winterson, Jeanette. 1985. *Oranges Are Not the Only Fruit.* New York: Grove, 1997.

Margaretta Jolly

Teaching Jo Spence's
Putting Myself in the Picture:
Pedagogy and Life Writing
in and outside the University

"I'll be so proud of you Jo when you get your degree and learn to be ashamed of me." Thus Jo Spence captioned one of the auto/biographical photographs in her 1988 series Mother and Daughter Shame Work: Crossing Class Boundaries. Dressed as her mother in pinafore and hairnet and leaning on a broom, Spence peers up at the viewer from the stooped position she has assumed to pick up some milk bottles. We are forced to look down on her, but we also confront the gaze of a woman we know to be positioning herself ironically with us. Through the peculiar division of the self-portrait, Spence confronts her own shame: of her working-class upbringing, but also of her distance from her mother (Meskimmon 148).

The political and psychoanalytic as well as theatrical and narrative qualities that define Jo Spence's photography have made it a popular teaching tool in universities, especially in women's studies and life writing courses. A British photographer who worked her way from Main Street commerce to the art world, Spence is best known for her autophotographic explorations of class, gender, and family; her pioneering "phototherapy" with Rosy Martin and Terry Dennett in the early 1980s; and her documentation of her breast cancer before her death from leukemia in 1992. Courses that feature Spence's work range from Experimental Photography and Queer

Strategies in Studio Practice at the University of North Carolina, Chapel Hill, to The Private Self: Forms and Traditions of Life Writing at the University of Strathclyde to Imaging Women, Body and Identity at Anglia Polytechnic University.[1] Indeed, Dennett, Spence's former partner and now curator of the Jo Spence Memorial Archive, offers "to assist students and others world-wide, who are doing projects or theses on Spence and her special areas of interest" (6).[2]

Spence herself did not enter higher education until she was in her midforties. Indeed, she begins her "political, personal and photographic" autobiography *Putting Myself in the Picture* with a story of educational exclusion: "After leaving school at thirteen (having failed my exams for entry to 'the Tech') I was put through private secretarial college for two years by my parents, both of whom worked in factories and wanted 'something better' for me" (14). She learned photography on the job as an unskilled assistant, got a political education in working-class and women's struggles in the 1960s, and received her cultural education when she branched out from her secretarial job at the Education Division of the British Film Institute in 1976 to teach and to prepare exhibitions, with some trepidation, herself (134). It was unsurprising that when Spence went on to Central London Polytechnic to study photography in 1980, she angrily rebelled against her guilt-stricken semiotics tutors for the contradictions between their radical theory and conservative institutional practice (92–93).

It is with the class politics of education in mind that I explore Spence's autobiographical approach to photography and the subsequent use of her texts in life writing courses, including my own teaching for the Workers' Educational Association and the University of Exeter. Spence's development as an artist and teacher, largely outside the academy, shows that autobiographical methods, placed alongside the teaching of autobiography as a subject, bring together intellectual, personal, and political levels of discovery in ways that the academy could learn from. In *Putting Myself in the Picture* Spence not only describes the story of how a professional photographer comes to turn the camera on herself. In photographically staging selves that she feels have been unrepresented or repressed, she also puts into the picture the hidden ideologies that construct the gaze of the high street photographer, the documentary maker, the compiler of family albums, the pornographer. This approach to photography, she suggests, is difficult for conventional pedagogy to understand:

I've had a lot of flak for my work on the mistaken assumption that it is some kind of narcissism rather than politically motivated investigation. Using the camera in these ways has shown me that I have no fixed identity and that my subjectivity is always in process rather than a "positive" or "negative" thing to be spoken about from outside. Critical academics have found it difficult to comprehend an endeavour to find a "subject language" when they are so highly trained as professional managers of knowledge, deeply implicated in concealing their own feelings and class histories. I've also had positive feedback from people all over the world, encouraging me to go on making it safe for others to dig into their histories, repressed feelings and fantasies. I see my artworks as a kind of "politicised exhibitionism" about particular psychic and social issues which have enraged me. In this respect I have used myself as a kind of case study. ("Woman" 94–95)

Although here Spence used postmodern terminology to present the self as a linguistic, historical, and psychological construct, her pedagogical allegiances were always much more experiential. From the early 1970s, she was deeply involved in community education. Influenced by the workers' theater, film, and photo movements, the libertarian free school movement, and the theory of Augusto Boal, she and Dennett formed a grassroots teaching organization, Photography Workshop Ltd., which operated from an old hospital ambulance converted into a mobile darkroom (Dennett 2). Part of its brief was "to encourage the photographic recording of personal, group and local history by those involved, with or without the assistance of professional photographers" (*Putting* 65). Throughout the 1980s, Spence ran women's workshops that built on feminist ideas of consciousness raising, oral history, and radical psychotherapy movements. Her Faces Group project, for example, is outlined in *What Can a Woman Do with a Camera?* (Spence and Solomon) as one of several practical suggestions of autophotographic exercises that readers can do for themselves:

Invite women who "do not like their own faces" to come to a meeting to discuss this phenomenon. Each participant would bring an informal portrait, with room/window lighting, as a way to open up discussions. It is easier to talk about pictures than real faces. In the group we organised it transpired that each person wondered what on earth the others did not like about their faces, and what had brought them to the meeting. . . . Such a group could be a useful way of dealing with anxiety in a supportive situation. Building on this there is potential for its reversal through "public" display, fun and pleasure. People brought make-up, clothes, wigs, props—anything that could contribute to confronting old fears and creating new fantasies. We broke up into pairs. Working without mirrors we trustingly offered up our faces to a partner who could do whatever kind of make-up she liked. After this initial stage, which was fearful and downright funny, people dressed up and photographed each other. The activity moved then into writing. The dressing-up clothes and make-up were removed and people spent five minutes gazing at themselves in their mirrors. Now was the time to write what they were feeling. (Spence and Solomon 165–66)[3]

Spence's personalized methods of teaching, which assert her mutual indebtedness to academic and community education, presented a political challenge to the academy. Just this conncection lay behind my first encounter with Spence's work in the classroom. While doing my PhD at the University of Sussex, I audited a semester's evening course Working with Life History Documents at the university's Centre for Continuing Education, taught by Jo Stanley, who after Spence's death had edited her collected works, *Cultural Sniping: The Art of Transgression*. Like Spence, Stanley worked part-time in higher education; both interested in and at odds with it, she described herself as "a freelance writer and cultural worker originally from a Liverpool working-class family" (Stanley, qtd. in Spence and Solomon 192). She had us bring in photocopies of family photographs and, in the manner of gestalt therapy, write on them what we felt that body parts were saying, having played anthropologist with one anothers' photographs in the light of Spence's examples (see Stanley). Such a psychoanalytic approach bears obvious risks, especially for the academically aspiring students of university evening classes who know they will be conventionally assessed. I was thus intrigued to hear that the women's studies master's degree at the University of York also successfully used Spence-style autophotography, in an academic course on race, "as a method for articulating whiteness" (Kaloski-Naylor and Broughton 106). Significantly, the course was held off-campus and facilitated by lecturers, Ann Kaloski-Naylor and Trev Broughton, who were steeped in community education and activism. When I was subsequently employed to teach for the Workers' Educational Association, I could not resist trying out my own autobiographical use of Spence's work, discovering for myself possibilities for the mutual education of university and other education providers.

Founded in 1903, the Workers' Educational Association (WEA) is the major voluntary adult education organization in Britain, providing over ten thousand courses each year for over 110,000 students. To teach for it, one must join a local branch run voluntarily, often by ex-students or other tutors, as well as be trained by regional paid workers. Brighton Women's WEA, for whom I taught Life/Lines: Autobiography for Women, is explicitly guided by feminist, antiracist, and socialist ideals. The students who chose to attend my ten-week evening course were mostly white women of mixed social class and economic background, their ages ranging from the thirties to the sixties, who had an already developed interest in writing and to some extent feminism and sexuality. My job was to provide them with friendships, relaxation, and personal development as much as with knowledge or skill, though the WEA is now, like all education providers in Britain, under pressure from market-oriented state funders to show transferable skills as the learning outcome.[4]

I discovered that a judicious amount of academic material, in the form of short excerpts of auto/biographical texts, was crucial not only as preparation for exercises in life story, reminiscence, and guided auto/biographical writing but also as a source of personal and creative as well as intellectual satisfaction for the group. Therefore as a preface to my adaptation of Stanley's exercise, in which students collaged, colored, and captioned photocopied enlargements of family or self-portraits, I discussed Spence's essay "Woman in Secret" and conducted a timed writing exercise under the same title. By gently bringing in psychoanalytic, sociological, and historical theories of the self, I encouraged students to consider secrets for their pleasures as well as dangers, as Spence herself does. Academic discussion thus protected the creative, even in a course where personal reflection, physical comfort, and accessibility were priorities (tea breaks! soft chairs!). The students voted to follow the course with an autophotography day school centered on the theatrical exploration of our alter egos, and we used some of the photographs of our guises as cleaners, belly dancers, aviators, and sex kittens in an exhibition and ongoing writers' group.

As for typical undergraduate education, Spence's practical approach to theory is a reminder that auto/biographical exercises are one of the best means of teasing students toward the academic. Very often when university students are allowed to write more personally, the stories that emerge concern educational anxiety and aspiration. These stories can then be used as material to explore the value (as well as limits) of the academic register toward which students are struggling—for example, by offering an aesthetic reading of their work. Portraits and self-portraits are of course even more accessible than life writing, intensifying the possibility for inclusion and identification among students. By the same token, the possibilities for critical surprise are more dramatic.

My subsequent approach to teaching life writing to undergraduate and graduate students has been to end the course with a session on photography, at least half of which is given over to practical work. Spence's family album imagery, for example, works well alongside Roland Barthes's *Camera Lucida* in establishing critical comparisons between life writing and visual auto/biography. Spence provides the personal and gendered analysis missing from Barthes, while both writers establish photography as the trace of what is missing or unconscious in all photography. I ask students to analyze one another's photographs in the academic terms of looking for the "studium" and "punctum" (Barthes 26–27); for the relation of gazes between photographed and photographer, especially when these involve the inner divisions of a self-portrait (Bruss); for the question of mortification that Barthes so lyrically sees in the photograph's frozen transience and that Spence literally stages through photographs of her body. Students then creatively doctor photocopies of their photographs in the way I describe above. It is important to add that this method requires establishing ground rules of respect and privacy and involves a closing moment in which I ask students to "de-role-play" by thinking about what they have explored and where they will be going after class. I also give students the option of sitting out the exercise by doing something more academic or not showing their work—though to date none has taken up the offer.

Of course, the use of auto/biographical method outside the university is largely based on humanist ideologies of individual self-development rather than the more explicitly political agendas of much higher education in the arts and certainly of Spence's socialist, feminist agitprop. But in the context of today's economic fundamentalism, these two positions are much closer allies than they used to be. The flowerings of popular autobiography, self-portraiture, and art therapy in the 1970s were all sustained by libertarian interpretations of older humanist ideas of "the intelligence of feeling" and "self-expression" (Atkinson 138–39; Jolly), and although we may wish to modify some of the romantic excesses of this individualism, in part by the kinds of deconstruction of identity that Spence argued for, the emphasis on the practical is more relevant than ever in today's conceptual climate. If praxis, as the integration of theory and practice, is the highest expression of understanding, it may also be the best remedy for undoing the class repression that Spence identified in "professional managers of knowledge" ("Woman" 94). Autobiographical—and even photographic—praxis is precious not just because it cannot be economically quantified but because it is a gateway between different educational institutions, from schools to access courses, adult education to higher education. In this, the avant-garde is both inside and outside the university.[5]

Appendix
Two Class Plans: Workers' Educational Association: Secrets

Working with Photographs, Part 1

Family albums: the mystique of the photo. Reading: Jo Spence, "Woman in Secret"

7:30–8:15. Discuss how Spence organizes the article around the idea of the secret—and only later divides the topic into good and bad secrets. Define the difference: essentially it's about whether the secret is chosen or imposed. What kinds of secrets: class, sexuality, ugliness, family division, or power struggle. Discuss Spence's idea of what is invested in a family album and how to go beyond it; show her work on it. Talk about what photo is taken, by whom, how preserved. What experiences do you regret not having a visual record of? Discuss her idea of photo therapy and how she used it in relation to her breast cancer. Consider the idea of the photo as objectifying and discuss how photography exploits and builds on the objectification of women's bodies.

8:15–8:30. Tea

8:30–9:00. In pairs, tell the story of your photos. For each photo, consider what the person wanted to show, what you think it really shows, what it conceals (secrets), and how it has been preserved. Think how each photo can tell a story and be used on your life time line. If you like, give your photos to the other person to analyze first before you discuss them.

9:00–9:20. Writing exercise: Put one of your photos on your life time line and public chronologies, and write a short piece describing the "woman in secret." Alternatively, write about the moment that the photo was taken and what it was for.

Working with Photographs, Part 2

Bring colored pencils, pens, scissors, glue, old magazines, frames, *What Can a Woman Do with a Camera?* and other books on women and photography.

7:30–7:40. Briefing for tonight's task: adapt, re-create, re-vision some images of your past. This can be done as a creative or artistic exercise in itself, much as writing auto/biography or family memoir is a creative interpretation. It can also be done in a more personal way, exploring what the original photo represented or even hid and what it can be made to speak. You will do this work in two stages, with feedback in between. Introduce work other women have done with photography, through photomontage, in books on women photographers, and so on. These books will be available for you to browse if you want to take a break or get ideas.

7:40–8:05. Jo Stanley exercise. Creatively doctor your photos; for example, cut them, write on them, add to them, do speech bubbles, make parts of the body speak to each other. Color them in. Do a frame. Put bits of different photos together. Give them a caption. Write across, behind, or around them. Mount them as a collage.

8:05–8:30. Give each other feedback in pairs, but don't judge or assess the other person's work—either artistically or psychologically. Instead, find out what the person was exploring, and reflect on this. Don't even necessarily give your own interpretation, but simply let the person talk for a few minutes.

8:30–8:50. Tea

8:50–9:10. Develop your work to further realize what you wanted it to be. If you have done all you can visually, write an accompanying text. Or write about what wasn't photographed that you wish had been.

9:10. In groups of three, show your work and explain it. If you are willing, display your work on a table and talk the class through it. (This is valuable and personal work that students should protect, perhaps by making a special folder for it.) Finally, to "de-role-play," everyone should say something about what they are going to do when they leave the class.

Notes

1. For the University of North Carolina, Chapel Hill, courses, taught by Elin O'Hara Slavick, see www.unc.edu/~eoslavic/pedagogy/photography.html; for the course at Strathclyde, taught by Sarah Edwards, see www.strath.ac.uk/departments/English/privateself.html; and for the course at Anglia Polytechnic University, taught by Gina Wisker, see www.apu.ac.uk/dso/catalogue/cambridge/Forward_Planners/level_4_mdf?WS_WomensStudies?WSM2003.DOC.

2. Dennett can be contacted at Dennett@GMS.net.

3. Dennett suggests that the workshop was only partially successful.

4. The WEA is funded largely by students' own fees (which are on average half the cost of courses with university continuing education departments—for example, £3.50 per class for a full-wage earner) but also subsidized by central and local governments, particularly if local branches and districts can conform to criteria that aim to get unemployed people into work or further education.

5. Recent government recommendations for using photography in schools could only have delighted Spence: "Looking at, talking about and making photographs in and for a variety of contexts offers all children a means through which they can explore and ultimately express their self identity. . . . Work on photographic self representation can best be organized around the following five areas: the examination and evaluation of those images with which students are familiar; the practical exploration of ways of making self representations; how self images are understood and received in different contexts; how students come to realize

their intentions through controlled use in making self images; the examination and interrogation of stereotypes" (Isherwood and Stanley 41–42).

Works Cited

Atkinson, Dennis. *Art in Education: Identity and Practice*. London: Kluwer, 2002.

Barthes, Roland. *Camera Lucida: Reflections on Photography*. Trans. Richard Howard. New York: Hill, 1981.

Boal, Augusto. *Theater of the Oppressed*. New York: Urizen, 1979.

Bruss, Elizabeth W. "Eye for I: Making and Unmaking Autobiography in Film." *Autobiography: Essays Theoretical and Critical*. Ed. James Olney. Princeton: Princeton UP, 1980. 296–320.

Dennett, Terry. "The Wounded Photographer: The Genesis of Jo Spence's Camera Therapy." *Afterimage* 1 Nov. 2001. 22 Dec. 2003 < http://www.findarticles .com/cf_dls/m2479/3_29/807575514/p1/article.jhtml >.

Isherwood, Sue, and Nick Stanley, eds. *Creating Vision: Photography and the National Curriculum*. Manchester: Corner House, 1994.

Jolly, Margaretta. "Teaching Carolyn Steedman's *Landscape for a Good Woman*: A Comparative Perspective on Pedagogy and Life Writing in British University and Adult Education Contexts." *Auto/Biography* 10.1–2 (2002): 35–40.

Kaloski-Naylor, Ann, and Trev Broughton. "Teaching Whiteness." *White?Women: Critical Perspectives on Race and Gender*. Ed. Heloise Brown, Madi Gilkes, and Kaloski-Naylor. York: Raw Nerve, 1999. 91–112.

Meskimmon, Marsha. *The Art of Reflection: Women Artists' Self-Portraiture in the Twentieth Century*. London: Scarlet, 1996.

Spence, Jo. *Cultural Sniping: The Art of Transgression*. Ed. Jo Stanley and David Hevey. London: Routledge, 1995.

——. *Putting Myself in the Picture: A Political, Personal and Photographic Autobiography*. London: Camden, 1986.

——. "Woman in Secret." Spence and Solomon 85–96.

Spence, Jo, and Joan Solomon, eds. *What Can a Woman Do with a Camera?* London: Scarlet, 1995.

Stanley, Jo. *Writing Out Your Life-Story: A Handbook for Women*. London: Scarlet, 1997.

Georgia Johnston

Teaching Queer Lives

The haunting distinctions between queer and straight autobiography suggest that queer autobiography should be taught in any course on autobiography in general and that a course on queer autobiography alone would necessarily and powerfully teach students about social conformity and oppressions. For some students at lower curricular levels, such autobiographies might become vehicles for encountering depictions of gay life. "We have a duty," George E. Haggerty argues, to provide "all our students" with "the tools they need to achieve a sexual identity in a society that is determined to make that identity an impossibility. That duty includes being open . . . to the sexualities of texts and the sexualities of students" (12). Such an introductory course in queer autobiography would present diverse life experiences through the thematics of the lives, while also "recovering a history which has thus far been neglected or obscured" (Alderson and Anderson 5). The course would counter what Cheshire Calhoun notes as "the principal, damaging effect of a heterosexist system" on gays and lesbians—gay and lesbian displacement "from both the public and private spheres of civil society so that lesbians and gays have no legitimated social location, not even a disadvantaged one" (2).

Gay autobiographies differ from straight autobiographies in ways analogous to the differences between masculine and feminine autobiography

336

analyzed by Estelle Jelinek and explored more fully in anthologies such as *Life/Lines* (Brodzki and Schenck), *American Women's Autobiography* (Culley), *The Private Self* (Benstock), and *Women's Life Writing* (Coleman). As in many women's autobiographies, queer textual formation, expectations of script, and multiplicity of the I all counter what one expects from an autobiography depicting a life supported by dominant Western patriarchal culture. But between gay and straight life texts, distinctions arise also because of contrasting relations to society and politics, particularly as they relate to ideologies of normalcy and realities of safety.

At upper levels of the curriculum, where I teach semester-long courses in autobiography, I include theories of autobiography alongside primary texts. Taught with theories of autobiography, queer autobiography powerfully exposes the seams of autobiographical inscription itself, since the course allows me to introduce theories of the subject, of culture, of language discourse—theories endemic to studies of all autobiography. Queer autobiographies mark these theoretical issues in relation to straight autobiography and straight culture, providing a textual commentary on the supposedly normal scripts of autobiography, in terms of both textual traditions and ideologies of the I. In other words, gay and lesbian life writers present, resist, and expose ideological constructions of both the self and the genre.

Autobiographers are not always explicit about their sexualities, queer or straight, particularly in autobiographies before the late twentieth century. Readers must look for the "variations, fluctuations, blurrings, coded signals, and lapses into mimicry or a void" that Catharine Stimpson finds in lesbian literature ("Zero" 379). Queer life representation has always had much to do with what is not said. Julia Watson writes of the "unspeakable" and the attempts to decolonize women from patriarchal systems so as to permit both women's and specifically lesbian representations. Her observations correspond to Brian Loftus's understanding of textual silence in lesbian discourse and to what Eve Kosofsky Sedgwick establishes as the queer trope—the closet and its "epistemology"—incorporating what is silenced even while that absence is always known. In addition, multiple I's correspond with multiple subject positions of same-sex relations. Elizabeth Meese connects Virginia Woolf's, Vita Sackville-West's, and Gertrude Stein's autobiographies to her own contemporary lesbian autobiographical address, positing a defiantly lesbian form of address to a lover, who, along with the letter writer, also becomes that lesbian autobiographical I.

An upper-division course can proceed through (1) analysis of the gay and lesbian doubling of the narrative I and audience; (2) the gay and lesbian life writer's use of the closet as a space, as a narrative form, and as a censoring device; and (3) the gay and lesbian life writer's use of the palimpsest as narrative technique producing multiple layers to take meaning outside of (policed) experience. Different types of life writing texts add to an understanding of these experiential constructions—from private (even secret) diary to public autobiography; from case studies, such as Freud's *Dora*, to experimental fantasies, such as Woolf's "biography" *Orlando*; from texts relying on the other, the lover, for voice, such as Stein's *Autobiography of Alice B. Toklas* or *Lifting Belly*, to texts that eulogize a lover, such as Paul Monette's *Elegies* or Adrienne Rich's "Twenty-One Love Poems." Texts such as Anne Lister's diaries and Stein's autobiographies—which I would argue, appropriating Leigh Gilmore's words, "play with certain expectations about how and whether lesbian authors write lesbian texts, and what such a claim might mean" ("Anatomy" 227)—are central to a course on queer autobiography, in part because they emphasize the artificial construction of the queer (or any) life.

Presenting queer autobiographies from a range of historical periods can keep queer from being read as essentialist. Teaching texts of the eighteenth and nineteenth centuries, such as excerpts from Lister's diaries and Herculine Barbin's memoir, helps a class concentrate on the controlled roles for men and women and on the construction of gender performances. Lister (1791–1840) wrote the sexual commentary in her diary in code, a "crypt hand" (Frangos 47)—as if, according to Caroline Eisner, she was "on paper, dividing her deviant self from her public self" (29). Creating a doubled text with a closet of safety, Lister constructs a lesbian identity that combines the traditional masculine ownership and management of an estate, the acquisition and control of her lover's (Ann Walker's) neighboring estate, and lesbian sexual conquest and practice. Because Lister wrote the lesbian parts of her diary in code, she was able to remain a figure of normality during her lifetime. The violence toward her sexuality is seen in posthumous events. When her nephew, with an aim toward publishing the diaries, broke the code, he was advised to destroy them (Lister 240). Barbin, a hermaphrodite, records her/his experiences in a world that at first regards him as a girl and then, on his redefining his gender, treats him as a man. Barbin's memoir shows a deliberate attempt to pass as a man rather than accept the role of woman in which he had been brought up. In contrast to Lister's ability to manipulate her role, Barbin's confusion over gender, initially because of lesbian sexual experiences, along with Barbin's subsequent suicide, show the tragic consequences of Barbin's inabilities to perform gender.

Early-twentieth-century texts, such as Woolf's *Orlando*, Stein's texts, and Vita Sackville-West and Nigel Nicolson's *Portrait of a Marriage*, help students understand the legal issues and censorship that create the need for disguise. Teaching such life writing texts in the context of the trial of Rad-clyffe Hall's novel *Well of Loneliness* introduces students to queer autobiography's coded and fantastical narrative. Teaching such texts alongside the case studies in Havelock Ellis (chs. 3 and 4) and Freud develops under-standing of how modern theories of lesbian and gay male perversion have power over queer representation. The resulting self-censorship in early-twentieth-century queer autobiography enacts the double deviation that Jean Starobinski identifies in all autobiography. The theories of Leigh Gilmore's "mark" of the I and Paul de Man's creation of writer through the written I both predict a reading of this queer palimpsestic subject. Such theories pinpoint the dilemma of the early-twentieth-century queer I, who had to find a way both to emerge from yet remain in silence. Stein in particular writes a palimpsestic text, presenting one text for audiences in the know and another for audiences who cannot understand queer narrative. The texts written for publication, and therefore to be read by both straight and queer readers, are of much interest for their silences, their evasions, their self-policing, and their disguising of sexual desire. Alice's voice in Stein's *Autobiography of Alice B. Toklas*, for instance, gives way to Gertrude's, providing a template in an autobiography class for talking about the signature in terms of lesbian interchange (see Stimp-son, "Gertrice"; and Meese). Working with what is not said lets us enter into discussions of alternate discourses for gay autobiography (see Loftus).

Late-twentieth-century gay autobiographies can help a class focus on the queer need to eschew censorship. These autobiographies may be hos-tile to straight audiences. "*Rub their faces in it, Paulie*," Paul Monette's tex-tualized lover Stevie says. "*Nobody told us anything. You tell them*" (*Becoming* 144). Or consider Minnie Bruce Pratt, losing her children because she is lesbian and writing of "useless words" in trying to convey her story to a straight feminist woman colleague who doesn't understand Pratt's pain: "I don't say: / You've known for years who I am. Have you / never imagined what happened to me day / in and out, out in your damned straight world?" (68).

The determination to tell the story, despite policing and despite the closet, reflects the need of gay men and lesbians to teach their readers, to expose details of queer life, to change society through narrative. Samuel R. Delany's *The Motion of Light in Water* and his *Times Square Red, Times Square Blue* and Rich's "Twenty-One Love Poems" all tell sexual stories, sometimes graphically. Delany writes of the "notion of sexuality itself as always occurring partly inside language and partly outside it" yet also of the power of stories "to start further, operationalized investigation," adding that it is his "utopian hope . . . that in such stories as these such study might begin" ("Aversion" 20, 18). Students may be uncomfortable with the autobiographical details of sexuality and desire in these texts. And classroom discussion might need to include details about gay and lesbian culture that may upset students. For instance, teaching John Ashbery's "Self-Portrait in a Convex Mirror" in the context of gay autobiography may also mean teaching John Vincent's understanding of that title poem as incorporating cruising, thus taking into account cultural components of gay male sexuality that other audiences may not perceive. Despite the possible discomfort of students, however, autobiographers choosing exposure help advance a class conversation about the reciprocity between autobiography and cultural context. "Our sexualities and their representations are the raw material of volatile syllabi and classrooms," Stimpson notes, but "[i]f classrooms are to be of use, we must learn to speak together in them" (Preface xii).

Connecting queer autobiographies and theoretical texts may help us "learn to speak together." Teaching a theoretical and historicizing text such as Sedgwick's "Introduction: Axiomatic" helps students who are uncomfortable with the gay material to recognize parallel oppressions. Sedgwick narrativizes the gay dilemma of the closet from paralleled religious and straight perspectives—by depicting the plight of the Jew, Esther. Teaching Rich's "Compulsory Heterosexuality" makes students aware of some of the effects of discomfort or prejudice, since Rich shows how scholarly ignorance of lesbian materials results in inaccurate theorization of female psychology.

All these autobiographies share a dubious, fraught, ironic, and doubled relation with the closet, that cincture of silence that Sedgwick posits as the basis of gay interaction with language. Students and the instructor bring that relation to the closet, in varying degrees, into the class, not just in their reading of the autobiographies, but also through their own relations to language and culture. The process of creating awareness of that closet, and stepping outside of it, is one of the pleasures of teaching a course in queer lives.

Works Cited

Alderson, David, and Linda Anderson. Introduction. *Territories of Desire in Queer Culture: Refiguring Contemporary Boundaries*. Ed. Alderson and Anderson. Manchester: Manchester UP, 2000. 1–9.

Ashbery, John. *Self-Portrait in a Convex Mirror*. 1976. New York: Penguin, 1992.

Barbin, Herculine. *Herculine Barbin: Being the Recently Discovered Memoirs of a Nineteenth-Century French Hermaphrodite*. Introd. Michel Foucault. Trans. Richard McDougall. New York: Pantheon, 1980.

Benstock, Shari, ed. *The Private Self: Theory and Practice of Women's Autobiographical Writings*. Chapel Hill: U of North Carolina P, 1988.

Brodzki, Bella, and Celeste Schenck, eds. *Life/Lines: Theorizing Women's Autobiography*. Ithaca: Cornell UP, 1988.

Calhoun, Cheshire. *Feminism, the Family, and the Politics of the Closet: Lesbian and Gay Displacement*. Oxford: Oxford UP, 2000.

Coleman, Linda S., ed. *Women's Life Writing: Finding Voice / Building Community*. Bowling Green: Bowling Green State U Popular P, 1997.

Culley, Margo, ed. *American Women's Autobiography: Fea(s)ts of Memory*. Madison: U of Wisconsin P, 1992.

Delany, Samuel R. "Aversion/Perversion/Diversion." *Negotiating Lesbian and Gay Subjects*. Ed. Monica Forename and Richard Henke. New York: Routledge, 1995. 7–33.

——. *The Motion of Light in Water: Sex and Science Fiction Writing in the East Village, 1960–1965*. New York: Masquerade, 1996.

——. *Times Square Red, Times Square Blue*. New York: New York UP, 1999.

de Man, Paul. "Autobiography as De-facement." *MLN* 94 (1979): 919–30.

Eisner, Caroline L. "Shifting the Focus: Anne Lister as Pillar of Conservatism." *A/B: Auto/Biography Studies* 17.1 (2002): 28–42.

Ellis, Havelock. "Sexual Inversion in Men" and "Sexual Inversion in Women." *Sexual Inversion*. 3rd ed. Philadelphia: Davis, 1921. 75–263. Vol. 2 of *Studies in the Psychology of Sex*.

Frangos, Jennifer. "'I Love and Only Love the Fairer Sex': The Writing of a Lesbian Identity in the Diaries of Anne Lister (1791–1840)." Coleman 43–61.

Freud, Sigmund. *Dora: An Analysis of a Case of Hysteria*. 1905. New York: Simon, 1997.

Gilmore, Leigh. "An Anatomy of Absence: *Written on the Body*, *The Lesbian Body*, and Autobiography without Names." *The Gay '90s: Disciplinary and Interdisciplinary Formations in Queer Studies*. Ed. Thomas Foster, Carol Siegel, and Ellen E. Berry. New York: New York UP, 1997. 224–51.

——. "The Mark of Autobiography: Postmodernism, Autobiography, and Genre." *Autobiography and Postmodernism*. Ed. Kathleen Ashley, Gilmore, and Gerald Peters. Amherst: U of Massachusetts P, 1994. 3–18.

Haggerty, George E. "'Promoting Homosexuality' in the Classroom." *Professions of Desire: Lesbian and Gay Studies in Literature*. Ed. Haggerty and Bonnie Zimmerman. New York: MLA, 1995. 11–18.

Hall, Radclyffe. *The Well of Loneliness*. 1928. New York: Anchor, 1990.

Jelinek, Estelle. *The Tradition of Women's Autobiography: From Antiquity to the Present*. Boston: Twayne, 1986.

Lister, Anne. *Female Fortune: Land, Gender, and Authority: The Anne Lister Diaries and Other Writings, 1833–36*. Ed. Jill Liddington. London: Rivers Oram, 1998.

Loftus, Brian. "Speaking Silence: The Strategies and Structures of Queer Autobiography." *College Literature* 24.1 (1997): 28–44.

Meese, Elizabeth A. *(Sem)Erotics: Theorizing Lesbian: Writing*. New York: New York UP, 1992.

Monette, Paul. *Becoming a Man: Half a Life Story*. New York: Harcourt, 1992.

——. *Love Alone: Eighteen Elegies for Rog*. New York: St. Martin's, 1988.

Nicolson, Nigel, and Vita Sackville-West. *Portrait of a Marriage: Vita Sackville-West and Harold Nicolson*. London: Weidenfeld, 1973.

Pratt, Minnie Bruce. *Crime against Nature*. Ithaca: Firebrand, 1990.

Rich, Adrienne. "Compulsory Heterosexuality and Lesbian Experience." *Signs: Journal of Women in Culture and Society* 5 (1980): 631–60.

——. "Twenty-One Love Poems." *Dream of a Common Language: Poems 1974–1977*. New York: Norton, 1993. 25–36.

Sedgwick, Eve Kosofsky. "Introduction: Axiomatic." *Epistemology of the Closet*. Berkeley: U of California P, 1990. 1–63.

Starobinski, Jean. "The Style of Autobiography." *Autobiography: Essays Theoretical and Critical*. Ed. James Olney. Princeton: Princeton UP, 1980. 73–83.

Stein, Gertrude. *Autobiography of Alice B. Toklas*. New York: Harcourt, 1933.

——. *Lifting Belly*. Ed. Rebecca Marks. Tallahassee: Naiad, 1989.

Stimpson, Catharine R. "Gertrice/Altrude: Stein, Toklas, and the Paradox of the Happy Marriage." *Mothering the Mind: Twelve Studies of Writers and Their Silent Partners*. Ed. Ruth Perry and Martine Watson Browne. New York: Holmes, 1984. 122–39.

——. Preface. *Professions of Desire: Lesbian and Gay Studies in Literature*. Ed. George E. Haggerty and Bonnie Zimmerman. New York: MLA, 1995. xi–xii.

——. "Zero Degree Deviancy: The Lesbian Novel in English." *Critical Inquiry* 8 (1981): 363–79.

Vincent, John. *Queer Lyrics: Difficulty and Closure in American Poetry*. New York: Palgrave, 2002.

Watson, Julia. "Unspeakable Differences: The Politics of Gender in Lesbian and Heterosexual Women's Autobiographies." *De/Colonizing the Subject: The Politics of Gender in Women's Autobiography*. Ed. Sidonie Smith and Watson. Minneapolis: U of Minnesota P, 1992. 139–68.

Woolf, Virginia. *Orlando: A Biography*. London: Hogarth, 1928.

Trev Lynn Broughton

Cultures of Life Writing

When commentators want to prove the cultural and social significance of life writing in Britain or the United States, they point to the groaning shelves in the bookshops, to the best-seller lists, or to the academic courses and studies dedicated to the subject (Holmes 12; Law and Hughes 1–3). But the gesture does not tell us much about why and how life writing matters, or doesn't matter, at a particular moment. My master's degree elective Cultures of Life Writing, offered in the departments of English and women's studies at the University of York and delivered to postgraduates from a variety of cultural and disciplinary backgrounds, attempts to tease out such issues. I have outlined elsewhere some of the critical tendencies that have contributed to the current emphasis on autobiography as cultural artifact rather than solely or primarily as literary text (242–45). While in their titles or introductions, many recent critical volumes have aspired to move beyond the conventions of and challenges posed by life writing as a writerly craft to an engagement with "the functions which it can serve and has served in different societies, its *uses*" (France and St. Clair 4; Folkenflik), in practice this aspiration, with a few honorable, and mainly feminist, exceptions (Evans; Gagnier; Smith and Watson), has been pursued unevenly and indecisively. My aim is to open up the context of life writing to include not only production but, just as important, consumption and circulation—what Liz Stanley calls the "cultural politics" (3) of life writing.

How significant is it, for instance, that the development of feminist autobiographical studies has coincided historically with the rise of Reaganism and Thatcherism? In a deliberately provocative essay called "First Person Suspect; or, The Enemy Within . . ." Julia Swindells has asked whether, for the moment at least, "autobiography in Britain [is] . . . too hopelessly compromised (not *least* by 18 years of Conservatism) to service the politics of oppression" (40–41). To recognize this possibility is not to dismiss life writing as a political weapon of potential value to feminists but to acknowledge that it may be double-edged: that in reworking the relation between public and private, it may reshape what counts as political. Kay Ferres puts it thus:

> "[I]ncluding gender" involves not only the transformation of life narratives, but also the constitution of newly emergent publics. Biography can be a catalyst of dispute and disagreement about the public interest, as well as a document of public lives and careers. (305)

If one of the aims of postgraduate study in the humanities is to enable students to think self-reflexively about their ideas and approaches, then asking whether and how we, as women's studies or literary scholars, are being constituted as a public might be a step in the right direction.

Part of the first session is spent brainstorming the ways in which lives are inscribed in the society or societies with which the group is familiar. This discussion invariably generates between thirty and fifty genres of life writing—from the more obviously literary (biography, autobiography, religious confession, etc.) through the ephemeral (celebrity interviews, personal diaries, blogs and home pages, obituaries) to the bureaucratic (bank statements, dental records, visa applications, CVs, and so on). The group then provisionally arranges the items along various axes: relative literary value; greater or lesser value to the historian; size of intended audience; extent to which each item may disclose gender. The point of these deliberately fast and furious exercises is, needless to say, not to develop watertight distinctions but precisely to problematize distinctions: to demonstrate the complex and contradictory ways in which lives and contexts (disciplinary, technological, political) may constitute each other; to disrupt facile understandings of the relation between public and private—or between gender and genre—in late modernity. Such taxonomic problems suggest possible lines of inquiry for the rest of the course.

By this stage I hope that the group will understand what I mean when I offer a series of heterogeneous shorthand headings beginning "Life writing and. . . ." The list might include scandal, surveillance, ageing, crime, identity politics, feminist theory, the construction of dis/ability, the creative writing movement, health and illness, and—if I'm feeling brave or especially reflexive—the classroom. The group adds its own suggestions, which in the past have included personal advertisements, cyberspace, and self-help culture. Participants then each choose a topic and, with guidance, generate reading lists, preparatory tasks and questions, and exercises to undertake in class. Thereafter my role is to steer the discussions beyond the inevitable debates about truth, taste, and political correctness to an understanding of, or at least engagement with, what is at stake in such debates in any given context.

A typical seminar on John Bayley's *Iris: A Memoir of Iris Murdoch* gives a glimpse of how this approach works in practice. The first of a trilogy, Bayley's memoir of his eminent novelist-cum-philosopher wife, Iris Murdoch, offers reminiscences of their early life together as young Oxford dons in counterpoint with observations and reflections on their life since the onset of her Alzheimer's disease. Published while Murdoch was still living, the volume juxtaposes scenes of adventure and lush promise with tragicomic images of seedy decline. A dense thematic patterning, however, emphasizes Bayley's perception of the integrity of his wife's identity—and hence the unity of her work and story—rather than their disintegration. Bayley's avowedly partial version of his wife's life, and the multiple biographical role of sensitive consort, critic, and carer on which it is predicated, were widely and lavishly praised at the time, though Bayley's sweetly saintly reputation was later challenged with some vigor. The text's high profile in the media increased as challenges to its authority proliferated; at stake was not only the reputation of the writer herself (and of Bayley) but—Hollywood being involved—"the perceived character of an age and the people who inhabit it" (Aaronovitch). Indeed, the tendency of biographical controversy to inflate its own social significance while at the same time insisting on the uniqueness of its subject makes *Iris* a fascinating instance of the working of ideology in the marketplace of lives.

A preliminary reading divides the class along lines of taste: they love it or hate it. On further exploration these groups subdivide into those who

appreciate the work for the light it throws on an important woman of letters, those who simply enjoy it as a romantic tale of love triumphing over
infidelity and tragedy, and those who derogate its elitist "Eng. Lit." assumptions and Oxbridge parochialism; into those who deplore the spectacle—
and question the ethics—of a husband metaphorically undressing his
helpless wife in public and those who celebrate the work as making
poignantly visible what is usually hidden from view. The more theoretically attuned members of the group arrive fairly promptly at a metageneric
reading of the text: a reading that recognizes the way the Alzheimer's
topos catalyzes themes of identity and memory into an elegant exposition
of the impossibility of auto/biography and hence sees the text as a commentary on the ethics, hermeneutics, and politics of representing a subjectivity that is "always already" inaccessible (Bayley 71–72; 236).[1] The point,
however, is to situate this theoretical approach not as the final or privileged
reading but as one possibility among many, albeit one bristling with postgraduate credentials.

As the readings multiply, it becomes clear that they represent overlapping as well as mutually exclusive readerships. Many in the group, for instance, are scandalized (delighted *and* disgusted) by the couple's domestic
squalor. A little reading around in the scandal enables us to begin to locate
the *Iris* controversy within prevailing cultural and social crosscurrents and
to think of the ways in which such disclosures may cleave readers apart
over issues of interpretation, while paradoxically cleaving them to one another over perceptions of the wider stakes.

While no individual or group could be said to own any of these readings, it is at least possible to ask whether any of these versions of the text
have been sponsored in the press, whose interests the various readings
might serve, whether some have achieved more public assent than others,
and whether the unifying or sectarian tendencies have prevailed. It is usually
possible to get a sense of which reviewers, which media, and which organizations have interested themselves in a given text and—just as tellingly—
which have not.

The exercise the group set itself was to map publicly available responses to the Bayley-Murdoch story, looking for both patterns and aber-
rations. Some patterns were easily discernible: the schmaltzier packaging
of the book for United States consumers, for instance, seems to have
heightened North American critics' perceptions—or at least intensified
their accusations—of vulgarity, sentimentality, and poor taste. Elsewhere

we found the work of mapping done for us. When, shortly after Murdoch's death, in February 1999, sociologists at the University of Stirling surveyed the accounts of Murdoch's life offered in both the Bayley text and in newspaper obituaries, they found a marked tendency to "reproduce conventional narratives of the life course and of dementia, characterizing the deceased in terms of a moral career" (McColgan, Valentine, and Downs 97).

When one looked beyond critical and commemorative responses, the findings were more surprising and less easy to theorize. Although Bayley takes pains to distinguish their story and their partnership from many of the trench-humor jokes and narratives of heroism circulating among carers and their support networks (53–54, 85–86, 237, 262), academics, pundits, and medical institutions were relatively quick to co-opt Bayley's Iris as a paradigmatic Alzheimer's sufferer. The medical constituencies have frequently appealed to Bayley's account of his wife's decline and of his trials as a carer to back up generalizations about the disease and its consequences and, more recently, to boost both fund- and consciousness-raising activities (e.g., Henderson). On the other hand, paper-based and computer-mediated testimonies by sufferers and their carers seldom if ever cite, much less recommend, Bayley's text. This is not to imply that such testimonies exist in discursive isolation. They often cite other Alzheimer's narratives, recommend self-help texts, or direct the reader to both medical and charitable resources. In other words, our collective research suggested that attempts by powerful constituencies—including, in some instances, Bayley himself—to enlist (this version of) Iris Murdoch *on behalf* of the Alzheimer's community may have raised the profile of the problem of Alzheimer's but has done so in ways discontinuous with the concerns of key stakeholders—ordinary sufferers and carers themselves.[2]

We found an instructive comparison in another memoir of dementia, published a year later, which engaged with many of the same frustrations and sorrows but foregrounded the "unpalatable choices" (Grant, "True Confessions") forced on most families by the demands of work, the shortcomings of the welfare system, and the sheer failure of patience. Critically acclaimed and elegantly written, Linda Grant's *Remind Me Who I Am, Again* is far less notorious than Bayley's *Iris*, yet Grant's experience of publishing an account of her mother's illness forced her to rethink the relationship between professional writers and readers and between critics and other audiences. If confessional writers are doing their job properly, she argues, they "help people." "Empathy," she wrote later in "True Confessions," "is an important word missing from the critics' vocabulary." Noting the difference between her book and Bayley's, she nevertheless insists on the need for heterogeneous "personal" responses precisely because they are personal. "How," she asks, "are we to understand these conditions if no one is allowed to write about them, if they are so securely privatized that you can never make your own subjectivity public without being accused of cashing in on your own misery?"

Who are "we" and "you" here; who is doing the accusing; what is the relationship between these constituencies? How far—and with what limits—do the exigencies of the marketplace compromise what Swindells calls the politics of autobiographical use? What, for example, is the ideological function of the taboo against "cashing in on misery"? These are the kinds of questions I hope my students will address—questions that, I hope, will have relevance for feminist research in the twenty-first century. Kay Ferres reaches the same point through a different route:

> Another way to construe feminism's recent insistence on differences is to think of it as the basis from which desire can become action. Biography's traditional concern with the public life and career needs to be supplemented by an account of the continuing reorganization of the public sphere to accommodate newly emergent publics. What is still— and always—to be worked out is how to say "we." (319)

Notes

1. To students interested in this kind of reading, I recommend Smith.

2. The same pattern—of a homosocial elite discoursing to itself—is evident in other phases of the Iris Murdoch controversy (e.g., see Aaronovitch).

Works Cited

Aaronovitch, David. "The Iris Troubles." *Observer* 7 Sept. 2003. 16 Nov. 2006 < http://observer.guardian.co.uk/comment/story/0,6903,1036974,00.html > .

Bayley, John. *Iris: A Memoir of Iris Murdoch*. London: Abacus, 1998.

Broughton, Trev Lynn. "Autobiography and the Actual Course of Things." *Feminism and Autobiography: Texts, Theories, Methods*. Ed. Tess Cosslett, Celia Lury, and Penny Summerfield. London: Routledge, 2000. 241–46.

Evans, Mary. *Missing Persons: The Impossibility of Auto/Biography*. London: Routledge, 1999.

Ferres, Kay. "Gender, Biography, and the Public Sphere." France and St. Clair 303–20.

Folkenflik, Robert, ed. *The Culture of Autobiography: Constructions of Self-Representation*. Stanford: Stanford UP, 1993.

France, Peter, and William St. Clair, eds. *Mapping Lives: The Uses of Biography*. Oxford: Oxford UP, 2002.

Gagnier, Regenia. *Subjectivities: A History of Self-Representation in Britain, 1832–1920*. New York: Oxford UP, 1991.

Grant, Linda. *Remind Me Who I Am, Again*. London: Granta, 1999.

———. "True Confessions." *Guardian* 29 June 1999. 24 Nov. 2003 <http://www.guardian.co.uk/print/0,3858,3878934-103677,00.html>.

Henderson, Mark. "American Tests Offer New Hope on Alzheimer's." *Times* [London] 1 Mar. 2001: 7.

Holmes, Richard. "The Proper Study?" France and St. Clair 7–18.

Law, Joe, and Linda K. Hughes. "'And What Have *You* Done?': Victorian Biography Today." *Biographical Passages: Essays in Victorian and Modernist Biography*. Ed. Law and Hughes. Columbia: U of Missouri P, 2000. 1–17.

McColgan, Gillian, James Valentine, and Murna Downs. "Concluding Narratives of a Career with Dementia: Accounts of Iris Murdoch at Her Death." *Ageing and Society* 20 (2000): 97–109.

Smith, Sidonie. "Taking It to the Limit One More Time: Autobiography and Autism." Smith and Watson 226–46.

Smith, Sidonie, and Julia Watson, eds. *Getting a Life: Everyday Uses of Autobiography*. Minneapolis: U of Minnesota P, 1996.

Stanley, Liz. *The Auto/Biographical I: The Theory and Practice of Feminist Auto/Biography*. Manchester: Manchester UP, 1992.

Swindells, Julia. "First Person Suspect; or, The Enemy Within . . ." *Representing Lives: Women and Auto/Biography*. Ed. Alison Donnell and Pauline Polkey. Basingstoke: Macmillan, 2000. 33–42.

G. Thomas Couser

Quality-of-Life Writing: Illness, Disability, and Representation

One of the most significant developments in life writing in North America over the last several decades has been an upsurge in the publication of book-length accounts—from both first- and third-person points of view—of living with illness and disability. In the 1970s it was difficult to find any representation of certain somatic conditions in life writing; today one can find multiple representations of once stigmatic conditions such as HIV/AIDS and even of relatively obscure conditions like Tourette syndrome. Equally significant, perhaps, one can find autobiographical accounts of conditions that would seem to preclude first-person testimony—Down syndrome, locked-in syndrome, and (early) Alzheimer's disease. The proliferation of such narratives has not been universally welcomed,[1] and it presents challenges even for those who welcome it. One challenge is winnowing through this burgeoning literature for the most compelling and teachable accounts; another is approaching them respectfully but not uncritically.

These accounts deserve attention—and not just in courses devoted to life writing—for a number of related reasons. First, they remind us of the diversity of the human condition. Second, in portraying the body in extremis, they foreground the somatic basis of human existence, which is too often ignored in the humanities. Finally, they claim our attention as citizens because so many controversial issues in the arenas of public policy and public culture are bound up with variations in the form or function of our bodies. Abortion, eugenics and genetics, euthanasia and assisted suicide, health care and health insurance, and welfare only begin the list. Increasingly, to make decisions that often literally involve life or death, citizens need to understand illness and disability in cultural and historical context. With the aging of the North American population, the invention and application of new medical technologies, and a looming crisis in health care, disability literacy will become all the more desirable—and, indeed, indispensable—as an attribute of an informed public. Narratives of disease and disability demand attention today, then, in part because they epitomize quality-of-life issues crucial to public policy.

Whether regarded as disabilities or diseases, the conditions in question should be regarded as culturally constructed as well as somatic. To ignore either dimension is to oversimplify them. One entrée into the vexed relation between somatic variation and life narrative is to start with a phenomenon students readily recognize: the way deviations from somatic norms arouse dis-ease and curiosity and often provoke a demand for an explanatory narrative. The unmarked case—the "normal" body—can pass without narration; the marked case—the limp, the scar, the wheelchair, the missing limb—calls for a story. When entering a new situation or reentering a familiar one with an anomalous body, a person is often explicitly called to account: "What happened to *you*?"[2] One of the social burdens of disease and disability, then, is that they expose those affected to inspection, bold inquiry, and violation of privacy.

In effect, people with extraordinary somatic conditions are held responsible for them, in two senses. First, they are expected to account for them—even to complete strangers. Second, their accounts are expected to ease the anxiety of their auditors. Thus, despite the request for extemporaneous narration, often the answer to the question "What happened to you?" has already been determined, with the expectation that the narrative produced will affirm the preinscribed narrative. An obvious example is the expectation that someone diagnosed with lung cancer will admit to having been a longtime smoker—an acknowledgment that the subject has somehow brought the condition on him- or herself. Thus to have certain conditions is to have one's life written *for* one: that is one fundamental connection between life writing and somatic anomaly.

Given this context, autobiography is a particularly important form of life writing about illness and disability because by definition it involves self-representation. Too long the objects of others' classification and examination, disabled people have recently taken the initiative in representing themselves; in disability autobiography, disabled people assume the subject position. Whatever conditions one chooses to explore with this increasingly rich literature, it is helpful to address the agency and dialogical dynamics of representation, for people narrating anomalous somatic conditions always enter the domain of discourse from a position of belatedness, marginalization, and preinscription. Representation of the body in such narratives is not merely a mimetic but also a political act.

The very existence of first-person narratives makes its own point: people with X are capable of self-representation. The autobiographical act itself therefore models the autonomy and agency that the patients' rights and disability rights movements have fought for. One example is *Count Us In: Growing Up with Down Syndrome* (Kingsley and Levitz), a collaborative narrative by two young men with the syndrome in question. Not only is the title in the imperative mood, but it also puns on up and down, a bit of self-assertion through verbal play. Another is *The Diving Bell and the Butterfly*, Jean-Dominique Bauby's memoir of locked-in syndrome, which he laboriously "eye-typed," blinking to select each letter as an amanuensis recited the alphabet. Autobiography, then, can be an especially powerful way for disabled people to say and to show that they have lives.

Disability life writing is thus valuable as a way of raising questions concerning the ethics of representation. When persons are not capable of representing themselves, questions arise as to who has the right to represent them and what constitutes legitimate representation. A related issue, which can broaden perspective, is the matter of the medium used, whether visual or verbal. One way to approach this issue is to offer students representations of a single condition both in prose nonfiction and in documentary film. (The use of feature film, of course, raises another issue: whether the condition in question should be enacted by someone who actually has it. Typically, the actor does not have the condition, especially when a lead role is involved, and performances that entail mimicking a disabling condition are traditional Oscar nomination material.)

Tourette syndrome is a particularly interesting condition for these purposes, because it involves involuntary movements and utterances that are difficult to convey in print and that can be disturbing to observe. One might teach the documentary *Twitch and Shout* (Chiten) along with "Shane: Tourette's Syndrome" and Oliver Sacks's "Witty Ticcy Ray." This set of texts affords a prime opportunity to discuss the role of mediation and of agency. Though rooted in a medical perspective, "Shane" affords Sacks's subject a venue for talking back directly to Sacks, an opportunity lacking in his written case studies, with their third-person monological approach. *Twitch and Shout*, which presents a number of persons with Tourette, almost without medical testimony, offers a good contrast to the single-subject Sacks documentary. Such clusters of texts can assist students in exploring complex questions about the ethical obligations involved in representing others, especially when those others are unable to represent themselves or are subject to prejudicial assessment (Couser, *Vulnerable Subjects*).

A comprehensive history of life writing concerning disability and illness has yet to be written, but it is safe to say that there was not much in the way of autobiographical literature before World War II. War both creates and valorizes certain forms of disability, and after the war disabled veterans produced a substantial number of narratives. Polio generated even more narratives; indeed, polio may be the first condition to have produced a substantial autobiographical literature (Wilson). In the 1980s and 1990s, HIV/AIDS and breast cancer generated significant numbers of narratives, many of which challenge cultural scripts—if not of the conditions themselves, of personal attributes associated with them (homosexuality in the case of AIDS, femininity in the case of breast cancer).

A related phenomenon is the creation of small numbers of narratives concerning a large number of conditions, some quite rare and some only recently defined. Among these are, in alphabetical order, Alzheimer's (DeBaggio; McGowin), amyotrophic lateral sclerosis (ALS, or Lou Gehrig's disease; Robillard), aphasia (Wolf), Asperger's syndrome (Willey), asthma (Brookes), autism (Grandin; Williams), blindness (Kleege; Kuusisto), cerebral palsy (Sienkiewicz-Mercer), chronic fatigue syndrome (Skloot), cystic fibrosis (Rothenberg), deafness (Bragg; Cohen; Walker), depression (Styron; Slater, *Prozac*), diabetes (Roney), disfigurement (Grealy), Down syndrome (Kingsley and Levitz), epilepsy (Robinson; Slater, *Lying*[3]), locked-in syndrome (Bauby), multiple sclerosis (Mairs), obsessive-compulsive disorder (Wilensky), stuttering (Jezer), stroke (McCrum; Robinson; Sarton), and Tourette syndrome (Handler).

In the last quarter of the twentieth century, then, many disabilities and illnesses came out of the closet, and like life writing by women, African Americans, and gays, disability life writing can be seen as a cultural manifestation of a civil or human rights movement and should be taught as

such. Significantly, the upsurge in the personal literature of disability coin-
cides with the agitation for, passage of, and aftermath of the Americans
with Disabilities Act (1990). Thus the first flowering of disability autobiography, an important aspect of a disability renaissance, occurred in the
1990s. Acknowledging this connection helps not only to put these narratives in a useful historical context but also to remove the onus of representation from single narratives. No one narrative of any condition can
represent it, or the larger movement, definitively. But if narratives are
properly contextualized and approached, they won't be seen as doing that.
In any case, disability life writing, especially in the first person, should be
seen not as spontaneous self-expression but as deflecting or returning the
cultural stare, taking issue with arbitrary preinscribed narratives.

These narratives can be approached in a number of ways depending on
the context and abilities of students. My experience has been exclusively at
the college level, usually in upper-level (but not advanced) courses in disability literature or life writing, and it has mostly had to do with book-
length narratives. My sense is, however, that some material could be
successfully introduced to high school students. One approach that helps
students put any narrative representation in a large cultural and historical
context is to examine the texts in terms of which, and how many, of the
three major paradigms for the representation of somatic conditions they
draw on: the metaphorical (or symbolic), the medical (or individual), or
the minority (or political). Briefly, the metaphorical paradigm construes
the condition as a sign of some spiritual or moral condition; a classic example would be the belief that a crippled body (that of Shakespeare's
Richard III, for example) houses a corrupt soul. The medical paradigm simultaneously demystifies and pathologizes the condition, defining it as
nothing more than an anomaly or defect in the person's body, to be addressed by medical treatment or rehabilitation. The minority paradigm
views the condition as subjecting those who have it to oppression; that is,
it locates disability not in the individual body but in the body politic, or in
the interface between the individual body and the constructed world.
(Thus paralyzed individuals are immobilized not by their inability to walk
but by aspects of the built environment that impede wheelchair travel: lack
of curb cuts, ramps, and elevators.)

Of late, people with disabilities have been at pains to represent themselves in terms of the minority paradigm, but the other two paradigms are
often imposed on them, willy-nilly. The importance of the three-paradigm

perspective is that it enables, or requires, students to look beyond the immediate circumstances in a particular narrative and to examine the ways in
which various conditions are culturally constructed. To put it differently, this
approach should enable students to view writing by people with illnesses and
disabilities as postcolonial and thus to align them with writers from more familiar minority populations. One can enrich the three-paradigm approach
with a sense of particular rhetorical patterns that encode them (Couser,
"Conflicting"). A text that recommends itself for treatment in these terms is
Susanna Kaysen's *Girl, Interrupted*. Kaysen cleverly avoids ready-made for-
mulas in her account of her time in a mental hospital by eschewing continuous linear narrative. Instead, she produces a montage of short chapters
deploying very different sorts of discourse. Furthermore, her book literally
incorporates and interrogates the clinical documents that were used to diag-
nose, analyze, and eventually discharge her. (The recent feature film based on
the book helps make the subject available to students and also offers an alternative form of representation for comparison.)

If time allows, it is often instructive to read texts in pairs or sets. The
opportunity to compare and contrast works read side by side not only enables students to observe things about each example that they wouldn't
have noticed without the other but also helps prevent overgeneralizing
about particular conditions. A related approach is to pair a nonfictional
text with an equivalent fictional one. I have had good results teaching
Franz Kafka's *The Metamorphosis* and Herman Melville's "Bartleby the
Scrivener" back-to-back with Richard Galli's *Rescuing Jeffrey*, a father's
brief account of coping with his son's sudden paralysis.[4] It is one thing
for students to discuss the Samsas' response to Gregor's transformation as
a metaphor for a family's response to a suddenly acquired disability; it is
quite another for them to listen to a father explain and rationalize the urge
to have his teenage son's ventilator disconnected (without consulting
him) because his life seems (to the father) no longer worth living. Students may shrug off the death of Gregor or Bartleby as the inevitable result of their disabilities—after all, they're only fictional characters—but
they tend to respond very strongly to Galli's desire—and established legal
right—to "kill" his son. Not surprisingly, students suddenly get interested
in issues of euthanasia and assisted suicide, to which they had hitherto often been indifferent.

This last example illustrates the use of disability narratives to teach disability literacy. *Rescuing Jeffrey* can be an excellent springboard for discussing

difficult questions regarding quality of life. Students may be surprised to find that children under eighteen—even those like Jeffrey who are fully conscious—need not necessarily be consulted about their own fate. Current events will often supply further cases for discussion. Much life writing about disability can be taught as qualify-of-life writing because it addresses questions that are discussed under that rubric in philosophy, ethics, and bioethics. As such, they are crucial readings for citizens in a world with underfunded, often inadequate health care and with enormous technological capability to keep people alive and repair them but very little commitment to support or accommodate chronic disability. In an age as paradoxically body-conscious and body-effacing as our own, narratives of anomalous somatic conditions offer an important, if not unique, entrée for inquiry into the nature of the postmodern self, life writing, and contemporary citizenship.

Notes

1. In a review of my book *Recovering Bodies*, A. M. Daniels, a physician, attributed the recent proliferation of narratives of illness and disability to "the death of humility as a social virtue"; he went on to claim, inaccurately: "at one time, after all, only people of great or exceptional achievement, or with an extraordinary or exemplary tale to tell, would have written an autobiography."

2. See Lois Keith's *What Happened to You?* for a collection of life writing by women with disabilities that illustrates and responds to this cultural pattern.

3. Slater is rather coy about whether she actually has epilepsy; see my "Disability as Metaphor."

4. For a disability reading of "Bartleby," see Garland-Thomson.

Works Cited

Bauby, Jean-Dominique. *The Diving Bell and the Butterfly*. Trans. Jeremy Leggatt. New York: Knopf, 1997.

Bragg, Bernard. *Lessons in Laughter: The Autobiography of a Deaf Actor*. As signed to Eugene Bergman. Washington: Gallaudet UP, 1989.

Brookes, Timothy. *Catching My Breath: An Asthmatic Explores His Illness*. New York: Vintage, 1995.

Chiten, Lauren, dir. *Twitch and Shout*. New Day Films, 1994.

Cohen, Leah Hager. *Train Go Sorry: Inside a Deaf World*. Boston: Houghton, 1994.

Couser, G. Thomas. "Conflicting Paradigms: The Rhetorics of Disability Memoir." *Embodied Rhetorics: Disability in Language and Culture*. Ed. James C. Wilson and Cynthia Lewiecki-Wilson. Carbondale: Southern Illinois UP, 2001. 78–91.

——. "Disability as Metaphor: What's Wrong with *Lying*." *Prose Studies* 27.1–2 (2005): 141–54.

———. *Recovering Bodies: Illness, Disability, and Life Writing.* Madison: U of Wisconsin P, 1997.

———. *Vulnerable Subjects: Ethics and Life Writing.* Ithaca: Cornell UP, 2004.

Daniels, A. M. "Sick Notes." Rev. of *Recovering Bodies,* by G. Thomas Couser. *Times Literary Supplement* 24 Apr. 1998: 31.

DeBaggio, Thomas. *Losing My Mind.* New York: Touchstone, 2003.

Galli, Richard. *Rescuing Jeffrey.* New York: Algonquin, 2000.

Garland-Thomson, Rosemarie. "The Cultural Logic of Euthanasia: 'Sad Fancyings' in Melville's 'Bartleby.'" *American Literature* 26 (2004): 777–806.

Girl, Interrupted. Dir. James Mangold. Perf. Winona Ryder and Angelina Jolie. Columbia, 1999.

Grandin, Temple. *Thinking in Pictures.* New York: Doubleday, 1995.

Grealy, Lucy. *Autobiography of a Face.* Boston: Houghton, 1994.

Handler, Lowell. *Twitch and Shout.* New York: Dutton, 1998.

Jezer, Marty. *Stuttering: A Life Bound Up in Words.* New York: Basic, 1997.

Kafka, Franz. The Metamorphosis, *"In the Penal Colony," and Other Stories.* Trans. Joachim Neugroschel. New York: Scribner, 2000.

Kaysen, Susanna. *Girl, Interrupted.* New York: Turtle Bay, 1993.

Keith, Lois, ed. *What Happened to You? Writing by Disabled Women.* New York: New, 1996.

Kingsley, Jason, and Mitchell Levitz. *Count Us In: Growing Up with Down Syndrome.* New York: Harcourt, 1994.

Kleege, Georgina. *Sight Unseen.* New Haven: Yale UP, 1999.

Kuusisto, Stephen. *Planet of the Blind.* New York: Dial, 1998.

Mairs, Nancy. *Waist-High in the World.* Boston: Beacon, 1996.

McCrum, Robert. *My Year Off.* New York: Norton, 1998.

McGowin, Diane Friel. *Living in the Labyrinth.* New York: Delacorte, 1993.

Melville, Herman. *Bartleby the Scrivener: A Story of Wall Street.* 1853. New York: Simon, 1997.

Robillard, Albert B. *Meaning of a Disability: The Lived Experience of Paralysis.* Philadelphia: Temple UP, 1999.

Robinson, Jill. *Past Forgetting.* New York: Harper, 1999.

Roney, Lisa. *Sweet Invisible Body.* New York: Henry Holt, 1999.

Rothenberg, Laura. *Breathing for a Living.* New York: Dimensions, 2003.

Sacks, Oliver. "Witty Ticcy Ray." *"The Man Who Mistook His Wife for a Hat," and Other Clinical Tales.* New York: Summit, 1985. 92–101.

Sarton, May. *After the Stroke: A Journal.* New York: Norton, 1988.

"Shane: Tourette's Syndrome." *The Mind Traveler: Oliver Sacks.* BBC, 1998.

Sienkiewicz-Mercer, Ruth, and Steven B. Kaplan. *I Raise My Eyes to Say Yes.* New York: Houghton, 1989.

Skloot, Floyd. *The Night-Side: Chronic Fatigue Syndrome and the Illness Experience.* Brownsville: Story Line, 1996.

Slater, Lauren. *Lying: A Metaphorical Memoir.* New York: Random, 2000.

———. *Prozac Diary.* New York: Random, 1998.

Styron, William. *Darkness Visible: A Memoir of Madness.* New York: Random, 1990.

Walker, Lou Ann. *A Loss for Words: The Story of Deafness in a Family.* New York: Harper, 1986.

Wilensky, Amy S. *Passing for Normal.* New York: Broadway, 2000.

Willey, Liane Holliday. *Pretending to Be Normal.* London: Kingsley, 1999.

Williams, Donna. *Nobody Nowhere.* New York: Times, 1992.

Wilson, Daniel J. "Covenants of Work and Grace: Themes of Recovery and Redemption in Polio Narratives." *Literature and Medicine* 13.1: (1994): 22–41.

Wolf, Helen Harker. *Aphasia: My World Alone.* Detroit: Wayne State UP, 1979.

Hilary Clark

Teaching Women's Depression Memoirs: Healing, Testimony, and Critique

As a professor of English at the University of Saskatchewan, I teach courses in women's literature and life writing. For the Women's and Gender Studies Department I also occasionally teach a semester undergraduate course titled Women, Depression, and Writing. I will describe this course, its objectives, teaching challenges, and ethical issues, focusing on why the assigned reading has shifted from novels and stories to autobiographical writing recounting women's experience of depression.

This shift to life writing has followed my increasing sense that autobiography, although clearly drawing on fictive strategies in its reconstruction of the self, involves a more intimate investment of the self in narrative than fiction does. Paul John Eakin points out that in life writing, or "self-narration," narrative "is not merely *about* the self but rather in some profound way a constituent part *of* self." For this reason, "the writing of autobiography is properly understood as an integral part of a lifelong process of identity formation in which acts of self-narration play a major part" (101). In reading autobiography, we reflect on our own lives; as Nancy Miller puts it, "We read the lives of others to figure out how to make sense of our own" (137). Reading autobiography allows us to think about the process of self-narration or self-constitution itself. One objective of

Women, Depression, and Writing is to encourage such reflection in the context of gender and mental illness. The students—most of them white, middle-class women ranging widely in age and majoring in women's and gender studies, English, psychology, or sociology—learn not only about other women's experiences of depression but also about depression as a powerful cultural narrative or script that shapes women's identities. Students learn that this narrative can be rewritten to some extent and that writing the depression memoir can contribute to a healing or liberation from the scripts of helplessness and hopelessness that frequently mark the lives of women and contribute to depression. They learn, as Mark Freeman puts it, that in self-stories, "the self may be transformed from an object, prey to the potentially constrictive power of culture, to a willful agent: a creator, able to cast into question those stories thought to be 'given' and write new ones" (185–86). By assigning depression memoirs, I want to help students to reflect on their lives and to realize that they too can become authors of their own stories, their own lives.

When I first taught Women, Depression, and Writing, the reading list included rather technical readings on gender and depression, a bit of psychoanalytic theory, a few personal essays such as Nancy Mairs's "On Living behind Bars," and poetry and fiction by women sufferers: Anne Sexton's and Sylvia Plath's poems, for instance, or Marie Cardinal's autobiographical novel *The Words to Say It* and Virginia Woolf's novel *Between the Acts*. I taught one memoir: *Half-Breed*, by Maria Campbell, a Canadian Métis writer. Significantly, the personal essays and the memoir were most successful in stimulating self-reflection and reimagining of the students' lives.

Over the years, the general readings have gradually shifted from academic theories of women's depression to accounts based on interviews (e.g., Dana Jack's *Silencing the Self*), accounts foregrounding women's own stories. The narrative readings have also shifted, primarily from fiction to memoir and from well-known authors like Woolf to less canonical (and more current) writers like Lauren Slater and Meri Danquah. In the latest version of the course, we looked almost solely at autobiographical narratives. Though I could have assigned biographies and may still do so in the future, it is the healing act of writing one's own story—and the healing effects, for women, of reading that "self-narration"—that I have been most interested in exploring with students.

I wish now to look briefly at depression narratives as a genre, to identify some issues that guide my teaching of these texts. These narratives are best understood within the larger class of illness memoirs or autopathographies (Hawkins xviii), narratives that recount the onset, progress, and resolution of—or resignation to—an illness. Most of these narratives concern diseases such as breast cancer and AIDS or physical conditions such as epilepsy or diabetes. While a number of depression memoirs have been published—especially since William Styron's *Darkness Visible*—narratives of physical illness dominate the shelves of bookstores and receive more critical attention. Anne Hunsaker Hawkins and Arthur Frank have addressed the functions and strategies of narratives of physical illness. Hawkins observes that people tell illness stories to regain control over an interrupted or broken life, "to restore to reality its lost coherence and to . . . bind it together again" (3). The illness story also offers readers a "cautionary parable," "a disquieting glimpse of . . . the drastic interruption of a life of meaning and purpose by an illness that often seems arbitrary, cruel, and senseless" (2). Indeed, writers may convey the impossibility of reestablishing coherence, arguing that a neatly redemptive narrative falsifies the experience of serious illness as an acute interruption of a life (Rimmon-Kenan 22–23).

Illness narratives also bear witness to encounters with harsh, depersonalizing medical treatments and with medical institutions often as intrusive as the illness itself (Hawkins 2). Countering the institutionalized silencing of patients in the doctor-patient relationship, an illness memoir allows the sufferer or survivor to "reclaim" a voice (Frank 64) and encourages other sufferers to do the same—to resist being silenced by the very system that would heal them.

Owing perhaps to the stigma still attached to mental illness, narratives of depression and other mood disorders have not received as much critical attention. A memoirist of both physical and mental illness (multiple sclerosis and depression), Nancy Mairs has commented perceptively on what she calls, tongue only half in cheek, the "literature of personal disaster." She suggests that readers of such literature who are ill themselves may receive some consolation in their suffering: "The narrator of personal disaster, I think, wants not to whine, not to boast, but to comfort" ("Literature" 127). Writing a narrative of personal disaster is a way of coming to terms with a life that may be interrupted indefinitely by episodes of illness. As well, writing such a narrative allows one to analyze and negotiate the illness identity imposed, particularly on women, by a particular psychiatric diagnosis—an identity that almost always, in the Western biomedical context, involves seeing oneself as dependent indefinitely on medication. In *Speaking of Sadness*,

David Karp traces what he calls the "illness career" of people suffering from depression (56); he locates a point of crisis at which the sufferer must "go public" and get treatment. In doing so, the person is forced to adopt a new illness identity (62).

For both male and female sufferers, to be depressed in our culture is to take up a feminine role, and a woman who would write an empowering memoir of her illness must analyze and resist this gendering of depression and model this resistance to her readers. Mairs does this most insightfully in her personal essay "On Living behind Bars," which looks at the gender politics of her experience of psychiatric hospitalization in the 1960s. Women reading a memoir of depression need to read a "counterstory" that resists (to whatever extent) the "master narratives" (Nelson 150–51) of gender, scripts in which the feminine is the depressed and vice-versa.

When I began teaching Women, Depression, and Writing, I drew on a psychoanalytic model of depression based on Freud's essay "Mourning and Melancholia," which sees significant loss, and repressed anger over loss, at the core of depression. Accordingly, I organized the classes and readings around the losses women experience in their lives as women: the losses entailed in becoming an adolescent girl, a young mother, a menopausal woman, and so on. We also looked at social factors such as on-going discrimination, harassment, and violence against women, which themselves imply a terrible loss of agency and opportunity. "Women are in a continual state of mourning for what they never had"—the "worldly power" their brothers take for granted—Phyllis Chesler writes in *Women and Madness*, revising Freud (82).

The problem with such an overarching structure for the course, I found, is that the explanatory framework comes first. The women's stories do not generate the issues, at least not the main ones, for discussion. As the course has evolved, the emphasis has shifted to narrative and to the importance of analyzing and rewriting the gendered scripts that shape women's (indeed, everyone's) lives. For the most part now, the memoirs we study—individual women's stories of depression set in particular contexts of sexuality, race, and class—determine the shape the discussion takes. In the latest version of the class, we looked first at the wide range of explanations that have been given for women's depression. (Susan Nolen-Hoeksema's *Sex Differences in Depression* contains a useful general survey.) We also read excerpts from Karp and Frank on depression careers and postmodern illness narratives and evaluated their sociological spin on stories. But the students were always hungry for women's stories with which they could compare their own. While general ideas on depression, identity, narrative, medicalization, and stigma were read and discussed, the real excitement was in the individual stories making these issues come alive: Kay Jamison's *An Unquiet Mind*, Meri Danquah's *Willow Weep for Me*, Lauren Slater's *Prozac Diary*, Susanna Kaysen's *Girl, Interrupted*, Maria Campbell's *Half-Breed*, and the harrowing stories in Allie Light's documentary *Dialogues with Madwomen*—stories in women's voices, sometimes humorous, sometimes anguished, always reflective and in control. "I got through it," these voices say, "and you can, too." As much as possible, however, among the terrifying, funny, and sometimes tedious and self-indulgent details of these individual stories, I kept returning to what I identified as the basic functions of the depression narrative: repairing and healing a damaged life; witnessing to and critiquing the depersonalizing effects of the psychiatric institution, with its heavy emphasis on medication; and offering hope to other women in similar situations.

I've had small groups of three or four students prepare presentations on one of the texts; I encourage them to look at literary matters of style and general issues in writing depression and compare the different texts on these issues. But the jury is still out on these presentations as an assignment, since the results are sometimes often weak on analysis and heavy on paraphrase.

Students are also required to complete two other assignments: a short essay and a longer term paper. The first addresses issues in the popular representation of women's depression—stereotyping, stigma, the pressure to take medication—touched on in the memoirs. Students can look at newspapers, magazines, TV programming, movies, Internet sites, and self-help books. They usually know a lot about the popular media already, and the assignment encourages them to exercise their critical reading skills in analyzing text and especially images.

The term paper has taken a number of different directions. One option I always include is writing a narrative of depression—the writer's own or that of a woman close to her. Those unwilling to get personal can write a paper on a particular issue emerging from the depression memoirs. In the last version of the course, topics included depression and creativity; depression, illness identity, and medication; psychotherapies; and (based on the terrifying stories in Light's film) the role of early trauma in adult women's depression. Another option more specifically addresses life writing as such:

the student must read two biographies of a particular sufferer—Virginia Woolf, for example, or Sylvia Plath—and compare the biographers' construction of the woman's life and the place of depression within it. Another topic requires the student to read several life writing texts by a writer covered in the course—for example, Slater's "memoir" *Lying* and her *Prozac Diary*—and compare their constructions of the self.

In teaching life writing, one covers material that may affect students personally, sometimes viscerally. Fiction can also be traumatic to read, but because of their generally greater identification with autobiographical writing, students may be visited by traumatic memories while reading or find themselves looking at existing memories—indeed their whole lives—in new ways. For both writer and reader, life writing is "risky writing," to use Jeffrey Berman's phrase. In the first class I therefore offer a warning about potentially upsetting content. I am also prepared to do some debriefing if students are finding certain texts particularly upsetting, especially if a student is being retraumatized by reading about experiences she has undergone (for example, rape and childhood abuse). The instructor must strive to make the class a safe place for discussion of reactions to readings. If for some reason this environment cannot be created, the instructor should be available for individual discussions—always, however, with the proviso that she or he is not qualified to offer therapy. Discussing a course she taught on Holocaust narratives, Shoshana Felman has suggested that it can be effective to get students to write down their reactions. By analyzing their reactions in writing, they can often attain some distance from them.

All teaching has an ethical element, of course. Teachers of literature know that students identify with characters and authors, seeing themselves in their situations. Especially if they are still young, students are vulnerable to trauma and shame in encountering what Elaine Showalter has called "dangerous subjects"—for instance, racist and sexual violence, suicide attempts—subjects frequently found in memoirs of depression and other mental illnesses. To teach such material sensitively, Showalter suggests, the instructor must establish important principles, including "candor and clear labeling—telling students in advance that they may be offended and upset; contextualizing the topic with some sociological or historical background; [and] being prepared for some students to be shocked and upset no matter what you do, and allowing opportunities for them to respond" (126).

To teach a course on women's writing and depression, particularly on women's depression memoirs, is thus to teach a "syllabus of risk"; one must always anticipate depressive side effects (Berman, qtd. in Showalter 126), which can affect teachers as much as students. I find that I can only teach Women, Depression, and Writing at infrequent intervals, as the experience is usually—well, depressing. But I will not give up the course, for it exemplifies the risk and pleasure of teaching in the feminist classroom. Here, just as the boundaries between life and fiction are blurred in life writing, the boundaries between text and experience, teacher and student are put into question in each class. In the feminist classroom the healing, testimonial, and critical dimensions of illness narratives—and of autobiographical writing more generally—become vividly clear.

Works Cited

Berman, Jeffrey. *Risky Writing: Self-Disclosure and Self-Transformation in the Classroom*. Amherst: U of Massachusetts P, 2001.

Campbell, Maria. *Half-Breed*. 1973. Halifax: Formac, 1983.

Cardinal, Marie. *The Words to Say It: An Autobiographical Novel*. Trans. Pat Goodheart. Cambridge: Van Vactor, 1984.

Chesler, Phyllis. *Women and Madness*. 1972. New York: Four Walls, 1997.

Danquah, Meri Nana-Ama. *Willow Weep for Me: A Black Woman's Journey through Depression*. New York: Ballantine, 1998.

Eakin, Paul John. *How Our Lives Become Stories: Making Selves*. Ithaca: Cornell UP, 1999.

Felman, Shoshana. "Education and Crisis; or, The Vicissitudes of Teaching." *Trauma: Explorations in Memory*. Ed. Cathy Caruth. Baltimore: Johns Hopkins UP, 1995. 13–60.

Frank, Arthur W. *The Wounded Storyteller: Body, Illness, and Ethics*. Chicago: U of Chicago P, 1995.

Freeman, Mark. *Rewriting the Self: History, Memory, Narrative*. London: Routledge, 1993.

Freud, Sigmund. "Mourning and Melancholia." 1917. *Standard Edition of the Complete Psychological Works of Sigmund Freud*. Vol. 14. Ed. and trans. James Strachey. London: Hogarth, 1974. 243–58.

Hawkins, Anne Hunsaker. *Reconstructing Illness: Studies in Pathography*. 2nd ed. West Lafayette: Purdue UP, 1999.

Jack, Dana Crowley. *Silencing the Self: Women and Depression*. Cambridge: Harvard UP, 1991.

Jamison, Kay Redfield. *An Unquiet Mind: A Memoir of Moods and Madness*. New York: Vintage, 1996.

Karp, David. *Speaking of Sadness: Depression, Disconnection, and the Meanings of Illness*. New York: Oxford UP, 1996.

Kaysen, Susanna. *Girl, Interrupted*. New York: Vintage, 1994.

Light, Allie, dir. *Dialogues with Madwomen*. Women Make Movies, 1993.

Mairs, Nancy. "The Literature of Personal Disaster." *Voice Lessons: On Becoming a (Woman) Writer*. Boston: Beacon, 1994. 123–35.

———. "On Living behind Bars." *Plaintext*. Tucson: U of Arizona P, 1986. 125–54.

Miller, Nancy K. *But Enough about Me: Why We Read Other People's Lives*. New York: Columbia UP, 2002.

Nelson, Hilde Lindemann. *Damaged Identities, Narrative Repair*. Ithaca: Cornell UP, 2001.

Nolen-Hoeksema, Susan. *Sex Differences in Depression*. Stanford: Stanford UP, 1990.

Plath, Sylvia. *The Bell Jar*. 1963. Harper Perennial, 2000.

Rimmon-Kenan, Shlomith. "The Story of 'I': Illness and Narrative Identity." *Narrative* 10.1 (2002): 9–27.

Showalter, Elaine. "Dangerous Subjects." *Teaching Literature*. Oxford: Blackwell, 2003. 125–30.

Slater, Lauren. *Lying: A Metaphorical Memoir*. New York: Penguin, 2000.

———. *Prozac Diary*. New York: Penguin, 1998.

Styron, William. *Darkness Visible: A Memoir of Madness*. New York: Vintage, 1990.

Woolf, Virginia. *Between the Acts*. 1941. New York: Oxford UP, 1992.

Leigh Gilmore

What Do We Teach
When We Teach Trauma?

Autobiographical representations of trauma make an invaluable contribution to the study of literature and culture. They offer indispensable eyewitness accounts of large-scale and everyday violence and, through their elaboration of specific scenes of terror and trauma, provide an antidote to universalizing narratives about evil, suffering, and history. They also provide compelling texts through which to examine the complexities associated with such specificity, for all witness literature acutely reminds us that interpretation and documentation are two sides of the coin of representation. Without the consciousness to interpret and the occasion to organize a verbal account of a shattering experience, the facts in question remain disembodied. Trauma texts restore the human, in its myriad realizations, to the scene of violence. Some first-person accounts reach international and multigenerational audiences and are well integrated into general frames of reference. The experiences, as well as the figurations of the survivor, offered by Anne Frank, Elie Wiesel, and Primo Levi are central acts in the memorialization and documentation of the Holocaust. Yet many autobiographical accounts of trauma find smaller audiences, often because of a minoritizing view of the trauma and those who are suffering and sometimes because of formal challenges raised by the texts. Trauma enters the public sphere in a variety of ways, but the knowledge it offers often seems too hard to hear and is resisted. Specific accounts not only relate experiences of suffering but also challenge political, moral, and cultural views of power, injury, and redress. Fault lines run through the understanding of trauma because the experience and representation of trauma concern how power circulates at every level—from the intimate experience of suffering to its management by entities as diverse as governmental institutions, national and international law and policy, health care practices, and publishing. Anyone choosing to teach at the convergence of life writing and trauma finds interesting pedagogical and interpretive challenges, an abundance of compelling documents, and a pressing historical situation. Trauma inflects so much autobiographical material that we should probably admit that it has already chosen us and acknowledge this demand. This essay addresses some of the challenges raised by teaching autobiographical accounts of trauma and describes a particular course in this context.

The project of teaching trauma raises pedagogical questions in three related areas. The material itself: Are there unique risks in teaching materials that represent actual violence and suffering, or are these risks generalizable to pedagogies that critically examine other graphic materials (including fiction)? The setting: What sort of venue is a classroom for the study of trauma? In what ways does it differ from other settings in which trauma is examined, such as the clinic or the courts? Are there productive areas of overlap between the pedagogical and the therapeutic, or ought one not only to clarify but also to maximize the differences between them? Finally, there are the students: What are we asking of them when they undertake this challenge, and how do we prepare them for it? What are the effects of this study? Can it be claimed that students risk traumatization by studying representations of trauma, as Shoshana Felman did in her discussion of teaching a graduate seminar? Or is it more appropriate to say that students are shocked, saddened, titillated, or repulsed, but not traumatized per se? When students have strong reactions, how should we clarify the boundary between the experience of trauma and the experience of learning about trauma, even when that boundary is not fixed? How can we make our vocabulary better able to describe a student's entry into historical consciousness without making it indistinguishable from trauma? And if the potential for student traumatization is a matter of debate, what of the less hypothetical risk of retraumatizing students who have previously experienced trauma? How, ultimately, should we frame these issues about the material, the classroom, and the students so as not to inspire frustrated or defensive silence but to initiate an inquiry that does not specify in advance or foreclose the intensities of its engagement?

I move to particulars by way of a pragmatic point. Whether I am teaching a whole course or a single text on trauma, I begin with the spatial language of thresholds and boundaries. As material related to trauma moves into the classroom, we want to attend to this cultural transfer. Accounts of trauma enter courtrooms according to legal protocols of evidence and testimony; therapeutic settings establish rituals and procedures for listening and talking. I ask that we be aware of the ways in which classroom conventions and disciplinary norms work on this material and our responses to it. We notice, too, that when trauma crosses the threshold of the classroom through its place on the syllabus, other memories and experiences of trauma are already present among us. I shift from thresholds to boundaries to remind us that we should talk as if someone who had experienced trauma is in the room. I underscore that trauma stories are often present and that the settings in which they can be spoken include classrooms. I want neither to prohibit nor to require testimony. Instead, I give us permission not to testify, but also make it possible to consider that authorities on the topic are everywhere, including our classroom, who can and may speak testimonially.

I experimented with organizing an upper-division undergraduate course around scandal and truth telling in autobiographical representations of trauma. (The course was offered in an English department under the flexible rubric Studies in Nonfiction.) The concern with scandal arose pressingly enough from the recent memoir boom and its emphasis on representations of trauma, but it also offered case studies and a context focused on the cultural mechanisms by which traumatic materials enter the public sphere in contested ways. Our texts included *I, Pierre Rivière, Having Slaughtered My Mother, My Brother, and My Sister . . . : A Case of Parricide in the Nineteenth Century*, edited by Michel Foucault; *I, Rigoberta Menchú*, by Rigoberta Menchú; *Fragments*, by Binjamin Wilkomirski; and *The Kiss*, by Kathryn Harrison. Our questions were, What form had scandal taken in each case and why? Around what issues had it erupted, and through what mechanisms was it disseminated? On what materials did the scandal draw, and what effects did it produce around gender, race, and ethnicity? How was truth understood differently by those taking different positions on the scandal?

We began with Sigmund Freud's essay "Mourning and Melancholia" and sections from his *Beyond the Pleasure Principle* as a way to introduce critical language about the psychic and material forces that shape loss and self-representation. These works and others by trauma theorists (Caruth; Felman and Laub) were useful in shaping insights into how the subject of trauma and the subject of scandal were elicited, how such subjects and scenes differed, and how subjects, once elicited in particular ways, could respond. Freud offered a way to frame the temporalities of trauma; namely, the ways in which the subject could never adequately anticipate trauma and its aftermath, including scandal, or fully address or moot the views of others once scandal had erupted. Our focus on the temporality of trauma also illuminated the continuity between the runaway-train-like quality of scandal and the loss of control and meaning associated with trauma itself. Preliminary work with Freud and trauma theory was joined with an examination of the etymology of scandal to disclose the linguistic and cultural histories it bore, Trojan horse–like, within itself.

With some shared vocabulary in place about the relation of the psychic, the linguistic, and the material, we turned to Foucault's *I, Pierre Rivière*. This volume includes Foucault's introduction, Rivière's memoir, the testimony of experts and witnesses and the court proceedings of Rivière's trial, and essays by Foucault's contemporaries. From this text, we developed a sense of how scandals emerge: a crime occurs (later, we would see how criminality or impropriety need only be insinuated); the figure of the criminal emerges through accusation and acts, including writing; authorities and experts are produced who explain and judge (we would later see how judgment and authority can be uncoupled from expert status); disciplines and sciences of explanation and judgment emerge; and punishment is present. In our study of Menchú, Wilkomirski, and Harrison, we developed our own archives by gathering a range of sources, from reviews and magazine articles to literary criticism, anthropology, and political science. We considered our own historicity (why are we interested now?) and the differing geopolitical and historical contexts on which any particular account of trauma depends. In all cases, we paid attention to the mobile dynamics by which experts arose, to negative reviewing and its proximity to libel, to the vulnerability of First Amendment protections to media manipulation, and to the degree to which scandal revealed cultural islands of complexity around which the currents of gender, race, sexuality, and authority swirled.

Rivière's memoir issues from the position of the accused. His rhetorical situation is supercharged with the consequences of life and death. Not only does Rivière understand his position and those arrayed against him, he anticipates and addresses their concerns. The memoir reads as if he had been writing it in his head over the years during which his hatred of his mother mounted to homicidal intensity. It is a justification, steeped in the logic of contract, for the murder of his mother, sister, and brother. His seeming rationality makes him appear as the most confident of all the witnesses, experts, and authorities. As a result of studying Rivière, students grew more skeptical about any claims to superior knowledge and certainty. In contrast to Rivière, Rigoberta Menchú, who neither committed nor was accused of a crime, spoke from the pressing situation of documenting the civil war in Guatemala and seeking international support for those, like her, who opposed the army. Her testimonio did not anticipate the kind of antagonist it would acquire in the American anthropologist David Stoll (see also Rohter), who accused Menchú of distortion and outright lying. Our archival method had us gathering a range of opinions about her testimonio not so much to ask whether she had lied (such a question would have led us into scandal's trap) as to consider how this question had come to obscure the terms in which she presents her experience. We examined not only her representation of specific traumas—the murder of family members, the rape of her mother, harsh working conditions on the coastal plantations, being terrorized by the Guatemalan army, the impact of this trauma on her at the time she recorded her testimonio—but also the careful framing of secrets and discretion that mark Menchú's description of her project in her early chapters. We then examined Stoll's backtracking and equivocation over what he said and what he meant, as well as current debates about the changing definition of testimonio as a genre.

Wilkomirski published *Fragments* to great acclaim. In it, he claimed to have been a child survivor of the Holocaust and re-created that experience through an elliptical and lyrical account of terror from a child's perspective. He won literary prizes and was embarked on a successful speaking tour when his identity was challenged by the Swiss journalist Daniel Ganzfried, who asserted that Wilkomirski was really Bruno Dosseker, the adopted son of Swiss parents who had sat out the war in relative comfort. After commissioning an inquiry by the historian Stefan Maechler into the dispute, Wilkomirski's publisher withdrew the book, and Wilkomirski's public career as a child survivor of the Holocaust came to an end.

Because the students' awareness of these revelations followed closely on their reading the memoir, they did not feel like Wilkomirski's dupes. But they did differ over the value of what they had read. For some, it was the work of a disturbed person who had hitched his fragile megalomania to the Holocaust. They found him monstrously overreaching and ultimately pathetic and wanted to dispatch author and book. Others were willing to let go of their sense of Wilkomirski as a child survivor of the Holocaust without wanting to disavow their powerful encounter with its representation. Despite the fraudulence of Wilkomirski's stated identity, he had, they argued, not represented the Holocaust fraudulently. Nor, they insisted, had he strengthened the hand of Holocaust deniers, for Wilkomirski had imagined nothing more horrible than what had transpired historically. Their argument was that when trauma has a secure historical foundation, such as the Holocaust and the civil war in Guatemala, the autobiographer does not bear the burden of sole witness, and, as such, his or her account does not have the capacity to invalidate historical events.

We concluded with *The Kiss*, Harrison's memoir of adult father-daughter incest. Despite the prevalence of incest, this crime lacks the historical apparatus that gives it cultural solidity. Harrison, then, is a different historical witness, one whose truth and whose own claim on history is always potentially in doubt. The illegality of child sexual abuse is draped by privacy law and family law, cultural norms of silence around middle-class families and what occurs within them, confused notions of consent, and the gendering of sexual violence and power. We examined the personal nature of Harrison's negative reviews and the desire to silence her: one critic told her to "hush up" (Crossen). In addition to being ambivalent about telling family secrets, reviewers were confused by the coexistence of Harrison's talent and her traumatic experience. If the incest was so bad, they puzzled, why didn't she kill herself instead of writing this book? The very strength of the writing seemed to argue against her pain. Thus our focus on scandal revealed what studies in trauma and memory did not always foreground: the potency of gender. Gender functioned like a symptom of cultural anxieties related to revelation and exposure, which were themselves related to privacy and the control of dissonant views of the family in the public sphere. We concluded that scandal arises at the interpenetrated site of public and private, that the broaching of a perceived (and fictitious) barrier between the two is required for scandal to emerge, and that gender had animated the scandals that involved not only the women writers but also the figurations of violation and violence in Rivière and Wilkomirski.

By examining representations of trauma around which scandals had developed, we were able to place the impact of trauma within the contemporary histories of its experience, representation, and reception. But this focus also affected the class's sense of the ethical demand autobiographical representations of trauma make. How to sift the controversial claims and counterclaims without falling into reductive judgments? Given that testimonies of trauma are pouring out from all over the globe, that national and international tribunals and commissions are being convened in which to hear such testimony, and that the words of those who have suffered and survived seek a hearing, how will we listen, and how will we respond? Autobiography provides a compelling discourse through which to engage such questions.

Works Cited

Caruth, Cathy, ed. *Trauma: Explorations in Memory.* Baltimore: Johns Hopkins UP, 1995.

Crossen, Cynthia. "Know Thy Father." *Wall Street Journal* 4 Mar. 1997: A16+.

Felman, Shoshana. "Education and Crisis; or, The Vicissitudes of Teaching." *Testimony: Crises of Witnessing in Literature, Psychoanalysis, and History.* Ed. Felman and Dori Laub. New York: Routledge, 1992. 1–56.

Foucault, Michel, ed. *I, Pierre Rivière, Having Slaughtered My Mother, My Brother, and My Sister . . . : A Case of Parricide in the Nineteenth Century.* Trans. Frank Jellinek. New York: Routledge, 1992.

Freud, Sigmund. *Beyond the Pleasure Principle.* 1920. *Standard Edition of the Complete Psychological Works of Sigmund Freud.* Ed. and trans. James Strachey. Vol. 14. London: Hogarth, 1974.

——. "Mourning and Melancholia." 1917. *Standard Edition of the Complete Psychological Works of Sigmund Freud.* Ed. and trans. James Strachey. Vol. 14. London: Hogarth, 1974. 243–58.

Harrison, Kathryn. *The Kiss.* New York: Random, 1997.

Maechler, Stefan. *The Wilkomirski Affair: A Study in Biographical Truth.* Trans. John F. Woods. New York: Schocken, 2001.

Menchú, Rigoberta. *I, Rigoberta Menchú: An Indian Woman in Guatemala.* Ed. and introd. Elisabeth Burgos-Debray. Trans. Ann Wright. New York: Verso, 1984.

Rohter, Larry. "Tarnished Laureate." *New York Times* 15 Dec. 1998: A1+.

Stoll, David. *Rigoberta Menchú and the Story of All Poor Guatemalans.* Boulder: Westview, 1998.

Wilkomirski, Binjamin. *Fragments: Memoirs of a Wartime Childhood.* Trans. Carol Brown Janeway. New York: Schocken, 1996.

Additional Resources for Teaching Life Writing Texts: Cultural Approaches

Booth, Alison. *How to Make It as a Woman: Collective Biographical History from Victoria to the Present*. Chicago: U of Chicago P, 2004.

Braxton, Joanne. *Black Women Writing Autobiography: A Tradition within a Tradition*. Philadelphia: Temple UP, 1989.

Brophy, Sarah. *Witnessing AIDS: Writing, Testimony, and the Work of Mourning*. Toronto: U of Toronto P, 2004.

Chambers, Ross. *Facing It: AIDS Diaries and the Death of the Author*. Ann Arbor: U of Michigan P, 1998.

Danahay, Martin A. "Breaking the Silence: Symbolic Violence and the Teaching of Ethnic Autobiography." *College Literature* 18.3 (1991): 64–80.

Dunaway, David K., and Willa K. Baum. *Oral History: An Interdisciplinary Anthology*. 2nd ed. Walnut Creek: Alta Mira, 1996.

Eakin, Paul John, ed. *American Autobiography: Retrospect and Prospect*. Madison: U of Wisconsin P, 1992.

Foley, John Miles, ed. *Teaching Oral Traditions*. New York: MLA, 1998.

Franklin, Cynthia. *Writing Women's Communities: The Politics and Poetics of Contemporary Multigenre Anthologies*. Madison: U of Wisconsin P, 1997.

Geesey, Patricia, ed. *Autobiography and African Literature*. Spec. issue of *Research in African Literatures* 28.2 (1997).

Goldman, Anne E. *Take My Word: Autobiographical Innovations of Ethnic American Working Women*. Berkeley: U of California P, 1995.

Gugelberger, Georg M., ed. *The Real Thing: Testimonial Discourse and Latin America*. Durham: U of North Carolina P, 1996.

Heilbrun, Carolyn G. *Writing a Woman's Life*. New York: Norton, 1988.

Huff, Cynthia, ed. *Women's Life Writing and Imagined Communities*. New York: Routledge, 2004.

Kramer, Martin, ed. *Middle Eastern Lives: The Practice of Biography and Self-Narrative*. Syracuse: Syracuse UP, 1991.

Krupat, Arnold. *Ethnocriticism: Ethnography, History, Literature*. Berkeley: U of California P, 1992.

————, ed. *Native American Autobiography: An Anthology*. Madison: U of Wisconsin P, 1994.

Mascuch, Michael. *Origins of the Individual Self: Autobiography and Self-Identity in England, 1591–1791*. Cambridge: Polity, 1997.

Miller, Lynn C., Jacqueline Taylor, and M. Heather Carver, eds. *Intimate Partners: Voices Made Flesh, Performing Women's Autobiography*. Madison: U of Wisconsin P, 2003.

Moraga, Cherríe, and Gloria Anzaldúa, eds. *This Bridge Called My Back*. New York: Kitchen Table / Women of Color, 1983.

Neumann, Shirley, ed. *Autobiography and Questions of Gender*. London: Cass, 1991.

Ostle, Robin, Ed de Moor, and Stefan Wild. *Writing the Self: Autobiographical Writing in Modern Arabic Literature*. London: Saqi, 1998.

Padilla, Genaro M. *My History, Not Yours: The Formation of Mexican American Autobiography*. Wisconsin: U of Wisconsin P, 1993.

Perreault, Jeanne. *Writing Selves: Contemporary Feminist Autobiography*. Minneapolis: U of Minnesota P, 1995.

Reed-Danahay, Deborah E. *Auto/ethnography: Rewriting the Self and the Social*. New York: Berg, 1997.

Reynolds, Dwight, ed. *Interpreting the Self: Autobiography in the Arabic Literary Tradition*. Berkeley: U of California P, 2001.

Riesz, Janos, and Ulla Schild, eds. *Autobiographical Genres in Africa*. Berlin: Reimer, 1996.

Ritchie, Donald A. *Doing Oral History: A Practical Guide*. New York: Oxford UP, 2003.

Stanton, Domna C., ed. *The Female Autograph*. New York: New York Literary Forum, 1984.

Whitlock, Gillian, ed. *Autographs: Contemporary Australian Autobiography*. St. Lucia: Queensland UP, 1996.

————. *The Intimate Empire: Reading Women's Autobiography*. London: Cassell, 2000.

————. *Soft Weapons: Autobiography in Transit*. Chicago: U of Chicago P, 2007.

Wong, Hertha D. Sweet. *Sending My Heart Back across the Years: Tradition and Innovations in Native American Literature*. New York: Oxford UP, 1992.

Woodward, Kathleen, ed. *Figuring Age: Women, Bodies, Generations*. Bloomington: Indiana UP, 1999.

Miriam Fuchs, Craig Howes, and Stanley Schab

Life Writing Resources
for Teachers

Periodicals and Online Resources

A/B: Auto/Biography Studies (Autobiography Soc., U of North Carolina, Chapel Hill). Biannual journal on autobiography, biography, diaries, letters, and relations between life writing and other discourses.

American Memory. <http://memory.loc.gov/ammem/index.html>. Library of Congress site provides access to thousands of written and spoken texts and images, including extensive collections on American histories, literatures, technologies, and travel narratives.

Auto/Biography: An International and Interdisciplinary Journal (British Sociological Assn. Study Group on Auto/Biography). 1992–2006 triannual journal addressing theoretical, epistemological, and empirical issues relating to auto/biographical research.

Autopacte. <http://www.autopacte.org>. Managed by Philippe Lejeune. Provides extensive life writing bibliographies, information on journals and publications in several languages, notices of conferences and events, and links to a wide range of life writing and biographical resources.

Bibliographie des études en langue française sur la littérature personnelle et les récits de vie (Centre de Recherches Interdisciplinaires sur les Textes Modernes, Université Paris X). Bibliography of ongoing work in French from 1938 to the present.

Biography: An Interdisciplinary Quarterly (Biographical Research Center, U of Hawaiʻi P). Quarterly journal on the theoretical, generic, historical, cultural, and practical dimensions of life writing.

Bios: Zeitschrift für Biographieforschung und Lebensverlaufs analysen (Institut für Geschichte und Biographie der Fernuniversität Hagen). Biannual journal devoted to the study of life writing in its various forms.

La faute à Rousseau (Journal of l'Association pour l'Autobiographie et le Patrimoine Autobiographique). Triannual journal exploring "l'actualité et contribue à creer une culture de l'autobiographie."

Florilettres (Fondation La Poste, Paris; < http://www.fondationlaposte.org >). Newsletter for articles on books of correspondence and the study of epistolarity.

Hagiography. < http://www.kbr.be/~socboll >. Société des Bollandistes extensive Web site on hagiography, including research methods and results, events, and publications.

International Auto/Biography Association Life Writing discussion list: iaba-l @hawaii.edu. Contains postings on upcoming conferences, calls for papers, new publications, and scholarly queries.

Identity: An International Journal of Theory and Research (Soc. for Research on Identity Formation). Quarterly journal focusing on the problems and prospects of human self-definition over the life course.

Intramuros (Asociación por la Autobiografía, Madrid). Quarterly journal devoted to writing and research across a range of auto/biographical texts.

Journal of Medical Biography (Royal Soc. of Medicine). Quarterly journal focusing on lives of people in or associated with medicine.

Life Writing (Curtin U of Technology, Perth). Biannual journal featuring analytic and reflective writing on the self or selves and the roles of narrative in the creation of identity.

Lifewriting Annual (formerly *Biography and Source Studies*) (AMS Press). Annual journal publishing articles and reviews in auto/biographical theory and practice.

Memoria: Revista de estudios biográficos (formerly *Boletín de la Unidad de Estudios Biográficos*) (Unitat de Studis Biogràfics, U of Barcelona). Annual journal focusing on topics in life writing.

Memory (Psychology Press / Taylor and Francis). Journal for all forms of work on memory. Eight issues annually.

Les moments littéraires: La revue de l'écrit intime. Biannual review of work on chronicles, diaries, and similar texts.

Narrative (Soc. for the Study of Narrative Literature, Ohio State UP). Triannual journal exploring English, American, and European narrative in fiction, nonfiction, film, and performance art.

Narrative Inquiry (formerly *Journal of Narrative and Life History*) (Benjamins Publishing). Biannual forum for theoretical, empirical, and methodological work on narrative that conceptualizes, preserves, or hands down memories, experience, tradition, or values.

Narrative Psychology: Internet and Resource Guide. < http://web.lemoyne.edu/ ~ hevern/narpsych.html >. Created by Vincent Hevern, Le Moyne College. Introduction and interdisciplinary guide to resources, including bibliographies, course outlines, and pedagogical material on "the storied nature of human conduct."

The Narrative Study of Lives (Sage and American Psychological Assn.). Book series focuses on the teaching, learning, and working experiences of narrative research scholars.

New York Public Library. < http://www.nypl.org/research/chss/grd/resguides/ biography >. A guide to the New York Public Library's life writing resources.

Oral History (Journal of the Oral History Soc.). Biannual journal featuring articles from disciplines and practices that value orality, personal testimony, and remembering.

Oral History Association. < http://www.dickinson.edu/oha >. Web site with material on events and publications and guides to research, legal, and technological issues.

Oral History Research Office, Columbia University Libraries. < http://www .columbia.edu/cu/lweb/indiv/oral >. Information on Columbia's extensive archival collection, workshops, seminars, summer institute, and programs, including the September 11, 2001 Oral History Project.

Oral History Review (Oral History Assn., U of California P). Biannual journal exploring the recording, transcribing, and preserving of conversations with participants in important political, cultural, economic, and social developments.

Primapersona (Fondazione Archivo Diaristico Nazionale, Pieve Santo Stefano). Biannual journal for research on and recuperation of autobiographical texts.

Prose Studies (Frank Cass / Taylor and Francis). Triannual journal on the history, theory, and criticism of nonfiction prose of all periods, including autobiography, biography, the sermon, the essay, the letter, and the journal.

Prosopon (Unit for Prosopographical Research, Linacre College, U of Oxford). Online newsletter disseminating information on current work in subjects relevant to medieval prosopography. < http://www.linacre .ox.ac.uk/prosopon.html >.

Psychobiography. < http://www.psychobiography.com >. Created by William Todd Shultz, Pacific College. Bibliographies and other resources on psychobiography and personology.

Revue de l'A.I.R.E. (Bulletin de l'Association Interdisciplinaire de Recherche sur *l'Épistolaire*, Le Chesnay). Interdisciplinary annual journal of research on letters.

Stories of Life (UP of Rennes). Annual journal focusing on life narratives and identity construction.

Life Writing Centers, Programs, and Organizations

Arbeitskreis für moderne Biographik (Berlin; < http://www.akmb-online.de >). Emerging from a 2004 conference at the Herder Institut Marburg, links researchers exploring the theory, practice, purposes, and conventions of contemporary biographical writing.

Association Interdisciplinaire de Recherches sur l'Épistolaire (A.I.R.E.). Fosters interdisciplinary and international research into the history, theory, genre, and practice of letters.

Association pour l'Autobiographie et le Patrimoine Autobiographique (APA). Publishes *La faute à Rousseau*, a newsletter, bibliographies, and other occasional works; collects and maintains an archive; and conducts public events designed to "développer l'échange et la réflexion autour du phénomène autobiographique dans toutes ses dimensions."

Ludwig Boltzmann Institut für Geschichte und Theorie der Biographie (Vienna). International research institute whose main critical focus is applying insights from contemporary social science, anthropology, literary theory, and gender theory to the study of the methods of modern biographical writing; conducts conferences and exhibitions; supports writing of scholarly biographies.

University of British Columbia, Research in Women's Studies/Gender: Center for Studies in Auto/Biography, Gender, and Age. Explores auto/biography in its broadest interpretation, including life writing in written, oral, and visual forms, with a special focus on issues raised by gender and age throughout the life course.

University of California, Berkeley, Regional Oral History Office. Teaching activities focus on methods and meanings of individual testimony and social memory, and archival work focuses on oral and video history relating to Californian and United States history.

California State University, Long Beach, History Department Oral History Program. Instructional program focusing on the techniques and methods of oral history gathering and use in teaching and research, leading to a BA or MA in interdisciplinary studies.

Curtin University, Life Writing Research Unit. Publishes *Life Writing* and serves the Western Australian community interested in life writing in any of its forms by providing access to ongoing work, sponsoring lectures and meetings, and maintaining electronic lists and resources.

University of East Anglia, MA in Life Writing. Explores and analyzes the history, theory, and textual practice of biography and autobiography from classical to the postmodern.

University of Hawai'i–Mānoa, Center for Biographical Research. Publishes *Biography: An Interdisciplinary Quarterly* and a Biography Monograph series; supports courses, a lecture series, the *Biography Hawai'i* documentary series, and outreach activities.

University of Hawai'i–Mānoa, Center for Oral History. Programs, archives, and how-to guides on preserving and disseminating recollections of Hawai'i's people.

Indiana University, Center for the Study of History and Memory. Archival, pedagogical, and research activities focus on preserving, collecting, and interpreting twentieth-century history through first-person testimony and the interdisciplinary study of how people remember, represent, and use the past in public and private life.

La Trobe University, Unit for Studies in Biography and Autobiography. Offers classes, advises postgraduate work, supports research activities, sponsors conferences and lectures, and hosts visiting scholars.

University of London Goldsmiths College, Department of English and Comparative Literature, MA in Creative and Life Writing. Focuses on developing writing skills and critical awareness of relevant literary and cultural theory and the politics and practicalities of writing from the writer's point of view.

Monash University, MA in Biography and Life Writing. Offers an interdisciplinary approach to reading and writing life stories, including research technologies, legal and ethical issues, and interpretive and critical theories.

University of North Carolina, Chapel Hill. Publishes *A/B: Auto/Biography Studies*; maintains archives on North American slave narratives and first-person narratives of the American South; and through the Southern Oral History Program conducts archival, research, and teaching activities designed to foster an understanding of the American South.

Northwestern University, Foley Center for the Study of Lives. Affiliated with Northwestern's human development and social policy and psychology programs, conducts research on psychological, social, and life course development in adult years; offers conferences and lectures; and supports the Narrative Study of Lives monograph series.

University of Oxford, Prosopographic Research Unit, Linacre College. Dedicated to the study, promotion, and development of disciplines and methods of prosopography.

RITM (Centre de Recherches Interdisciplinaires sur les Textes Modernes). Publishes interdisciplinary research on modern texts, including the series *Récits de vie,* overseen by Philippe Lejeune, and *Écritures des voyages,* overseen by Gabrielle Chamanat.

University of Sussex, Centre for Life History Research and Mass-Observation Archive. Supports life history teaching and research, offers an MA program in life history research, and conducts courses and conferences; the archive includes primary sociohistorical source materials.

Working Lives. < http://www.econ.usyd.edu.au/wos/workinglives >. Program of the University of Sydney's Work and Organizational Studies unit. Supports research into the role of the individual in labor and social history and publishes Working Lives series focusing on labor and social history biographies.

York University, Faculty of Education, International Society of Educational Biography. Promotes study of the lives of educators and pedagogical improvements by adding biographical dimensions to the study of teaching.

Notes on Contributors

Timothy Dow Adams, professor of English at West Virginia University, is the author of *Telling Lies in Modern American Autobiography* (1990) and *Light Writing and Life Writing: Photography in Autobiography* (2000). He teaches autobiography, southern literature, Canadian literature, and photography and literature.

Arturo Arias is professor of Spanish at the University of Texas, Austin. He is the author of *Taking Their Word: Critical Dialogues, Central American Signs* (2007) and cowriter of the film *El Norte* (1984). He has published six novels in Spanish, books on Central American culture and literature, and a critical edition of Miguel Angel Asturia's *Mulata*. He edited *The Rigoberta Menchú Controversy* (2001).

Thomas J. D. Armbrecht, assistant professor of French, University of Wisconsin, Madison, teaches French theater as literature and in performance, queer studies, and twentieth-century French prose fiction. His works include a translation with critical introduction of *Wicked Angels*, a novel by Eric Jourdan (2006), and a forthcoming monograph on Marguerite Yourcenar and Julien Green.

Kathleen Boardman is associate professor of English and associate dean of the College of Liberal Arts, University of Nevada, Reno. She teaches composition and rhetoric, life writing, and Native American literature. She has published on gender and composition, literature and the environment, social issues and pedagogy, and collaborative autobiography and is coeditor, with Gioia Woods, of *Western Subjects: Autobiographical Writing in the North American West* (2004).

Alison Booth, professor of English at the University of Virginia, is the author of *How to Make It as a Woman: Collective Biographical History from Victoria to the Present* (2004), which received the Barbara Penny Kanner Prize of the Western Association of Women Historians. Her publications include *Greatness Engendered: George Eliot and Virginia Woolf* (1992) and an edited collection, *Famous Last Words: Changes in Gender and Narrative Closure* (1993). She is engaged in a project on the "homes and haunts" genre and literary tourism.

Sarah Brophy is associate professor of English and cultural studies, McMaster University. She teaches cultural theory, the memoir, and postwar British literature and culture. She is the author of *Witnessing AIDS: Writing, Testimony, and the Work of Mourning* (2004). She has published in *PMLA*,

Victorian Poetry, The Eighteenth Century: Theory and Interpretation, and *Essays on Canadian Writing*.

Trev Lynn Broughton is senior lecturer in English and women's studies, University of York. Her publications include *Men of Letters, Writing Lives: Masculinity and Literary Auto/Biography in the Late-Victorian Period* (1999). She is the editor of the four-volume resource collection *Autobiography* (2007) and coeditor, with Linda Anderson, of *Women's Lives / Women's Times: New Essays on Auto/Biography* (1997).

Suzanne L. Bunkers, professor of English, Minnesota State University, teaches and researches women's writing and diaries, survivors' literature, autobiography, memoir, and American literature. She edited *Diaries of Girls and Women: A Midwestern American Sampler* (2001), *"All Will Yet Be Well": The Diary of Sarah Gillespie Huftalen, 1873–1952* (1993), and *The Diary of Caroline Seabury, 1854–1863* (1991). She is the author of *In Search of Susanna* (1996) and coeditor, with Cynthia Huff, of *Inscribing the Daily: Critical Essays on Women's Diaries* (1996).

David Caplan is associate professor of English at Ohio Wesleyan University and the author of *Questions of Possibility: Contemporary Poetry and Poetic Form* (2004), *Poetic Form: An Introduction* (2006), and numerous articles on poetry and contemporary literature.

Sandra Chait, independent scholar, previously with the University of Washington, is the coeditor, with Elizabeth Podnieks, of *Hayford Hall: Hangovers, Erotics, and Modernist Aesthetics* (2005) and the author of numerous literary papers and reviews.

Julia Clancy-Smith is associate professor of history at the University of Arizona, Tucson. She published *Rebel and Saint: Muslim Notables, Populist Protest, Colonial Encounters (Algeria and Tunisia, 1800–1904)* (1994) and coedited *Domesticating the Empire: Gender, Race, and Family Life in the Dutch and French Empires* (1998) and a special issue of *French Historical Studies, Writing French Colonial Histories* (2004). She edited *North Africa, Islam, and the Mediterranean World from the Almoravids to the Algerian War* (2001) and is completing a book entitled "Migrations: Trans-Mediterranean Settlement in Nineteenth-Century North Africa."

Hilary Clark, associate professor of English, University of Saskatchewan, has published on Melanie Klein's unpublished life writing and has coedited, with Joseph Adamson, *Scenes of Shame: Psychoanalysis, Shame, and Writing* (1998). She is the editor of *Depression and Narrative: Telling the Dark* (forthcoming). In 2003 she published *The Dwelling of Weather: Poems*.

Julie F. Codell, professor of art history and English, Arizona State University, wrote *The Victorian Artist* (2003); edited *Genre, Gender, Race, and World Cinema* (2006) and *Imperial Co-Histories* (2003); coedited *Encounters in the Victorian Periodical Press* (2004); and wrote essays on life writing for *Life Writing and Victorian Culture* (2006), *Orientalism Transposed* (1998), the *Biography* special issue on narrative film and life writing (2006), and the *Encyclopedia of Life Writing* (2001). She is preparing a book on India under the British Raj.

Judith Lütge Coullie is professor of English, University of KwaZulu-Natal (formerly the University of Durban-Westville). She produced a CD-ROM on Roy Campbell (2004) and edited the anthology *The Closest of Strangers: South African Women's Life Writing* (2004). She coedited *Selves in Question*, a collection of interviews on southern African auto/biography (2006), and a volume on the work of Breyten Breytenbach (2004).

G. Thomas Couser is professor of English and director of disability studies at Hofstra University. His books include *Recovering Bodies: Illness, Disability, and Life Writing* (1997) and *Vulnerable Subjects: Ethics and Life Writing* (2003). His work has been assigned in Canada, the United Kingdom, New Zealand, and the United States in courses in American studies, rhetoric, deaf studies, political science, women's studies, and disability studies.

Martin A. Danahay, professor of English at Brock University, teaches Victorian studies, autobiography, and theory and practice of cultural studies. His books are *Jekyll and Hyde Dramatized* (2004), editions of H. G. Wells's *The War of the Worlds* (2003) and Robert Louis Stevenson's *Dr. Jekyll and Mr. Hyde* (1999), *A Community of One: Masculine Autobiography and Autonomy in Nineteenth-Century Britain* (1993), and *Gender at Work in Victorian Culture: Literature, Art, and Masculinity* (2005).

Kate Douglas is lecturer in the Department of English and Cultural Studies, Flinders University. Her teaching and research interests include contemporary life writing (in various media), cultural memory and commemoration, contemporary fiction and authorship, Australian studies, and postcolonial studies.

Richard Freadman is currently Tong Tin Sun Chair Professor of English at Lingnan University, Hong Kong. His publications include *Threads of Life: Autobiography and the Will* (2001), the coedited *Renegotiating Ethics in Literature, Philosophy, and Theory* (1998), and *Shadow of Doubt: My Father and Myself* (2003).

Miriam Fuchs coedits *Biography: An Interdisciplinary Quarterly* and is professor of English at the University of Hawai'i at Mānoa. She is the author of *The Text Is Myself: Women's Life Writing and Catastrophe* (2004), editor of

Marguerite Young, Our Darling: Tributes and Essays (1994), and coeditor, with Ellen G. Friedman, of *Breaking the Sequence: Women's Experimental Fiction* (1989). She has published on modernist authors, life writing, Djuna Barnes, Emily Holmes Coleman, H.D., Patricia Grace, and Queen Lili'uokalani.

Leigh Gilmore is the author of *The Limits of Autobiography: Trauma and Testimony* (2001) and *Autobiographics: A Feminist Theory of Women's Autobiography* (1994) and coeditor of *Autobiography and Postmodernism* (1994). Her essays are in *American Imago, Biography: An Interdisciplinary Quarterly, Fourth Genre, Genre, Genders, Journal of the History of Sexuality, Prose Studies,* and *Signs.* She is the Dorothy Cruikshank Backstrand Chair of Gender and Women's Studies at Scripps College.

Gabriele Helms taught in the Department of English, University of British Columbia. She published on auto/biography and Canadian literature and coedited, with Susanna Egan, *Autobiography and Changing Identities,* a special issue of *Biography: An Interdisciplinary Quarterly* (2001), and *Canadian Auto/Biography,* a special issue of *Canadian Literature* (2002). Her book *Challenging Canada: Dialogism and Narrative Techniques in Canadian Novels* was published in 2003.

Craig Howes is director of the Center for Biographical Research, the coeditor of *Biography: An Interdisciplinary Quarterly,* and professor of English at the University of Hawai'i at Mānoa. He is the author of *Voices of the Vietnam POWs* (1993) and essays on Victorian literature and life writing, including the afterword to *The Ethics of Life Writing* (ed. Paul John Eakin, 2004), and the coproducer of the television documentary series *Biography Hawai'i.*

Cynthia Huff, professor of English at Illinois State University, edited *Women's Life Writing and Imagined Communities* (2005) and coedited, with Suzanne L. Bunkers, *Inscribing the Daily: Critical Essays on Women's Diaries* (1996). She has published articles in *Prose Studies, Victorian Review,* and *Biography: An Interdisciplinary Quarterly.* She teaches life writing, women's literature, Victorian literature, feminist literary theories, pedagogical theory, and archival research.

Georgia Johnston, associate professor, Saint Louis University, has published on Gertrude Stein, Virginia Woolf, Lyn Hejinian, and Paul Monette in the journals *Biography: An Interdisciplinary Quarterly, Modern Fiction Studies,* and *Sagetrieb.* She is the author of *The Formation of Twentieth-Century Queer Autobiography* (2007). She teaches female modernism, autobiography studies, and queer textualities.

Margaretta Jolly, senior lecturer and codirector of the Centre for Life History Research, Centre for Continuing Education, University of Sussex, is the editor of the *Encyclopedia of Life Writing* (2001) and *Dear Laughing Motorbyke: Letters from Women Welders of the Second World War* (1997) and coeditor of *Critical Perspectives on Pat Barker* (2005). She is the author of *In Love and Struggle: Letters and Contemporary Feminism* (2008).

David Houston Jones, lecturer in French at the University of Exeter, is the author of *The Body Abject: Self and Text in Jean Genet and Samuel Beckett* (2000) and articles on contemporary fiction.

Daniel Heath Justice, Cherokee Nation, is associate professor of Aboriginal literatures at the University of Toronto. His research interests include Indigenous literatures, Native studies, and Indigenous intellectualism. He is the author of *Our Fire Survives the Storm: A Cherokee Literary History* (2006). He is coeditor of the journal *Studies in American Indian Literature* (*SAIL*) and has published articles on Native literature and Native studies.

Joanne Karpinski is associate professor of English at Regis University, Denver. She teaches cultural history, humanities, research techniques, comparative literature, and literary theory. She has published essays on Charlotte Perkins Gilman and is the editor of *Critical Essays on Charlotte Perkins Gilman* (1992). Her article on life writing and artifacts is in the *Encyclopedia of Life Writing*.

Jeraldine R. Kraver is associate professor of English and director of English education in the School of English Language and Literature, University of Northern Colorado, where she teaches literature and composition and language methods courses. She has edited two novels by Benjamin Disraeli and published in numerous journals and essay collections.

John Mepham was senior lecturer in English at Kingston University, London. He is the coauthor of a television screenplay, *Between Times* (1993), and the author of *Virginia Woolf: A Literary Life* (1991), *Virginia Woolf* (1992), and articles on other literary figures, film, and television. His teaching interests include life writing and Indian writing in English.

Susannah B. Mintz is associate professor of English at Skidmore College. She is the author of *Threshold Poetics: Milton and Intersubjectivity* (2003) and *Unruly Bodies: Life Writing by Women with Disabilities* (2007). Her teaching and research areas include seventeenth-century literature, life writing, the personal essay, and disability studies.

Joycelyn K. Moody is the Sue E. Denman Distinguished Chair in American Literature at the University of Texas, San Antonio, the editor in chief of *African American Review*, and author of *Sentimental Confessions: Nineteenth-Century Spiritual Narratives of African American Women* (2000). She specializes in African American literature and culture, nineteenth-century American literature, gender studies, and self-representation during the American slave era.

Ghirmai Negash is assistant professor of English and African literature at Ohio University. He formerly held positions at Leiden University and the University of Asmara, where he founded and chaired the Department of Eritrean Languages and Literature (2001–05). He is the author of *A History of Tigrinya Literature in Eritrea: The Oral and the Written 1890–1991* (1999), *Who Needs a Story? Contemporary Eritrean Poetry in Tigrinya, Tigre, and Arabic* (with Charles Cantalupo, 2005), and articles on African literature and orature.

Gail Y. Okawa, professor of English at Youngstown State University, specializes in multicultural literacy, multiethnic literatures (life writing), sociolinguistics, and pedagogy. She has published on pedagogies of language awareness, multicultural literacy/antiracism, and mentoring. She was a visiting scholar in residence at the Smithsonian Institution (2002) and the Center for Biographical Research, University of Hawaiʻi at Mānoa. (2002–03, 2006). She is writing a book on Hawaiʻi Japanese immigrants in mainland US Department of Justice internment camps during world War II.

Frances Freeman Paden teaches writing and gender studies at Northwestern University, where she has been named a Charles Deering McCormick Distinguished University Lecturer. Her projects include an English translation of medieval troubadour poetry in collaboration with William D. Paden, *Troubadour Poems from the South of France* (2007), and a book on the life and times of Adelene Moffat (1862–1956).

Iulia-Karin Patrut, research assistant at the University of Trier–German Research Foundation Collaborative Research Center 600: Strangers and Poor People, is currently working on written and oral representation of Gypsies in literary, ethnographic, and anthropological texts from 1850 to 1930. She is coeditor of *Ethnizität und Geschlecht. (Post-)Koloniale Verhandlungen in Geschichte, Kunst und Medien*, and her PhD dissertation was published under the title *Schwarze Schwester-Teufelsjunge: Ethnizität und Geschlecht bei Paul Celan und Herta Müller* (2006).

Kristine Peleg teaches English and women's studies at Century College and researches pioneer memoirs, both published and archival manuscripts. Her PhD dissertation at the University of Arizona explored Rachel Calof 's *Jewish Homesteader on the Northern Plains*, using a new translation of the original Yiddish manuscript.

James W. Pipkin is associate professor of English at the University of Houston. His primary teaching and research interests are nineteenth- and early-twentieth-century British literature, especially British Romantic poetry. He is the author of *Sporting Lives: Sports Autobiographies and American Culture* (2008).

Roger J. Porter, professor of English at Reed College, is the author of *Self-Same Songs: Autobiographical Performances and Reflections* (2002) and *The Voice Within: Reading and Writing Autobiography*, with Howard Wolf (1973). His research and teaching interests are autobiography and life writing, Shakespeare, modern drama, modern fiction, and travel writing.

Katrina M. Powell is associate professor of rhetoric and writing at Virginia Polytechnic Institute and State University. She teaches courses in autobiography, writing pedagogy, and research methodology, and her research interests include issues of self-representation across literary, professional, and personal genres. Her book, *The Anguish of Displacement: The Politics of Literacy in the Letters of Mountain Families in Shenandoah National Park*, is forthcoming.

Sarah Sceats is head of English literature and deputy head of the School of Humanities at Kingston University, London. She specializes in twentieth-century fiction and life writing and also teaches creative writing. She has published on Angela Carter, Doris Lessing, Rose Tremain, Margaret Atwood, and Betty Miller. She is the author of *Food, Consumption and the Body in Contemporary Women's Fiction* (2000) and is working on a book about women's fiction and a project on belonging.

Thomas R. Smith, associate professor and head of the Arts and Humanities Division at Penn State University Abington, is editor of *Lifewriting Annual*. He has contributed essays and articles to the *Bucknell Review*, the *Encyclopedia of Life Writing*, *Studies in Autobiography* (ed. James Olney, 1988), *Modernism/Modernity*, and *A/B: Auto/Biography Studies*, for whom he guest-edited the special issue *Autobiography and Neuroscience* (1998).

Gary Totten, associate professor of English at North Dakota State University, is the editor of *Memorial Boxes and Guarded Interiors: Edith Wharton and Material Culture* (2007). He has published essays on Simone de Beauvoir, Charlotte Perkins Gilman, and Theodore Dreiser. He teaches and does research in American literature and culture, travel literature, and aesthetic and cultural theory.

Gillian Whitlock is professor of English, media studies, and art history at the University of Queensland. She is the author of *Soft Weapons: Autobiography in Transit* (2007) and *The Intimate Empire: Reading Women's Autobiography* (2000). She is editor of a selection of contemporary Australian autobiographical writing in *Autographs* (1996).

Kenneth Womack, professor of English, heads the Division of Arts and Humanities, Penn State University, Altoona. He is editor of *Interdisciplinary*

Literary Studies: A Journal of Criticism and Theory and coeditor of *Year's Work in English Studies.* He coauthored, with Ruth Robbins and Julian Wolfreys, *Key Concepts in Literary Theory* (2002) and is the author of *Postwar Academic Fiction: Satire, Ethics, Community* (2001).

Michael W. Young, senior lecturer of English and director of academic assessment, La Roche College, contributed essays on Canadian diaries and letters before 1900, Robert Louis Stevenson, and sports in auto/biographies to the *Encyclopedia of Life Writing.* He has published essays on teaching literature through technology, teaching text and performance through sound scripting, and teaching children's literature, as well as short stories and poetry.

Index

Modern Language Association of America
Options for Teaching
Joseph Gibaldi, series editor